Aperture™ Exposed

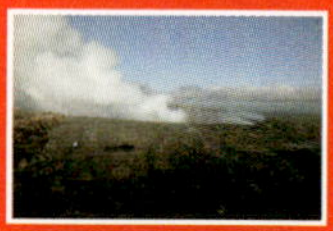
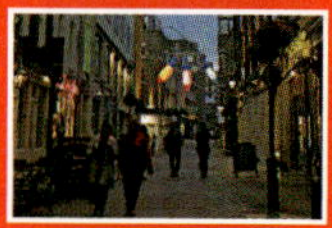
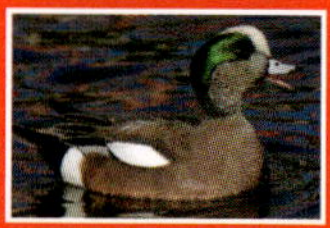
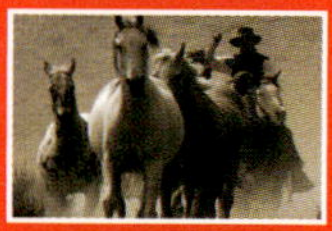
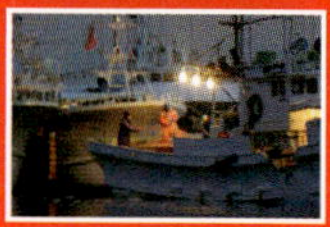

Aperture™ Exposed

The Mac® Photographer's Guide to Taming the Workflow

Ellen Anon

Josh Anon

WILEY PUBLISHING, INC.

Acquisitions and Development Editor: Pete Gaughan
Technical Editor: Scott Bourne
Production Editor: Vanessa Nuttry
Copy Editor: Kathy Carlyle
Production Manager: Tim Tate
Vice President and Executive Group Publisher: Richard Swadley
Vice President and Executive Publisher: Joseph B. Wikert
Vice President and Publisher: Dan Brodnitz
Book Designers: Franz Baumhackl and Lori Barra
Compositor: Side By Side Studios
Proofreader: Nancy Riddiough
Indexer: Ted Laux
Cover Designer: Ryan Sneed
Cover Image: Ellen Anon

Published simultaneously in Canada

ISBN-13: 978-0-470-04019-5
ISBN-10: 0-470-04019-X

For general information on our other products and services or to obtain technical support, please contact our Customer Care Department within the U.S. at (800) 762-2974, outside the U.S. at (317) 572-3993 or fax (317) 572-4002.

Wiley also publishes its books in a variety of electronic formats. Some content that appears in print may not be available in electronic books.

Library of Congress Cataloging-in-Publication Data is available from the publisher.

10 9 8 7 6 5 4 3 2 1

SYBEX®

Dear Reader

Thank you for choosing *Aperture Exposed: The Mac Photographer's Guide to Taming the Workflow*. This book is part of a family of premium quality Sybex graphics books, all written by outstanding authors who combine practical experience with a gift for teaching.

Sybex was founded in 1976. Thirty years later, we're still committed to producing consistently exceptional books. With each of our graphics titles we're working hard to set a new standard for the industry. From the writers and artists we work with, to the paper we print on, our goal is to bring you the best graphics books available.

I hope you see all that reflected in these pages. I'd be very interested to hear your comments and get your feedback on how we're doing. To let us know what you think about this or any other Sybex book, please send me an email at: sybex_publisher@wiley.com. Please also visit us at www.sybex.com to learn more about the rest of our growing graphics line.

Best regards,

Dan Brodnitz
Vice President and Publisher
Sybex, an Imprint of Wiley

To my family, for their encouragement.
Mutual support makes all things possible.
—Ellen Anon

To my family, for always setting the alarm
before the sun was up.
—Josh Anon

Acknowledgments

Ellen Anon

Sometimes you realize just how lucky you are. I have always felt blessed to have two extraordinary sons, each quite unique. But having the opportunity to write this book with Josh has driven the point home even more. And having Seth's continued support and perspective on things has helped keep me balanced at some of the more trying moments. As I said, I'm lucky! And I'm grateful for Jack's continued patience with and support of my erratic and demanding schedule.

I also realize how fortunate I am to have so many friends in the field who have gone out of their way to inspire me, encourage me, and further my career. People such as Arthur Morris, Joe and Mary Ann McDonald, George Lepp, Freeman Patterson, Rick Holt, Jon Canfield, Peter Burian, Charlotte Lowrie, Dee Cunningham, Art Becker, Walt Anderson, and Michael Nadler, among others, have been friends as well as colleagues. Without them I doubt I'd have accomplished anywhere near as much as I have. A special thank you to each of you! And thank you also to all the workshop participants and others I've met who encourage me in so many ways. Forgive me for not listing you individually, but I don't want to inadvertently leave someone out. You all know who you are, and I'm grateful to each of you!

Thank you also to Kirk Paulsen, Chris Gonzales, Melissa Horn, Patty Montesion, and many others at Apple who have made us feel like part of the team and helped us in so many ways.

Of course, Josh and I are thankful to the folks at Sybex for seeing the value in this project. Pete Gaughan has been outstanding as both acquisitions editor and development editor. We've appreciated his advice, encouragement, and wit as well as his patience and outlook. We were fortunate to have Scott Bourne agree to be the technical editor and ensure that everything in the book is accurate. Scott, who co-presented one of the first talks about Aperture at Macworld, offered some valuable suggestions along the way. In fact, the whole book team has been great. Our production editor, Vanessa Nuttry, kept things flowing smoothly, and our copy editor, Kathy Carlyle, made certain wc were communicating in English. Our compositor, Side By Side Studios, did an excellent job, as did our proofreader, Nancy Riddiough. Our sincere gratitude to the entire team, who made this project go smoothly!

Josh Anon

When you're a photographer, it's hard to describe how nice it is to have a family that not only accepts your desire to travel the world—getting up at insane hours and spending hours shooting the same rock (thanks, Dad and Seth!)—but also will be there shooting that same rock with you. It's also hard to describe what it's like having a mother who gets temporarily annoyed with you not because you're staying out late but because you're standing where she wants to be shooting from too, and how about moving over a little because she's your mother. Ah, family. However, as much as we joke that photography is a competitive sport, it's pretty exciting to have a chance to collaborate with my mother on what we believe will be the best book about the coolest new photographic tool. We've come a long way since you accidentally hit that Num Lock key (friggin' keyboard won't type letters, dang it!). Haven't we, Mom?

In addition to my family, I also extend a special thank you to my friends and coworkers. Every day, when I drive through the Pixar gate, I am still amazed at how smart and motivating you all are. I feel very fortunate to be in an environment where art and technology converge, and where I learn so much from everyone every day. To start, I'd like to say a special thanks to Michael B. Johnson for all the help and advice you've given me the past few years. For all the interesting photography discussions and support of our growing Pixar Photoclub, thanks to Ralph Hill, Arun Rao, J. Hee Soo Lee, Josh Minor, Mahyar Abousaeedi, Bjorn Leffler, and Ed Catmull. Furthermore, I owe thanks to three particular professors: Jack Tumblin (for getting me excited about what we can do with digital cameras beyond more megapixels), Dennis Glenn (for an amazing amount of support and insight into life, learning, and more), and Claudia Skerlong (who taught me to write well but probably figured that hell would freeze over before I wrote a book).

Echoing what Mom said, thank you to our photographer friends; I've been lucky enough to meet and shoot with some of you, and those whom I haven't met directly yet have inspired me with their images. Of course, special thanks to the people at Apple who have helped us and listened to our feedback. You all have done a great job, and we hope to continue to work with you in the future! Most important, to the wonderful people at Sybex without whom this book would not be possible, thank you!

Last, thanks to you, the reader. Without your support, this book would not be here.

About the Authors

Ellen Anon

Ellen Anon is an Apple Certified Trainer in Aperture and a freelance photographer who got her start with photography at age five. However, it remained a hobby as she took a very long fork in the road, eventually earning a Ph.D. in clinical psychology. In 1997, a broken foot forced her to take a break from her work as a psychologist, and she used the time to study photography. She debated briefly whether to build a traditional darkroom in her home or create a digital darkroom. Because she's not fond of being closed up in small dark spaces with strong smells of funky chemicals, she opted for the latter. Ever since, photography has been a two-part process for her. Making the image in the field is step one, and optimizing it is step two.

Ellen is passionate about photography and the digital darkroom and enjoys sharing her expertise both by teaching and by writing. She has been fortunate to co-lead photography workshops with Arthur Morris, Photoshop workshops for Joe and Mary Ann McDonald, and her own Photoshop-in-the-Field workshops. (See www.sunbearphoto.com for upcoming courses.) She also presents seminars in various locations and is an instructor for the high school scholarship programs at the North American Nature Photography Association (NANPA) summits. Recently, she was honored to be one of the VIP Pro Photographers consulting with Apple on Aperture.

Ellen cowrote *Photoshop for Nature Photographers: A Workshop in a Book* (Sybex, 2005) with Tim Grey, and she contributed to Jon Canfield's *Print Like a Pro* (Peachpit, 2005) and Charlotte Lowrie's *Camera Raw Studio Skills* (Wiley, 2006). Ellen was the technical editor for several recent books on digital photography. Her articles and images have been published in *Nature's Best*, *eDigital Photo, Shutterbug, Popular Photography*, Sierra Books' *Mother Earth,* Photoworkshop.com, and various calendars, billboards, and more.

Photography has taken Ellen to locations from Hawaii to South Africa to Japan and has paved the way for her to meet all sorts of wonderful people. Her husband and two sons, all of whom are quite skilled with cameras, sometimes travel with her. Fortunately, they adapt to her crazy schedule and willingly plan vacations around her photographic destinations.

Josh Anon

Josh Anon has been a nature photographer for 10 years, although his interest in photography started when he received his first Kodak 110 camera at the ripe old age of four. He attended Northwestern University in Evanston, Illinois, and received a B.S. in computer science from the McCormick School of Engineering and Applied Science. His research focused on high dynamic range imagery, and he worked both in the Distributed

Learning Center building distance learning solutions and as a senior residential network consultant providing computer networking support to thousands of students.

After graduation, Josh began working at Pixar Animation Studios in Emeryville, California, where he has worked on *Finding Nemo* (uncredited), *The Incredibles,* and *Cars.* Currently, he is a layout technical director doing cinematography, and his past responsibilities have included rendering optimization, Linux and Mac software development, and model optimization.

His photographic work, which has appeared in a variety of publications, is currently represented both by EcoStock in Seattle and independently. He has traveled the globe, searching for the next great picture, be it diving 100 feet deep on the Great Barrier Reef or walking along Chicago's Michigan Avenue. On the weekends, Josh teaches photography and leads workshops. Josh also writes software for Lightbox Software (www.lightboxsoftware.com), including Lightbox, one of the first professional-quality image management programs for Mac OS X. More recently, he wrote Aperture2iLife, which allows Aperture users to quickly access their Aperture projects in iLife.

When not shooting, making cartoons, or coding, Josh can be found on his road bike, playing the violin, skiing, and learning to kite surf.

Foreword

The photographic world is in a state of transition. Long gone are the simple days of viewing and editing slides atop a lightbox. Make no mistake: the digital train has left the station. Where you choose to board is up to you, but rest assured that train is on its way to a new horizon, with no turning back.

Within a short period, even the occasional digital shooter can amass gigabytes of information, comprising thousands of images. What to do with the original images captured and how to make the most of each image are perplexing problems we all currently face. Photographers making the transition from film to digital quickly realize there is much to learn to make the most of a captured image. Moreover, the thought and implementation of a digital workflow often overwhelm both novice and professional photographers alike.

Software programs now abound for every aspect of digital photography. While some are highly specific in task, others are multifaceted. Many programs allow the photographer to import, browse, view, edit, and share images—but none so far has the power of Aperture. This new program gives the digital photographer the means to import, edit, organize, convert, browse, and search for images through a hierarchy that's easy to understand and to implement.

A photographer who wants to succeed professionally must be able to quickly and easily archive, retrieve, and submit images via both electronic transmission and the printed page. Aperture provides basic image processing in a nondestructive manner, complete with web galleries, book layouts in high-resolution PDF application, slideshows, contact sheets, and more.

Aperture is a powerful and sophisticated program, but regardless of how sophisticated a program is, it is of little benefit to end users unless they can fully comprehend it. *Aperture Exposed: The Mac Photographer's Guide to Taming the Workflow* makes it easy to adopt Aperture as part of your workflow. With this book, Ellen and Josh have unlocked all its doors with concise, easy-to-understand text and illustrations. *Aperture Exposed* is sure to benefit all those wishing to ease their workflow worries.

—Charles Glatzer
M. Photog., renowned and award-winning professional photographer, photographic educator, and host of "Shoot the Light" Instructional Photographic Workshops (shootthelight.com).

Contents

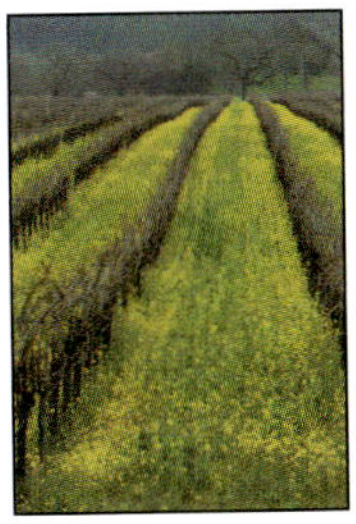

Chapter 3 Viewing Images 53

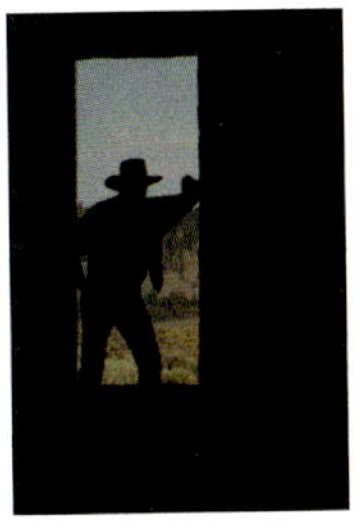

Chapter 4 Finding the Keepers 83

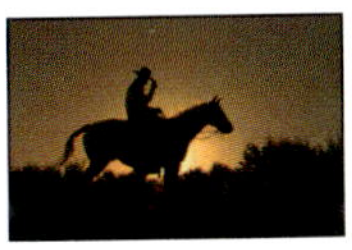

Chapter 5 Nondestructive Image Processing 115

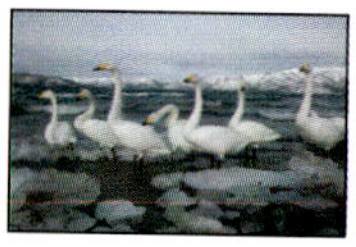

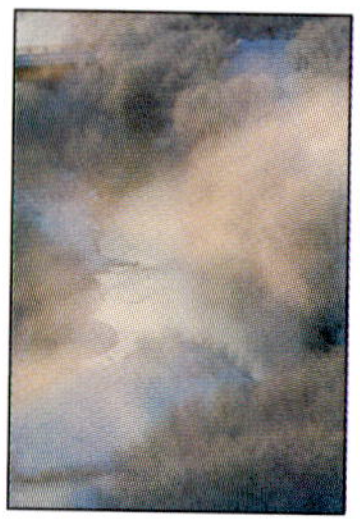

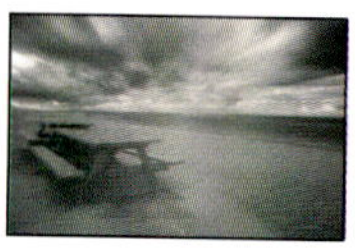

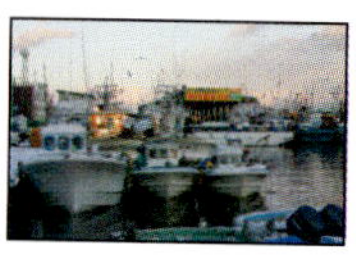

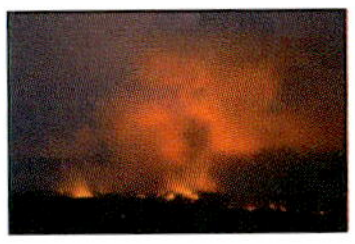

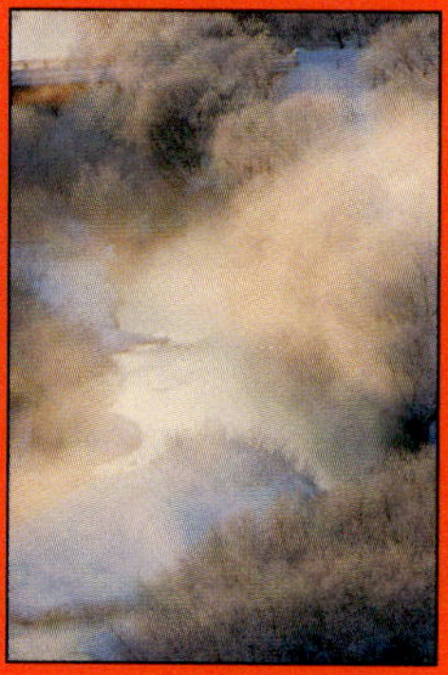

“dramatically different software means that the user will face

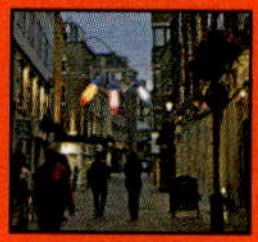
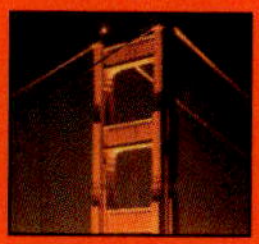
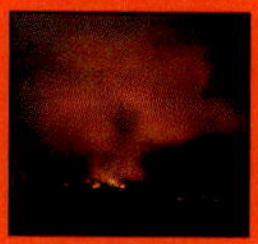

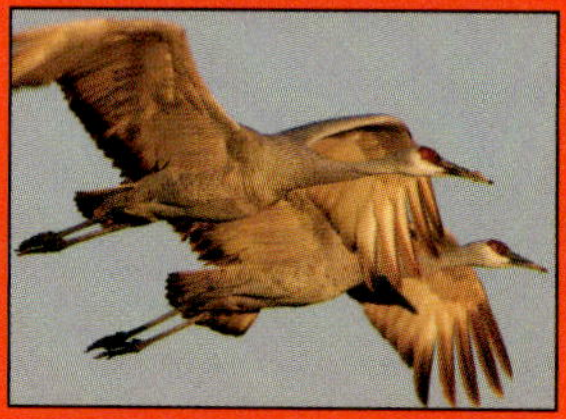

a learning curve”

Introduction

Photography has undergone a major evolution, from a film-based industry to a digital one, in a relatively short period of time. Digital cameras have evolved quickly from the initial low-resolution cameras produced for NASA, followed by the Kodak DCS cameras for photojournalists that had 1.3 megapixel sensors and cost a small fortune, to much higher-resolution cameras that have become the mainstream tools of many photographers—professional, enthusiast, and amateur. A variety of software programs evolved along with the cameras to help photographers optimize and organize their photos. Many of those programs alternated between focusing on the needs of graphic designers and those of photographers. Apple's Aperture is the first major application to focus entirely on the needs of photographers, providing us an elegant way to efficiently import, edit, rate, keyword, optimize, output, and manage images in whatever format we choose, including RAW.

New, dramatically different software means that the user will face a learning curve. Even software that is destined to make our lives easier and workflow smoother can initially be frustrating as we struggle to figure out how to complete each step. After we've mastered the basics, it may take a while to learn all the tricks and advanced techniques that may ultimately become second nature to us. *Aperture Exposed: The Mac Photographer's Guide to Taming the Workflow* explains all the basics of using the program so that you can quickly and easily incorporate Aperture into your regular workflow. Once you've done that, the book reveals many advanced techniques to increase your productivity.

Aperture Exposed is clearly written, by photographers, in an easy-to-follow style that invites you to master each step and concept rather than leaving you feeling overwhelmed and confused as some books do. It focuses on the practical knowledge and skills you need to get up and running with Aperture and then offers more advanced tips so that you get the most out of the program. The book is designed so that you can read it cover to cover or just seek out particular topics and read relevant sections as necessary.

Note: We have a companion web page where we share some files with you. You can use these files to experiment with the concepts we're covering and to help master using the different tools. Get the companion files at www.sybex.com/go/apertureexposed.

Who Should Use This Book

Aperture Exposed: The Mac Photographer's Guide to Taming the Workflow is for every photographer who is starting to use Aperture or considering purchasing Aperture. Photographers who have been using Aperture since its initial release will find useful advanced tips throughout the book and especially in the last chapter, which is devoted to advanced topics.

When brand new software is released, one of the challenges is making people feel comfortable with the new interfaces and tools and helping them use it productively. Most of us have a tendency to hesitate a bit with new software, not knowing exactly how to accomplish our goals and not wanting to spend time feeling frustrated. *Aperture Exposed* clearly explains how to use Aperture and all its features. We take you step by step through using Aperture so that you can quickly adapt your workflow to it, without wasting time wondering how to do something. If time is valuable to you, this is the book for you! We'll show you how to use Aperture to create an efficient, customized twenty-first-century digital workflow.

You can read this book cover to cover or you can opt to use it as a reference book, referring to whatever sections you need at any particular moment. We've written it to be used both ways. The bottom line is, this book will make it easy for you to adopt Aperture into your routine.

What's Inside

Here is a glance at what's in each chapter.

Chapter 1: Welcome to Aperture begins with a summary of the workflow and a basic explanation of Aperture. It goes on to define the terminology associated with Aperture, such as libraries, projects, albums, smart albums, versions, HUD, inspectors, and so on.

Chapter 2: Importing and Organizing Your Images covers the various ways to bring images into Aperture, including importing directly from a memory card as well as from other sources such as folders on your hard drive and iPhoto libraries. It also explains stacking and setting up projects and albums, including smart albums.

Chapter 3: Viewing Images explains the variety of ways that Aperture lets you view and compare images. It also explains how to customize your Aperture interface to make your Aperture workflow faster.

Chapter 4: Finding the Keepers covers image selection and rating, using keywords and metadata, finding images using the Query HUD, using the vault for backup, and general backup tips.

Chapter 5: Nondestructive Image Processing introduces you to all of the image optimizing tools available within Aperture, from the basic tools such as cropping and straightening to detailed explanations of using the quarter-tone Levels tool. We show you how to use each tool and how to make batch changes.

Chapter 6: Exporting Images explains how to configure the export presets and how and when to export images, including how to place images in email. This chapter also covers how and when to open images in an external editor such as Photoshop.

Chapter 7: Printing covers the basics of a color managed workflow, including monitor calibration and using printer/paper profiles. Printing single images or a series of single images, contact sheets, and montages, as well as soft proofing, is explained.

Chapter 8: Creating Web Content shows how to create web galleries and web journals. In addition, it covers some advanced techniques for creating your own web templates.

Chapter 9: Creating a Book covers the steps to take to create a custom book, from setting up the album to selecting a theme, customizing pages, and proofing the book to ordering it.

Chapter 10: Advanced Aperture presents some additional techniques to help make your workflow more efficient, including using Automator as well as ways to open your images in other RAW converters. There is also a troubleshooting section to help guide you in case you have problems with Aperture.

What's on the Companion Website

The companion website—www.sybex.com/go/apertureexposed—contains a variety of sample images and demo files for your use in practicing the techniques discussed in the book. Use them to follow along with the text and try out new techniques and tools as they are presented. Taking the time to use these images will reinforce what you're reading.

How to Contact the Authors

Both of us welcome feedback from you about this book or about books you'd like to see from us in the future. You can reach Ellen by writing to ellenanon@mac.com or Josh at joshanon@mac.com. For more information about Ellen's workshops and photography, visit her website at www.sunbearphoto.com. To learn more about Josh, visit www.joshanon.com.

Sybex strives to supply you with the latest tools and information you need for your work. Please check www.sybex.com for additional content and updates that supplement this book. Enter the book's ISBN—**047004019X**—in the Search box (or type **Aperture Exposed**), and click Go to access the book's update page.

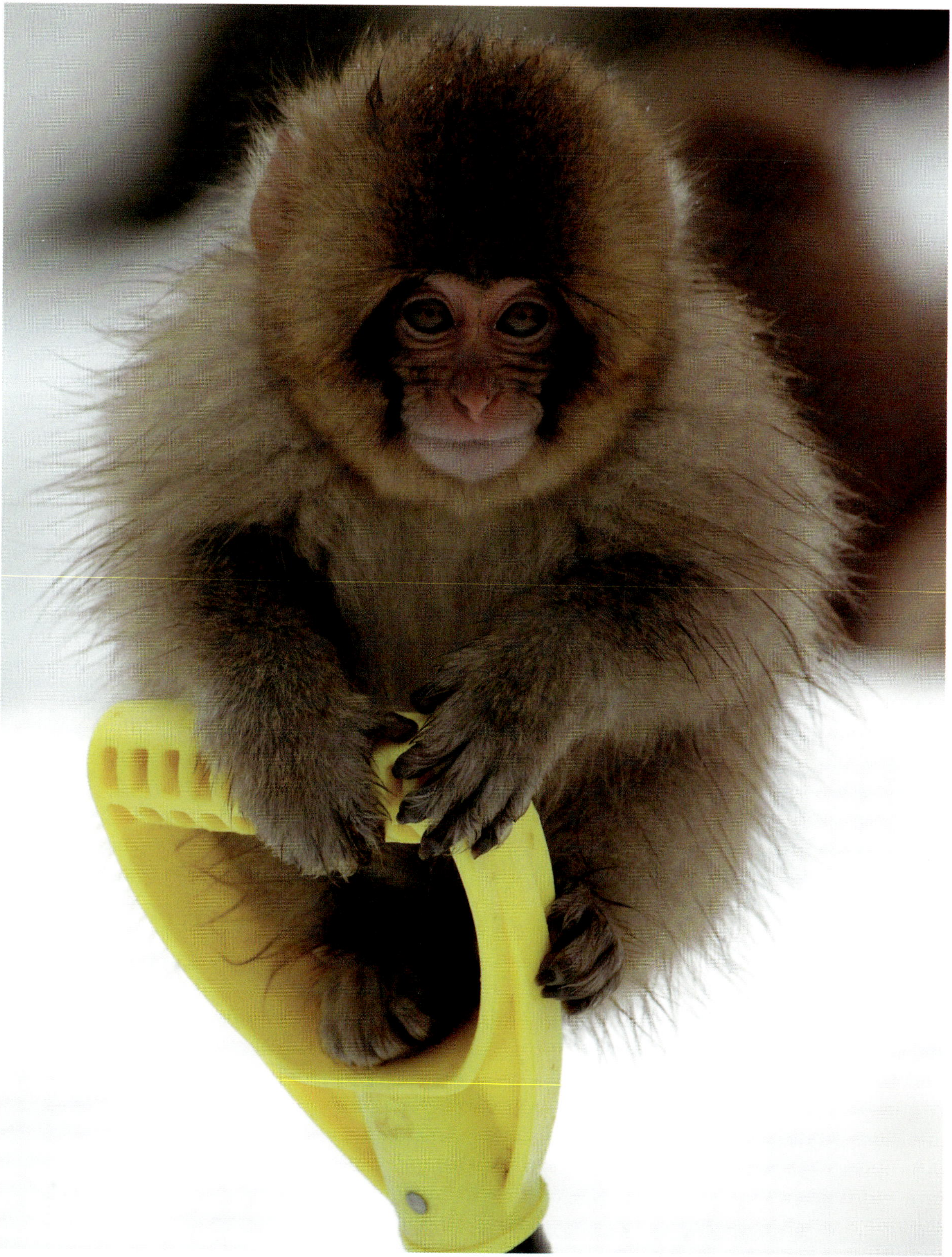

1 Welcome to Aperture

Going out in the morning to shoot gigabytes of photos is easy. Editing and organizing those photos is a little harder. Ten years ago, editing and organizing photographs was easy. You'd lay your slides across a lightbox, grab a loupe, and discard any image you didn't like. After you selected your images, you'd label the slides and store them in sheets within organized folders.

For many photographers, one of their biggest frustrations with digital photography is the lack of a similarly simple and elegant workflow. Throughout this book, we'll show you how Aperture allows you to reclaim that workflow freedom and do more than you ever imagined possible with your images.

Chapter Contents

What Is Aperture?

Over the past few years, digital images have replaced slides, and many pieces of software, from Adobe's Bridge to Apple's iPhoto, have replaced the lightbox/loupe/slide sheet combination. Unfortunately, easy-to-use programs often can't meet the demands of a professional photographer, and the programs that can meet those demands often aren't very easy to use.

Apple's Aperture program aims to strike a balance, providing both power and ease of use. Over the next few hundred pages, we'll show you how to incorporate Aperture into your workflow. We're confident that once you see everything Aperture can do and how easy it is to use (with a little bit of help at first), you'll never yearn for slides again.

Aperture's goal is to make it as simple as possible for photographers to import, select, annotate, organize, and share their images, regardless of file format or experience level. The process of managing and organizing photos is commonly called a *workflow*. Photographers tend to have a range of workflow styles, ranging from just copying the images from the camera to the computer and never really organizing them, to importing and organizing in iPhoto (Apple's consumer-oriented photo management tool), to extensive work in a third-party digital asset management program.

In fact, many of the concepts in Aperture are similar to iPhoto. However, iPhoto was designed to work with JPEG files, and Aperture was designed from the ground up to work with RAW files. As far as Aperture is concerned, a RAW file is just another image file, basically similar to a JPEG file. This makes working with a RAW file in Aperture as easy as working with a JPEG in iPhoto. This does not mean that Aperture handles only RAW files. Aperture can import and work with many image formats, from RAW to PSD to JPEG to TIFF.

Why Shoot RAW?

If Aperture can work with JPEGs, why should you bother shooting RAW? One big reason is that a RAW file contains more information than a JPEG. A JPEG can contain only 16.7 million (that is, 2^{24}) possible colors, whereas some RAW files can contain 68.7 billion (that is, 2^{36}) colors. That is over four thousand times more colors than a JPEG file can contain. Also, settings such as white balance are not actually applied to the image stored in the RAW file until you view it, meaning that you can change those settings without losing any data. When you shoot JPEG, settings like white balance are permanently applied to the image data as soon as the camera writes the image file to its storage card.

Because RAW files contain more information and the adjustments haven't been forcibly applied to the image, some image adjustment operations, such as highlights and shadows, can be performed only to a RAW file. Furthermore, JPEG is a lossy format. The first time the camera saves the image, it throws away information from the sensor, and each time you save the JPEG file, it will throw away more information. By starting with a RAW file and working with a lossless format such as TIFF, you'll be working with all the information that the camera can capture and you won't lose any data as you continue to work with the image.

The Photo Library

When you import your image into Aperture, the digital image file is stored in the Aperture photo library. (We will discuss importing your images in Chapter 2, "Importing and Organizing Your Images.)" A library is simply a special folder on your hard drive that contains every image file you import into Aperture, as well as information about each image. By default, Aperture places your library folder in the Pictures directory in your Home directory. If you want to see it, in the Finder, you could select Go > Home and click the Pictures directory. You can change the library's location, perhaps to an external hard drive, under the Aperture preferences. Also, if you're importing pictures from iPhoto's library or from somewhere else on your hard drive, Aperture will copy the images to its own library and leave your original files untouched. Figure 1.1 shows Aperture's Welcome screen, which is designed to get you started importing images into Aperture.

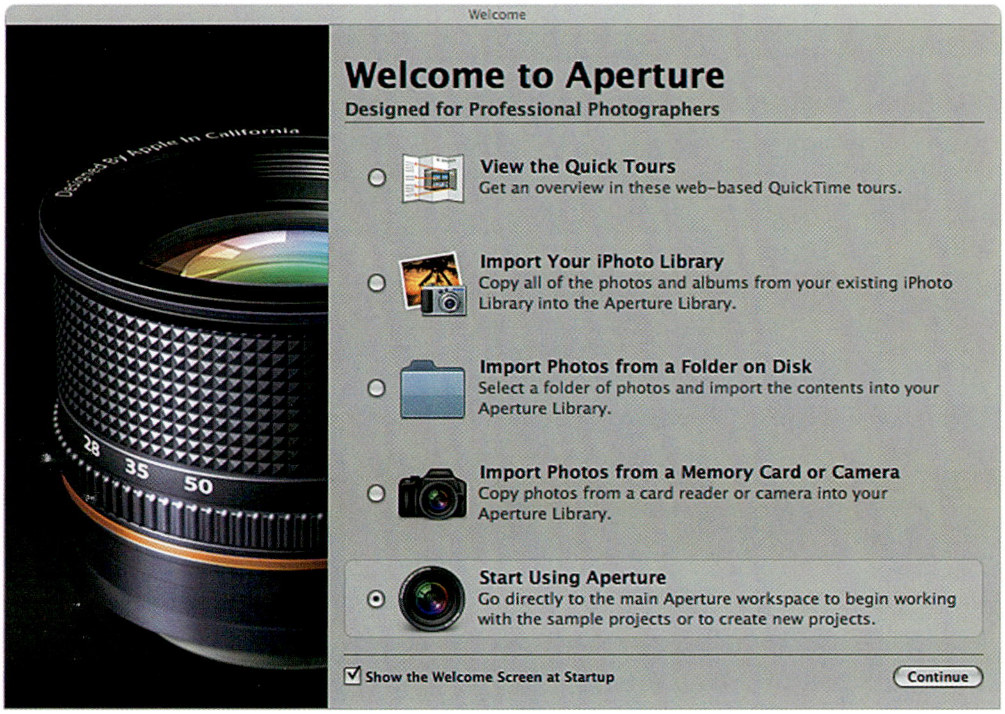

Figure 1.1: The Aperture Welcome screen

Unlike other file management programs that let you scatter your images wherever you want to put them and then help you browse those folders, Aperture manages your photos for you. Aperture is what digital photographers call a digital asset management tool (DAM). Because DAMs allow you to quickly search for and view your images, many people prefer using DAMs to scattering their files all over their computers. Furthermore, because you only interact with your images through the DAM, your images rarely get lost. DAMs often provide tools to help you share your work via slideshows, email, and more. The one downside to using a DAM is that you must interact with your images via the DAM: you can't go into the Finder and rearrange your images. However, for many people, not having to deal with manually rearranging your files isn't a disadvantage. It's an advantage.

If you were to look at the photo library on your hard drive, it would appear as a file and not a folder that you can look inside, as seen in Figure 1.2. Aperture saves your photo library as a special type of folder called a *bundle,* which is a folder that appears in the Finder as a file, discouraging people from looking inside. You don't have to worry about what's inside the bundle because again, Aperture is a DAM. Instead of using the Finder to find, open, and move your images around, you do everything from within Aperture and let Aperture figure out what to do with your image files. Within Aperture, everything starts with your photo library.

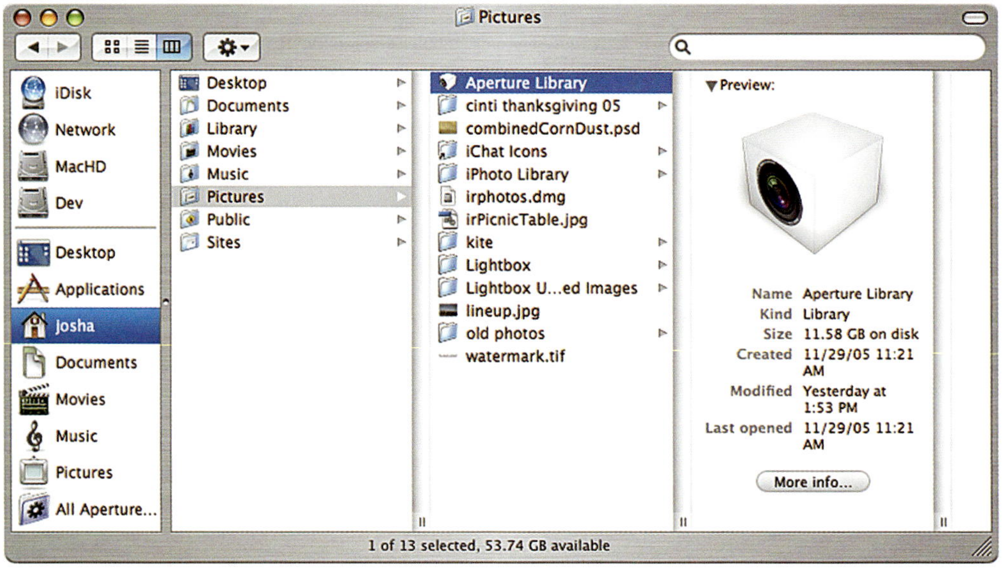

Figure 1.2: The Aperture photo library

Aperture allows you to have only one photo library active at a time. That means that all of the images you actively work with inside of Aperture are stored within the same folder on your hard drive. One library is beneficial because all of your photos are in one place, but having only one library can also be a pitfall because your hard drive can hold only so much data. If you don't edit carefully, Aperture's photo library can take over your hard drive. The program provides a way to export certain parts of your photo library to a format that you can move elsewhere and reimport later. (You can even import those photos to another computer, which we will talk more about in Chapter 6, "Exporting Images.)" However, Aperture does not provide a way to browse these exported files without reimporting them to your photo library.

Note: Creating additional photo libraries is easy. Under Aperture's Preferences, you can select your photo library's location. To create a new library, select a folder that doesn't already contain a photo library. To switch photo libraries, you must change the preference to point to whatever photo library you want to use and restart Aperture.

Peeking Inside the Photo Library

For the advanced user, if you really want to look inside your Aperture library, you can Control-click (right-click if your mouse has two or more buttons) the library icon in the Finder and select Show Package Contents. This opens a new window that lets you browse the bundle just as if it were another folder. We'll discuss the contents of your photo library more in Chapter 10, "Advanced Aperture." We'll also explain how you can always get to your images so that if something goes wrong with Aperture, your photos will still be safe. Additionally, because you can access your photos directly, you can use another program to convert your RAW files and then import the converted file into Aperture.

Projects

Back in Aperture, within your library, you create projects to group your images. A project is a virtual collection of images, albums, and other files you create using the photos in the given group, such as web galleries or books. Projects appear in the panel on the left, as seen in Figure 1.2, which is called, appropriately enough, the *Projects panel*. If the Projects panel is hidden, pressing W or choosing Window > Show Projects will reveal it. You can create a project by choosing File > New Project (⌘+N). You can rename the project by selecting it, pressing Return, and typing a name. Figure 1.3 shows the project in detail, highlighting a project, album, and folder. We'll discuss each container in the next few sections.

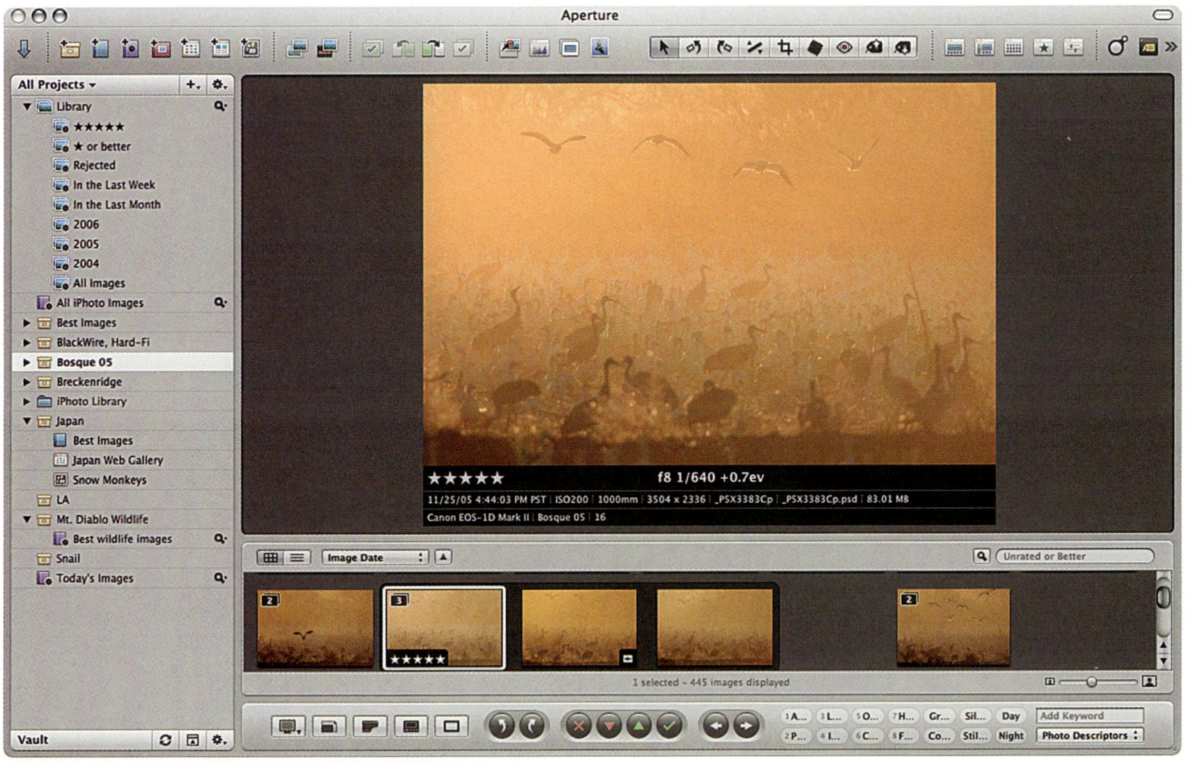

Figure 1.2: The Aperture user interface, showing the Projects panel, Viewer, and Browser

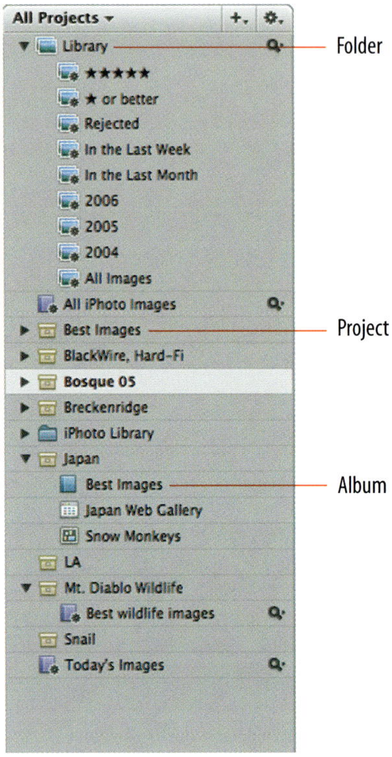

Figure 1.3:
The Aperture Projects panel

Projects provide a handy way to do large-scale grouping of your photos. For instance, if you are shooting in Yosemite one week and in King's Canyon the next, you could create two projects called "Yosemite" and "King's Canyon" and separate your images accordingly, or you could create one project called "California National Parks" and just put all of your images in there. If you were going on an assignment to take photos of California parks for a magazine, you would probably choose the latter because it would organize all of your images for the assignment into one project. If you were shooting for a stock agency, the former would be more useful because later, you could quickly find and grab an image from Yosemite for your stock agency without having to sort through King's Canyon images too. As another example, rather than just having one project called Weddings, you could make one project called Smith Wedding and another project called Jones Wedding. We'll cover projects more in Chapter 2, including how to move images between projects.

Note: As you name your projects, albums, and folders, use only letters, numbers, and spaces. Other special characters and punctuation, from colons to brackets, might cause problems down the road. For example, third-party programs and scripts that work with Aperture's photo library may not handle filenames with slashes correctly, as Mac OS X uses a slash to indicate a directory.

Albums

Generally, though, you'll want an even finer grouping for your images than projects provide. For instance, if you were shooting slides, you might have a group of slide sheets for waterfalls and another group for wildlife within your Yosemite folder. Aperture has a similar notion called *albums*. Albums appear in the Projects panel, shown in Figure 1.3, grouped under the project within the album. You can also create folders within each project to contain your albums and other files, such as web galleries, associated with your images. You create folders by selecting File > New Folder (⌘+Shift+N). To put items into the folder, drag and drop albums and files into the folder.

Note: Unlike an album, a folder cannot contain images, and unlike a folder, an album cannot contain non-image files.

Unlike physical slides, photos within Aperture can exist in multiple albums. That way, if you have a slide that falls into multiple categories, you can put the slide into each category. For instance, on a multiday shoot, you might first organize your photos into albums depending on when you took the photo. At the end of a shoot, you would have albums named from "Yosemite 11/05 AM 1" to "Yosemite 11/05 PM 3." Then, you could make an album named "Yosemite Best" and pick out and copy your top images into that album so that you could quickly show people your best images. Then, you might make another album named "Yosemite Wildlife" that you'd copy wildlife images into so that if your stock agency wanted a picture of a deer in front of Half Dome, you could quickly look in one album rather than sort through all of your albums to find the image that the agency wanted. Similarly, a wedding photographer can create albums for subcategories such as bride portraits, wedding guests, wedding party, ceremony, etc. To create an empty album to copy images into, select the project you want the album to be in, and select File > New Album (⌘+Option+L).

Note: You can also make an empty album by selecting the project you want the album to be in, clicking the + button next to the All Projects text, and choosing New Empty Album.

A Summary of Key Terms

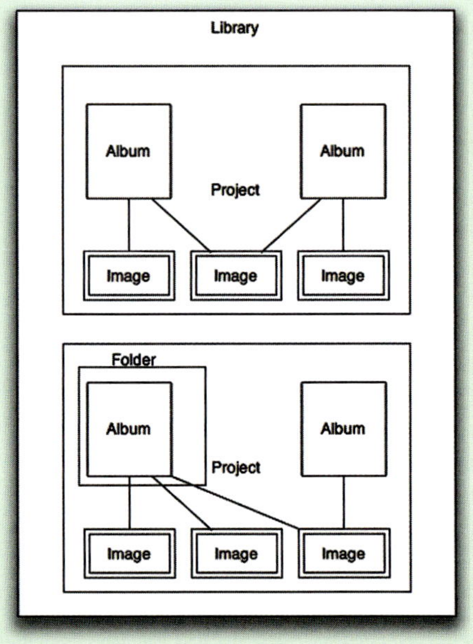

The diagram provides a visual representation of the relationships among the library, projects, albums, and folders.

Library A special folder on your hard drive that contains every image file you import into Aperture, as well as information about each image.

Project A virtual collection of photos, albums, and other files that you create using the photos in the given group, such as web galleries or books.

Album A grouped collection of photos that exists within a project.

Folder A container for albums and other files, but not images.

Metadata "Information about the information": data about the image, such as exposure or copyright. Each metadata entry contains a "field," such as shutter speed, and a "value," such as 1/30 sec.

Smart Album An album whose contents are based on the metadata in each image and a user-defined query.

Stack A collection of images that are related in some way, usually images that were taken within a short timeframe of a similar subject.

Browser A panel that lets you see a sortable, filterable table or a thumbnail view of all of your images within the album or project.

Viewer A panel that lets you view the full version of your image or images.

Light Table A view that lets you arbitrarily position and resize images.

Filmstrip The full-screen version of the Browser.

Heads-Up Display (HUD) A partially transparent window containing controls to interact with your image, from making adjustments to setting metadata.

Inspector A panel or window that lets you see details related to an item such as a photo.

Master The original image that you imported into Aperture.

Version The modified version of the master file, stacked with the master. It can be a reference to the master, if you're making changes within Aperture, or a new image file, if you've opened the file in an external editor.

Vault A copy of your photo library that can be automatically synced to your library or that your library can be restored from.

Metadata

Within each album, you can label each image with metadata. Metadata is data about the image, ranging from exposure information to copyright information that is attached to the image.

Back in the days of slides, you had to remember where and when you took each image. Although you might have a rough idea as to what exposure and lens choice you used for the image, information you might tediously cram on a slide label, you probably couldn't remember the details. If someone asked you exactly how you took a photo, it was nearly impossible to determine if the image you took with your 16–35mm lens was set at 16mm or 18mm, f/5.6 or f/6.3, and at 1/250 or 1/500 of a second.

Digital cameras automatically capture and record tons of information, from exposure and compensation to (in some cases) GPS data. This information is *metadata* that is automatically attached to digital photos. For each piece of metadata, there is a "field" such as shutter speed and a "value" such as 1/30 sec. Aperture allows you to add additional metadata, such as your name and address, to each image, and it lets you tag each image with keywords. In fact, you can set Aperture to add metadata to each image as it's being imported. Figure 1.4 shows Aperture's *Metadata Inspector* for the given image. An inspector is a panel or window that lets you see specific details, such as metadata, related to an item, such as a photo.

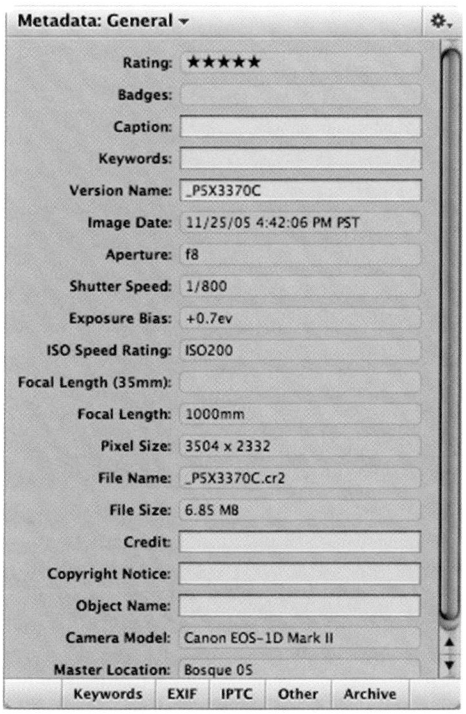

Figure 1.4: The Aperture Metadata Inspector

Once you've imported the image into Aperture, you can edit some of its metadata, add or remove keywords, and apply a rating to each image. Ratings help you quickly edit through the images you shoot. Images that you dislike, perhaps due to composition or focus, are called *rejects* and are flagged with an X, and images that you really like are called *selects* and are flagged with five stars. Other images can be rated from one to five stars or left unrated.

However, metadata goes beyond rating and exposure. Aperture allows you to tag each image with keywords. You can bring up the Keywords window (Figure 1.5) by pressing Shift+H or by choosing Window > Show Keywords HUD. This display contains a hierarchical listing of keywords that you can drag and drop onto images. You can also add your own keywords, reorganize them, and drag and drop groups of them onto images. We will explain how to do this customization in Chapter 4, "Finding the Keepers."

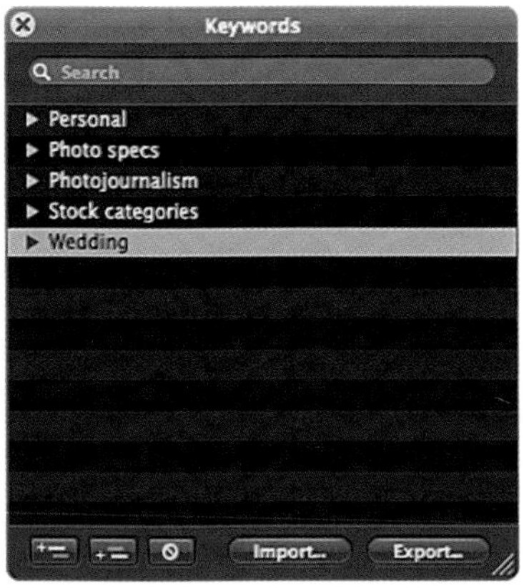

Figure 1.5:
The Keywords HUD

Keyword controls, as seen in Figure 1.6, appear at the bottom of the main window in the control bar. You can use them to apply groups of keywords with one click. If the control bar isn't visible, you can show it by choosing Window > Show Control Bar (Shift+D). You can reveal the keyword controls by choosing Window > Show Keyword Controls (D).

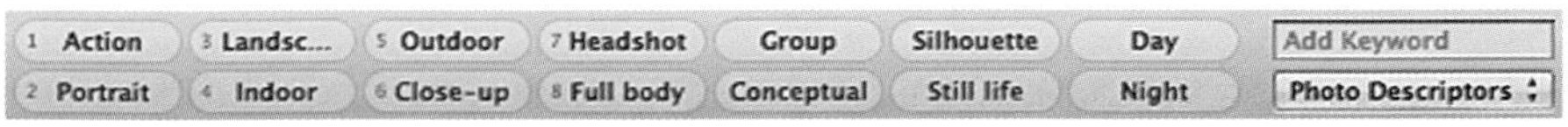

Figure 1.6: The keyword controls within the control bar

Continuing the earlier example, when you're in Yosemite, you can have Aperture automatically tag each image with "Yosemite" and "California" keywords on import (we'll explain how in Chapter 2). You can also automatically add your name, copyright information, and contact information. As you're viewing and rating your images, you can add keywords such as "wildlife" to the images with wildlife and more specific keywords such as "deer," "squirrel," "tourist," and "half dome" to the appropriate photos. You might also want to rate any image that you really like as either four or five stars and flag any image that you don't like as a reject. Rejected images aren't deleted right away, and we'll show you how to retrieve a rejected image in Chapter 4. By applying this metadata, you can quickly set up a smart album to automatically show your best wildlife images from Yosemite.

Note: You can quickly rate a five-star image (a *select*) by selecting the image and pressing the slash key (/). For any image you don't like (a reject), select the image and press the 0 key to reject it.

Smart Albums

One big benefit of Aperture is the ability to create a *"smart album."* A smart album is an album whose contents are based on the metadata in each image and a user-defined query. Smart albums can be global for your entire image library or local to each project.

To create a smart album, select the project you want to contain it, and choose File > New Smart > Album (⌘+Shift+L). A Query panel, shown in Figure 1.7, will appear to help you set up the album.

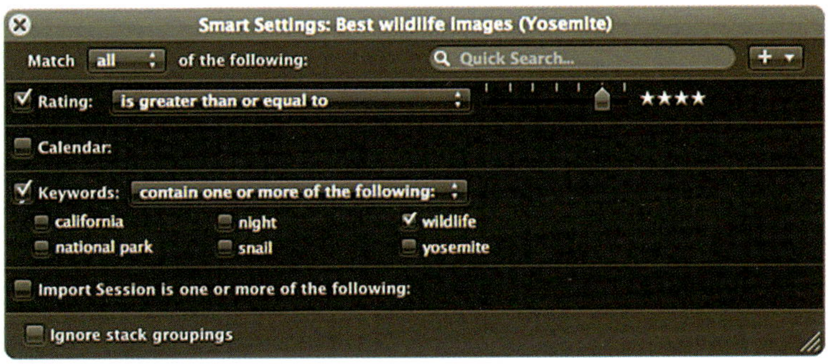

Figure 1.7:
The smart album query HUD

To quickly see your wildlife images, assuming you've tagged them all with a "wildlife" keyword, you can make a smart album with a query for keywords containing "wildlife." Similarly, if you want an album with your best images, you can make another smart album by querying for ratings greater than or equal to four stars. If you want to see your best wildlife images, you can make a smart album with both queries, by querying for ratings greater than or equal to four stars and keywords that contain "wildlife." Figure 1.7 shows what this combined query would look like. Note that this smart album query is set to match "all" criteria (an "and" operation) and not "any" criteria (an "or" operation). This will give us pictures that are of wildlife *and* four stars or better and not pictures that are of wildlife *or* four stars or better.

The next day, after you import, tag, and rate your new images, if you were to click your "best wildlife" smart album, it would automatically be updated with your best wildlife photos from earlier that day. You don't have to manually copy your photos into the album. Smart albums can significantly enhance your workflow, and we'll discuss them in depth in Chapter 2.

The Library Project

Let's broaden our view from fine-grained keywords back to the overall photo library at the top of the Projects panel. There you'll find an item called *Library*, as shown in Figure 1.8. The Library is the collection of all the images in all the projects and albums in

Aperture. It comes preloaded with several smart albums, such as all five-star images, all images from 2005, and all rejected images. All Images shows you every image that you've imported into Aperture.

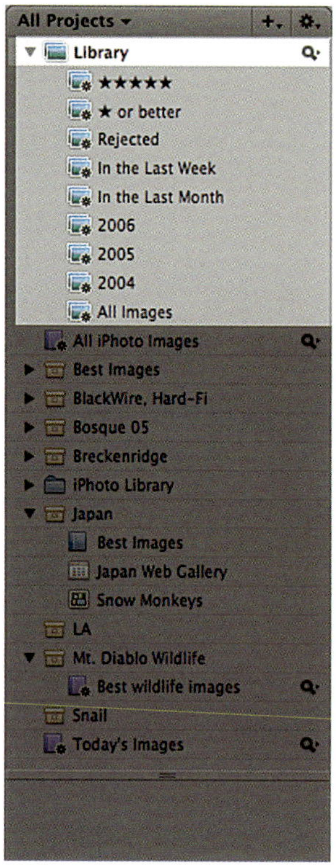

Figure 1.8:
The Projects panel with the Library project highlighted

If you want to define items that use images from multiple projects, you can add your own albums and other items into the Library project. Any items you add will appear at the top level of the Projects panel, alongside your other projects, and not underneath the Library project. This is different from what happens when you add an item, such as an album, to a project and the new item appears as a child of the project.

Importing Images

Above the Projects panel is the Import panel, shown in Figure 1.9. The Import panel lets you bring images into Aperture from either your hard drive or a digital storage device, such as a compact flash card. You can bring up the Import window by clicking where you want to import pictures from within the Import panel (either a storage card or a disk) and selecting the project into which you want Aperture to import the images. Aperture will display an arrow with the tail indicating the source and the arrowhead pointing to where the images will be imported. On the right, you will see a panel with image previews, metadata, and other controls for grouping images.

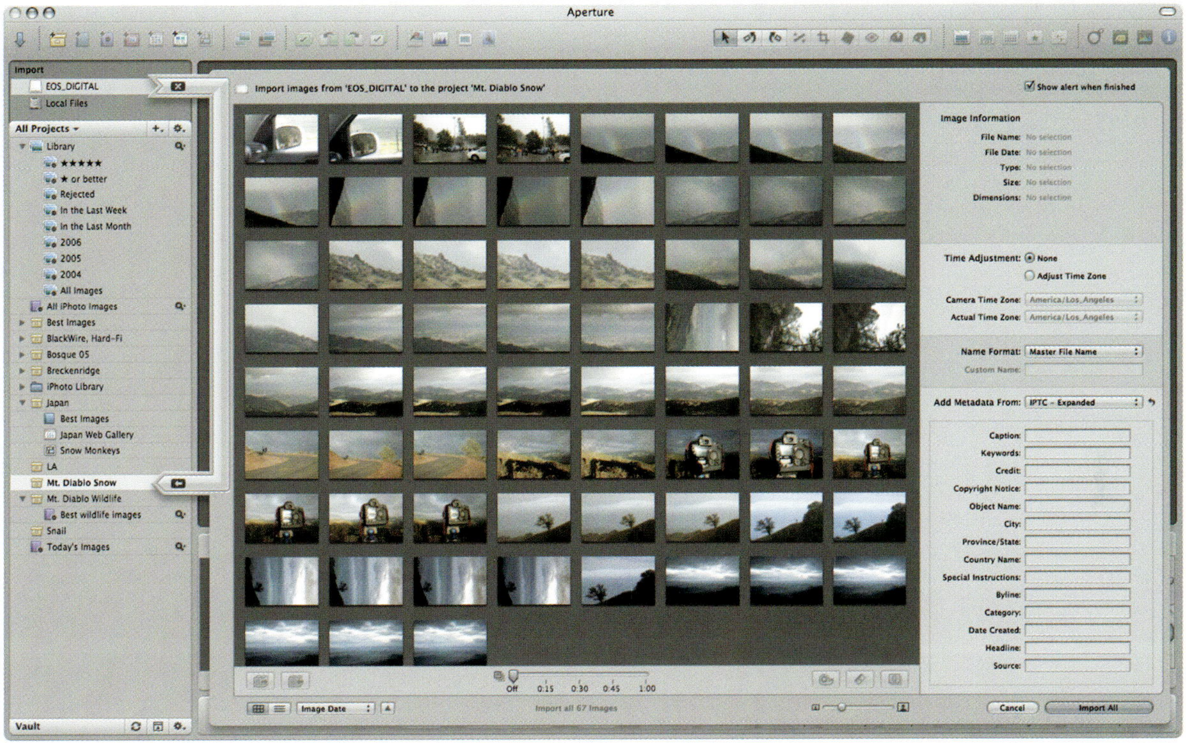

Figure 1.9: The Import panel and window

Stacking

If you're like many photographers, you tend to shoot in bursts. You point your camera at the bear that's running at you, fire off the largest burst you can, and run for your life hoping that you've captured the picture of a lifetime. Later on, when importing your images so that you can recount the escapade to your friends with some visual aids, you will want to group the related set of images from each burst together and pick the best images. In Aperture, these photos can be grouped together into a *stack*.

A stack is a collection of images that are related in some way, usually images that were taken within a short timeframe of a similar subject. When you're importing your images, you can tell Aperture to automatically stack images by time, and you define this time period by using the Time slider at the bottom of the Import window seen in Figure 1.9. As you change the auto-stacking duration, Aperture will visually group and collapse your photos into an expandable stack. The buttons along the bottom will let you close or expand all stacks and manually edit the image groupings (splitting or joining images) in each stack. After importing, you can also manually add and remove images from a stack, and you can expand them to view specific images within the stack, and more.

By stacking related images, finding your best images for a given pose/subject is easy. For instance, the storage card with your bear photos would have a burst of photos, a pause, and another burst of photos. You might tell Aperture to stack images taken within 1 second of each other. This would give you have a handful of stacks for each time you stopped to take photos of the charging bear. Later on, you can compare images within each stack and select your best image from each time you stopped to shoot.

Metadata

The metadata controls on the right side of the Import window let you add captions, keywords, location, and other bits of metadata to the photos you're importing. Aperture also provides a time zone adjustment tool that will automatically correct the date and time stamp in your photos' metadata in case you didn't reset your camera's time zone while shooting—something we've all forgotten to do at least a hundred times As soon as you have your thumbnails stacked, your metadata set up, and you're ready to import, select the images you want to import (or don't select any image to import every image) and click the Import button. Aperture will import your photos in the background and allow you to start viewing the full version of the first image before the second image has finished downloading. We'll discuss importing in greater detail in Chapter 2.

Browsing and Viewing Images

The center portion of the screen in Aperture's main window, as seen in Figure 1.10, has two portions, the Viewer and the Browser. The Browser is where you can see a thumbnail view or a table view of your images within the selected album or project and select images to view. The Viewer shows the selected image.

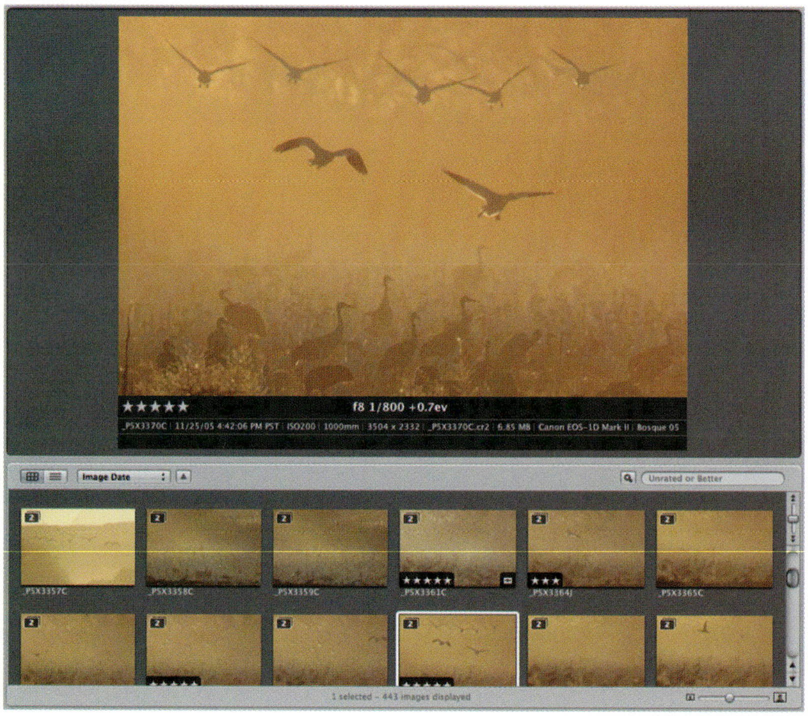

Figure 1.10: Aperture's image viewer and Browser

Aperture is not limited to viewing just one image at a time. In fact, it offers five different ways to view your images, including a way to view multiple images at once so you can compare two non-stacked images and a special viewing mode to compare images within a stack.

Often, you don't just want to view the images in the stack, you want to sort the stack with your best image on top. Aperture provides the Stack Compare mode that lets you show two images from a stack at once, keeping your pick on the left and showing another image from the stack on the right. In Chapter 3, "Viewing Images," we'll show you how to select the best image by promoting and demoting the images in the stack. The new pick replaces the one on the left and the Viewer adjusts to let you continue sorting through the stack. After you finish sorting through the stack, the best image appears on the top of the stack.

Sometimes it's easy to pick which image is better, because one image will be out of focus or have a bad composition. At other times, you'll need to look closely at the image and perhaps pick the one with the better catch light in the eye. Aperture provides a digital loupe that you can pull up nearly anywhere you can see an image by pressing (`), (not a single quote; this key is variously known as the accent grave, backtick, or tilde key) or by selecting View > Loupe. The Loupe provides a quick way to see part of an image at 100 percent magnification or higher, and the Loupe will actually grab its data from the original RAW file and convert the data on the fly. We'll cover the Loupe more in Chapter 3, but for now, Figure 1.11 shows what the Loupe looks like.

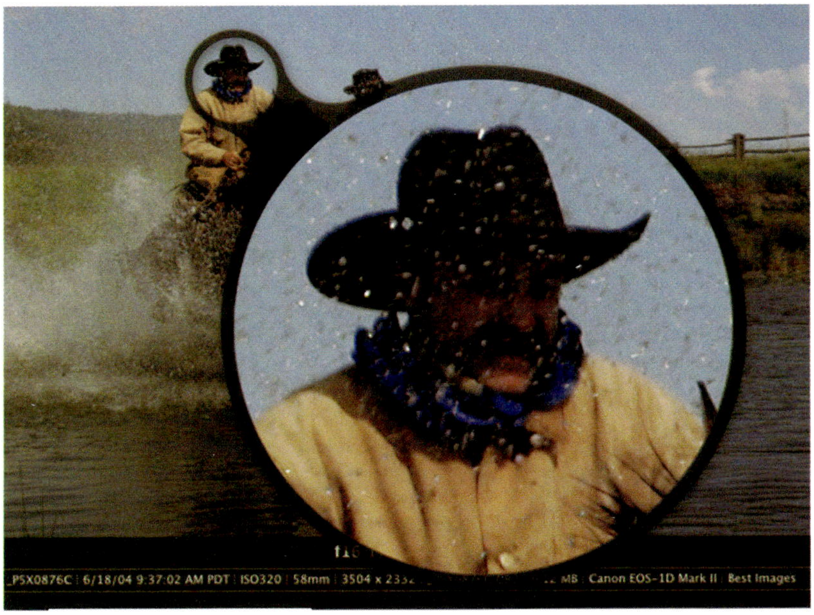

Figure 1.11: The Loupe

Proxy Images

When you first select an image, Aperture loads a proxy image while loading the full image in the background. The proxy image is smaller than 1024 × 1024 and should not be used to judge sharpness. Furthermore, you cannot loupe the proxy image. You will see a status icon saying "loading" until the full image is ready, at which point the large image will appear to sharpen and an image will appear in the Loupe. After the current image has loaded, Aperture will preload the next image in your browser so that when you switch to it, you'll have a shorter load time.

Sometimes a loupe isn't enough, and you want to zoom in and view the image at 100 percent. To zoom the Viewer to 100 percent, press the Z key or select View > Zoom To Actual Size. When zoomed in, Aperture overlays a small rectangle representing the image with a red rectangle representing the portion you're looking at, as seen in Figure 1.12. You can drag the red region around to scroll over the image.

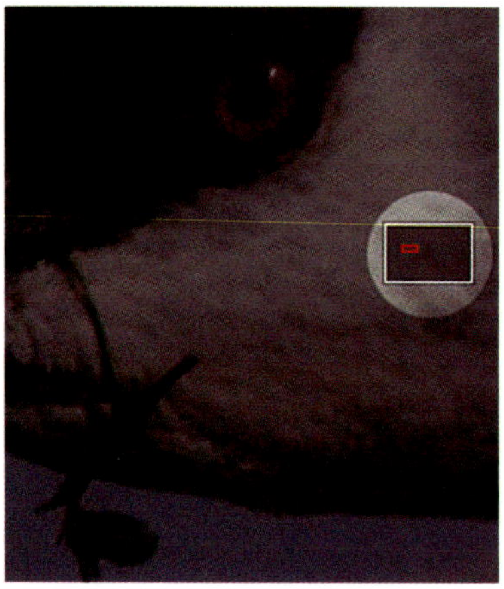

Figure 1.12: The small rectangle with the visible area in red

Note: When you press Z to zoom in, Aperture will automatically zoom the image to wherever your cursor is, assuming your cursor is on the image.

If you want to compare multiple images in detail, you can select each image and press Z to zoom in on all of them. In addition to scrolling each image individually, Aperture also allows you to *lock scroll* the images. By holding down the Shift key as you scroll one image, the other images automatically scroll in exactly the same way. For instance, to compare a catch light in an animal's eye to an eye positioned in roughly the same spot in your images, ⌘+click the images to select them, press Z, and while holding down the Shift key, drag the red rectangle around to scroll the visible region over the animal's eye. Once you've picked the best image, you can rate it as a *select* by pressing the button with the green check in the control bar or by pressing the backslash key (\).

Light Tables

Sometimes, picking the best images isn't as simple as comparing focus and catch lights between similar shots. Back in the days of slides, it was nice to be able to just spread our slides out on a lightbox, arrange them in some arbitrary fashion, and pick our favorites. Aperture digitizes this concept and moves it forward by providing a light table view. In Aperture, a light table lets photographers select some images, drag and drop them onto the light table, and arbitrarily move them around, rotating and scaling as desired and providing the ultimate visual organization tool. You can use the light table for a variety of purposes, from comparing similar images side-by-side to trying out image arrangements for a website to creating a photomontage. Figure 1.13 shows a sample light table.

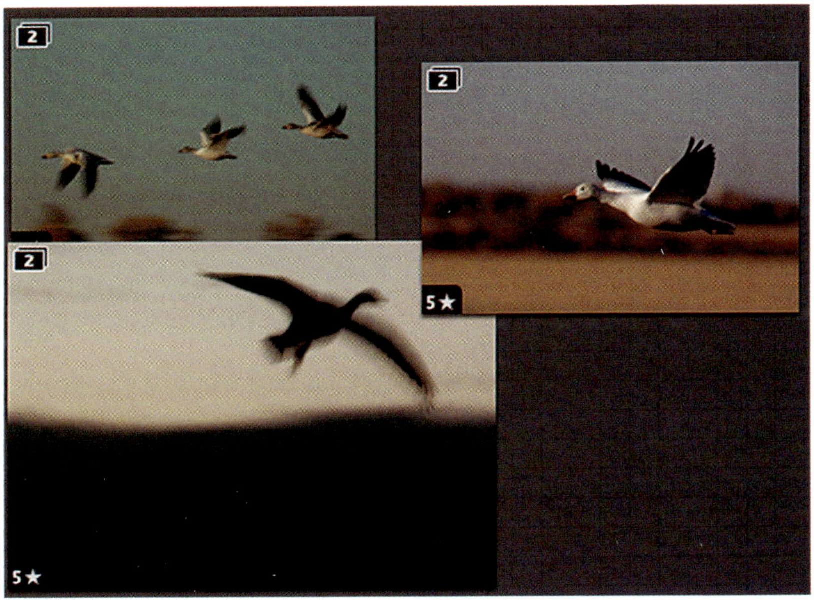

Figure 1.13:
A sample light table

We'll discuss the light table more in Chapter 3. If you want to explore a little before you get there, you can create a new light table in a fairly straightforward process:

1. Select some images in the Browser.
2. Choose File > New From Selection > Light Table. A new item will appear in the Projects panel to represent your light table, and within the light table, you will see the familiar Browser/Viewer layout.
3. To place an image, drag it from the Browser onto the light table.

You can use a light table for everything from moving images around in order to compare them to creating a collage of photos that you'll print. Plus, if you want to see an image's detail, you can even pull up a loupe to view it on the light table.

Full Screen Mode

Sometimes you just don't have enough space to really see your image, even with the Loupe, perhaps because the Projects panel and inspector are taking up too much space. To maximize the amount of space devoted to your image, you can go into Full Screen mode.

Unlike full screen modes in other programs, Full Screen mode in Aperture is more than just a slideshow, and Chapter 3 will cover all of the different things you can do in it. Part of this power comes from two special heads-up displays (HUDs). HUDs are partially transparent, small sets of tools that are quickly accessible, and they can be hidden or locked on the screen for even quicker access. Through the HUDs, you can do nearly everything that you can do in Windowed mode, from rotating images to viewing metadata. The first HUD is called the Filmstrip (Figure 1.14), and it provides a way to jump through images. The Filmstrip can be either docked to an edge of the monitor, hidden, or docked and set to avoid the image (it positions itself so that it doesn't cover the image). In case you're wondering, you can even use the Loupe in the Filmstrip.

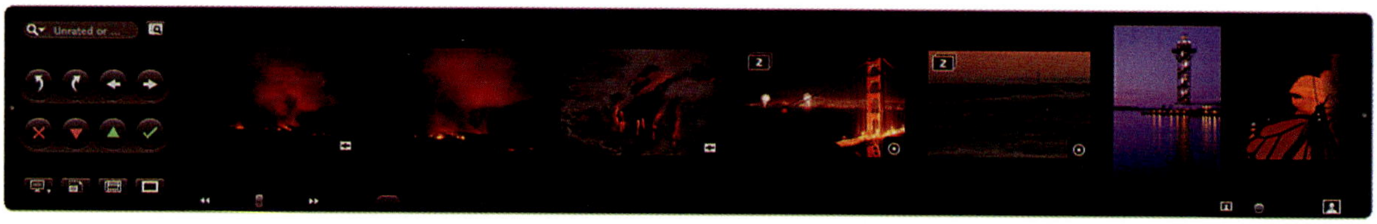

Figure 1.14: The Filmstrip

The second main HUD is a toolbar (Figure 1.15) docked to the top of the screen and hidden until you move your cursor near it. This non-customizable toolbar provides quick access to a number of common functions ranging from expanding stacks to cropping. All of these buttons have hotkeys, and once you learn the hotkeys, you can avoid wasting screen space with this toolbar.

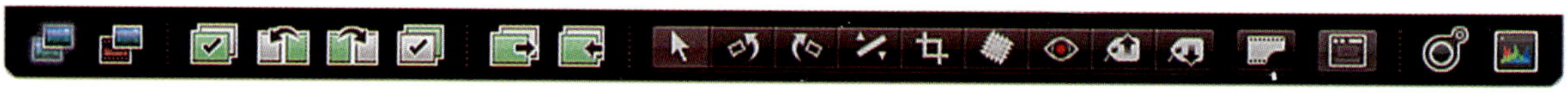

Figure 1.15: The Full Screen toolbar

Adjusting Images

The Filmstrip and the Full Screen toolbar are available only in Full Screen mode. However, Aperture has other HUDs, such as the Adjustments HUD that provides quick access to Aperture's image enhancing tools and is shown in Figure 1.16, and you can pull them up in Windowed mode. You can bring up the Image Enhancing Tools HUD by pressing H or by choosing Window > Show Adjustments HUD. We will cover the adjustment tools in depth in Chapter 5, "Nondestructive Image Processing." These tools include exposure adjustment, color correction, white balance, a histogram, and more. These tools are considered nondestructive because you can always remove the adjustment or change its properties without actually modifying the pixels in your original, master image file. In fact, throughout this book, you will see references to your master image, and the *master* is simply the original file that you imported.

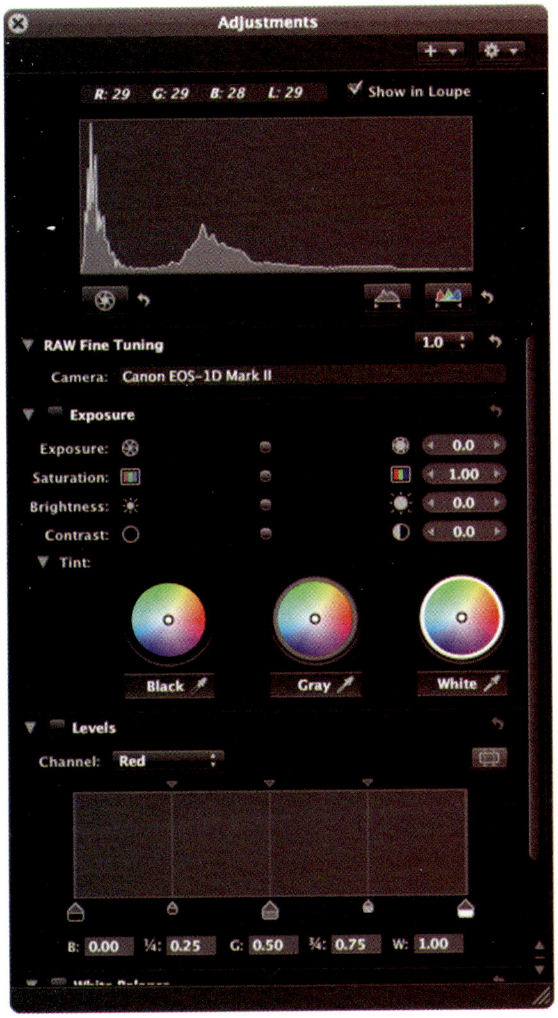

Figure 1.16:
The Adjustments HUD

In Aperture, each adjustment is actually a filter that's applied to your image. Think of a filter as a step on an assembly floor, and each time you view an image, Aperture assembles the image you see by taking the master and running its pixels through the assembly line. That way, you're always working with the original pixels in a nondestructive way, and you can always change your mind about various adjustments and their values. In fact, after you've made some adjustments, if you were to go look at your image in Photoshop, you wouldn't see the various changes you've made within Aperture; you would only see the original image. The filters you've applied to each image are stored within Aperture, and the only way to make an image file with your changes so that you can see them outside of Aperture is to export your image, as covered in Chapter 6.

Unlike Aperture, most other image editors are destructive. In them, once you've changed the image (unless you used a layer adjustment mask or some other more advanced technique), the only way to modify that change is to undo everything else you did after that change and/or start over—from scratch. Plus, if you actually look at the file after you work with it in other programs and click Save, you will see only see your modified image stored in the file; you won't see the original image anymore (unless it's a layered file). Again, if you were to look at the image that you modified within Aperture, you would see the original image, not the modified one, and a list of steps telling Aperture how to create your modified image. Chapter 5 will explain nondestructive editing in depth and how to incorporate it to your workflow.

Another benefit to Aperture's method of storing instructions for changes rather than changing the image itself is that the set of instructions you apply to a given image can be "lifted" from one image and "stamped" onto one or more other images, another topic that we will cover in Chapter 5. For instance, if you accidentally set the camera's white balance incorrectly, you can quickly correct it in one image and apply that correction to other images taken under similar lighting conditions. However, if you decide you like the incorrect white balance better than the corrected white balance in one image, you can remove the correction just by turning off those choices.

If you want to experiment with an image, perhaps to see what it might look like with a different white balance setting and compare the two images side-by-side, you can make a new *version* of the master instead of duplicating the master and creating a copy of the original file. A version is a reference to the master file with a different set of filters applied. Furthermore, because Aperture stores information about the changes to an image, rather than the image with the changes applied, creating a new version of an image uses very little disk space.

Note: You can always get a new, fresh version of a photo with no adjustments by selecting Image > New Version From Master (Option+G).

External Editors

Despite their destructive nature, for many of us, an image-editing program such as Adobe Photoshop is essential to our workflow. Aperture provides many of the basic tools we use to modify images, especially for RAW conversion, but it is by no means a Photoshop replacement. Whenever we want to make complicated changes to an image, we need to go to an external editor, which is set within the Aperture preferences.

Note: Opening a RAW file in an external editor from within Aperture isn't easy, but we'll show you how to hack Aperture so that you can get to the RAW file in Chapter 10. That way you can convert it using a different RAW converter if you want.

You can open an image quickly in your external editor by pressing ⌘+Shift+O or by choosing Image > Open With External Editor. Aperture automatically makes a new version of the image for you. Unlike the New Version From Master command, the version created with this command is tied to a new master image file, either a TIFF or PSD file, depending on your preferences, with all of your enhancements applied. Aperture has to make a new file because programs like Photoshop can't access or understand

Aperture's internal list of changes; they can work only with a new image file with the changes applied. The downside to using this new file is that you consume disk space every time Aperture has to make a new image file for your external editor; a RAW file converted to a 16-bit TIFF can be 100MB or larger.

After you make your changes in your editor, click Save (not Save As) and go back into Aperture. After a few seconds, you'll see the thumbnail for the new image version update with your changes. The version of the image you worked with in your editor is automatically stacked with your original image, and you can set it to be the stack pick by selecting it and pressing ⌘+\. Alternatively, you can extract it into its own stack by selecting it and pressing Option+Shift+K. Keep in mind that some of things you can do in an external editor, such as converting to CMYK, will prevent Aperture from reading the edited image. In case you're wondering which buttons to press to make sure color management from Aperture to print stays consistent, we'll answer that question and more in Chapter 6.

Sharing Images

Once your best images are selected, keyworded, and tweaked, it's time to share them with the world. You can share images from inside of Aperture through books, websites, prints, slideshows, email, and exporting them.

Books

Aperture lets you create books from numerous templates and provides the ability to customize each template.

Note: You can start a book from anywhere in Aperture by selecting some photos and then selecting File > New From Selection > Book.

Your first choice is to determine whether you want a small or large book. If you pick a large book, what style do you want? Perhaps you want to create a special occasion book for your cousin's wedding, with its white background and ample room for writing wedding stories. Perhaps you're preparing a book of stock images for a submission to a stock agency, and you prefer a professional black background with limited text. Either way, the process of making a book is the same: pick your template, drag images onto the book pages, move them around, and add/remove/modify the pages. Figure 1.17 shows what the book layout feature looks like, and Chapter 9, "Creating a Book," will show you all the secrets of bookmaking in Aperture. When you're ready, either you can print the book to a high-resolution PDF for self-publication, or you can click Buy Book to have your book printed using Apple's print service. Keep in mind, however, that even though Aperture's books are higher in quality than those you can order in iPhoto, the image quality is not on par with prints from high-end inkjets.

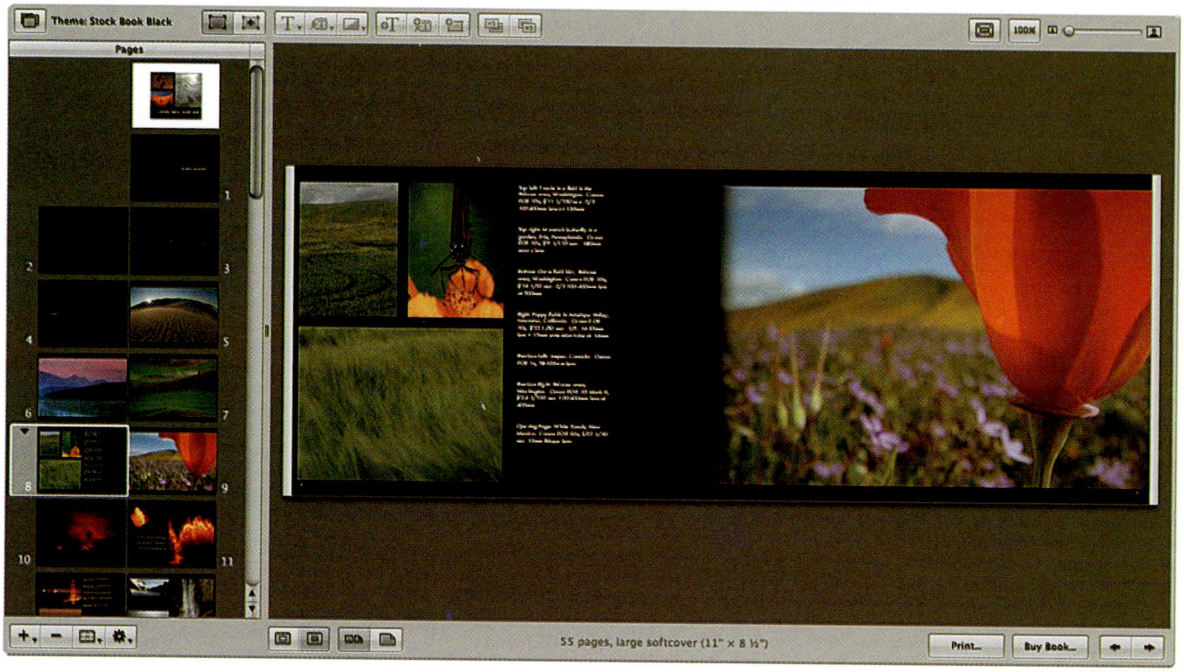

Figure 1.17: The Book Layout view

Web Pages

Books are so 1999. In today's world, everyone wants to see a web page of your work. Don't worry—you don't have to know HTML to make a professional-looking site. Aperture provides the tools you need to make two types of web pages. The first type is a *web gallery*. A gallery includes an index page with thumbnails of each of your photos, and a detail page showing a large version of the image for each, as well as optional and customizable metadata for each image. The second type of site is a *web journal*. The main difference between a journal and a gallery is that a journal is focused on photos and text (including, but not limited to, metadata), whereas a gallery only lets you place images and metadata. Figure 1.18 shows what the two types look like in a web browser.

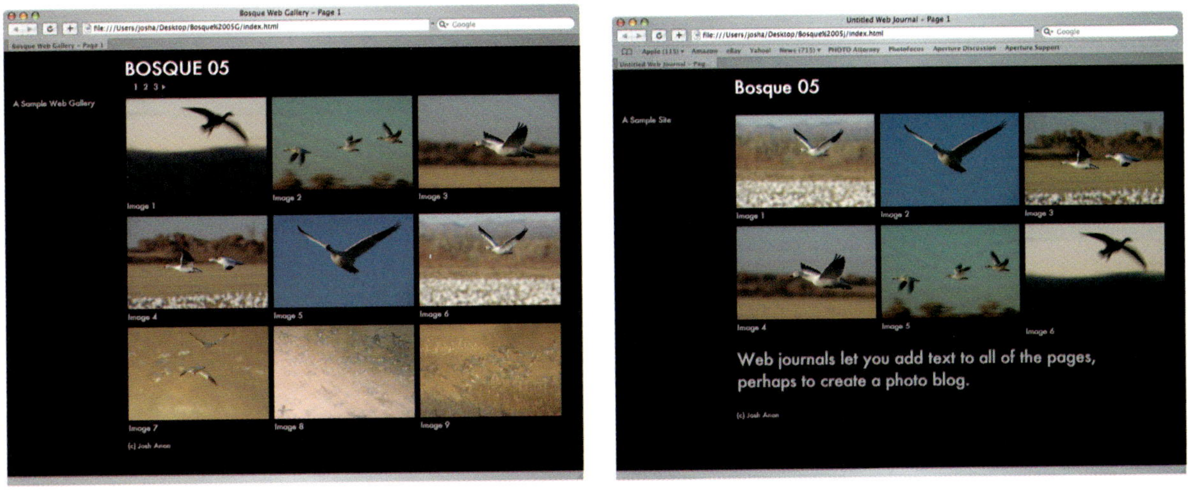

Figure 1.18: A sample web gallery (left) and a web journal (right)

Chapter 8, "Creating Web Content," will cover creating websites from start to finish. Both types are created the same way you create a book—select your images, and choose File > New From Selection > Web Gallery (or Journal). Also like a book, you can drag and drop to rearrange images, double-click text to edit it, and change your theme. Creating web pages in Aperture provides one big advantage over other programs—they're live. This means that within Aperture, you're actually looking at a web browser. You can click links to see what happens, and you don't have to worry about your site looking different when you view it outside of Aperture.

When you're ready to publish your site, you can save it to a folder on your computer, a folder that you can upload to a server or move to wherever you want, or you can automatically publish it to a .Mac account with one click.

Note: If you're worried about someone else taking credit for your image, you can specify that Aperture should automatically apply a watermark to every image you export. Select the watermark from within the Aperture > Presets > Web Export menu. Isn't it great to be able to share your work without being afraid of not getting credit? We'll show you how to add watermarks to your exported images in Chapter 5, and we'll cover watermarks with websites in Chapter 8.

Printing

As great as web pages are, sometimes you or your clients just want to see a contact sheet of your images or perhaps a print of one or two of them. In Aperture, printing your images is as simple as selecting the image or images you want to print (or just choosing File > Print Images to print all images) and choosing how you want to print them. Chapter 7, "Printing," will cover printing in detail, including creating your own print presets.

Aperture has two bundled print presets, one for contact sheets and the other for single images. For contact sheets, you specify either a desired number of pages or a desired number of rows and columns, and Aperture will configure its print job to meet your request. You can also select what type of metadata to display with the contact sheet and how big the font to print it should be. Figure 1.19 shows the Print panel with contact sheet printing selected and some options, such as metadata, enabled.

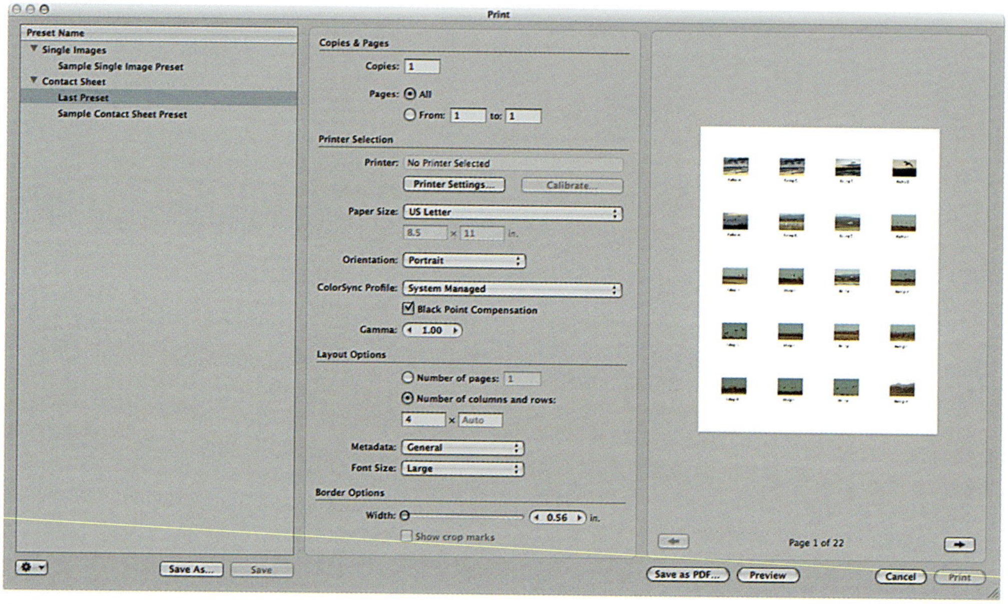

Figure 1.19: The contact sheet Print panel

Note: If some of the options in this panel are a bit confusing, don't worry. We'll explain them to you in Chapter 7.

For a single image, you can explicitly set the size to scale your image to, from filling to fit the page to a custom size, perhaps 8.5 × 12.5. We'll discuss color management with printing more in Chapter 7. One important point to remember is that if you select the System Managed ColorSync profile, make sure to turn color management off in your print driver after you click Print. Otherwise, you'll get a double-color-managed image, but the print won't be twice as good.

Slideshows

Sometimes, when a client is sitting with you, you might like to share what you've been shooting. A slideshow of your images can be quite effective. Aperture has six preset slideshow modes, including dissolve and manual, and you can choose Edit from the Slideshow Preset menu to create your own preset mode or modify one of the built-in ones. Figure 1.20 shows the Edit panel and some of the options that you can configure. These options include manually advancing the images or having Aperture time the images to match music you picked from your iTunes library. You can also set the slideshow to show up to 10 × 10 images at once, instead of the usual one-at-a-time, providing a way to easily see sequences of images within the slideshow. We'll cover slideshows more in Chapter 3.

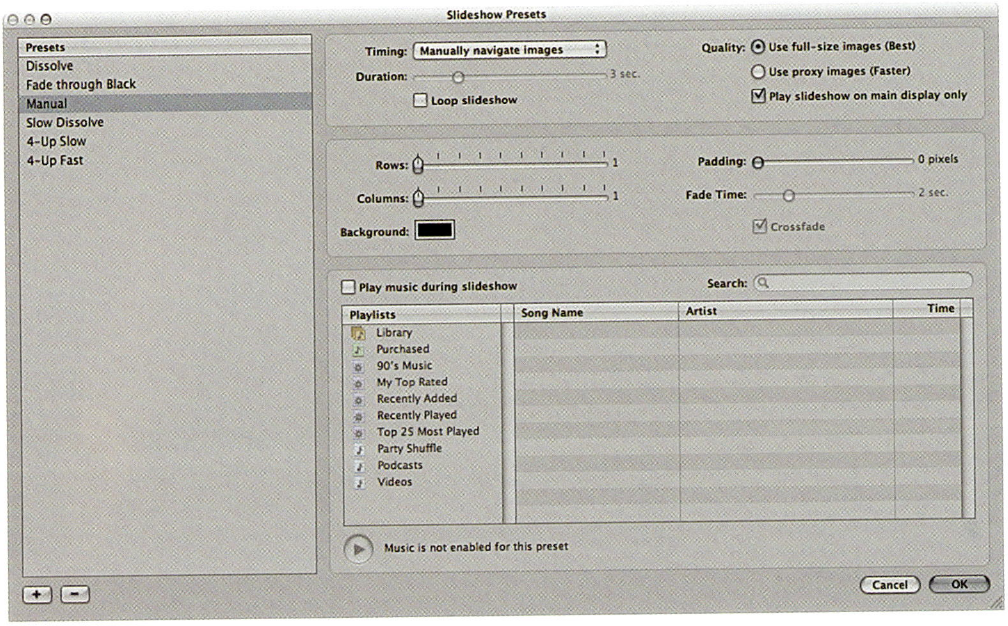

Figure 1.20: The various slideshow options

Note: You can set the slideshows to use the smaller preview files that Aperture creates for each image, rather than the full image, allowing your slideshow to run smoothly if you're trying to show large files.

Email

Speaking of smooth, it would be hard for Aperture's email tool to get any easier to use. Under Aperture's Preferences, you set your preferred email program and the file format to which you want your emailed images to be reformatted, such as Medium JPEG. Then, simply make sure your email client is open, select some photos in Aperture, and choose File > Email (Option+E). A copy of your image will automatically be reformatted to the format you specified under Preferences, optionally with a watermark. Aperture will create a new, blank message with your photos in your mail program. See Chapter 6, "Exporting Images" for more detail.

Exporting Images

Despite all of these slick ways to share your images, sometimes you just want to export the file from Aperture to use elsewhere, perhaps to send to a print service. We'll cover exporting in depth in Chapter 6. For a quick overview, if you want to export the master image, such as a RAW file, select the image you want and choose File > Export Master (⌘+Shift+S). You can select to keep the filenames or rename them based on image date, version number, or custom text. If you're exporting multiple images, Aperture will automatically append an index number to each image. Figure 1.21 shows some of the options you have for naming your images when you export them.

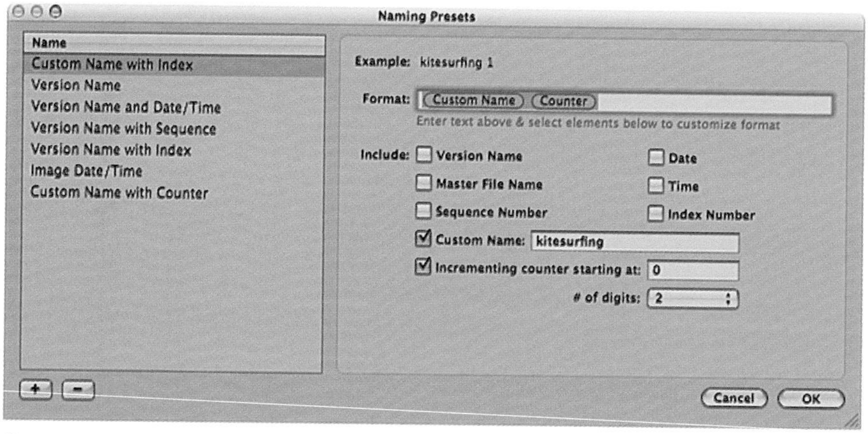

Figure 1.21: The Naming Presets panel

If you've altered your image in Aperture (for example, cropped it or changed the exposure) and you want to export the modified image, select File > Export Version (⌘+Shift+E) instead of Export Master. This type of export provides the same flexible naming scheme that Export Master does, but it allows you to select the type of image file you want, as Aperture can't give you a new RAW file with your changes applied. You can pick from a variety of image types, ranging from a full-sized 16-bit PSD file to a JPEG that fits within a 640 × 640 square. Keep in mind that Export Version uses the same export settings as the Mail exporter. In other words, if you have a particular type, such as Email Medium JPEG, set to add a watermark, Export Version will also add the watermark if you pick that format, in this case Email Medium JPEG.

Vaults

A common reason to export your images is to back up your work. Rather than exporting thousands of images, Aperture provides a way to automatically clone your photo library elsewhere, perhaps to an external hard drive. This backup of your images is called a *vault*, and you can have multiple vaults wherever you'd like them, as long as the drive you select for the vault has enough free space. Vaults are shown in Aperture in the bottom of the Projects panel, and you can see them by selecting Window > Show Vaults. Once you have set up a vault, the panel will look similar to Figure 1.22.

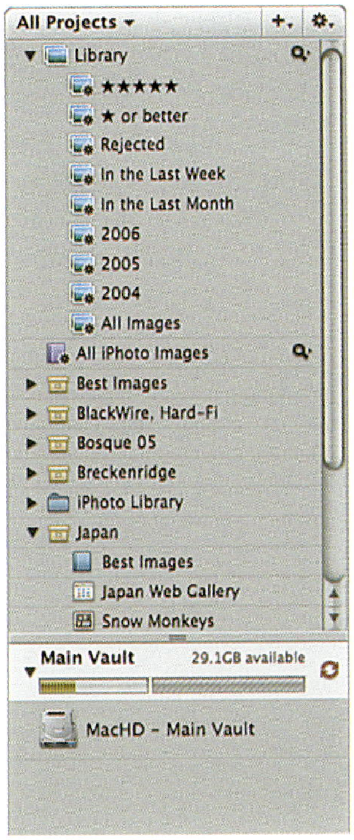

Figure 1.22:
The Vaults panel with a sample vault

When you sync your vaults after you make changes to your Aperture library, only the changes that you've made since the last sync are copied. Your entire library, potentially gigabytes of data, is not copied. Because only the changes are copied, syncing your vaults can be very fast, depending on your changes.

If something happens to your photo library, you can restore your library, or set up a copy of your photo library on another computer by selecting File > Vault > Restore Library. The panel you see in Figure 1.23 will appear, and you can select a vault file. Aperture will replace the contents of your photo library with the data from the vault. We will cover backup more in Chapter 4, including tips on how to safely store your backups.

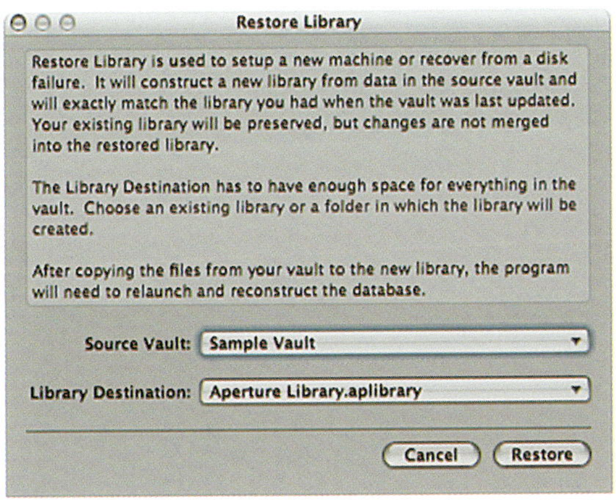

Figure 1.23:
Restoring from a Vault

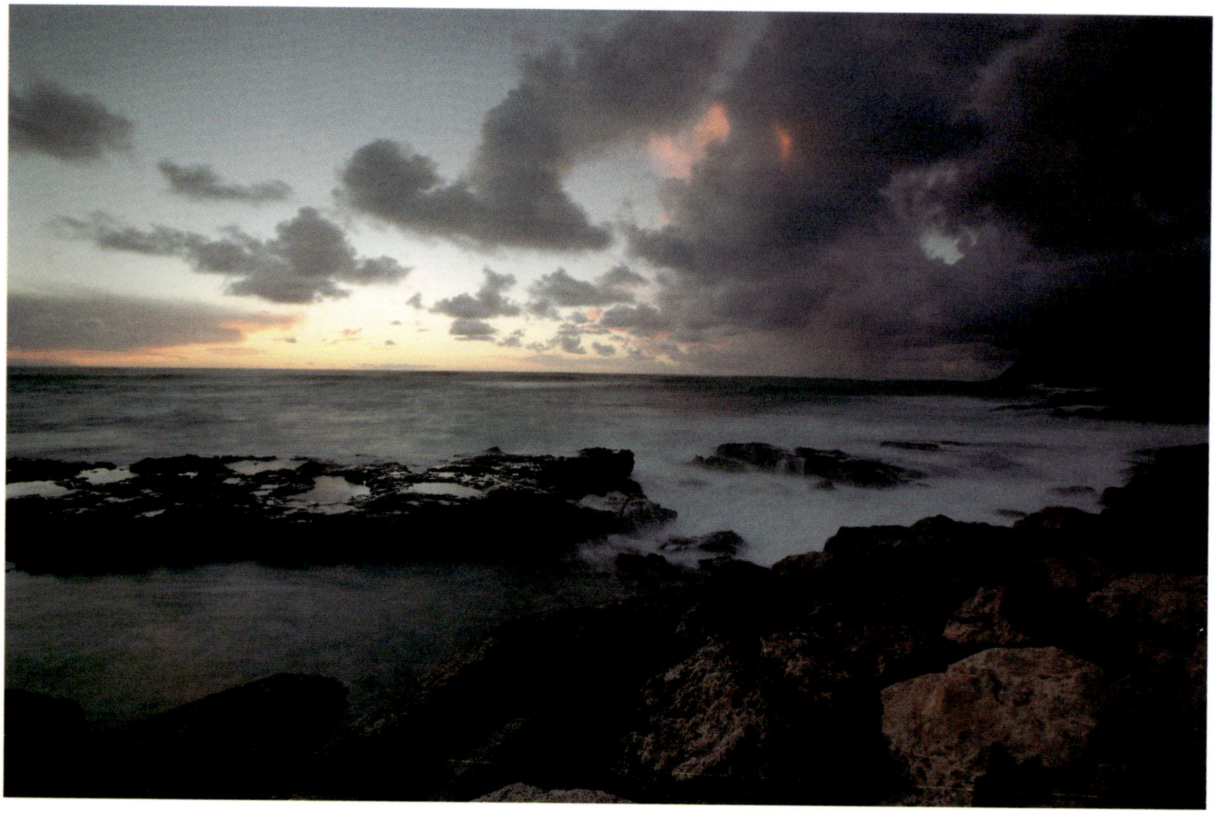

Importing and Organizing Your Images

For many photographers, the first hurdle with digital photography is getting images from the camera into the computer. Then, once the images are on the computer, it's easy to get confused as to where each folder is, what image is in each file, and where the files are from, given their obscure filenames and general lack of organization. In Aperture, Apple has simplified the process so that importing can be as simple as attaching your camera to the computer and clicking a button. The more advanced user can stack images, attach metadata, and do much more before importing.

2

Chapter Contents

The Import Panel

Aperture lets you import images from four different places: iPhoto, disk drives, cameras, and storage cards (such as a compact flash card). To import your images from a storage card, either directly attach your camera to your computer or attach your storage card and reader to the computer. Then open Aperture and choose Window > Show Import Panel. After a few seconds, your storage card will appear as an import source. Click the card to bring up the Import panel.

> **Note:** You can set Aperture to automatically launch when you attach a camera by selecting Aperture from the When Camera Is Connected, Open field in the Aperture preferences. If iPhoto launches automatically, quit iPhoto and then change the When Camera Is Connected setting within Aperture.

The Import panel, shown in Figure 2.1, has four main parts. Part 1 shows thumbnails of the images on your card. By using the controls on the bottom in Part 2, you can change the view from a thumbnail view to a table view and you can also change how the images are sorted. Part 3, directly below the view, consists of stack controls. Part 4, on the right, allows you to adjust metadata.

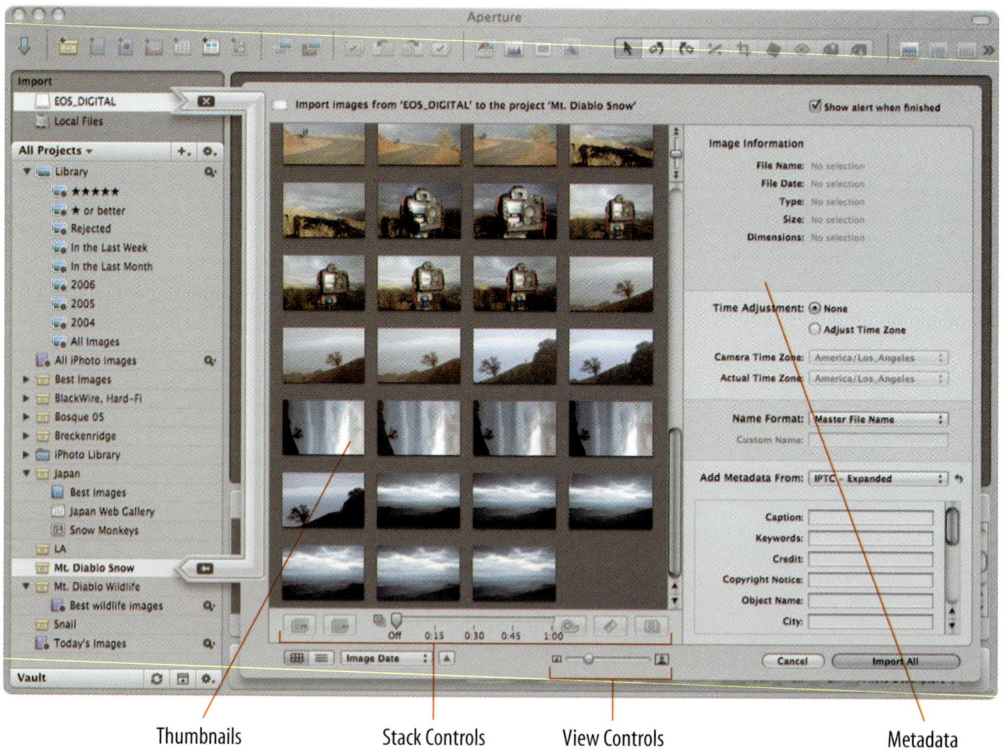

Figure 2.1: The Import window

Importing from a Camera

As far as Aperture is concerned, importing directly from a camera or from a storage card is exactly the same process. The only thing that differs is how you physically connect the device holding your photos to the computer. When you select the source from the Import panel and the Import window appears, Aperture automatically will generate low-resolution thumbnails for your images. These are thumbnails only; you cannot loupe them, and you shouldn't use them to judge exposure and color. If the program hasn't generated a thumbnail yet, it will show a gray box until it has. You can make the thumbnails larger or smaller by using the slider at the bottom of the window to the left of the Cancel button.

RAW Support in Aperture

Unlike programs such as Adobe Photoshop, Aperture relies on Mac OS X for its RAW support. As Apple adds support for more RAW formats, rather than updating Aperture, you'll need to update your operating system (OS) to get that support. As of early 2006, Mac OS X 10.4.5 supports most Canon and Nikon cameras and a few cameras from other manufacturers, such as Sony and Konica Minolta. You can find a complete list at http://www.apple.com/aperture/raw/.

Aperture also has some support for DNG, but as of early 2006, this support is quite limited. You can quickly and easily test whether or not Aperture will be able to import your image by trying to open it in Preview (inside your Applications folder).

If your RAW format is not currently supported, you can still use Aperture if your camera supports simultaneously shooting JPEGs. Aperture will import both the RAW and JPEG files. Although you won't be able to view the RAW file, you can access the JPEG by selecting Images > New Version From Master JPEG. If Apple adds support for your RAW file to Mac OS X, your RAW files will automatically be usable once you update your system and launch Aperture.

The controls shown in Figure 2.2 let you modify how Aperture displays the thumbnails. You can switch between a thumbnail view and a table view, and when you're in a thumbnail view, the pop-up button lets you pick which field to use to sort your images. The arrow will let you toggle between sorting them in ascending and descending order. If you're using a table view to see your thumbnails, you can click the column headers to sort your images by that field. Clicking a second time on the column header will reverse the sort order.

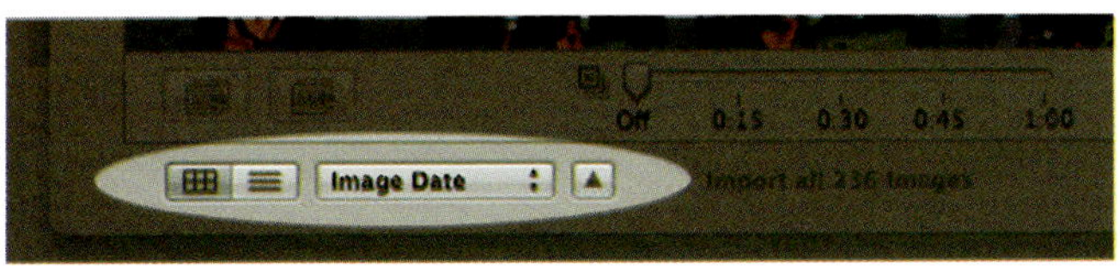

Figure 2.2:
The view display controls

When you click an image, Aperture displays basic information about the image, such as file size, in the top-right portion of the Import window. When you select two or more images, Aperture activates an additional control that will allow you to combine the images into a single stack.

Right above the top of the scroll bar in the importer's Image view is a scrolling acceleration control that you can use when you are trying to look at a large number of images. If you grab this control and move it up or down, Aperture will scroll in that direction. The farther you drag the control from the center, the faster Aperture will scroll through your images.

Stacking Images in the Import Window

The Import window has controls to manually and automatically stack images. As we discussed in Chapter 1, "Welcome to Aperture," a stack is a group of related images—for instance, a group of images taken within a short period of time or a burst of photos. Directly below the center of the Thumbnail view, there is a slider with labels underneath it ranging from Off to 1:00, representing one minute. If you grab this slider and move it to the right, Off changes to 0, and Aperture automatically starts stacking your images. It stacks images taken within whatever time duration you specify in the slider; if you move the slider to 0:30, it will stack images taken within 30 seconds of each other. In the Thumbnail view, Aperture creates a darker region around each stack, as shown in Figure 2.3, and it adds a label showing how many images are in the stack. If you're using the Table view to look at your images, Aperture displays a stack as a group that you can open by pressing the small triangle in the left-most column. Stacks aren't limited to time, however, and you might stack a series of bracketed exposures or alternative horizontal and vertical compositions of a subject. You can set up these non-time-based stacks manually.

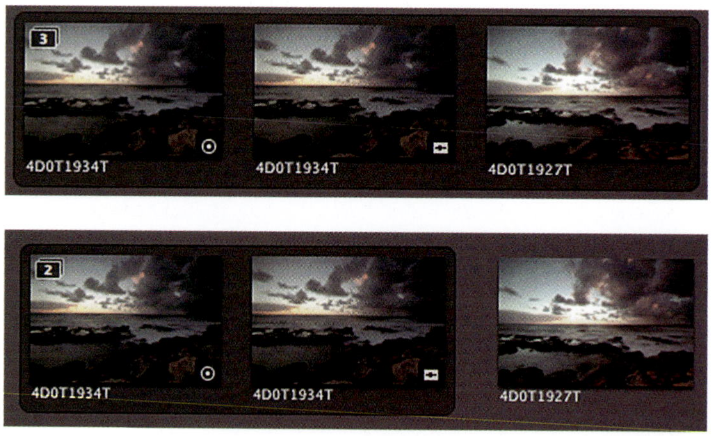

Figure 2.3:
In grid view, Aperture creates a dark region around each stack and adds a label displaying how many images are in the stack.

If you are unhappy with how Aperture automatically stacked some of your images, you can manually edit the stacks using the buttons at the bottom of the Import panel (Figure 2.4). If you'd like to split the stack into two or more stacks, select the first image that you'd like to remove from the stack and click the Split Stack button or choose Stacks > Split Stack. The image that you selected and any images to its right in the stack are split into their own stack. The second part of Figure 2.3 is what the stack turns into if you select the third image and click the Split Stack button . Rather than splitting the stack, if you just want to extract one item from the stack, select the item and choose Stacks > Extract Item. To completely unstack all images, you can either drag the autostack slider to Off (if you've only stacked images automatically based on time) or click the Unstack All Stacks button .

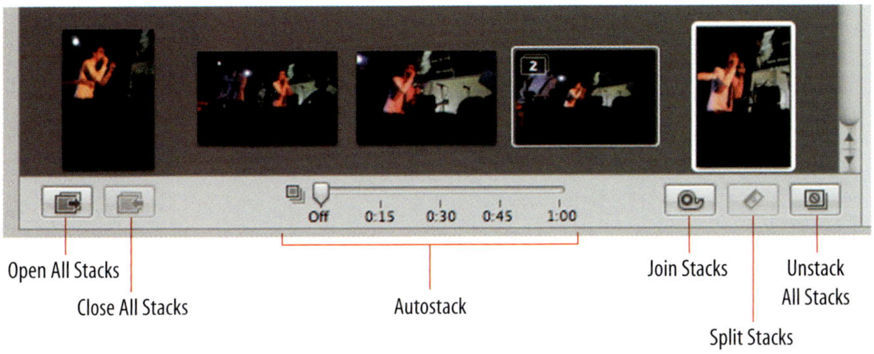

Figure 2.4: The stack editing buttons

In addition to manually unstacking images, you can select images you want to stack and manually stack them. To join an image to a stack, select the image to add and select an image in the existing stack, and click the Join Stacks button or choose Stacks > Stack.

Note: To select a range of images, Shift+click the first and last images you want to select. To select images that aren't next to each other, ⌘+click the images to toggle their selection state.

Once you have set up your stacks, Aperture provides a few utility functions to help you work with stacks. To quickly navigate between stacks, you can choose Stacks > Previous Stack and Stacks > Next Stack. If you'd like to jump to a stack and select the entire stack, you can choose Stacks > Select Previous Stack and Stacks > Select Next Stack.

When you're viewing stacks, you can expand and collapse the stacks to save screen space. To collapse all stacks, click the Close All Stacks button at the bottom-left of the Import window or select Stacks > Close All Stacks. To expand all stacks, click the Open All Stacks button on the bottom-left of the Import window or select Stacks > Open All Stacks. To expand a collapsed stack or collapse an expanded stack, select the stack and choose either Stacks > Close Stack or Stacks > Open Stack. The available menu item will change depending on whether you click a collapsed stack or an expanded stack. Expanding and collapsing a stack does not change how images are stacked; these commands change how you view the stack.

Note: You don't have to stack your images in the Import window. You can stack your images later, after importing them.

I Shoot with RAW + JPEG: Why Do I Only See My RAW files in the Importer?

Aperture's goal is to make working with RAW files as easy as working with JPEG files. To support that workflow, Aperture prefers the RAW file to any other format. If you shoot RAW and JPEG files, Aperture will not display your JPEG files in the importer's file listing. However, when you click Import, Aperture will import the JPEG file too. If you explore your photo library, as we will discuss in Chapter 10, "Advanced Aperture," you'll see the JPEG file grouped with the RAW file.

The only place that Aperture even acknowledges there is a JPEG file with your RAW file is in the Images > New Version From Master JPEG menu item. (We'll explore working with versions in Chapter 5, "Nondestructive Image Processing.") You can select the version that command creates and Export Master to access the JPEG outside of Aperture. Even though Aperture doesn't do much with the JPEG files, it can still be useful with programs that don't support RAW and for data recovery if a RAW file is corrupt. Additionally, if Aperture doesn't yet support your RAW file format, you can still import the RAW file into Aperture. As long as you also import a simultaneously-shot JPEG, you can use the New Version From Master JPEG command to see and edit your images.

Metadata

Often, each group of images you import will have some common element, be it the photographer, the location, or the keywords. You can tediously set this information later, after you've imported the images. However, setting your metadata values while you import your images with Aperture is easy. You can't set individual values for each image in the importer, however. The metadata values you set here are for all images in the import group.

Aperture provides a number of metadata sets; each set contains a variety of different fields. The sets range from Caption Only, where you can set the caption, to IPTC Expanded, which is arguably the most useful and where you can set values for fields including Keywords, City, and Byline. The Add Metadata From pop-up, which is shown at the top of Figure 2.5, lets you pick which set to use. If you enter a value in one field, such as Caption, and switch to a different metadata set, Aperture preserves the values you entered in the other sets. Chapter 4, "Finding the Keepers," will discuss how you can use metadata, such as keywords, to help you find your best images.

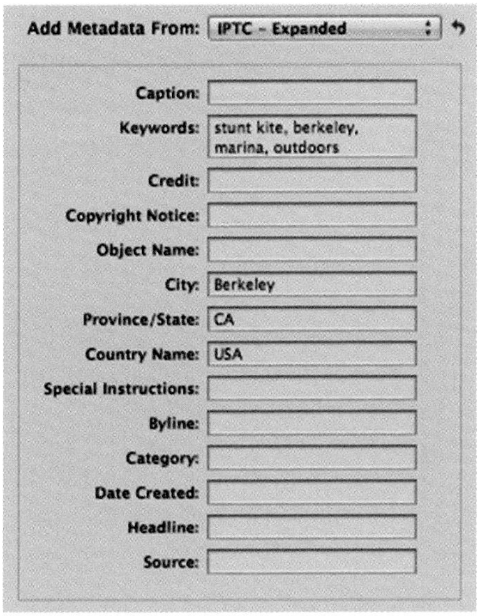

Figure 2.5: The Import window's Metadata view showing the IPTC – Expanded metadata with some sample values.

After you import your images, you can add additional metadata, including custom values for each image, and you can edit the information you set while importing.

Bulk Renaming

Some people insist that computers speak a different language. When you look at images from digital cameras and see filenames like 4D0T9821, you do have to wonder what language you're reading. If you really wanted to, you could go into the Finder, rename your images, and then import them into Aperture, but it is far easier to have Aperture rename your images as it imports them.

The Name Format pop-up, directly above the Metadata view in the Import window, allows you to pick how, if at all, Aperture will rename your images. The useful default options are:

Master File Name Your image will not be renamed.

Custom Name with Index You specify a name, and Aperture will add a number to the filename each time you import, always starting at 1.

Custom Name with Counter You specify a name and starting number, and Aperture will rename each image to that name and the next number, starting at the number you specify.

If these built-in naming formats are not enough, you can choose Edit from the bottom of the Name Format pop-up to create another custom name. Aperture will open the Naming Presets window in Figure 2.6. To use this dialog, click the + button in the lower-left to add a new naming preset, and then name the new format. We're going to create a format called Date, Master, and Counter, which will have the image date, master filename, and a counter.

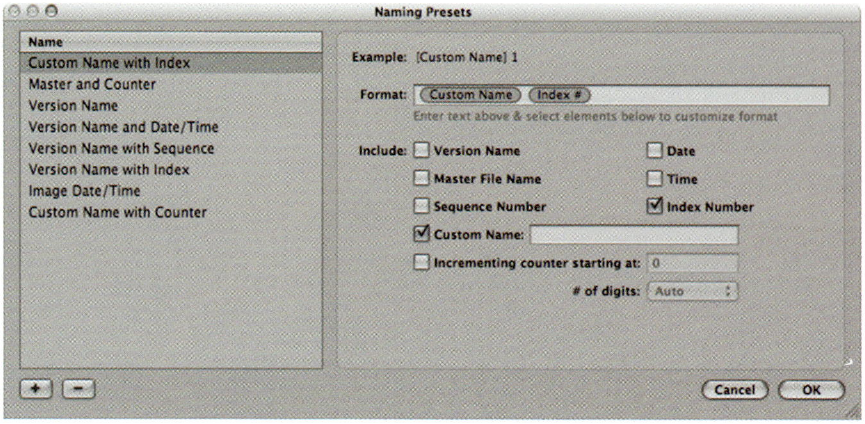

Figure 2.6: The Naming Presets window

On the right side of the Naming Presets window, you'll find a preview of what your naming preset looks like, a text field where you can manually rearrange and add text to the naming format, and various check boxes to add/remove fields from your custom name. Follow these steps to customize our naming preset:

1. Start by unchecking Version Name. The text field at the top will now be empty.
2. Select Date so that the image name will be the first part of the new name.
3. To add a bit of separation between the date and master name, let's add an underscore (_) instead of a space between the two fields. Click in the text field, after the Date placeholder, delete the space that Aperture added, and type an underscore.
4. Check the Master File Name check box, and again click in the text field and add another underscore.
5. Complete the new naming preset by checking Incrementing Counter Starting At. For our purposes, start at 1 and let the number of digits in the counter vary.

Note: Experiment with the number of digits in the counter, and watch the sample filename at the top of the window change.

When you're satisfied with how the sample filename looks, click OK to save your naming preset. If you're having trouble, try to match the naming preset settings you see in Figure 2.7.

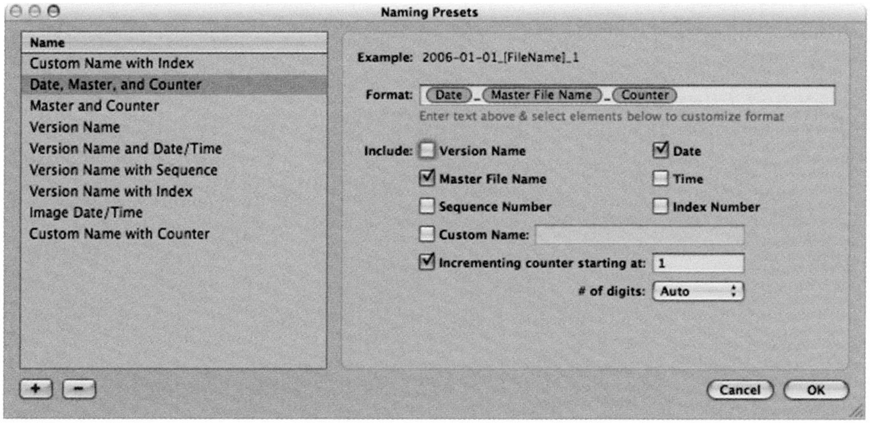

Figure 2.7: Naming preset values for a custom Date, Master, and Counter format

If you pick a name format aside from Master File Name, Aperture will display the file's new name in red, in the top-right portion of the Import window. Counters do not work in this Preview panel, however, and if you specified a naming format with a counter, Aperture will show the starting number you specified as the counter number for all of your images.

Time Adjustment

Many photographers travel all over the world. Usually, they remember to change their watches when traveling between time zones, but they don't change their cameras' clocks. If you're importing images from multiple cameras, for instance, you can become confused when the combined images don't appear in the correct order because one camera was set slightly different. Depending on where you traveled, you might think your sunset photos are actually sunrise photos if you were to look at the image's date/time information. Such confusion could be even more disastrous if you were on a photojournalism assignment or were interviewing subjects and you needed to know exactly when you saw something. Suffice it to say, if your images have the wrong dates and times, things can get messy.

Aperture again comes to the rescue by making it simple to adjust time zones. Directly above the Bulk Renaming view in the Import window, you'll find the Time Adjustment view seen in Figure 2.8. To activate this view, click in the circle next to Adjust Time Zone. Then, set the Camera Time Zone field to your camera's time zone, and set the Actual Time Zone to the time zone in which you were shooting. Once set, you'll see another red field appear in the top-left corner labeled Adjusted File Date. This field shows you the image's date after being adjusted to the new time zone. Again, remember that Aperture will apply this adjustment to all of the images you're importing in this group and not just to the selected images.

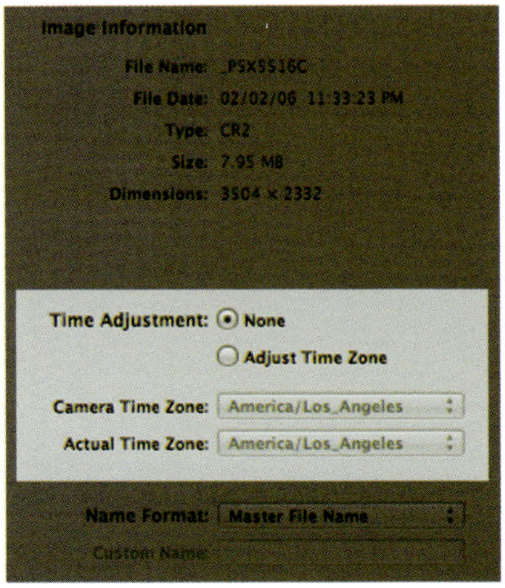

Figure 2.8: The Time Adjustment view

Projects

As we discussed in Chapter 1, projects are containers for images and their associated files, such as albums, light tables, and web galleries. Whenever you import images into Aperture, you must pick a project into which to import your images. If you haven't opened the Import window yet, you can create a new project by choosing File > New Project or by clicking the + button next to the All Projects text in the Projects panel and choosing New Project.

When you open up the Import window, the tip of the arrow whose tail is your storage card and whose middle is the Import window will point at the project Aperture will import the photos into. Try clicking different projects to watch the arrow change, such as in Figure 2.9 where we switch between the Best Images and Mt. Diablo Snow projects. If you decide to make a new project, after opening the Import window, you can click Library to cause Aperture to create a new project when you start importing your images.

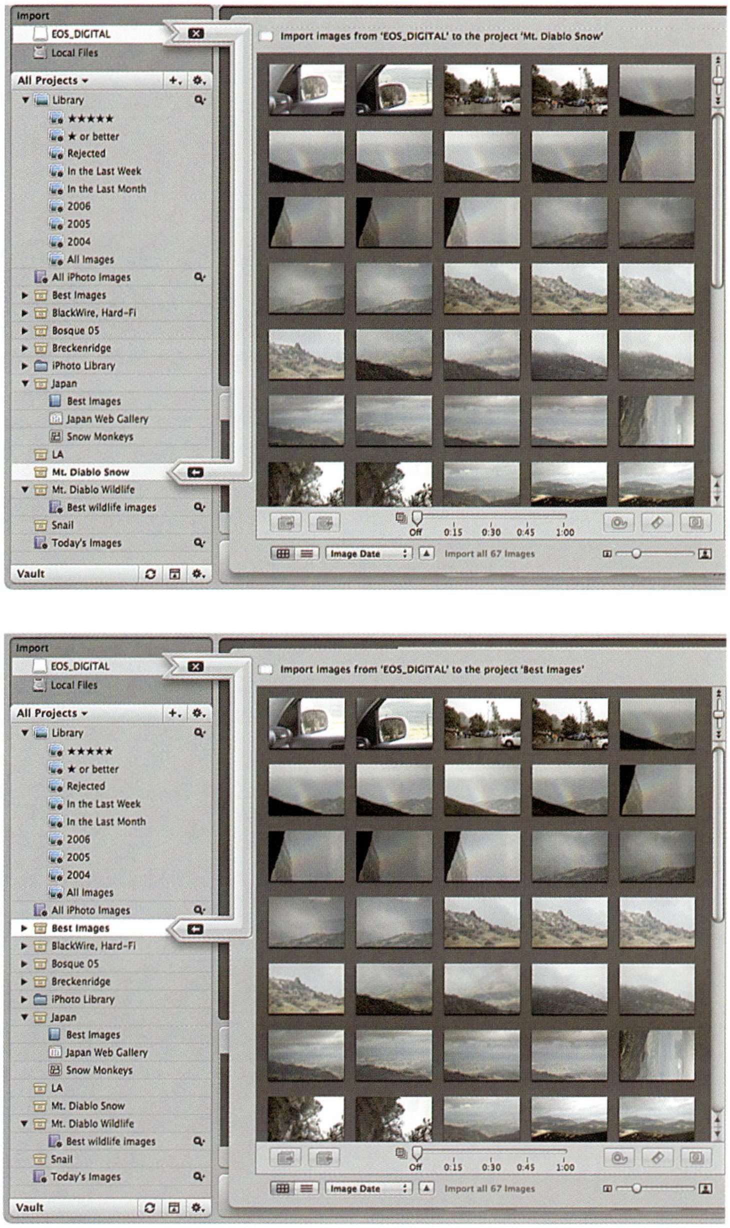

Figure 2.9:
The arrow points from the storage card to the project where your images will be imported.

Note: If you have an album (excluding smart albums) set up within a project, you can select the album instead of the project so that Aperture will import your images into the project and add them to the selected album.

Task List

Once you've stacked your images, set your metadata, set up your filename format, set the correct time zone, and picked your destination project, you can pick which images you'd like to import into your photo library and click the Import Images button in the bottom right of the Import window. If you'd like to import all of the images, either select all of the images and click the Import Images button, or deselect all of your images by clicking in an empty area in the Thumbnail view, and then click the Import All button at the bottom right.

Note: When Aperture imports your image, it automatically creates a thumbnail and a version of the image that you can manipulate.

Once Aperture has started importing, the Import window will disappear, and Aperture will import your photos in the background. You'll see a spinning icon in the Projects panel while Aperture imports your photos. If you'd like more information about what Aperture is doing, you can bring up the Task List.

To open the Task List, shown in Figure 2.10, select Window > Show Task List. The Task List provides a list of the tasks Aperture is performing in the background and how far along they are. If you change your mind and decide to cancel your import job, select the import task and click Cancel Task. To close the window, click the Done button. Alternatively, to cancel your import task, you can select File > Import > Cancel Import.

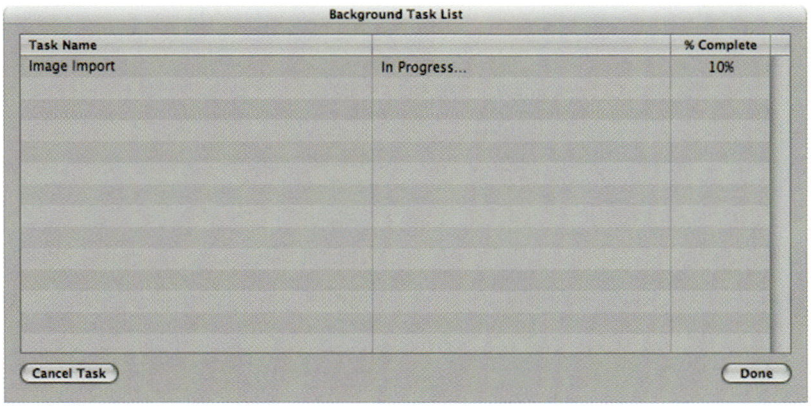

Figure 2.10: The Task List

After Aperture is finished importing, assuming you had Show Alert When Finished checked in the Import window, a dialog box will prompt you to eject your card, erase and eject your card, or do nothing. Ejecting your card is the most useful option because you will still have a backup of your images (until you reformat and use the card again) if something goes wrong. Clicking Done will dismiss the dialog without ejecting your card or erasing your images, and you'll have to manually eject the card later by selecting it in the Finder and choosing File > Eject.

Importing from a Disk

Aperture has a few different ways to import your images from a disk, such as your hard drive or a CD. The simplest method is to use the Import window, just as you do when you import from a compact flash card. To bring up the Import window on a disk, make sure the Import panel is visible. If it's hidden, you can reveal it by selecting Window > Show Import Panel. After you select a disk, the Import window will open. The Import window will have a browser on the top, as seen in Figure 2.11, which will let you browse your hard drive to find the images you want to import. Everything else in the Import window, from stacking to time zone adjusting, works exactly as it did when you were importing from a storage card.

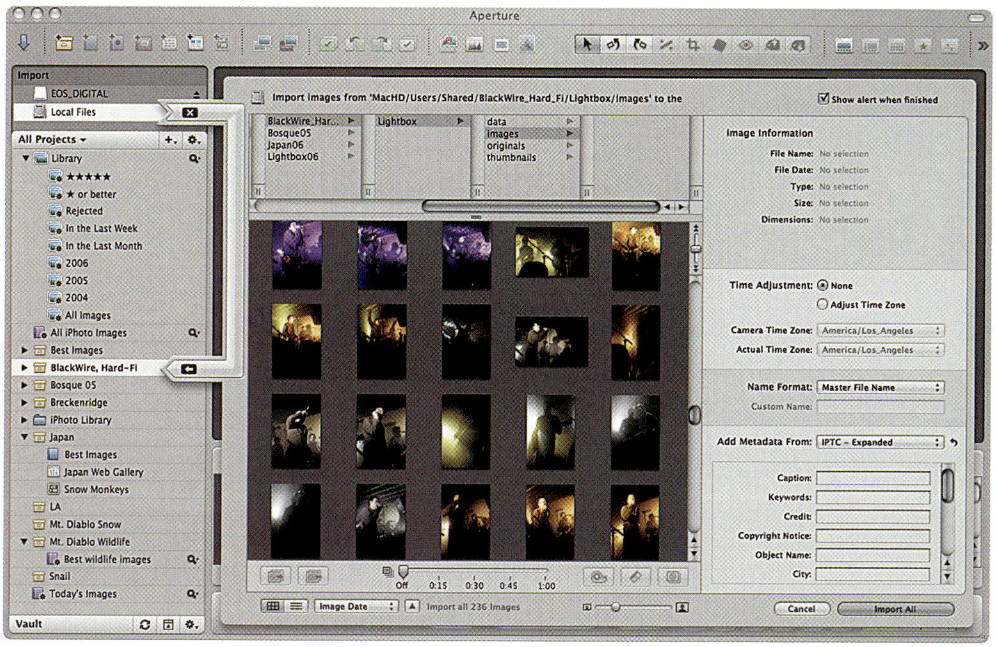

Figure 2.11: The Import window shows a browser when you're importing from a disk.

Note: The companion website, www.sybex.com/go/apertureexposed, provides a handful of RAW and JPEG files for you to import. Experiment with the various methods of file importing described in this section. Use the Import window and try dragging and dropping to import the images into Aperture.

However, you might already have a folder structure set up with your images from before you started using Aperture. If you use the Import window, Aperture will lose your folder structure. Instead, Aperture has a special command that will let you import a folder of images (or perhaps a folder of folders of images), preserving the hierarchy. You can find this command under File > Import > Folders Into A Project.

Note: If you are importing large groups of files from your disk, try importing a small subset first to make sure that everything is configured properly. If that small subset works, then finish importing your images.

As an example, let's say you have a Weddings folder with Smith Wedding and Jones Wedding subfolders. Furthermore, let's say each subfolder has images within it. When you choose Folders Into A Project, Aperture brings up an open panel. Navigate to your Weddings folder, select the Weddings folder, and click Open. Aperture will create a new project called Weddings, and the new project will have two albums called Smith Wedding and Jones Wedding.

Let's say that your folder structure is actually a bit more complicated, and you also have a Page Wedding folder within your Weddings folder. Inside this folder, you have your images and another folder called Rehearsal Dinner. When you import the Weddings folder, Aperture will create a folder for Page Wedding with two albums inside. One album will be called Images From: Page Wedding and the other will be called Rehearsal Dinner. The Images From: Page Wedding album will have the images within the Page Wedding folder itself, and the Rehearsal Dinner album will have the images that were in the Rehearsal Dinner folder.

Note: If you open your RAW files in another converter before you bring them into Aperture, check your settings in that converter. Make sure that your converter does *not* embed its settings into the RAW file. Embedding these settings can prevent Aperture from being able to read the RAW file, and the only way to import it to Aperture would be to convert it to a TIFF, PSD, or similar file and then import the converted file. A sidecar file, such as the one Adobe Camera Raw creates, is safe.

If you have deeper folders within folders, Aperture will continue to make folders and albums, matching the structure you had on your hard drive. The top-level project will contain all the images from all of the subfolders, though. If you have a folder with a large number of images, consider splitting the folder up into multiple projects.

Note: A project can contain at most 10,000 master images.

Drag and Drop

One feature that Apple has always done quite well is letting users drag and drop files to perform different functions. In Aperture, you can drag and drop images and folders from the Finder to have Aperture import these files in different ways.

The simplest operation would be to select some images in the Finder and to drag and drop them onto an existing project in Aperture. Note that you can only drop the images onto a project—you can't drop them onto an album or other file. If you select a folder, along with some images, in the Finder and drop those onto a project, Aperture will add all of the images to the project, and It will create an album (or folder of folders if your folder has subfolders) in the project with the images in the folder. If you grab just a folder and drag it onto an existing project, Aperture will import your images and turn the folder into an album. If the folder has subfolders, Aperture will make a new subfolder containing albums for each subfolder.

If you drag the image, or images and folder, onto a blank area in the Projects panel or onto the Library, Aperture will make a new project and then import your images. Again, if you select a folder with your images, Aperture will try to preserve your existing structure. If you just grab a folder and drag it onto the Projects panel, Aperture will make a new project with an album representing the old folder. As expected, if you drag a folder with subfolders onto the Projects panel, Aperture will make a new project with a new folder with albums within the folder representing the old subfolders.

Note: If you import a layered TIFF or PSD file, Aperture might flatten the image when you open it in an external editor. To avoid this flattening, do not adjust the image within Aperture and make sure that the external editor file format (under Preferences) matches your image format. We'll cover this issue more in Chapter 6. You can always access the layered file by Exporting Master, as we cover in Chapter 6, "Exporting Images," or by directly accessing the master file as we cover in Chapter 10, "Advanced Aperture."

Importing from iPhoto

Importing your existing images from iPhoto is quite straightforward and fairly automatic. Start by selecting File > Import > iPhoto Library. An Open panel will appear, and you'll need to navigate to your iPhoto library, which is usually found in ~/Pictures. The tilde character (~) represents your home directory, which you can get to by clicking the Finder icon in the dock and selecting Go > Home. Once you've selected your library, click Choose, and a progress bar will appear as Aperture imports your iPhoto library.

If you have a large iPhoto library, with more than a thousand images, having Aperture import your entire library can take a long time. If you only want a particular part of your iPhoto library, you are better off either using the File Import panel to import part of your iPhoto Library folder, or dragging specific images from iPhoto onto the Aperture project that you want to use to store your images.

Note: Even though you work with JPEGs within iPhoto, Aperture will transfer your RAW files if you import from iPhoto 5 or newer.

You might expect Aperture to create a new project called iPhoto and import your images into there, or perhaps you expect Aperture to import your iPhoto images into a selected project. It does neither. Instead, Aperture makes a top-level folder called iPhoto Library. Inside that folder, Aperture does its best to preserve your folder and album structure from iPhoto. It does *not* import smart albums from iPhoto, however. Toward the bottom of the folder is another folder called Rolls. The Rolls folder has multiple projects inside, one project for each group of photos you imported into iPhoto.

Note: To consolidate the images you imported from iPhoto, create a new project under Rolls. Drag and drop images from the other projects into it, creating one project containing multiple rolls. Even if you move an image between projects, it will still appear in any album it's in. Just be cautious of the 10,000 images per project limit.

In addition to your folder and album structure, Aperture will also transfer the keywords for your iPhoto images. It will also add an "iPhoto Original" keyword to your image. Later in this chapter, we'll show you how to set up an iPhoto smart album using that keyword.

Note: If you have keywords set on your iPhoto images, make sure that none of them start with an "at" symbol (@) before importing into Aperture; if a keyword does, Aperture will crash when importing that photo. For the technical-minded, Aperture uses Apple's Cocoa framework, and an @ symbol has a special meaning with key-value coding. It indicates an array value. If a keyword starts with @, Aperture will expect an array value, and since the keyword isn't an array, Aperture will crash.

Organizing Your Photos

As we mentioned earlier, all of your images are contained within projects. If you click a project, you will see all of the images within that project in the Browser. You can make the Browser larger by clicking the gray bar between the Browser and the Viewer and dragging the bar toward the top. To move an image to another project, drag and drop it onto that project's icon. To copy an image to another project, hold down the Option key while dragging the image. To completely delete an image, select it and choose File > Delete Master Image And All Versions. If you have only one version of the image, such as the one that Aperture automatically creates when importing, you can also pick File > Delete Version (⌘+Delete). Because this action cannot be undone, Aperture will prompt you to make sure that you want to move these images to the Trash.

Note: To change the Browser grid view's background color, adjust the Grid View Background Level slider under Aperture > Preferences.

To further help you manage your projects, albums, and other organizational files, there are two special menus to note in the Projects panel. These menus are represented by the icons to the left of the All Projects text +▾ | ⚙▾. The menu on the left is

The Add To Library menu, and the menu on the right is the Project Action menu. The Add To Library menu provides quick shortcuts to commands to create new items, such as projects. The Project Action menu provides quick access to a few project management commands, such as Add To Favorites. To flag a project as a favorite project, select the project and choose this menu item. Later on, to remove it from favorites, select the project and choose Remove From Favorites from the Project Action menu. To filter your Projects Panel so that you see only your favorite projects, click the All Projects text and select Show Favorites. To switch back to seeing all projects, select Show All from the same menu.

Aperture also allows you to display multiple projects in the Browser. If you ⌘+click a project in the Projects panel, Aperture will create a new tab in the Browser for the second project. You can switch between tabs to determine the project you see. If you'd like to open the project in a separate browser, Option+click the project. The Browser will split to display the new project Figure 2.12 shows what the Browser looks like after selecting the project Bosque 05, ⌘+click Breckenridge, and then Option+click Bosque 05. To close a project in the Browser, click the X next to its name in the Browser. You can open as many browser tabs as you would like.

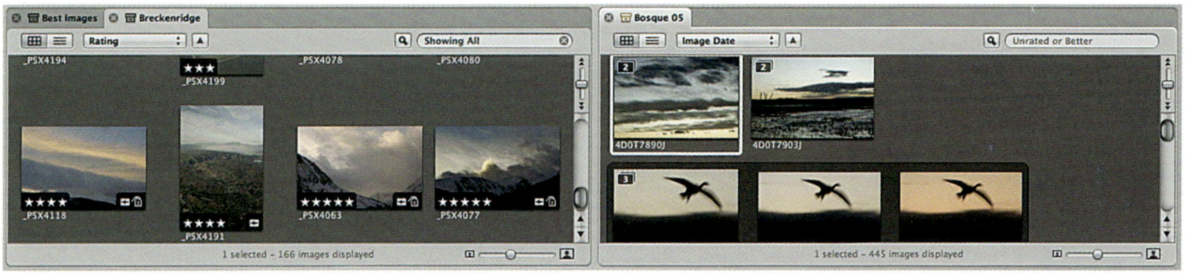

Figure 2.12: The Browser showing multiple projects in tabs (on the left) and splitting the Browser to show two projects.

You can also change how Aperture displays images in the Browser. You can use the Table View icon and the Grid View icon to switch the view. If you were to have multiple browsers up at once, each one could have its own view style.

In Grid view, you can change the sort criteria by using the pop-up next to the Table/Grid View buttons, and you can change the sort order from ascending to descending by clicking the Sort button. Also in the Grid view, you can customize the background color by choosing Aperture > Preferences and adjusting the Grid View Background Level slider. You can also change the thumbnail size by using the slider in the lower-right portion of the Browser. The maximum height and width for images in the browser is 512 pixels.

In the Table view, if you select View > View Options, you can change the settings under List View Columns to adjust which columns Aperture displays. To sort by a particular value, click the table column header, and to reverse the sort order, click the column again.

You can also quickly search for an image in the Browser by clicking in the search field in the top-right portion of the Browser and entering some text. Aperture will search your caption, filename, and other text fields to find this string, and it will adjust the Browser to show you any image that has the specified string. We'll show you how to change this search field's scope, meaning which fields it searches, in Chapter 4. To clear the search string, either click the X in the text field or delete the text you typed into the field.

We will discuss metadata in-depth in Chapter 4, but if you would like to see some information about the selected image, you can bring up the Metadata Inspector, seen in Figure 2.13, by choosing Window > Show Inspectors. This inspector lets you see metadata embedded in the image, such as your shutter speed, and you can also see any keywords or other values you set when importing the photo. You can switch to other metadata sets, just like you did in the Import window, by clicking the Metadata: General popup and selecting the other sets. To switch back to the general set, click the Metadata pop-up and select General.

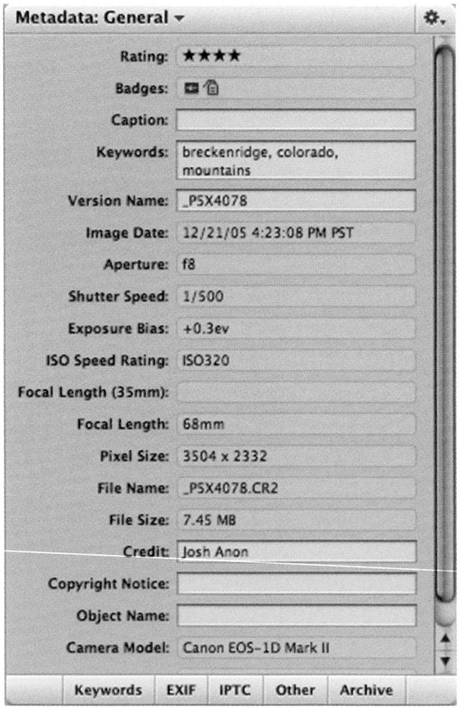

Figure 2.13:
The Metadata Inspector

Working with Stacks

If you didn't stack your images when you were importing them or if you changed your mind as to how they should be stacked, you can edit your stacks from within the Browser. Aperture even provides the same Auto-Stack tool you saw in the Import window. To bring up that tool, select Stacks > Auto-Stack (⌘+Option+A). Just like in the Import window, you can drag the slider to set the time frame Aperture should use for grouping your images. To manually create stacks, select two or more images (or two stacks, or a stack and more images) and select Stacks > Stack (⌘+K).

Note: Stacks are designed to be groups of different versions of one image (e.g. different exposures of a subject) and not groups of different versions of two or more images (e.g. different subjects).

For viewing, you can open or close stacks individually by selecting Stacks > Open/Close Stack, or you can expand or collapse all stacks by selecting the appropriate menu item under the Stacks menu.

Note: The shortcut for opening and closing a stack is Shift+K. This shortcut works everywhere in Aperture, even in Full Screen mode, which makes it quite useful.

There are a variety of ways to unstack images. If you just want to pull one or more versions out of a stack, open the stack, select the images, and select Stacks > Extract Item. If you want to split a stack after a given image, select the first image in the new stack and select Stacks > Split Stack. To completely unstack an image, you can either select the image and then pick Stacks > Unstack or right-click/Control-click the image and select Unstack.

Throughout Aperture, you'll periodically see references to a *stack pick*. A stack pick is the image on top of the stack, presumably your best image from the stack (Chapters 3 and 4 will show you how to find and view your best images). When you use a stacked image in a light table, web gallery, or book, Aperture will automatically use the stack pick. If you want to use another image from the stack in one of these collections, without changing the stack pick, you can set that image to be the *album pick*. Expand the stack by choosing Stacks > Open Stack, select the image, and choose Stacks > Set Album Pick. A stack can have a different album pick for each album it's in, and each stack can have its own album pick. Chapter 5, "Nondestructive Image Processing," covers album picks and versions in more detail in its "Understanding Masters and Versions" section.

Albums

When you're happy with your project setup, the next step is to create an album to hold a subset of your images. To make a new, empty album, select the project you want to create the album in and choose File > New > Album (⌘+Option+L), and then click the Add To Library menu and choose New Empty Album, or right-click/Control-click the project and select New > Album. To rename your album, select the album and press the Return key. You can drag and drop images from your projects and other albums onto the new album to add them to that album. When dragging between albums, the default action is to copy the image into the new album. To move the image instead, hold down the Option key while you drag and drop the image to the new album.

Note: If you drag an image from a project onto an album in a different project, even if you hold down the Option key while dragging, Aperture won't copy the image into the second project. It will copy or move the image to the second project only if you drop it on that project itself.

If you know which images you'd like to put into the album, you can select the images and choose File > New From Selection > Album, click the Add To Library menu, and choose New Album From Selection, or right-click/Control-click the project, and choose New From Selection > Album.

When you're ready to delete the album, select it and choose File > Delete Album (⌘+Delete), or right-click/Control-click the album and choose Delete Album. If you want to delete an image from an album without deleting it from your photo library, select the image and choose Images > Remove From Album. You can also select the image and press the Delete key. If you're trying to remove a stack from an album, make sure the stack is closed before you try to remove it, as Aperture won't allow you to remove an open stack. To permanently delete a version of an image, select the version and choose File > Delete Version. Similarly, to delete an image and all versions from your photo library, choose File > Delete Master Image And All Versions. If this seems like a lot of confusing information, don't worry. We'll cover all of these situations in Chapter 5, "Nondestructive Image Processing," under "Understanding Masters and Versions."

After you've made a few albums that you want to keep, you might want to group them together. For instance, if your project is called Smith Wedding and you have albums for the rehearsal dinner, pre-wedding family-bonding activities, the wedding itself, and the reception, you might want to group the pre- and post-wedding albums into two groups. To do so, make a new folder in your project either by selecting File > New Folder or by choosing New Folder from the Add To Library menu. Name your folder appropriately, and then drag and drop your albums onto the folder. You can also manually create folders within folders, and put other files, such as light tables, into the folders. We'll show you how to make them later.

Smart Albums

One of Aperture's big features is its ability to create a smart album. As we mentioned in Chapter 1, a smart album is an album for which you define a query using various criteria, and Aperture will automatically figure out which images should be in that album. You don't (and can't) manually add or remove images to a smart album.

Creating a smart album is fairly straightforward. Pick the project with the images you want to use, or select Library to make the smart album global. Choose File > New Smart > Album, right-click/Control-click the project, and select New Smart > Album; or click the Add To Library menu and select New Smart Album. A new album icon will appear, and in addition to having a slightly different icon than a plain album, you'll see a magnifying glass to the right of the album name, and a HUD similar to the one in Figure 2.14 will automatically appear. The various listed fields contain the criteria you can use to set up your smart album, and you can activate the criteria by clicking the check box on the left. You can add additional criteria, such as date or EXIF fields, by clicking the + button on the top-right of the query HUD.

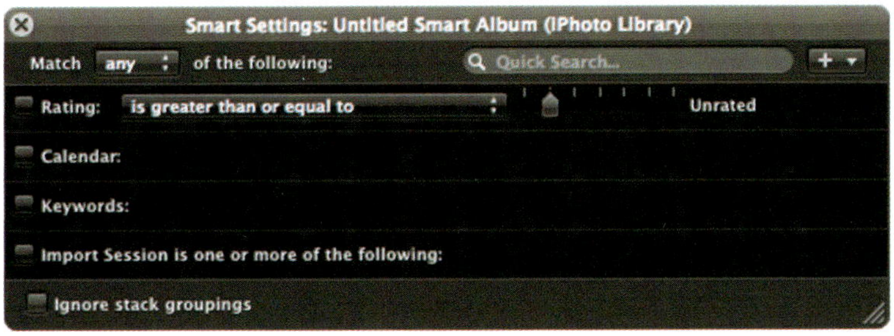

Figure 2.14:
The smart album query HUD

The easiest way to set up your smart album is to think explicitly about what you want to have in the album and to be able to express your desires in simple, discrete sentences. For instance, on Canon cameras, you can extend the ISO range to include ISO 50 and ISO 3200. You might want to make a smart album to show you all of the images you shot in this extended ISO range. You could express that thought in a discrete way by saying that you want to see images whose ISO is less than or equal to 50 or greater than or equal to 3200. To set up that query, set the Match pop-up on the top-left portion of the screen to Any. This will gives you the "or" part of your query. To add an EXIF criteria using the + button and set it to read "ISO Speed Rating Is Greater Than Or Equal To 3200," and you'd add a second EXIF criteria set to read "ISO Speed Rating Is Less Than Or Equal To 50."

Note: You can search for arbitrary text in filenames, captions, and other text fields by selecting the Text criteria.

As another example, let's say you want to see any image you took today at ISO 3200. This query will have two parts: the date is within the past day and the ISO is 3200. Add those two fields, date and EXIF criteria, because they don't come in by default. Set the Match pop-up to All, so that Aperture performs an "and" operation on your criteria. If you set it to Any, Aperture will give you any image at ISO 3200, along with every image you took within the past day.

One particular smart album you might find useful is Today's Images. This smart album lets you see everything you've shot today, regardless of which project or album stores it. You'll want to set up this smart album in the Library project, and you can set it up by using the criteria Image Date Is In The Last 1 Day. With Today's Images, you'll always have quick access to your most recent images.

Earlier in the chapter, we mentioned that you can set up a smart album to see all of the images you imported from iPhoto. The trick is to set up a smart album that looks for the keyword "iPhoto Original." We'll cover keywords more in Chapter 4, but in short, they provide an additional bit of metadata on your images that you can use as criteria for your smart albums. To set up this album, select Library and choose File > New Smart > Album (⌘+Shift+L). Check the Keywords box, and click the check box next to iPhoto Original. Your smart album query will look like Figure 2.15.

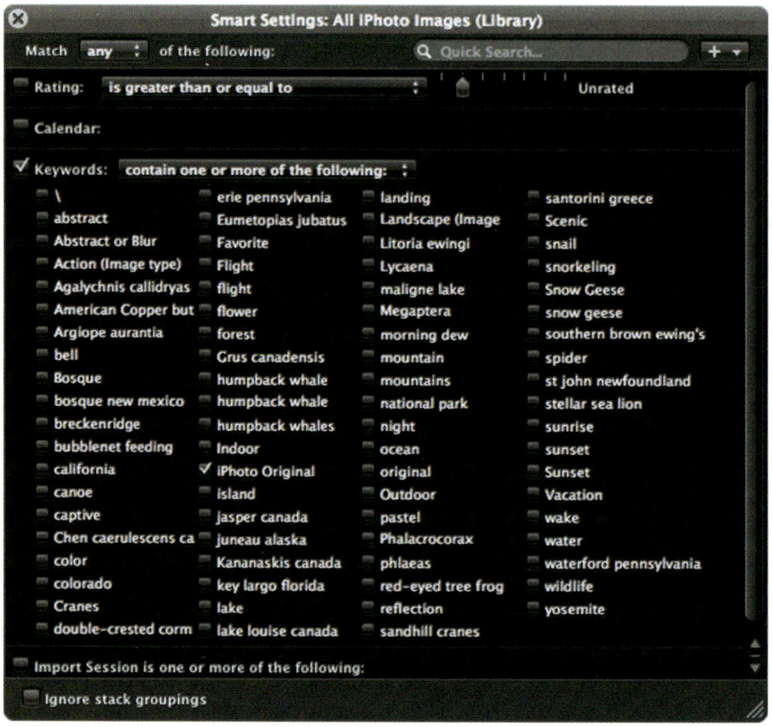

Figure 2.15: A sample smart album query to find all the images you imported from iPhoto.

If you imported a lot of images from iPhoto, you might want to further restrict this smart album by date. For instance, you could set up iPhoto 2004 and iPhoto 2005 smart albums that have the same keyword criteria but that also have date criteria. Make sure to set your Match pop-up to All for these smart albums.

Note: To set up two or more similar smart albums, start by setting up the first one. Then right-click/Control-click that album, and choose Duplicate Smart Album. Then modify the copy's criteria.

The calendar field in Figure 2.16 is a bit unintuitive. This field displays a Calendar view that you use to determine which capture date, as set in the image's metadata, or range of dates that Aperture will use to populate the smart album. When you activate the field, it will show you three months at a time, and you can use the arrow keys to change which months you're viewing. You can select a range of dates by clicking the first date and shift+clicking the last date, and you can toggle individual days by ⌘+clicking them on the calendar. If you select a range of days in one month and then advance the display far enough that you don't see those days anymore, they will still be selected. You just won't see them unless you scroll the calendar back to that month. If, for example, you take a trip every Thanksgiving and you want to see all of your photos from all the trips you've taken, you can use the calendar criteria to select the days from every year that you took a Thanksgiving trip.

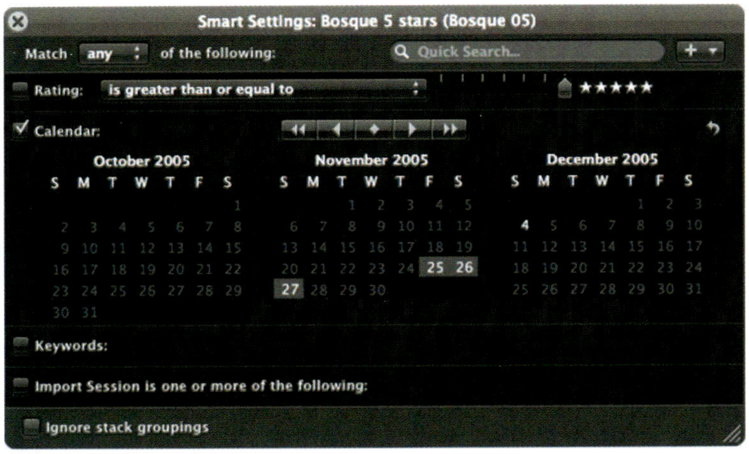

Figure 2.16:
The calendar query field with a range of dates selected

You can always change the contents of a smart album by clicking the magnifying glass to the right of the smart album and adjusting the criteria. If you want to delete the smart album, select it and choose File > Delete Smart Album.

Note: You cannot manually drag and drop images onto a smart album.

Now that you've learned how to use Aperture to organize your images, it's time to learn how to view your images in detail so that you can pick your best images and reject your bad images.

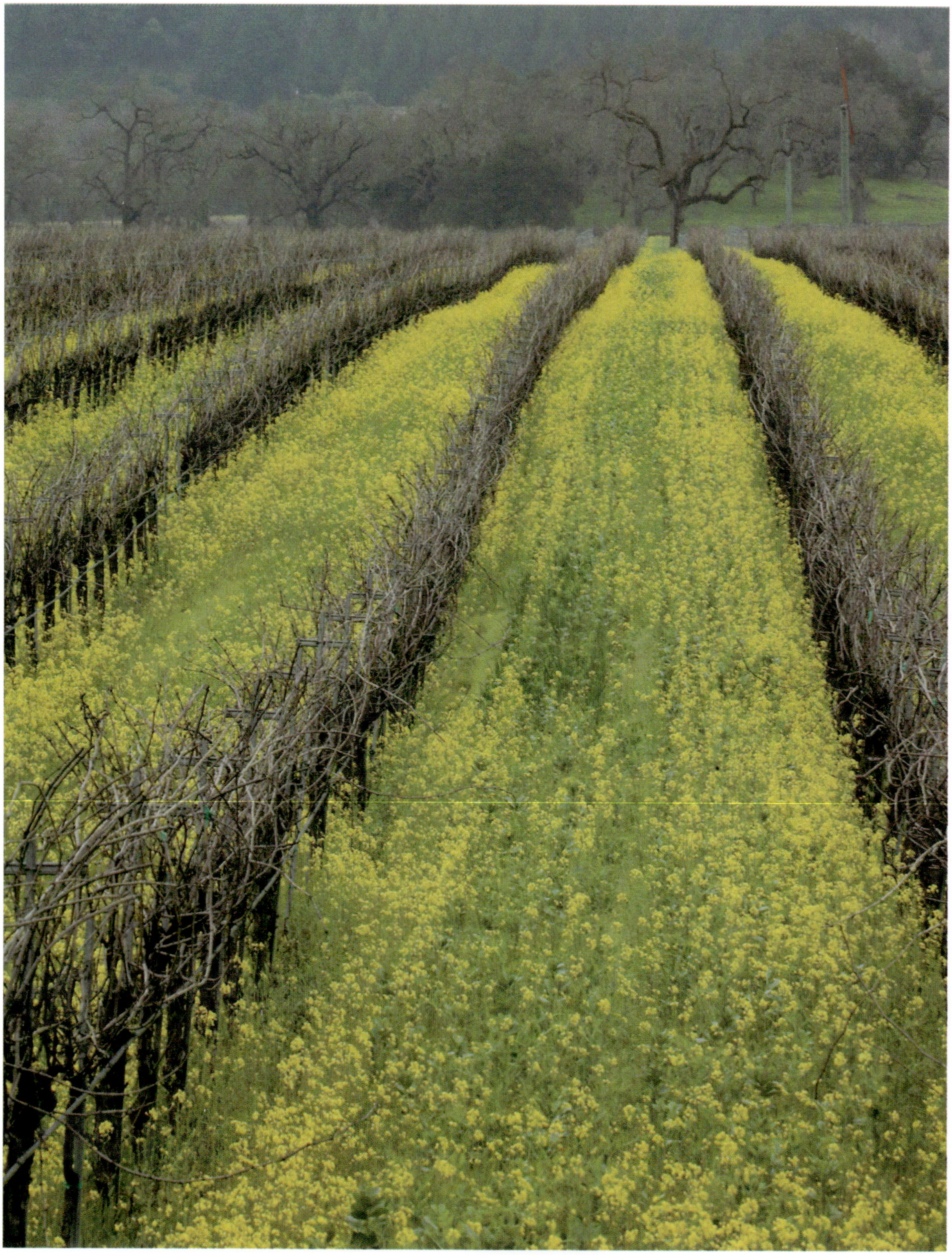

Viewing Images

One of Aperture's most powerful features is the variety of ways it allows you to view and compare images. Gone are the days of tediously arranging windows and zooming around to try to compare your images. Aperture's innovative tools allow you to easily view and compare your images separately or together, making it easy to find your best shots. Furthermore, viewing images in Aperture consists of more than just looking at your photos in a predetermined layout; light tables let you spread your images out on a virtual table, where you can resize and reposition them to your heart's content.

3

Chapter Contents

Viewing Images in Aperture

When you first launch Aperture, the Viewer is the panel directly in the center at the top. To make the Viewer larger or smaller, click and drag the gray strip between the Viewer and the Browser. By now, you've probably discovered that as you click to select images, Aperture shows your images in the Viewer. In fact, Aperture's default viewing mode is called Multi, and if you select multiple images, Aperture will show all of your images in the Viewer at once.

Viewing Modes

At the bottom of the screen, in the control bar, you will see the Viewer Mode button ( ). If the control bar is hidden, reveal it by choosing Window > Show Control Bar. When you click this icon, a menu pops up listing the five different modes for the Viewer (we'll discuss the additional menu items for a dual-screen system later). The five viewing modes are

Multi: See multiple images in the Viewer

Primary: View only one of several selected images

Three Up: View up to three images in the Viewer

Compare: View one fixed image and one or more selected images

Stack: View and compare images within a stack

As we already mentioned, the first mode, Multi, allows you to see multiple images at once in the Viewer, as seen in Figure 3.1. As you select more images, Aperture makes your already-selected images smaller so that more images can fit onto the screen. However, Aperture won't shrink your images below a certain size. If you select numerous images ("numerous" varies depending on the size of your screen, for instance, on a 15" high-res Powerbook G4 with the Viewer as large as it will go, you can display nine landscape images at once), Aperture will display a message in the Viewer letting you know how many images you have selected that aren't being displayed.

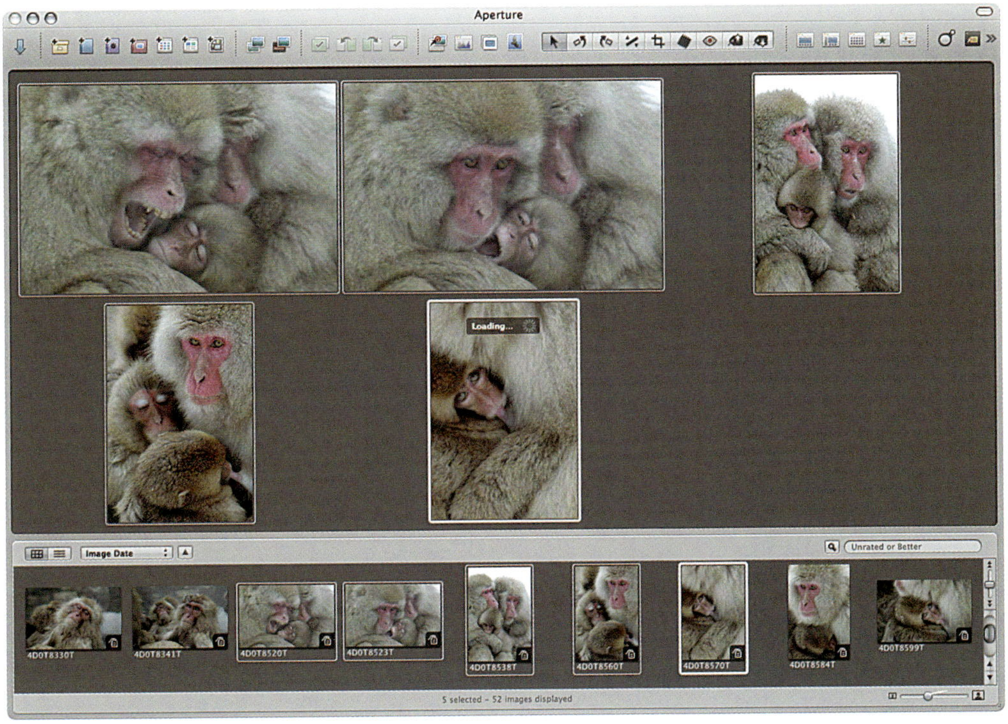

Figure 3.1: Viewing multiple images at once

The second viewing mode is called Primary. Sometimes, you intentionally select a group of images because you want to do something to them as a group. You might want to give them the same rating or export several versions of each of them, but you only want to see one image in the Viewer—perhaps because you noticed a spot of dust on one image that you want to fix before exporting. Primary mode lets you select a group of images and view only your primary image in the Viewer. As you can see in Figure 3.1, Aperture draws a thin, white selection rectangle around each selected image in the Browser, but the primary selection has a bolder rectangle. Change your primary selection by using the arrow keys on your keyboard or by using the arrow buttons on the control bar. If you have a group of images selected and arrow between them, Aperture will change only the primary selection. If you arrow to the image before or after your selected images, Aperture will deselect all of your images and select the image you arrowed to. If you hold down ⌘ and Option while using the arrow keys, Aperture will stay within your selected images.

Note: If you hover your cursor over the buttons in Aperture's control bar (for example, the arrow buttons), Aperture will bring up a tooltip with the hotkeys for other commands, such as Next Within Selection.

The next viewing mode is Three Up. The Three Up mode is similar to the Multi mode in that if you select multiple images, the Viewer will show them all at once. The difference between the two modes is that when you select a single image, Three Up mode will still show multiple images. It will show the image before and the image after your selected image. Additionally, Three Up mode respects expanded stacks; if you expand a stack containing three images and click the middle image, the Viewer will show all three images in the stack. If you close your stacks and sort by image date, Three Up mode provides a convenient way to quickly compare images that were taken in different bursts but around the similar time.

Note: If you select the first or last image in the Browser in Three Up mode, Aperture will show only the next or previous image, respectively.

However, Aperture has two special modes for comparing images. The first is, appropriately enough, called Compare. The idea behind Compare is to pick an image you want to compare to other images and display both images at the same time. Then, you change the second image you're viewing. If you find one that you like better, you can set that to be the image to which you compare other images.

To begin, select the image that you want to use as your compare image and either press Return or select Edit > Set Compare Item. Aperture will automatically put you into Compare mode, and your compare image will have an orange rectangle around it. Then, select another image (or images), and Aperture will show both images next to each other. As you use the arrow keys to move between images, Aperture continues to show the same compare image, but it changes the second image it's displaying. To use the second image as the new compare image, just press Return and Aperture will swap images. Press Option+arrow to make the next or previous image be the new compare. When you're comparing images, the various commands, such as rating an image, will affect the selected secondary image. To make those commands affect the compare image, hold down Option while pressing the specific command key. For instance, to rotate the secondary image to the left, press the left bracket ([). To rotate the compare image to the left, press Option+[. To exit the Compare mode with the compare image selected, press Option+Return or choose Edit > Select Compare Item. To exit the Compare mode with nothing selected, press ⌘+Return or choose Edit > Clear Compare Item.

Compare mode is quite useful for comparing images that aren't stacked (and for comparing images within stacks if you select the images and use the next/previous within selection keys), ⌘+Option+right/left arrow on the keyboard or screen, but Aperture provides an even better way to compare stacked images. The idea behind the final viewing mode, Stack, is to sort your images as you compare them within your stack, and when you're done looking through the stack, your stack pick should be on top.

After you select a stack you want to sort, expand the stack and put your viewer into Stack mode. As seen in Figure 3.2, Aperture automatically selects the image on the top of the stack as the current pick, and it shows you the next image on the right. If you like the compare image on the left more than the image on the right, just press the right-arrow key to move to the next image in the stack. To promote an image in the stack, choose Stacks > Promote (⌘+[). To demote an image, select Stacks > Demote (⌘+]). Aperture will visually flip your images to indicate your change in the stack sorting. When you find the image you like the most in the stack, you can either promote it until it's at the top or choose Stacks > Pick (⌘+\) to put the image on top. To exit Stack mode, set your viewer back to some other mode, such as Multi mode.

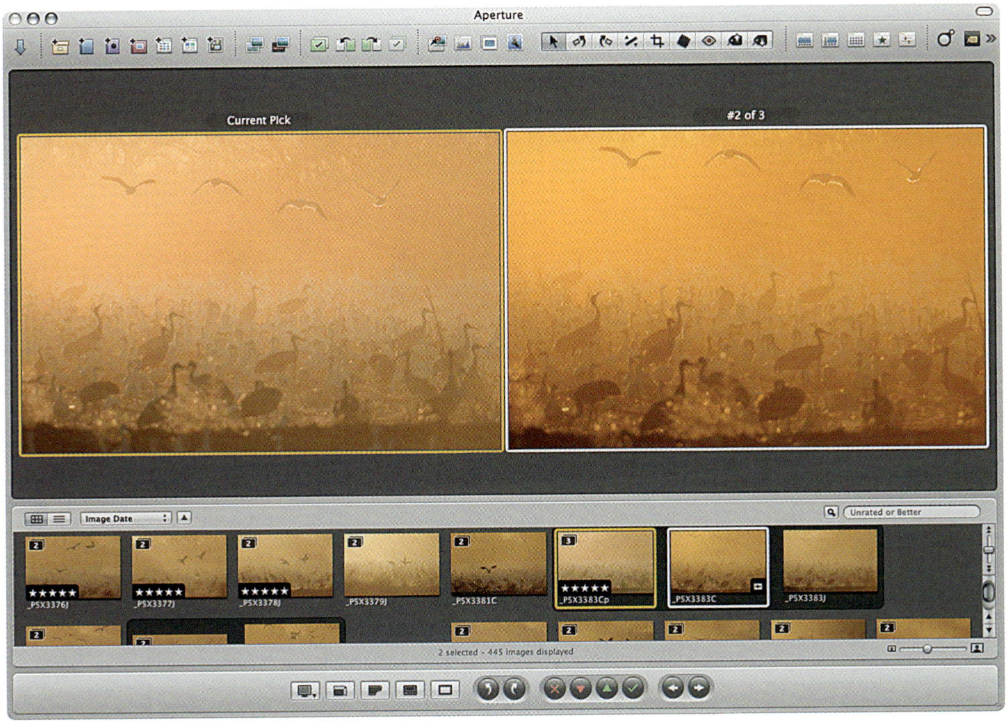

Figure 3.2: Viewing images in Stack mode

Note: You can change the Viewer's background color by opening up Aperture's preferences (Aperture > Preferences) and changing the Viewer Background Level slider.

To the right of the Modes button on the control bar, you'll find another set of useful commands. The first is the Zoom button ( ). When you select this button, or choose View > Zoom to Actual Size (Z), Aperture automatically zooms each image in the Viewer to 100 percent. Aperture also automatically overlays a small gray box, as seen in Figure 3.3. The small gray box represents the entire image, and a smaller red rectangle inside it represents the visible part of the image. Scroll around your image by dragging the small red rectangle within the larger box. You can also pan around the image without using the small rectangle by holding the spacebar while dragging. If you have multiple images open in the Viewer, Aperture lets you scroll each image at the same time by holding the Shift key while dragging the red rectangle in one of the images. Shift+spacebar will also pan through all the images at once.

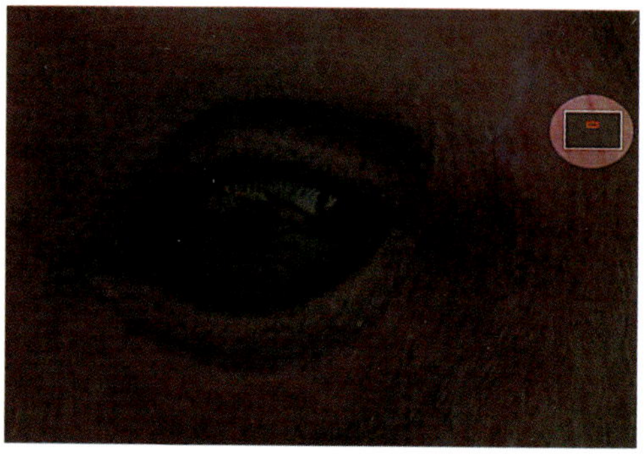

Figure 3.3:
The Zoom navigator

Note: Position your cursor over an image in the Viewer and press Z. Aperture will automatically zoom the image to 100 percent centered on where your cursor is on the scaled image. If you are viewing multiple images when you press Z, Aperture will zoom the one your cursor is in to that position, and it will zoom the others to their centers.

The second button, Show Master Image (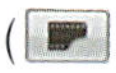) will automatically show the master file for an image. If you've opened a file in an external editor or are looking at the original RAW file, you're already viewing the master file. Yet if you've made various adjustments to your image in Aperture, when you select a version of your image and choose Show Master, Aperture will show you the unadjusted RAW file. To reveal the master, select View > Show Master Image (M).

The third button, Full Screen (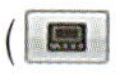), will switch Aperture into Full Screen mode. We'll discuss Full Screen mode later on in more depth, as it's quite useful. The last viewing button in the control bar, Primary Only with the 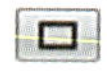 icon, toggles affecting the primary image only. As we mentioned before, when you select multiple images, the main selection is called the primary image. Whether or not you're in Primary mode, the adjustments you make to an image in the Enhancement panel and the values you type into the Metadata Inspector affect only the primary image. However, by default, keywords and ratings affect every selected image. If you want to affect only the primary image when you set these fields, toggle the Primary Only button on. You'll find this button useful when you're viewing multiple images in Multi mode, but you want to set the ratings and keywords on each image separately. Table 3.1 summarizes these buttons so that you can review them.

▶ Table 3.1: Button Summary

Button	Icon	Function
Zoom Viewer		Zoom to 100%
Show Master Image		Show master image
Full Screen		Full screen mode
Toggle Primary Only		Primary image only

One other useful option that affects the Viewer, which doesn't have an icon in the control bar, is the View > Highlight Hot Areas (Option+Shift+H) command. When active, this control will overlay bright red on any pixel in the image whose value is above a certain brightness threshold. Set this threshold in Aperture's Preferences using the Hot Area Display Threshold slider. Figure 3.4 shows a sample image with a very bright area and Highlight Hot Areas active

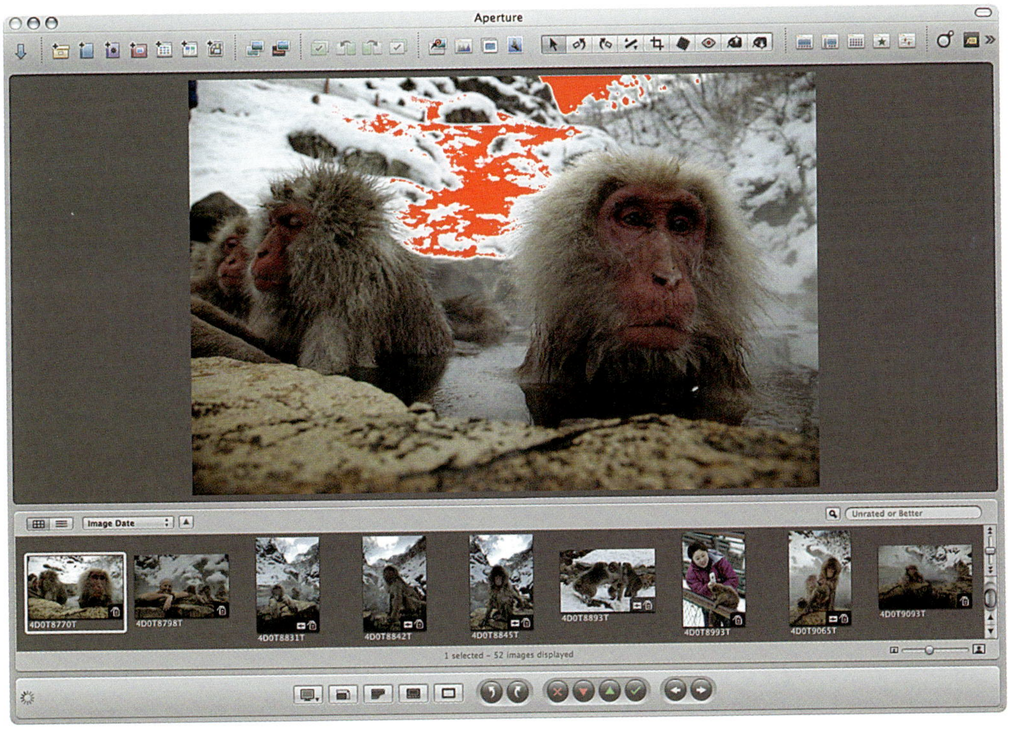

Figure 3.4: A sample image with Highlight Hot Areas enabled

Louping Your Images

Many people consider the Loupe to be one of Aperture's most useful tools. As its name implies, this tool allows you to digitally loupe your images, quickly viewing a portion of the image at its actual size or larger. To bring up the Loupe, select View > Loupe or press the backtick key (`). The circular overlay in Figure 3.5 will appear. The Loupe has two parts: the smaller sample area and the larger display area. The sample area follows your cursor around, and the display area shows the zoomed-in version of the sample area. The display area will also swing around to stay on the screen as you move your mouse to the screen edges. You can bring up the Loupe anywhere in Aperture, but the display area will show only a zoomed-in view if your mouse is over an image. However, you can use the Loupe on almost any image, including the Browser and the Viewer.

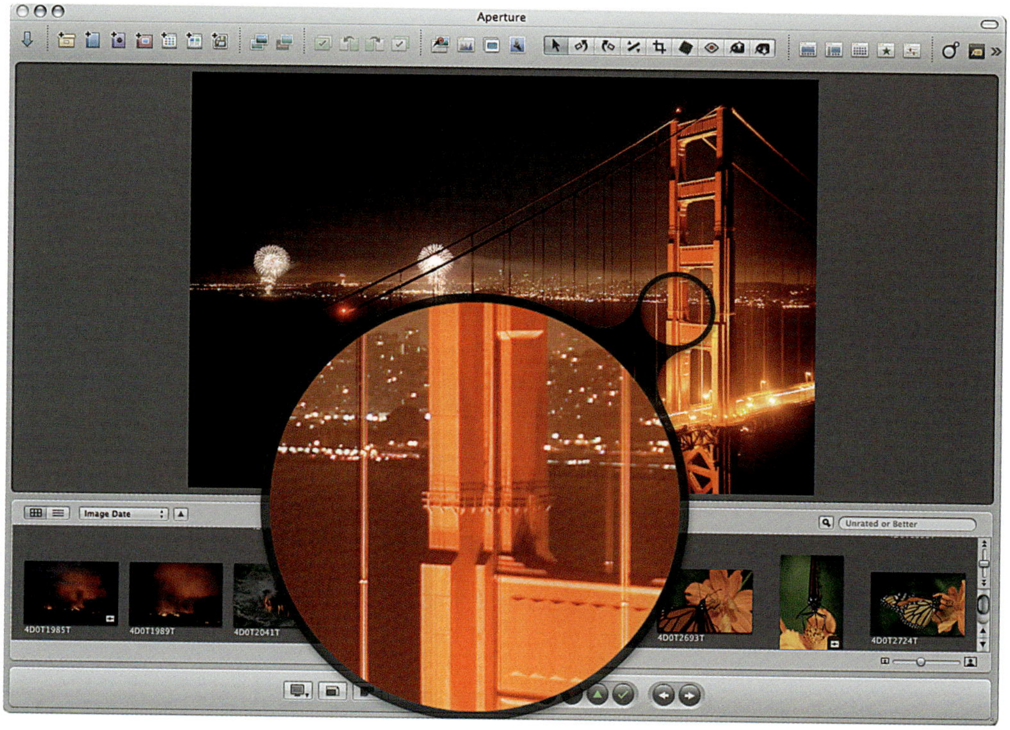

Figure 3.5: The Loupe

Sometimes, you want to zoom in more than 100 percent. Depending on the size of your screen, you might want to change the Loupe's display area size. To make the Loupe larger, select View > Increase Diameter (⌘+=). To make the Loupe smaller, select View > Decrease Diameter (⌘+-).

Similarly, to zoom in, use ⌘+Shift++, and to zoom out, use ⌘+Shift+_. As you change your zoom level, the sample area on the Loupe will become larger or smaller, indicating that the display area is showing a smaller or larger part of the image.

> **Note:** In Aperture 1.0, when you zoom in, Aperture will blend the pixels, giving you a visually smooth image. In Aperture 1.1, you will see the individual, unblended pixels when you zoom in.

In numerous cases, the Loupe is more efficient than zooming in on an image. For instance, if you want to see if your subject's eye or face is sharp, you can move the cursor over her face and bring up the Loupe. If you have multiple images in your viewer, such as in Compare mode, you can use the Loupe to compare catch lights in your subjects' eyes or to compare other details in the images. Unfortunately, there is no way to lock a loupe in place to compare the detail in two areas side-by-side. The Loupe always travels with your cursor.

Accessing a Color Meter

In Aperture 1.1, Apple added a color meter tool that lets you sample the color values in your photo. There is also a sample size option that allows you to specify how large of an area Aperture should sample from.

To sample a color value, make sure the Adjustments inspector (press I) or HUD (press H) is visible. If the color meter fields at the top (Figure 3.6) are not visible, select Show Color Value from the Action menu. As you move your cursor over your image or thumbnail, the color meter at the top of the inspector will display the currently sampled color.

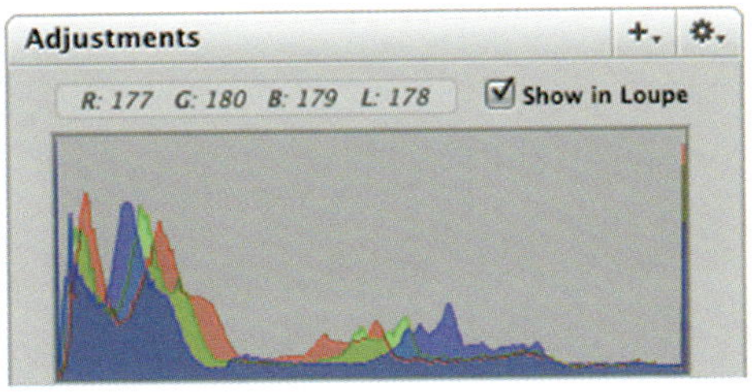

Figure 3.6: Aperture 1.1.'s color meter

To use the loupe to sample a color and display its values, select the Show in Loupe checkbox and loupe an image. You will see a display similar to Figure 3.7 where a small box indicates the sample region within the loupe. To change the sample size, select the Action menu and pick a new size, from 1 × 1 px to 7 × 7 px.

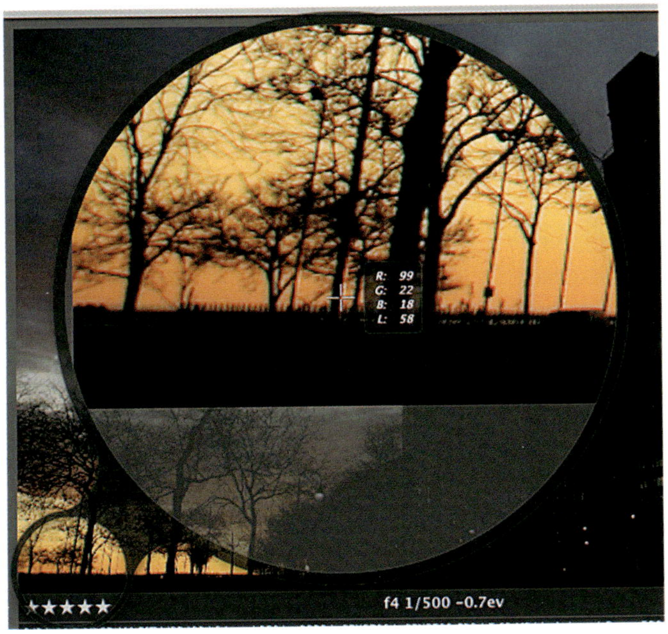

Figure 3.7: The loupe can be configured to show color values.

To sample a color in a mode other than RGB, select the Action menu and choose either CMYK or LAB. The Color meter fields will automatically update to show these new values.

Unfortunately, if you're using Aperture 1.0, there is no built-in color meter. Thankfully, Mac OS X has a built-in color meter that you can quickly bring up from within Aperture. To do so, double-click a project or an album name so that Aperture will switch to its Text Editing mode. Then, right-click/Control-click the text, and choose Font > Show Fonts. The Font panel will appear, and you'll see two colorwells at the top. The buttons on it will display solid blocks of color. Click one of the colorwells, and the panel in Figure 3.8 will appear. Close the Font panel, and click in the blank space in the Projects panel so that Aperture stops editing your project's name. The Colors panel stays, floating above everything else.

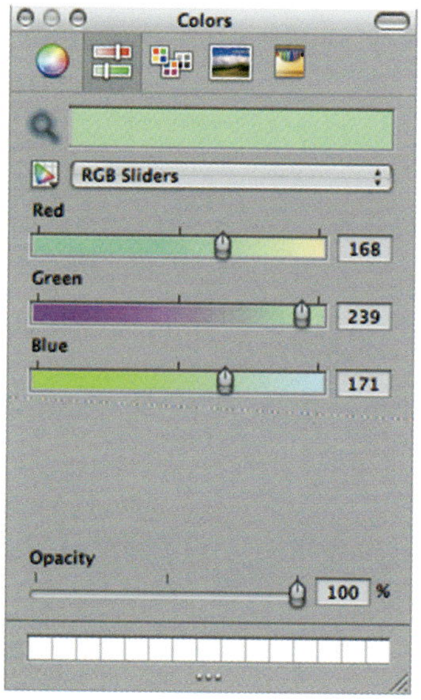

Figure 3.8: The Colors panel

Within the Colors panel, multiple buttons appear across the top in the toolbar and indicate various ways to pick colors. If the buttons aren't visible, click the lozenge in the top-right portion of the window to expose the toolbar. When you click the Color Sliders button ( ), the Colors panel will display sliders representing red, green, and blue. If you see only one slider for grayscale or four sliders for CMYK, switch the pop-up menu to RGB Sliders. Near the top of the panel is a Magnifying Glass button ( ). Click this button to bring up a magnifying glass that you can move around your monitor with your cursor. When you find a color that you want to sample, simply click it. The RGB sliders will change to show you the sample's color numerically.

As another alternative, Mac OS X has a built-in DigitalColor Meter application (see Figure 3.9) under /Applications/Utilities. When you run it, it will show you the RGB value of the pixel wherever your cursor is. Make it float above your open windows by selecting DigitalColor Meter > Preferences, and checking Float window above other apps. To sample only one pixel, make sure that the Aperture Size slider is all the way to the left, giving you a one-pixel sample.

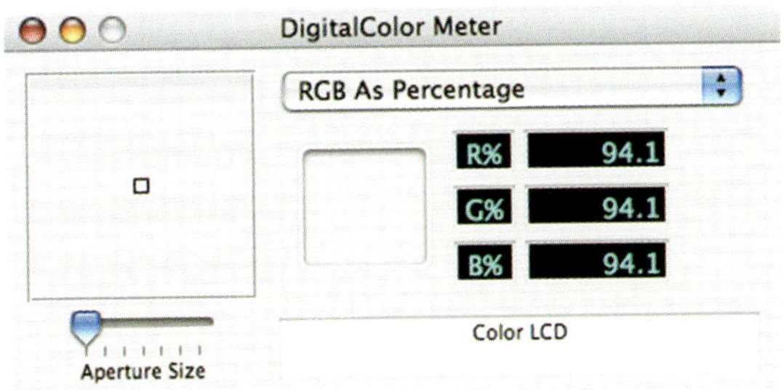

Figure 3.9: The DigitalColor Meter application

Onscreen Proofing

One common problem photographers must deal with is using different color spaces for different devices and digital images. There are literally books devoted to this topic, such as Tim Grey's *Color Confidence* (Sybex, 2004). The short story is that different devices, such as printers and displays, display color differently, and they cannot always display the same amount of colors. For instance, a monitor can display more colors than a printer can print. The obvious question people have when they're working with an image is "What will my image look like on this other device?"

Color calibrating your monitor is the first step toward answering this question and solving the color management problem. By using tools such as ColorVision's Sypder 2, you can accurately profile how your monitor displays color. That information lets your computer's color-management system (often ColorSync) convert between devices (such as a monitor and printer) properly so that colors are consistent across devices. However, even with a calibrated monitor, your colors will look slightly different when they're printed because, as we just mentioned, a monitor can display more colors than a printer can print.

Assuming your monitor is color-calibrated, Aperture comes to the rescue with its soft-proofing tool. This tool allows you to choose the color space with which to view your image, giving you a rough idea of how your image will look when it's reproduced elsewhere.

To enable onscreen proofing, make sure that View > Onscreen Proofing (Option+Shift+P) is checked. If it's not, select that menu item to enable it. The menu right below it (View > Proofing Profile) contains all of the various color profiles that Aperture can use to display your image. As an example, if you have a printer profile installed (these profiles usually come either from the driver CDs with the printer or from the manufacturer's website), select it to see what your image will look like when printed. Choose the Web Safe Colors profile to see what your image would need to look like to be viewable in all web browsers on all color platforms. That profile usually doesn't look too good because it forces your image to use a very limited number of colors.

If you are completely in doubt as to what color space to use, especially if your monitor isn't calibrated, try sRGB. sRGB represents the average, uncalibrated monitor, and this is what your image would probably look like if you emailed it to someone.

Viewing Metadata

While viewing your images, you may find it useful to see metadata for each image. For a single image, you can just look at the Metadata panel. However, that panel might be hidden, and it's hard to discern important bits of metadata, such as exposure information, from less important bits, such as the copyright notice. Also, if you're looking at multiple images, the Inspector won't show you information for all of the images; it only shows information for the primary selection. Aperture again comes to the rescue and allows you to customize the Viewer so that it shows some metadata with the image.

To display metadata with the image, select View > View Options (⌘+J) to bring up the window shown in Figure 3.10. From this panel, you can customize the metadata display for each of Aperture's viewing tools, such as light tables. For now, we're concerned with the Viewer options. Click the check box to enable viewer metadata displays. The pop-up menu lets you choose the metadata set you'll display with the image. The default set, General, is actually quite thorough and lets you see the important information, such as exposure and date, at a glance. You can display the metadata below or over the image. Displaying your metadata below the image is probably a better choice, because you can still see your entire image. However, each image will take up more screen space. Two radio buttons, labeled Set 1 and Set 2, let you set up two different ways to display metadata for the Viewer and Browser and toggle between them (Shift+Y to change the viewer set and Shift+U to change the browser set). Hide the metadata by unchecking the Viewer check box in the View Options window or by setting the metadata set to None.

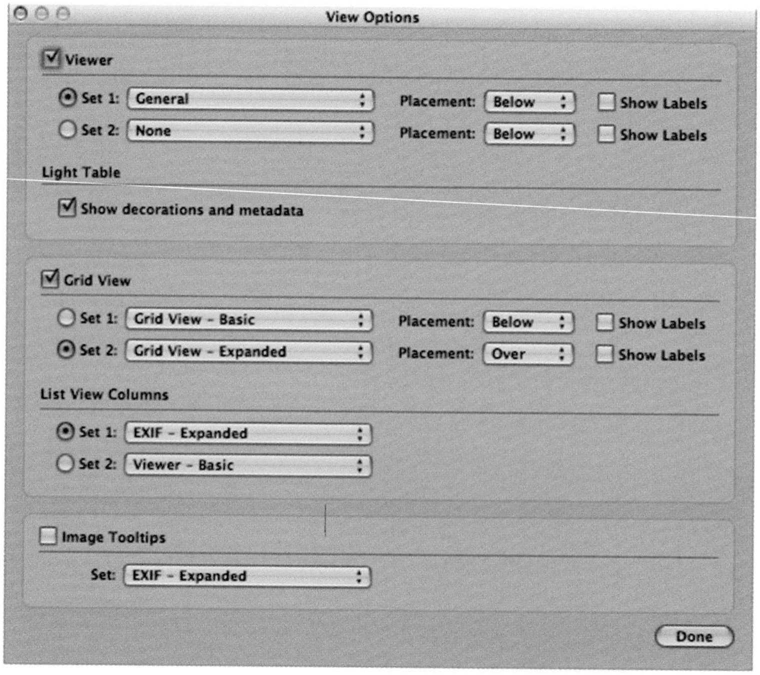

Figure 3.10: The View Options window

You can also quickly hide and show your selected metadata set for the Viewer, the Browser (in Grid mode), and light table independently. Under the View menu, you'll find the Metadata Overlays menu with check boxes next to each view onto which you want Aperture to overlay metadata. Toggle the menu item to hide and show the overlay. The Change Viewer Set and Change Browser Set commands let you toggle between the two metadata sets you set up in the View Options window.

Tooltips are another way to see your image's metadata without taking up screen space. A tooltip is a small display that appears when you leave your cursor floating over an image. The display goes away as soon as you move your cursor. To enable or disable tooltips, toggle View > Image Tooltips (T). You can change the information that Aperture displays in the tooltips under the Image Tooltips section of the View Options window. Another way to show or hide tooltips is to check or uncheck the Image Tooltips check box.

Badges

Aperture uses small icons, called *badges,* to indicate whether you've set keywords ( ), made adjustments ( ), or opened the image in an external editor ( ). There is also an icon for when the master image is unavailable or corrupt ( ).

When stacking images in Chapter 2, "Importing and Organizing Your Images," you saw the badge that Aperture places on a stack indicating how many images are in that stack . Later, when you place images on a light table, you'll see a badge ( ) indicating the number of times an image has been placed on a given light table.

As you'll find in Chapter 4, "Finding the Keepers," Aperture also places badges for the image's rating from Reject to Five Stars . As you'll see in Chapter 8, "Creating Web Content," and Chapter 9, "Creating a Book," if you're using low-resolution images for your book or web site, Aperture will place a small badge ( ) indicating that your image quality on the final document will be too low.

Window Layouts

As we show you how to display more and more data within Aperture, you might find yourself running low on screen space. The easiest answer solution is to customize your screen layout by hiding, resizing, and rearranging parts of the interface. Aperture has a single-window interface (meaning that you can't open your Viewer, Browser, or Project panel in their own windows). To resize each area of the interface, click in the gray area next to each area that you want to resize and drag your mouse left/right or up/down, depending on how you want to resize your views. In standard Mac terminology, two or more views are said to live in a "split view" if they have a special divider in the middle that lets you resize the views. In Aperture, there is a split view with the Project panel, Browser/Viewer combination, and inspectors. Then, there is a split view between the Browser and Viewer as well as the between the adjustment and metadata inspectors. Figure 3.11 shows some of the areas that you can drag to resize Aperture's views.

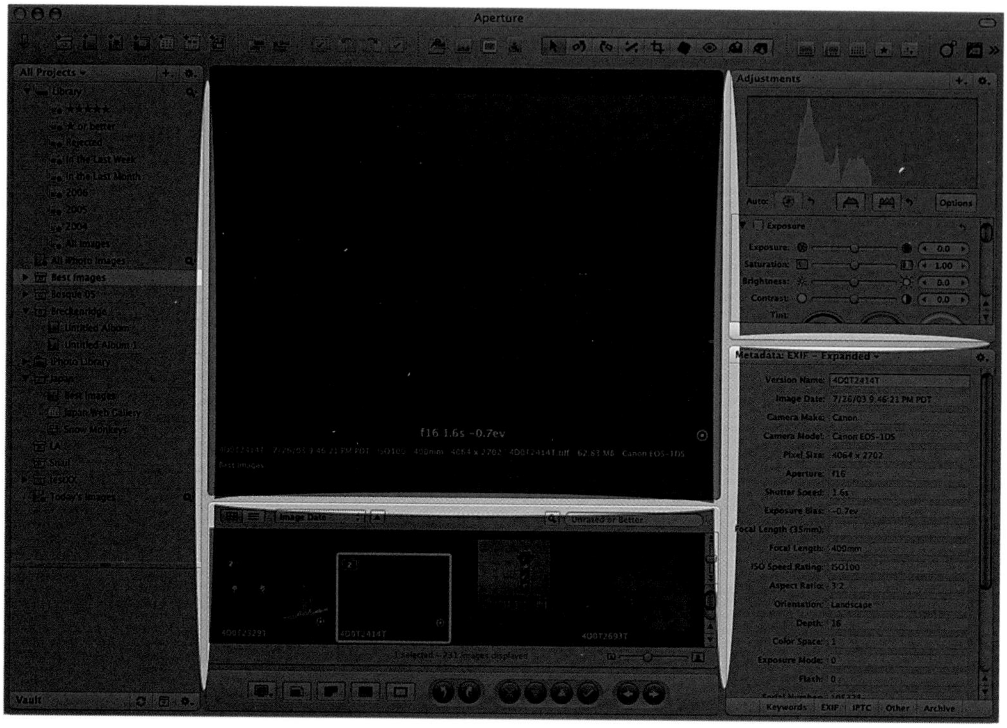

Figure 3.11: Areas that you can click and drag to resize the various views in Aperture

You can also rearrange the Browser and the Viewer. The default is for the Browser to be on the bottom and the Viewer to be on the top. Window > Swap Workspace (Option+W) will flip these views around so that the Viewer is on the bottom and the Browser is on top. Window > Rotate Workspace (Shift+W) will rotate the Browser so that it's vertical instead of horizontal. This can be useful if you want to have the Browser open while you're viewing large vertical images. When rotated, Swap Workspace will move the Browser from the left to the right side of the Viewer.

Sometimes, resizing and rearranging takes too long, and you just want to hide parts of Aperture's user interface (UI) that you don't need. Under the Window menu, you'll find commands to hide every part of the UI, except the Browser. After you hide the views, the Window menu will change so that commands show each view. If you want to make the Viewer as large as possible, hide each part of the UI except the Viewer, and use the resize control to make the Browser as small as possible.

Given how customizable Aperture's interface is, you will probably find yourself frequently rearranging it to best suit the specific task you're working on, be it organizing images into albums or viewing and rating images. Unfortunately, even when you know all of the shortcuts, it takes time to rearrange the view for each task. Aperture again comes to the rescue and provides a number of preset layouts. You can access these layouts under Window > Layouts or by using the buttons in the toolbar. Figure 3.12 shows the default set of layout buttons that Aperture provides.

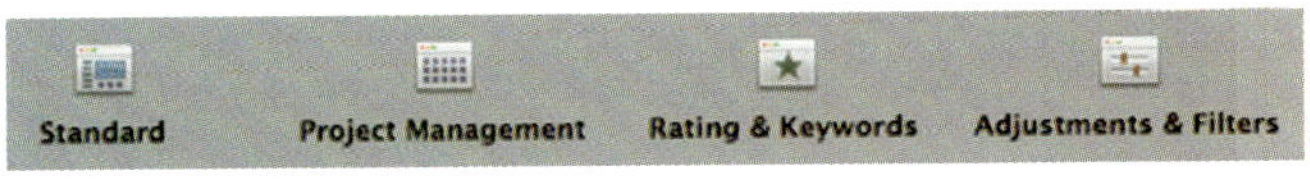

Figure 3.12: The default set of layout buttons you'll find in Aperture's toolbar

Aperture's default set of buttons includes, from left to right, standard, browser-oriented, rating-oriented, and adjustment-oriented layouts:

Standard The standard layout provides the Projects Panel, the Viewer, and the Browser. When you switch to this layout, Aperture will also hide your inspectors and minimize the Browser.

Browser The browser-oriented layout is useful for organizing your images into albums. In this layout, Aperture shows only the Projects panel and the Browser, and it makes the Browser as large as possible.

Rating When you switch to the rating layout, Aperture shows you a vertical, two-column-wide browser on the left and a large viewer on the right. This layout is designed to help you focus on the images in this collection. It hides the Projects panel, and it provides a bit more context for each image by showing more images in the Browser than the other layouts.

Adjustment The last layout is the adjustment layout. It is quite similar to the rating layout, but it includes the Adjustments Inspector view. In addition to providing more context for each image, this layout provides a quick way to access other images' adjustments and metadata for the Lift And Stamp tool. We'll discuss this tool more in Chapters 4 and 5, but the general overview is that the Lift And Stamp tool provides a convenient way to make bulk adjustments.

Note: None of the predefined layouts are locked, meaning that even after you choose one, you can still hide, rearrange, and resize the views to meet your workflow.

One more layout, maximize viewer, is quite useful, but it is not included in the toolbar by default. To access it, you'll need to customize Aperture's toolbar. Select View > Customize Toolbar or right-click/Control-click the toolbar and select Customize Toolbar. Aperture will bring up a sheet, as seen in Figure 3.13, showing all of the different buttons you can put into the toolbar. Additionally, the pop-up in the bottom left of the screen lets you display the button icon only, the button text only, or the button icon and text in the toolbar. From here, you can add items to the toolbar by dragging and dropping the buttons from the sheet onto the toolbar. Remove existing buttons from the toolbar by dragging them out of the toolbar and letting go, similar to how you remove items from Mac OS X's Dock.

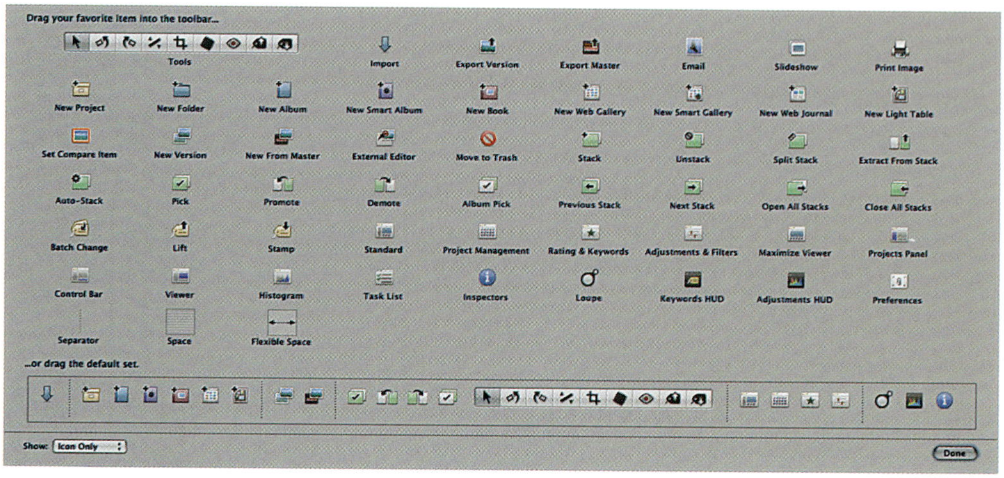

Figure 3.13: The Customize Toolbar sheet

Let's customize the toolbar by adding the Maximize Viewer button.

1. Grab the Maximize Viewer icon (Maximize Viewer) and drag it up with your other layouts.
2. When you have it positioned where you want it, let go, and Aperture will add that button to the toolbar.
3. Click the Done button in the customize sheet, and click the Maximize Viewer button to see how it works.

Note: Aperture's toolbar is a Mac OS X standard toolbar. You can customize the toolbar in other applications, such as the Finder, in exactly the same way. right-click/Control-click the toolbar, choose Customize Toolbar, and rearrange the buttons as desired.

Other viewing-related buttons in the customize toolbar sheet include buttons to hide and show the Projects panel, the control bar, and the Viewer. You'll find them immediately after the layout buttons, and you add them to the toolbar the same way you added the Maximize Viewer button. Because all of these buttons have hotkeys, we don't recommend that you waste toolbar space with them. We recommend that you learn the hotkeys instead.

If you ever want to reset the toolbar to its default state, grab the large strip at the bottom of the Customize Toolbar sheet, below the Or Drag The Default Set text, and drag the large strip onto the toolbar. Click the lozenge button in the top-right of the window to show and hide the toolbar.

Full Screen Mode

Despite the numerous customizations you can make to Aperture's user interface, sometimes it's still too busy, especially with the menu bar and the Dock. For these cases,

Aperture provides a Full Screen mode. Enter Full Screen mode by either clicking the Full Screen button ( ) in the control bar, choosing View > Full Screen, or pressing F. By default, in this mode, all you see is your image over a black background. Exit Full Screen mode by pressing Esc.

If you move your cursor to the top of the screen, a toolbar containing some common Aperture controls, such as New Versions From Master and Show Adjustments HUD, will slide down (Figure 3.14). Lock the toolbar into place and keep it visible all of the time by toggling the Always Show Toolbar button ( ). We don't recommend keeping this toolbar visible because all of the buttons have hotkeys, and it's better not to lose precious screen real estate to an unneeded button.

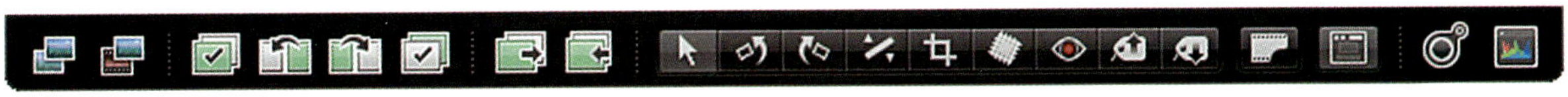

Figure 3.14:

Note: Hover your cursor over buttons in the toolbar for a second to reveal a tooltip with the button's function.

If you move your cursor to the bottom of the screen, the Filmstrip (Figure 3.15) will appear. The Filmstrip is similar to the Browser in that it shows thumbnails of your images, but it also includes common controls from the control bar, such as the Increase Rating and Decrease Rating buttons as well as the Exit Full Screen button ( ). These controls function the same way they do in Windowed mode. And yes, in case you're wondering, you can loupe images in the Filmstrip just as you can in the Browser.

You'll also find the familiar Viewing mode control, but there are two additional sets of options in the Full Screen button. The first option is the choice between On and Auto. This option determines whether or not the Filmstrip is always visible (On) or if it's visible only when you move your cursor near it (Auto). The second option is whether or not to enable Avoid. When set, the Viewer will resize so that the Filmstrip never overlaps the image. If you're using Full Screen mode to edit your images, having the Filmstrip set to always be on and to avoid overlapping an image is useful. That way, you can quickly access any image in the current collection without overlapping the image. If you're presenting images to someone, such as a client, hiding the Filmstrip is more useful so that it's there if you want to jump to a particular image, but the main focus is on the current image.

Note: Your full screen viewing mode controls are independent of your Main Viewer's control. For instance, your Main Viewer could be set to Multi while your Full Screen Viewer is set to Primary.

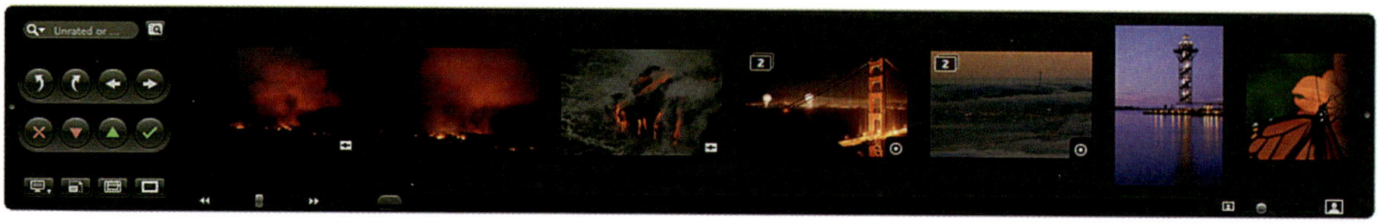

Figure 3.15:

In the Filmstrip, there is also a scrolling acceleration control, a slider with double arrows on both sides, similar to the one in the Browser, that lets you scroll anywhere from very slowly to very quickly through your images. Use the J, K, and L keys to (respectively) scroll to your previous images, stop scrolling, and scroll to your next images. Pressing J or L multiple times will cause Aperture to scroll through your images faster.

Note: The J, K, and L keys will also scroll a browser when Aperture isn't in Full Screen mode.

If you don't like where the Filmstrip is by default, you can reposition it. Click in the Filmstrip's blank area by the buttons, and drag it around the screen. As you move your cursor to the left and right side of the Viewer, the Filmstrip will become vertical to fit on the side of the screen. As your cursor nears the center top and bottom, the Filmstrip will become horizontal, stretching across the screen. If you want, you can even drop the Filmstrip in the center of the image. Setting the Filmstrip to Auto and dropping it in the center can actually be useful because you don't have to move the cursor to the far edges of your screen to reach the Filmstrip. As soon as you move your cursor away, the Filmstrip goes away. However, if you are trying to loupe or make adjustments to the image, this setup can be annoying since the Filmstrip will always pop up when you approach the center of your image.

Resize the Filmstrip along its long dimension by clicking and dragging the small dot at either end. You can't make the Filmstrip display more than one row or column (depending on whether it's horizontal or vertical), though. By using the slider between the two Picture icons (), you can change the size of the Filmstrip's thumbnails. Figure 3.16 shows what we consider to be the most useful setup. The Filmstrip is along the left side of the screen, because most Apple displays have more space horizontally than vertically. This position doesn't take space away from an already-smaller vertical image. By setting it to always be visible, we can easily see what the next and previous images are or what the other images in the stack are.

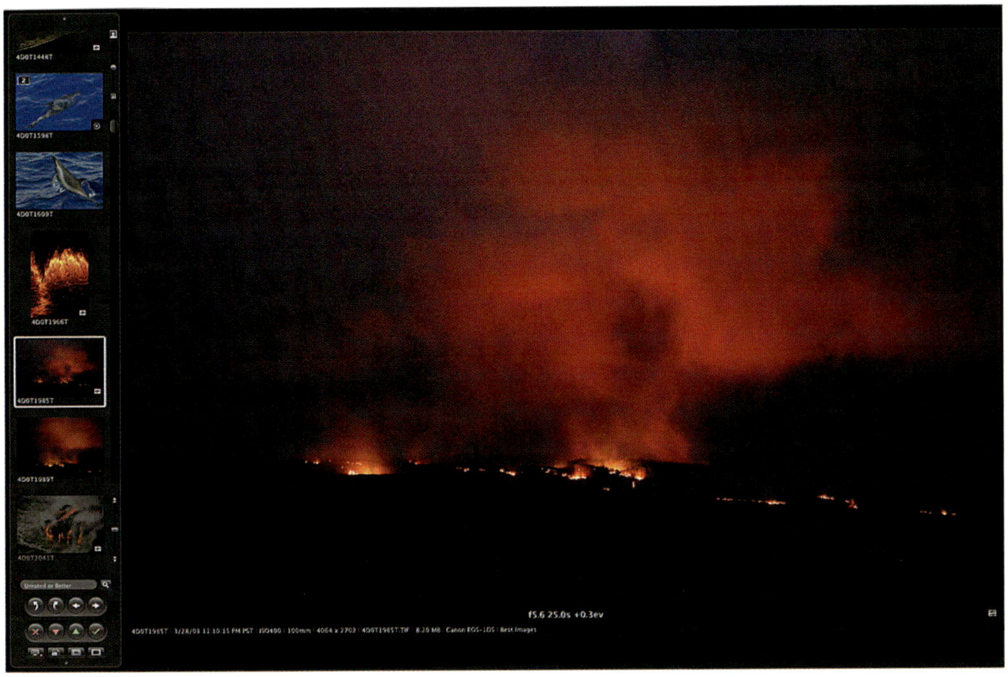

Figure 3.16: A sample full screen setup

If you're used to working in Windowed mode, you've probably used the Adjustments panel. This panel is the unmovable, Opaque Inspector you use to make your image adjustments. In Full Screen mode, there are no fixed items except for the toolbar at the top of the window and the Filmstrip. Instead, Aperture provides heads-up displays (HUDs) that you use to make your adjustments. A HUD is a partially transparent window that floats above your image, and you can quickly hide and quickly display it. Bring up the Adjustments HUD by clicking the Adjustments icon () in the toolbar or by pressing H. We'll explore the controls more in Chapter 5, "Nondestructive Image Processing."

Note: Bring up Aperture's HUDs in Windowed mode by either using the same hotkey as in full screen mode (H), clicking the button in the toolbar, or choosing Window > Show Adjustments HUD. By using the HUDs, you can hide the inspectors and maximize the amount of screen space used for actually viewing each image.

Aperture provides a second HUD, called the Keywords HUD, which you can use to adjust your image's keywords. Bring it up by pressing Shift+H. We'll explore keywords in depth in Chapter 4.

Try editing and rating your images in Full Screen mode. We're sure that you'll find its simplicity and elegance quite useful. Take advantage of Aperture's hotkeys, too, so that you're not always reaching for the mouse or exiting Full Screen mode to perform basic tasks. You'll find a handy tipsheet for the Aperture hotkeys included with Aperture's manual. To get you started learning Aperture's hotkeys, Table 3.2 lists the hotkeys for the items in the Full Screen toolbar.

Table 3.2: Toolbar Hotkeys

Command	Hotkey
Duplicate Version	Option+V
New Version From Master	Option+G
Pick	⌘+\
Promote	⌘+[
Demote	⌘+]
Set Album Pick	⌘+|
Open All Stacks	Option+'
Close All Stacks	Option+;
Select	/
Rotate Left	[
Rotate Right	]
Straighten tool	G
Crop tool	C
Spot And Patch tool	X
Red Eye tool	E
Lift tool	O
Stamp tool	Shift+O
Show Master Image	M
Loupe	`
Adjustments HUD	H

Viewing Options with Multiple Monitors

It's becoming more and more common to have more than one display. For instance, many nature photographers have a laptop with an uncalibrated display and a color-accurate display at home that they plug their laptop into to adjust their images. Believing the adage that he who dies with the most pixels wins, other fortunate photographers have dual-30" displays. Aperture allows you to take advantage of both displays.

Note: Products such as the Color Vision Spyder2 Pro Studio let you calibrate two monitors attached to the same computer.

Note: If you're connecting a laptop to an external display, make sure that your monitors are set to *span* and not *mirror* in System Preferences. The external display will act like more screen space instead of mirroring what's on your main display. However, as of press time, only the MacBook Pro and PowerBook are able to span monitors.

In both Full Screen and Windowed mode, you'll see two sections under the Viewing Modes button. The first section, which is always visible, is labeled Main Viewer. The second section, which is visible when you have multiple monitors connected, is labeled Secondary Viewer. You'll always find a Secondary Viewer submenu in the View menu, but it's useful only when you have more than one monitor. The Primary Viewer refers to the Viewer on the screen where the menu bar is. The Secondary Viewer is the other screen.

Note: To change the primary screen, select System Preferences > Displays. Under the Arrangement tab, you'll see two rectangles representing your screen. Drag the white area near the top of the primary screen, which represents the menu bar, to the other rectangle to switch primary screens.

The secondary display modes are

Desktop: Aperture does not use this monitor.

Blank: Displays black on the secondary screen.

Span: Distributes the images in the Viewer over both screens.

Mirror: Shows the same image(s) in the primary and secondary displays.

Alternate: Shows one alternative image in the Secondary Viewer.

If you don't want one of these monitors to display an image, set that viewer to Desktop. To set it to black, choose Blank. Span will spread the selected images over both screens. However, because you will have different sets of images on each display, you might find this viewing mode distracting especially if one monitor is not calibrated or if the monitors are at different resolutions so that the Viewers will not line up properly.

Mirror is quite useful for presenting images to groups of people. It shows a copy of whatever you have in your Primary Viewer against a black background. For instance, your MacBook Pro might be connected to an external display that faces the audience. You could leave Aperture in Windowed mode, giving you access to all of your controls, while mirroring the image on the second display, making it seem like a presentation with no work.

The last viewing mode is Alternate, and this mode is useful when you select multiple images. This mode will always show one image in the Secondary Viewer, even if the Main Viewer is set to Multi. This mode is useful if you want to see a number of selected images in the Main Viewer, but you want to view one image at a larger size. Additionally, if you select two images to compare, you can compare larger versions of your image on separate viewers instead of smaller versions in the same viewer, but again, be alert to color and resolution differences between your monitors.

Light Tables

As we mentioned in Chapter 1, part of Aperture's goal is to bring the simplicity and elegance of working with slides to digital images. One of the biggest benefits to slides was that you could lay a bunch of them on a light table and move them around to explore different compositions, stories you could tell, or to see similar images together. Aperture has a virtual version of the light table, taken a few steps further, where you can put images together, resize them, move them around, and even print the layouts when you're finished, which we'll discuss in Chapter 7, "Printing."

To create an empty light table, select File > New > Light Table. It will appear in the Projects panel, and you can rename it as you would an album. To delete it, select it in the Projects panel and choose File > Delete Light Table. Create a light table with various initial images by selecting images in the Browser and choosing File > New From Selection > Light Table.

Note: If you have multiple light tables in a project, create a folder called Light Tables to contain them.

Each light table contains an implicit album of images, images you can see in a browser and in the light table itself with the images you've placed onto it. Add images to the Light Table album by dragging them from a browser and dropping them onto the light table file in the Projects Panel. To remove them from the album, select the images and choose Images > Remove From Album (Delete).

When you switch to a light table, such as the one shown in Figure 3.17, one of the first things you'll notice is that the Browser has additional icons. The first new icon on the left is the Show Viewer For This Browser button (). When you press this button, Aperture will switch the contents of the Viewer from a light table to a Normal Viewer, respecting the Viewing Modes button in the control bar. Use this button if you want to adjust an image in your light table or compare images in the light table's browser to determine which image you wanted to place onto the light table.

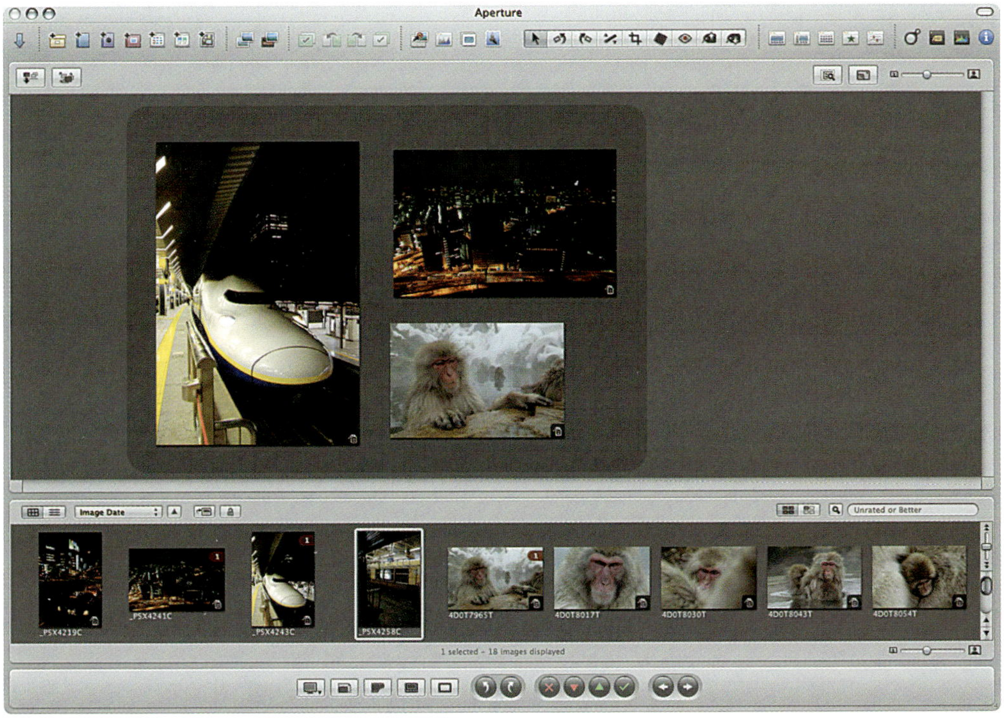

Figure 3.17: A sample light table and browser

The next button from the left is the Lock This Browser To The Viewer button ( ). This button is present in a number of special viewing modes, such as Light Table mode, Web Gallery mode, and Book Editing mode. If you have multiple albums open or projects that contain images you want to use on your light table open, you can select those images without leaving the Light Table Viewer (or whatever mode you're in). Understanding this button is a bit easier if you actually try using it.

1. Select a light table in the Projects panel so that you see it in the Viewer.
2. Option+click another album or project to split the Browser into two views. If you click an image in the second album, you'll see the Viewer change to show that image.
3. Click on one of the images in the light table's browser, and watch the Viewer switch back to a light table.
4. Press the Lock button. As you click images in the other project, Aperture will select those images, so that you can drag and drop them onto the light table's browser, but the Viewer will stay locked to the light table instead of switching to the new image.

On the right-hand side, to the left of the search field, are two new buttons, Show All Images and Show Unplaced Images ( ). When you put an image from the Browser onto the light table, we say that the image is *placed*. These buttons let you toggle between seeing every placed and unplaced image you've added to the light table's implicit album and just seeing only unplaced images.

Placing an image onto the light table is easy. Grab it in the Browser, and drag it onto the light table. After you drop the image onto the light table, notice that its browser icon has a small maroon icon with a "1" on it (Figure 3.18). This icon indicates that you've placed the image. Because there is a number on the icon, you might think you can place multiple copies of an image onto a light table, but this is not the case.

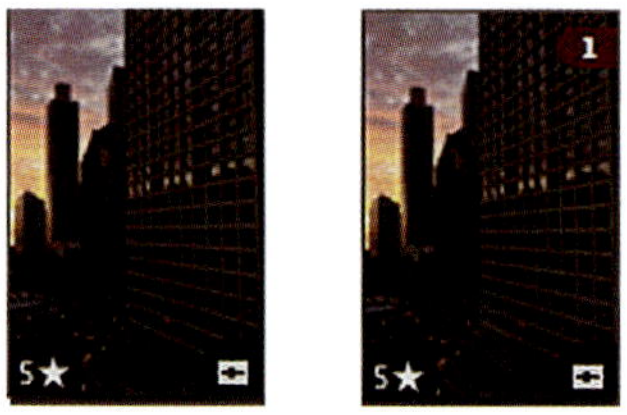

Figure 3.18:
The thumbnail on the left hasn't been placed onto a light table; the thumbnail on the right, with its small badge in the upper-right corner, has been placed.

Note: To place multiple copies of the same image, select the image, choose Images > Duplicate Version (Option+V), open the stack, select the new version, and choose Stacks > Extract Item (Option+Shift+K). You'll have two identical yet separate images that you can place onto the light table.

Once an image is on the light table, you can move it around, resize it, and change its layer order. To move an image around, drag the image wherever you want to put it. If you want the light table to expand, drag the image to one of the light table's edges, and the light table will expand in that direction. To select multiple images, which you can move around simultaneously, ⌘+click the images in the light table or select the images in the Browser using various combinations of Shift+clicking and ⌘+clicking. If you Shift+click in the light table, Aperture will determine where each image is in the Browser and select all of the images between the images you clicked. As usual, Aperture will draw a white border around the selected images and a thicker white border around the primary selection.

When you hover the cursor over an image in the light table, Aperture will show small, gray squares along the edge of the image. These squares represent points that you can drag to make the image larger or smaller. As you resize the image, you'll notice that Aperture always preserves the image's aspect ratio—you can't distort it. However, the square you pick to resize the image determines in which direction Aperture grows the image. For instance, if you grab the middle square on the right-hand side, Aperture will keep the left side fixed and make its width changes on the right side. The height changes will be divided equally along the top and bottom. On the other hand, if you were to click and drag the lower-left corner square, Aperture would keep the top and right sides fixed and grow or shrink the image on the left and bottom sides. To restore the image to its original size, right-click/Control-click the image and choose Reset Selected Size.

As you resize and reposition your images, you might find that you have overlapping images. Sometimes, you actually do want the images to overlap, but you might not like the order in which they are overlapping. To bring any image to the front, click it. However, if the image is completely hidden, or you want to expand a number of overlapping images to see all of them at once, Aperture has an exposé-like feature. Move your cursor over an image in the overlapping pile, and press the Uncover button ( ) at the top of the light table, or press Shift+X. Aperture will expand the overlapping area and keep the picture initially under your mouse centered, as seen in Figure 3.19. This will allow you to select one of the covered images. Once you click the image you want to be on top, Aperture will collapse the area, and you'll find the selected image at the top of the pile. Shift+X without choosing an image to collapse the area as it was before.

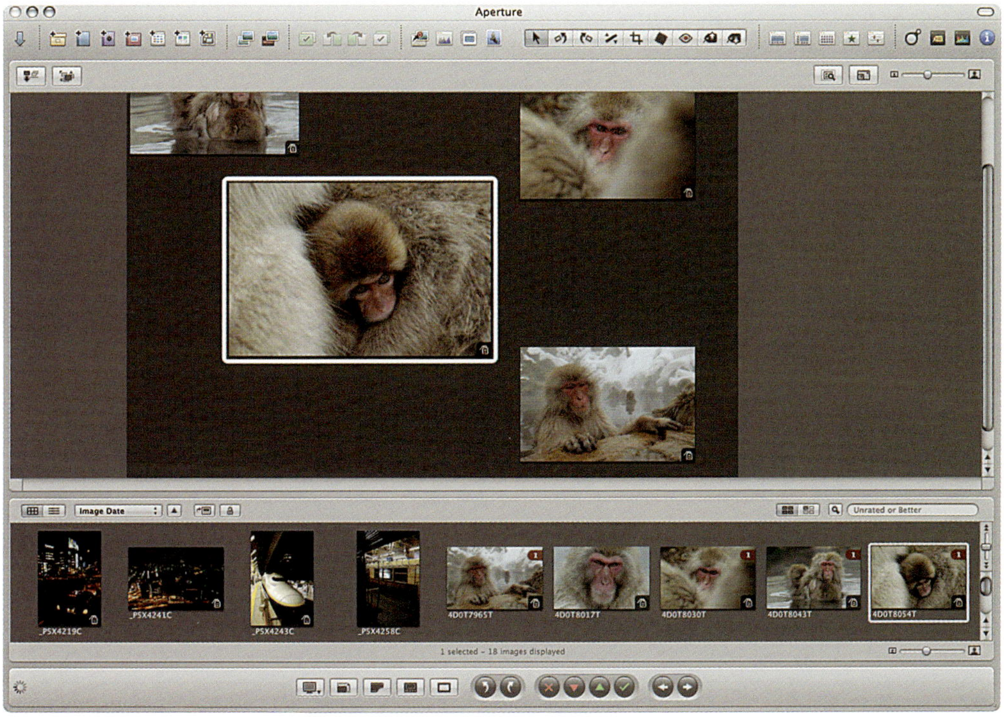

Figure 3.19: Uncovering an image in the light table

Perhaps you don't want your images to overlap at all; you want a more standard, grid-like layout. As a starting point, select the images you want to arrange, right-click/Control-click them, and choose Arrange. Aperture will automatically spread the selected images and avoid any overlap. You can arrange the all images automatically by Control-clicking in an empty area on the light table, and choosing Arrange All Images.

Furthermore, if you select multiple images and right-click/Control-click, you'll see two submenus labeled Align and Distribute. The commands under the Align menu will arrange the selected images to all line up neatly, perhaps at the top edge or the vertical center of the image. The Distribute menu's commands will look at the total space occupied by the selected images and determine how to distribute that space so that there's equal spacing between each image either horizontally or vertically.

If you want to remove an image from the light table, either select it and press the Put Back button ( ) or right-click/Control-click the selected image and choose Remove From Light Table.

After a while, your light tables can grow rather large. If you have lots of blank space around the edges, perhaps you accidentally expanded the light table when you didn't mean to expand it. Right-click/Control-click in an empty area, and choose Minimize Size. Aperture will automatically shrink the light table to the smallest size it can while still bounding all of your images. If you want to see the entire light table at once, press the Scale To Fit All Items button ( ) which will zoom the Viewer out so that you can see the whole light table. You could also right-click/Control-click in an empty area and choose Zoom To Fit. If you want to zoom in or out even more, use the slider at the top-right of the light table to adjust its scale to your desire.

If you don't want to change your zoom level, but you want to quickly move to part of the light table, then the Navigator is your answer. Either click the Navigator button ( ) or right-click/Control-click the light table and choose Navigator. The light table will temporarily zoom out with most of it darkened, as in Figure 3.20. However, a lighter rectangle represents the part of the light table at which you were looking. Drag this rectangle around to the new part of the light table you want to see. When you let go of the mouse, Aperture will scroll the light table to this new area. To exit the Navigator and return to your previous view, click within the rectangle.

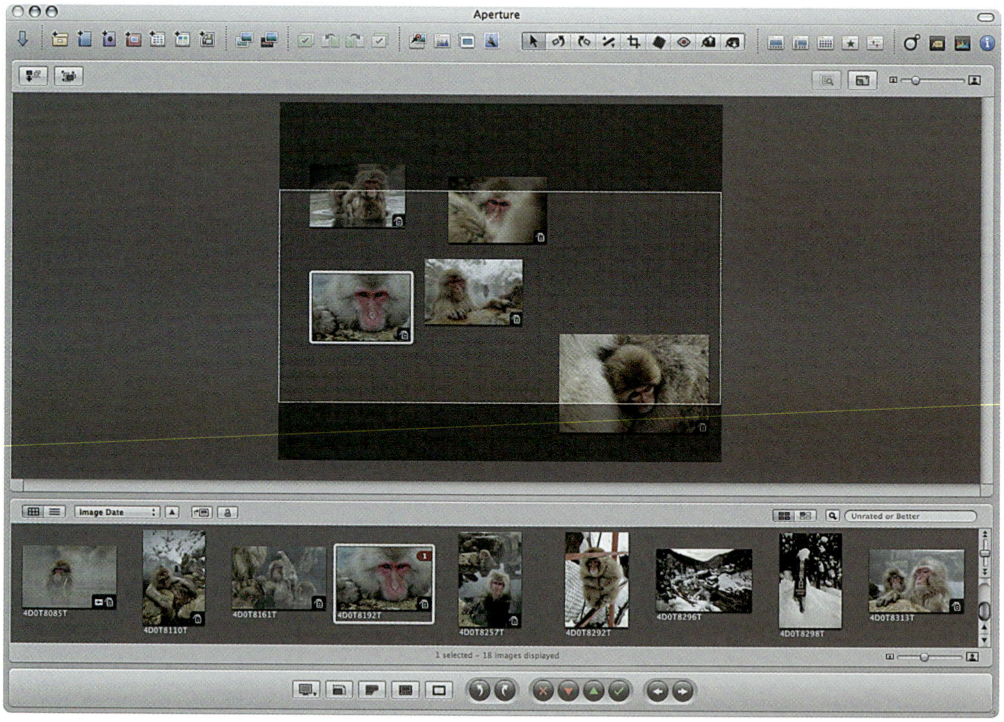

Figure 3.20: The Light Table Navigator

In summary, Control-clicking the empty light table area activates a context menu where you can choose the following:

Minimize Size Makes the light table as small as possible to contain your images

Arrange All Items Automatically arranges your images

Zoom To 100% Displays the light table at its actual size

Zoom To fit Displays the entire light table in the window

Navigator Access the light table navigator

Once you're happy with your light table's layout, you have a variety of options. You can use its layout as a sample design for a book (we'll cover books in Chapter 8) or website. You can select and print part of the light table, creating custom contact sheets or collages, which we'll cover in Chapter 7. You can bring up the Print panel, but instead of printing the light table, you can save it to a PDF and use another application to convert it to a JPEG for a website. The possibilities are limited only by your imagination.

Slideshows

One of the greatest benefits to digital asset management programs like Aperture, where you organize photos into albums and smart albums, is that you have multiple collections of images, with each collection potentially having overlapping contents, at your fingertips. For instance, if you have a 5-Star Best Images smart folder for each project and one for the entire library, you always have your best images from both your current project and for all other projects at your fingertips.

If you want to share one of these albums with someone, you can bring it up in the Viewer, maybe even in Full Screen mode. If you want to really impress them, Aperture provides an advanced slideshow tool you can use instead. This slideshow tool lets you add music and transitions to your images, and it lets you show more than one slide at once.

Note: Place the images for your slideshow into their own album. That way, you only have to select the images for a given slide show once and can just run a slide show on that entire album in the future.

To start a slideshow, select the images you want to show and choose File > Slideshow. To make a show from all of the images in an album, clear your selection by clicking an empty area in the Browser, and choose File > Slideshow. When you choose this command, the Run Slideshow window in Figure 3.21 appears. From there, you can choose one of Aperture's predefined slideshow modes or define your own.

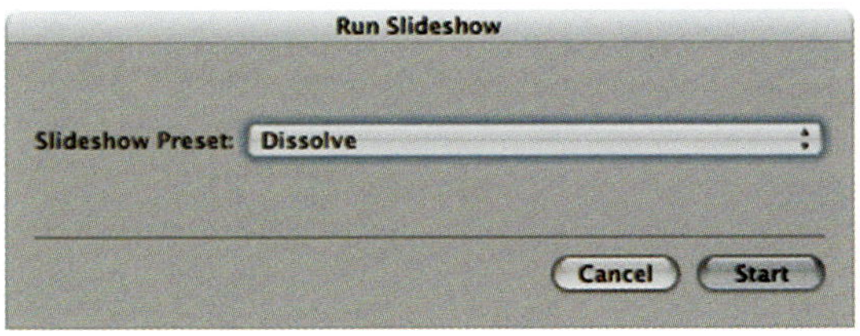

Figure 3.21: The Run Slideshow window

To create your own preset or modify an existing one, choose Edit from the pop-up menu in the Run Slideshow window. Aperture will open a window similar to Figure 3.22. On the left is a list of all of the preset slideshow modes. You can create a new mode by pressing the Add button (+), or you can edit an existing mode by selecting it and changing its options. To remove a preset, select it and press the Remove button (−).

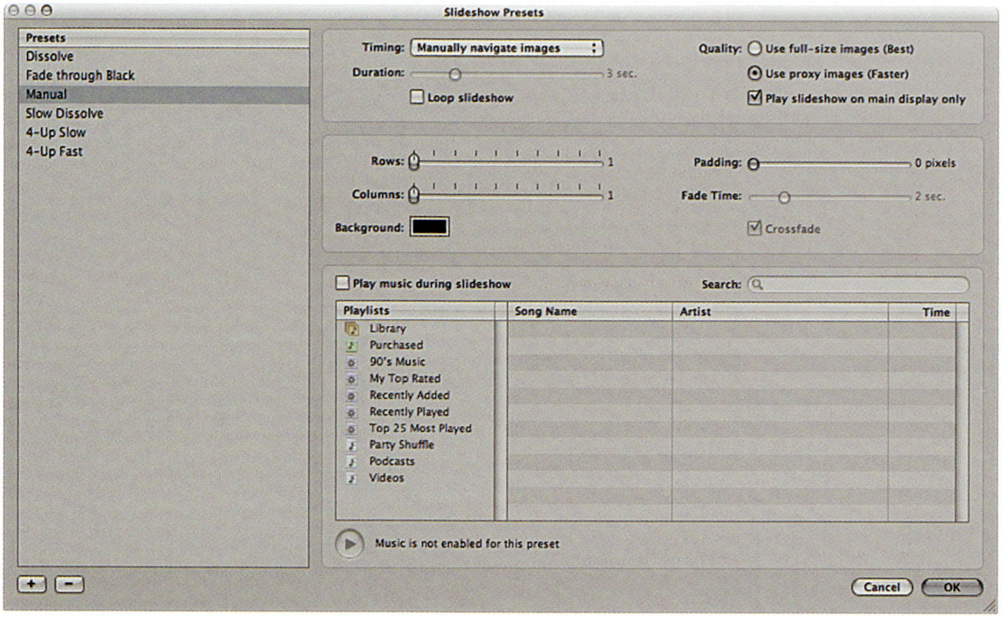

Figure 3.22: The Slideshow Presets window

Your first option is how you want to time the show. The timing pop-up has options to manually time the show (you manually advance each slide), show images for a fixed duration (which you set with the Duration slider), or to fit the show to music (Aperture will determine the length of a song you select and divide that time by the number of slides in the show). You can also choose to loop the show or stop the show after reaching the last slide. If you have more than one monitor, you can mirror it on both displays or play it on the main display only.

Your next choice determines the display quality. Aperture keeps a relatively small 1,024-pixel (along the longest dimension) proxy image for each RAW file. It shows this image to you in the Viewer, for example, while it's loading the RAW file. When you're running a slideshow and plan to have the slides display for a very short duration, Aperture might not have enough time to load the full image and prepare it for display in the slideshow. Instead, it gives you the option to use proxy images, which it can prepare very quickly for display. In general, unless you're presenting on a high-resolution display or focusing on the tack-sharp nature of each image, these proxy images will be sufficient for a slideshow. However, if every slide will display for 5 to 10 seconds or more and you are using a projector or monitor with a resolution higher than 1024 × 768, then configuring Aperture to use the full-size images in the slideshow should be safe.

The next set of options, in the middle in the Slideshow Presets window, determines how Aperture displays each image. On the left, you can choose the number of rows and columns to display. Aperture's slideshows can show more than one image at a time. You can set it to display up to one hundred images at once. As Aperture runs the show, it will add more images to the screen until it's reached the specified number of rows and columns, and then it will replace each image, still displaying the specified number of rows and columns, until it runs out of images. In other words, it builds up to the number of images you want to see at once, and then it always shows that many images at once. Press the colorwell to display a color picker to choose your show's background color.

The controls on the right affect how Aperture builds the slideshow. Padding controls how much space appears between the images as well as at the edges of the screen. Aperture will shrink each image so that it provides the amount of padding you specify. Fade time affects how long it takes for each image to appear. If you uncheck Crossfade, Aperture will fade the existing image to black and then fade in the new image over the specified amount of time. Set the Fade Time to 0 to have images simply appear without fading.

The bottom area provides an iTunes interface to access your iTunes songs and music. If you want to have background music during your slideshow, check the Play Music During Slideshow box. Preview a song by double-clicking it in the table or by selecting it and pressing the play button below the table.

Once you're happy with either your new preset or the changes you've made to an existing preset, click OK. The Run Slideshow window will appear again. You can select your preset, and click Start to run the show. Press Esc to close the show at any point.

Now that you know how to view and compare your images, it's time to learn how to use Aperture to find and save your keepers.

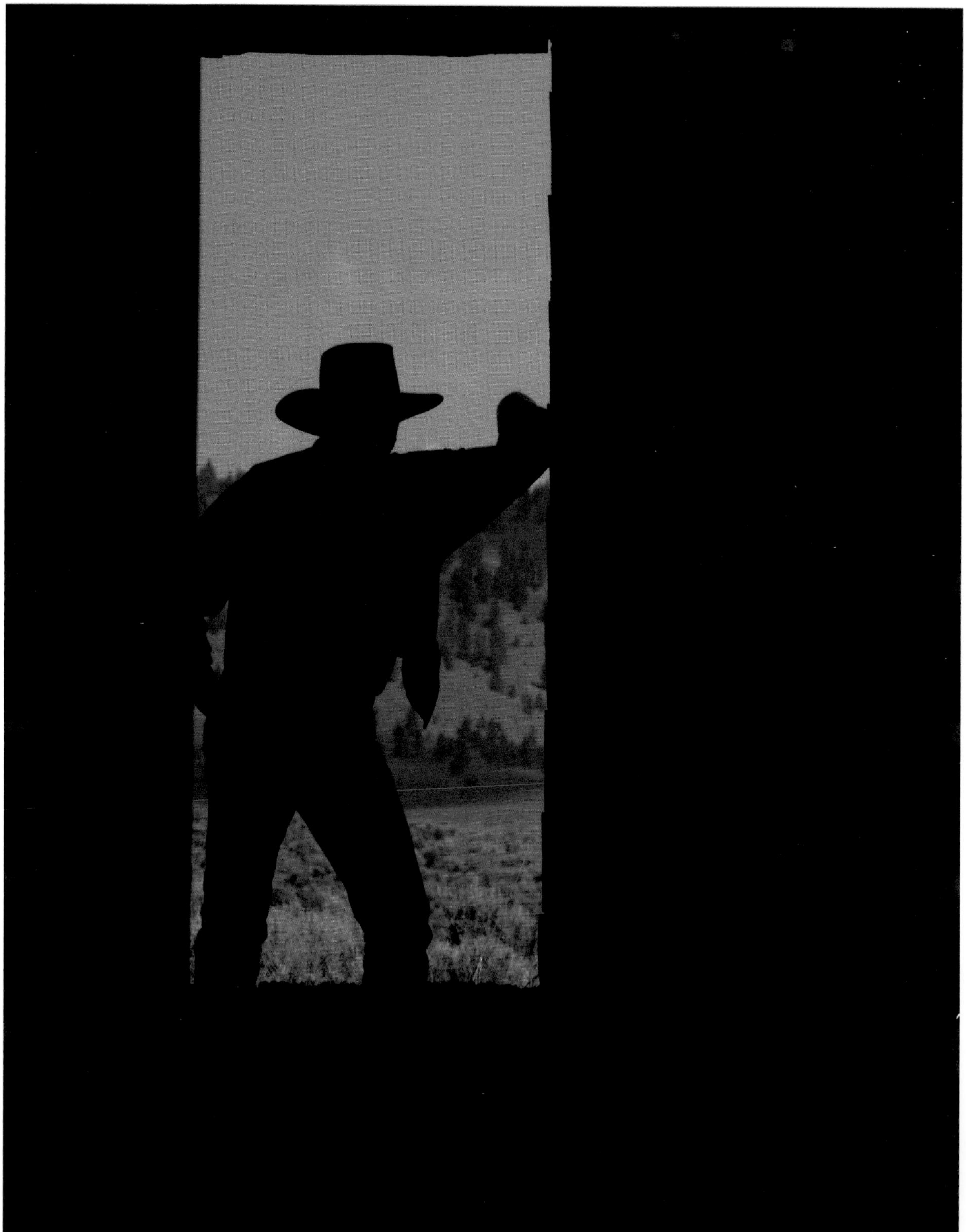

Finding the Keepers

With digital photography, many photographers end up shooting more images because it costs just as much to take one photo as it does to take one hundred. However, there is a hidden cost—you need to edit and store those additional photos. Some photographers try to keep every image, buying more hard drives when needed, but this is simply impractical because they never use the bad photos. In reality, you need to keep only a fraction of what you shoot. Aperture provides powerful tools, from keyword sets to backup vaults that help you find your best images now and in the future.

4

Chapter Contents

Metadata, Keywords, and Ratings

In previous chapters, we discussed some of the basics of adding keywords to your images (such as how to select the image and enter the keywords in the Inspector), but one important point we glossed over is why you should care about keywords and other image metadata. Put simply, metadata helps you find and organize your images. As we'll show you in this chapter, Aperture lets you search for images based on their metadata, and it lets you define smart albums (and other smart containers, such as smart web galleries) based on metadata, including keywords and ratings.

Understanding Metadata Formats

Before we delve any deeper, we need to sort through some of the acronym soup that makes up metadata. At some point, you've probably heard someone mention a type of metadata, be it EXIF, IPTC, or XMP. The most common type is EXIF metadata, which contains information about the exposure, such as exposure time, compensation, focal length, etc.. EXIF data is useful for everything from a learning tool to understand how camera settings change the image to contributing to using direct-print printers, where you hook the camera up to the printer directly.

Note: Originally EXIF was just for JPEG images, but now many RAW files, especially those based on the TIFF file format, store information using EXIF tags too.

EXIF (Exchangeable Image File) This type of information can also help you edit your images. As a simple example, if you took two photos of a macro subject, one at f/8 and one at f/11, you might decide that you want the one with more depth of field, but it might be hard to determine exactly which one that is. By looking at the EXIF data, you can quickly see which it is and pick that image over the other. As you may have already discovered, Aperture can read EXIF data if it's available.

IPTC (International Press Telecommunications Council) This was originally known as Information Interchange Model (IIM) metadata. It's designed to contain higher-level information about an image, such as where it was taken and who owns the copyright. Typically, you cannot edit EXIF data, but you can edit IPTC data. After all, the camera knows that the image was shot at $\frac{1}{60}$ sec (data stored in the EXIF metadata), but it doesn't know who pressed the shutter button (information you would add to the IPTC data).

XMP (Extensible Metadata Platform) This is a new metadata "container" developed by Adobe that has been gaining traction over the past few years. The idea here is that you create an XML schema (XML is a generic way of presenting data using tags and values, similar to the HTML that websites use) to describe what type of metadata you're adding, and an application adds data using that schema to the file. At the same time, another application could add a completely different set of metadata to the file, also using XMP, just by using a different schema. In other words, XMP is just a way of storing sets of data, and the data stored is completely up to the application. As an example, Photoshop will store the IPTC metadata you edit using XMP, data that other applications can read and use, and Adobe's Camera Raw converter can also save your conversion settings in XMP using its own schema, data that many other applications can't read. Unfortunately, Aperture doesn't support XMP. It supports only EXIF and IPTC metadata.

Note: When you edit file information in Photoshop, it stores a non-XMP header in addition to its XMP data. Aperture can read the data, including the keywords, in this non-XMP header when you import the image.

Viewing Metadata in Aperture

In Chapter 3, "Viewing Images," we covered how to use the View Options window (View > View Options or ⌘+J) to display metadata above or below each image or as a tooltip. It's useful to have Aperture show metadata below each image because this mode lets you see metadata in Windowed mode, Full Screen mode, and in the Browser in the same way. However, the Inspector is another more useful display that is available when you're not in Full Screen mode. The Inspector is on the right side of the screen and is shown in Figure 4.1. If it's not visible, you can show it by choosing Window > Show Inspectors or by pressing I.

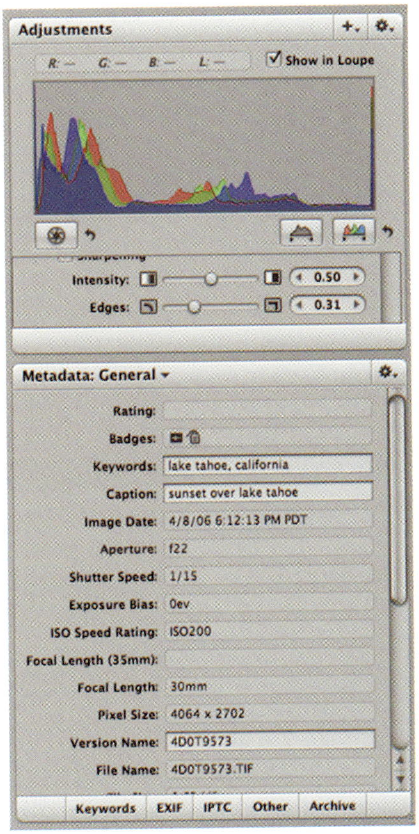

Figure 4.1: The Aperture inspectors in Windowed mode

The histogram is one of the most important pieces of metadata for an image, although it is not actually metadata in the traditional sense. However, many photographers do consider its data to be a type of metadata because the histogram provides information about the image, and we'll talk about it here.

Aperture calculates and displays the histogram when it's needed, as opposed to metadata, such as EXIF data, that it stores in its database. The histogram is at the very top of the Inspector; it's actually part of the Adjustments Inspector. If it's hidden, you can display it by selecting Show Histogram from the Action menu (✿) at the top of the Inspector.

Understanding Histograms

A histogram represents the number of pixels in an image at each luminance from black, on the far left, to white, on the far right. Contrary to what some people believe, there is no one "correct" histogram. A medium close-up of a blonde bride in a white wedding dress will have peaks toward the right side with very little data on the left, whereas a picture of a groom in a black tuxedo will have peaks on the left side toward the black but also will have peaks on the right for his white shirt. Each exposure could be perfect, but the histogram will still have those peaks. At the same time, if the image of the bride only has primarily a peak at the extreme right of the histogram, then much of the image is going to be pure white, without detail, and the image is probably overexposed. Similarly, the image is probably underexposed if there is a peak at the extreme left side of the histogram. Other books, such as *Photoshop for Nature Photographers* by Anon and Grey (Sybex, 2005), cover histograms in more detail.

Histograms are incredibly important for editing images because they provide an objective way to judge exposure. If you know roughly where you should see peaks in a histogram for a given image, you can make initial judgments about an image's exposure, regardless of the lighting conditions and monitor you're using to view your images. This is particularly important if you're using a laptop to view your images because the apparent brightness of the image will vary with the viewing angle of the monitor. In Chapter 5, "Nondestructive Image Processing," we'll cover Aperture tools that you can use to adjust your image's exposure and change the histogram.

Below the Adjustments Inspector, you'll find the Metadata Inspector. As we mentioned in Chapter 3, you can make the Inspector larger or smaller by clicking and dragging the gray area between the metadata and adjustments inspectors up or down. At the top of the Metadata Inspector, there are two menus, indicated by the two down arrows. The menu on the left lets you pick which metadata set Aperture shows in the Inspector. We'll discuss how to customize these sets in a bit, but for now, observe how Aperture shows the current set name next to the Metadata text when you switch sets. The Action menu (✿) contains the commands we'll use to customize those metadata sets.

Within the Metadata panel, you'll find various fields and values, depending on which metadata set you're viewing. For example, the General set includes fields from EXIF metadata, such as Shutter Speed and Exposure Bias, along with fields from IPTC metadata, such as Caption. This set also includes the Aperture-specific metadata fields Rating, which you set for each image, and Badges (see Chapter 3), which appear depending on what modifications you've made to an image.

Some fields have a dark gray background, whereas some have a light gray background; Figure 4.2 shows two such fields. The dark gray fields are not editable values. These are values that are set elsewhere in Aperture, such as Rating, or that you can't change, such as Shutter Speed. The other fields, such as Caption, with the light gray background are fields that you can click and then use to enter information. To set your image's caption, as an example, click in the Caption field, enter a value, and press Tab to confirm your change.

Figure 4.2: The File Name field, with a dark gray background, can't be edited. The Version Name field, with a light gray background, can be edited.

Customizing Metadata Sets

At the bottom of the Metadata Inspector, you'll see five buttons that you can use as follows:

Keywords: View and edit the image's keywords.

EXIF: View all EXIF fields and values.

IPTC: View all IPTC fields and values.

Other: View Aperture-specific metadata, such as custom keywords.

Archive: View Information for where and when an image is stored in a vault.

These buttons allow you to modify what metadata Aperture displays in the current set as well as showing you additional metadata about the image that might not be visible in the current set. For instance, when you click the EXIF button (or press Ctrl+E), an additional panel will open, and if you scroll down, you'll see the fields in Figure 4.3.

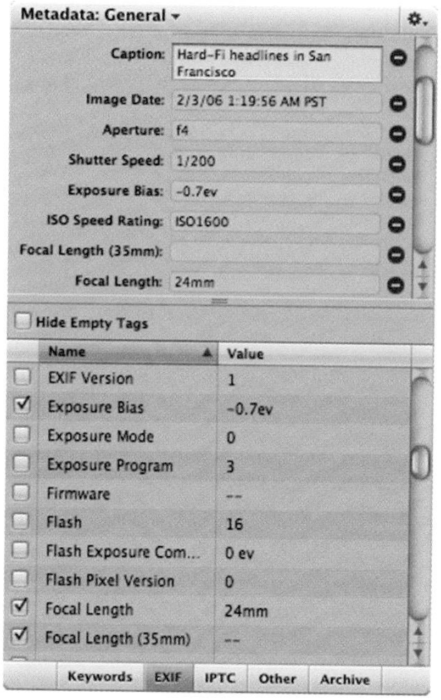

Figure 4.3: The Metadata Inspector displaying all available EXIF data

Some fields, such as Depth, have a value (in this case, 16 means that you have a 16 bit/component image) but are not checked. If you check the box, Aperture will add Depth to the bottom of the current metadata set.

When the buttons at the bottom of the Metadata Inspector are active, Aperture will draw Remove icons (⊖) next to each field in the Inspector. Click this button if you want to quickly remove a field from the current set. You can also click and drag each field—click the field name—to rearrange your metadata's order, perhaps grouping File Name and Version Name next to each other.

Some of these buttons have additional options at the top of their respective panels. For instance, the Keywords panel and Archive panel have buttons labeled Include In Summary. In other panels, such as the EXIF panel, Aperture simply presents lists of fields and values, such as Focal Length, that you can choose to show or not show. However, fields like Keywords include many subvalues, specifically individual keywords. The Keywords panel contains controls for the potentially numerous values of only one field, Keywords. At the top, the Include In Summary button gives you the option of whether or not to display all of the data you see within the panel.

You can also directly manipulate keywords in this panel. To add a keyword, enter it into the text field at the top of the panel and click the Add icon (⊕). To remove an existing keyword, click the Remove button (⊖) to the right of the keyword. Manually entering each keyword can be a bit tedious, and we'll show you better and faster ways to set keywords later on in this chapter.

Under the EXIF and IPTC panels, you'll find the Hide Empty Tags button. Both the EXIF and IPTC specifications have a large number of possible metadata fields, fields that not all cameras write to or that users care to edit. In other words, you often end up with a lot of metadata fields with no values for them. Checking this button hides any field that doesn't have a value so that you don't even have the option to display it in the metadata set.

Sometimes, it makes sense to keep these values hidden, especially for IPTC metadata. However, at other times, you'll want to see the field because you want to edit it. As an example, let's add the Special Instructions IPTC field to our metadata set.

1. Under the IPTC panel (you can open it by clicking the IPTC button or by pressing Ctrl+I), uncheck Hide Empty Tags.
2. Find Special Instructions, and check it.
3. Recheck Hide Empty Tags. Aperture will display the Special Instructions field in the metadata set, but it won't be visible in the IPTC panel.
4. Enter a value (for example, **Put this image on the cover!**) into the Special Instructions field and press Tab to confirm your change.
5. To work around a bug in Aperture 1.0, select another panel (e.g., EXIF) and then switch back to IPTC. You'll see Special Instructions and the value you entered listed in that field.

If you clear the value you set and toggle between panels, you'll notice that even though Special Instructions remains in the metadata set, you don't see it in the IPTC panel because it doesn't have a value set.

Adding Custom Metadata

At the top of the Other panel, as shown in Figure 4.4, you'll see two special text boxes with the placeholder values New Custom Metadata and Metadata Value. These text boxes let you add your own custom metadata to your images.

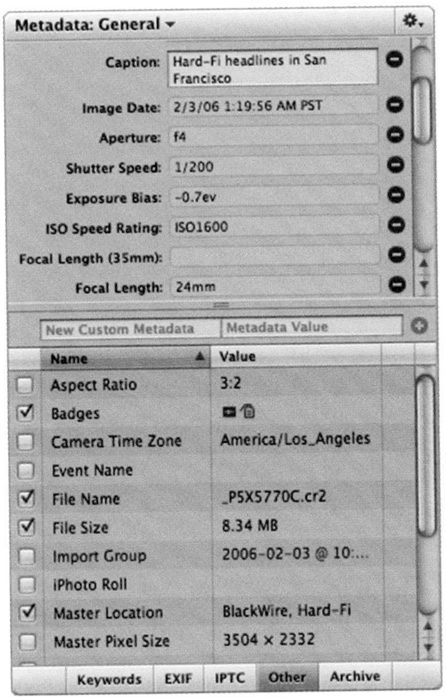

Figure 4.4: The Other panel with the custom metadata fields at the top

Stock photographers, to use a simple example, often have unique IDs for each image, often consisting of the category, image date, and image number. A stock photographer using Aperture might wish to create a special Stock Code field that you can edit for each image. To do so, simply enter **Stock Code** into the New Custom Metadata field and click the Add button (⊕). To view the stock code in the current metadata set, scroll down the Other panel until Stock Code is visible and check it. The field will be available for all the images (you don't have to manually add the field to every image), and you can set it on each image to whatever value you want.

> **Note:** Any custom metadata fields you add are available only within Aperture. They are not stored in the file's metadata when you export the file, and they are not directly readable outside of Aperture.

Creating New Metadata Sets

So far, we have shown you how to customize your existing metadata sets only. If the sets Aperture provides, such as General, meet your needs fairly well except for a few fields, then customizing an existing set is probably more useful than creating a new one.

However, there will be times when you'll want to show only certain fields for a specific purpose, and knowing how to create completely custom metadata sets will be useful. Additionally, any metadata set you create within the Inspector is available everywhere else in Aperture. Continuing the previous stock-code example, you might create a metadata set called Stock Data, which has the image name and stock code. Then, if you set the Browser to show the Stock Data set for each image, you could see your image's stock code just by glancing at it in the Browser.

As we mentioned earlier, the Action menu contains commands to help you create new metadata sets. Figure 4.5 shows the available commands. Follow these steps to make a keywords-only custom metadata set. We're designing this set with minimal information so that you can use it in the Browser where space is at a premium.

1. To create a blank metadata set, select New Set from the Action menu (⚙). You could also start with an existing metadata set by switching to that set and choosing Duplicate Set.

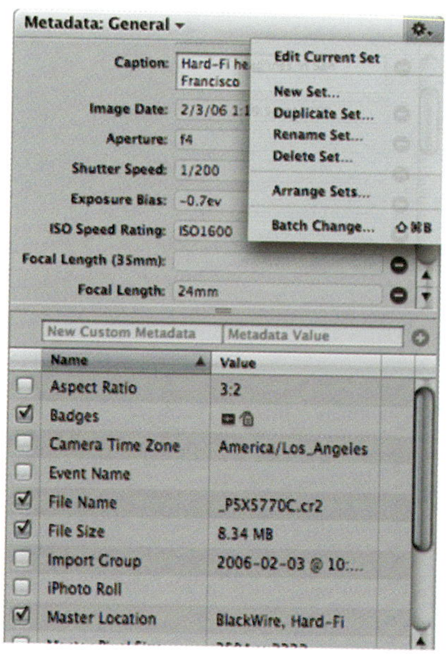

Figure 4.5:
The Metadata Inspector's action menu

2. A sheet will appear asking you to name the set. Leave it set to Untitled. The Metadata Inspector will now be completely blank, and if you look at the panels for the various metadata buttons, you'll see that nothing is checked.
3. After creating the empty metadata set, click the Keywords button.
4. Check Include In Summary to finish making the metadata set.
5. To clean up the title, choose Rename Set from the Action menu.
6. In the Rename sheet, set the set's name to Keywords Only.

When you're done, your Metadata Inspector should look like Figure 4.6. To examine this set, bring up the View Options (View > View Options or ⌘+J), and under Grid View, select Keywords Only from the pop-up for the active set.

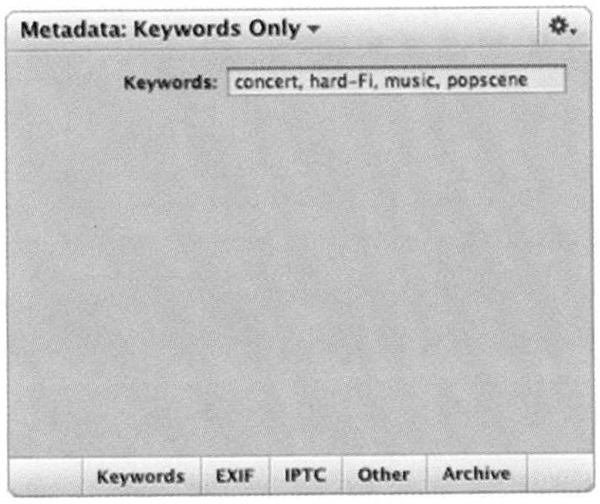

Figure 4.6:
The Keywords Only metadata set

To finish cleaning up, we're going to rename this set **Grid - Keywords Only** and move it up with the other Grid sets. To do so, perform these steps:

1. Select Arrange Sets from the Action menu. Aperture will display the sheet, shown in Figure 4.7, which lists all of your metadata sets.
2. Double-click a set to rename it. Double-click Keywords Only, and rename it **Grid - Keywords Only**.
3. To rearrange a set, click and drag it within the Table view to where you want it to be; move our Keywords set up with the other Grid sets.

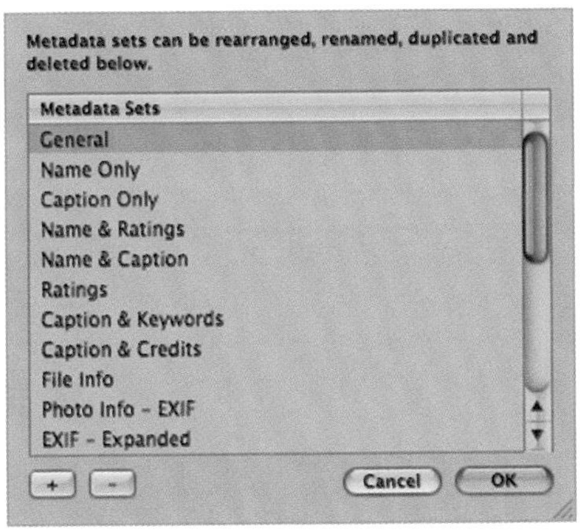

Figure 4.7:
The Arrange Sets sheet

To delete a set, select it and click the Remove button (-). To add a new set, select it and click the Add button (+). Aperture will make a copy of the currently selected set for you to use. When you're done editing, click OK to confirm your changes or click Cancel to lose your changes.

Using Keywords

Up until this point, we've periodically mentioned how to add keywords, but each time we've discussed them, we've only mentioned typing them in one by one. Furthermore, aside from some simple examples, we've yet to tell you why keywords matter. In truth, keywords aren't a requirement for shooting digitally, but they are quite helpful for finding images, sorting images, and selling images. For instance, if you shoot a music festival, there will be a variety of bands throughout the day. If you add a keyword with each band's name to the appropriate image, you could easily make smart websites (a topic we'll cover in Chapter 8, "Creating Web Content") that have each band's picture by using the keyword in the smart website's image criteria. Having a collection of websites looks better than having one massive one—but even if you have one massive site, by tagging each image with the band's name, your clients will be able to quickly tell which image is which band because Aperture can display keywords in its website metadata. Keywords are also useful for filtering and finding images within Aperture.

When you're ready to start tagging individual images with keywords, one useful trick is to take advantage of the Ratings And Keywords layout. As we covered in Chapter 3, Aperture has a handful of built-in interface configurations that are optimized for various tasks. The Ratings And Keywords layout, for example, maximizes the amount of screen space devoted to the Browser and viewer by hiding the Inspectors panel and Projects panel. The Ratings And Keywords layout also shows the control bar and keyword controls, which we will cover in depth in the next section. To switch to this layout, choose Window > Layouts > Ratings And Keywords or press ⌘+Option+R.

Applying Keywords

So far, the simplest way we've shown you to add a keyword to an image is to select it and enter the keyword into the Metadata Inspector. There is actually an easier way. In the control bar, Aperture can show keyword controls in the right section, as indicated in Figure 4.8. If these controls are not visible, show the control bar by choosing Window > Show Control Bar (or press Shift+D) and the keyword controls by choosing Window > Show Keyword Controls (or press D). If you need more screen space for your keyword controls, hide the inspectors by selecting Window > Hide Inspectors (or press I).

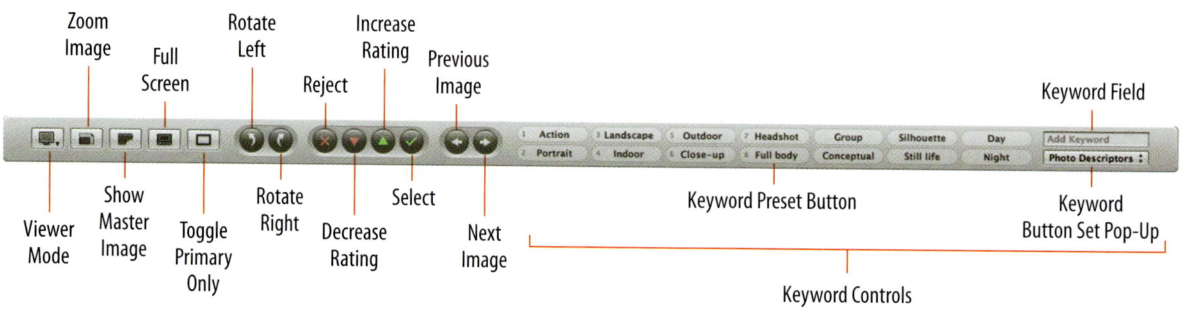

Figure 4.8: The control bar and keyword controls

Once the keyword controls are active, to add a keyword to an image (or group of images), select the image(s), enter the keyword into the text field on the top right, and press Return. You can quickly jump to this field by pressing 9, the hotkey for Metadata > New Keyword. As we'll discuss shortly, each button in the keyword controls also contains a keyword preset. To assign the keyword on the button to your image, click the button or press the associated number from 1 to 8 on your keyboard. These buttons are customizable, and you can have multiple button sets.

When you manually enter a keyword, Aperture will try to automatically complete the keyword so you won't have to type as much. For example, Figure 4.9 shows the Autocomplete List that Aperture opened when we entered the letter I into the keyword field. The list contains a hierarchical item, Image Type, which we expanded to see its children. The overall Autocomplete List contains a number of built-in keywords along with any keywords you've added to your images. To close the Autocomplete pop-up and continue typing, press Esc. To reopen the pop-up, press Option+Esc (make sure that your cursor is at the end of the text you've entered and that the text isn't selected).

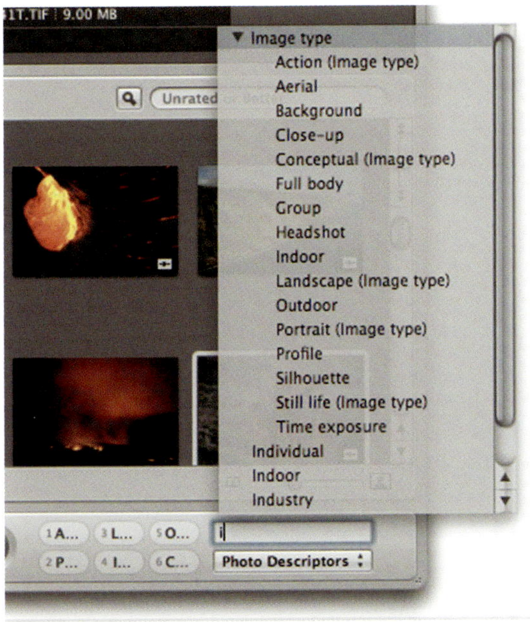

Figure 4.9:
Aperture's Autocomplete options

Size Limits on Metadata

When you export images, as we'll cover in Chapter 6, "Exporting Images," Aperture will embed your IPTC metadata, including keywords, into your image's metadata. In general, to avoid issues with some image viewers, you'll want to limit the sizes of your different values as indicated in Table 4.1.

▶ Table 4.1: IPTC Field Lengths

IPTC Field	Length and Purpose
Caption	Up to 2,000 characters describing the image
Keywords	Up to 64 characters divided into a list of words
Credit	Up to 32 characters naming the photographer or agency
Copyright Notice	Up to 128 characters listing the copyright information
Object Name	Up to 64 characters used to identify the image, similar to a stock code
City	Up to 32 characters for the city you took the image in
Province/State	Up to 32 characters for the state you took the image in
Country Name	Up to 64 characters naming the country you took the image in
Special Instructions	Up to 256 characters with any special using instructions
Byline	Up to 64 characters for the byline text
Category	Up to 3 characters for the ANPA category codes
Date Created	Up to 16 characters holding the date you took the image
Headline	Up to 256 characters for the image's headline
Source	Up to 32 characters to name the group or individual providing the image

Note: If you have multiple images selected, as we covered in Chapter 3, clicking the Primary Only button ( ) will cause Aperture to add the keyword only to the primary selected image and not to every selected image.

Keyword Sets

As you apply keywords, you'll eventually notice that there are a number of common keywords you use, depending on what you were photographing. For instance, you might flag images as **action**, **landscape**, **portrait**, or a combination. In fact, if you look at the left side of the keywords controls, you'll see those particular keywords as well as small numbers next to each.

As we mentioned in the last section, the buttons on the keyword controls contain a variety of keywords that you can apply to an image, either by clicking the button or by pressing the number on the keyboard shown next to the button. Furthermore, you can customize these buttons. The default set of keywords, Photo Descriptors, contains common keywords you can use to describe an image. If you click the pop-up in the bottom-right corner of the keyword controls, you can switch sets. The Wedding (Details) set, for instance, contains keywords you would use on photos from a wedding that weren't of the bride, groom, or other attendees—they're keywords to describe photos of the other details, such as the cake.

Even though the built-in keyword preset buttons cover a wide range of categories, you can also customize them or create your own. At the bottom of the Keyword

Sets pop-up, choose the item labeled Edit Buttons, and Aperture will open the panel in Figure 4.10.

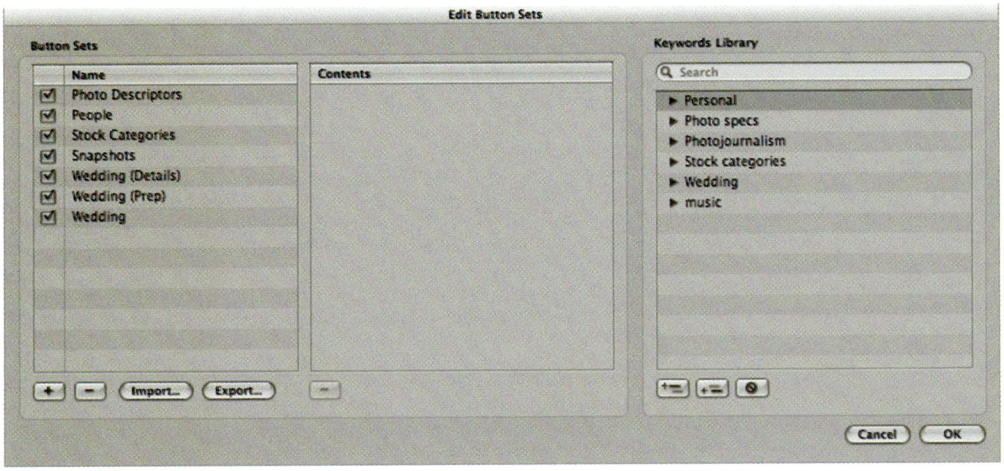

Figure 4.10: The Edit Button Sets panel

The Edit Button Sets panel contains three columns in two groups. On the far left is a table view with all of the available button sets. The middle column, activated when you select a button set, lists the keywords in that set. The two columns on the left comprise the button sets group.

The Keywords Library appears in the right column. This hierarchical outline view lists all of the built-in keywords along with any keywords you've manually added to your images. As you would expect, you can click the disclosure triangles next to each group of keywords to expand the group. Also as expected, you can use the search field at the top to filter the keywords to look for substrings among your keywords. Furthermore, by using the buttons below the Keywords Library and by dragging and dropping, you can create new categories and subcategories of keywords.

As an example, let's create a new keyword category for parades.

1. Click the Add Keyword button ( ), and Aperture will make a new entry.
2. Enter **Parade** to rename the category.
3. Click the Add Subordinate Keyword button ( ) and add various keywords associated with parades, such as **balloons**, **food**, and **clowns**.
4. Select the food keyword and click Add Subordinate Keyword.
5. Add various types of foods, perhaps **hot dogs**, **hamburgers**, **cotton candy**. If you make a mistake, you can remove a keyword by selecting it and clicking the Remove Keyword button ( ).

Note: If you already have a keyword selected when you click the Add Keyword button, Aperture will add the new keyword at the same level as the selected keyword. In other words, if you've expanded a group and click Add Keyword, Aperture will add the new keyword within that group.

At this point, you should have a keyword group labeled "Parade" with some keywords in it, and one of those, "food," should also have keywords beneath it. Your Keyword Library view should look like Figure 4.11.

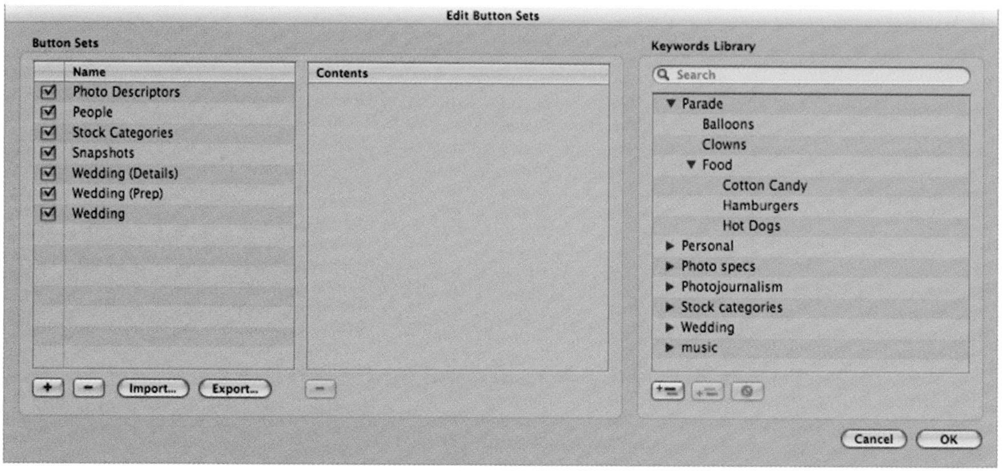

Figure 4.11: The Keywords Library view with the Parade group setup

The next step is to make a button set for these new parade keywords.

1. Under the Button Sets table at the far left, click the Add New Button Set button (+).
2. Rename the new entry that Aperture gives you to **Parades**. The button set can have, but doesn't have to have, the same name as the group you made in the Keywords Library. In fact, a button group can contain keywords from your entire Keywords Library and not just one group.
3. Select the parade set. The middle column, Contents, should be empty.
4. From the Keywords Library, drag the parade keyword to the Contents column and let go. Aperture automatically adds the parade keyword to your button set. One thing you might not expect is that even though you pulled the parade group over, Aperture only copied the parade keyword and not its children.
5. Open the parade group and continue dragging keywords. You can drag multiple keywords at one time by selecting multiple keywords and dragging them to the Contents column. (Shift+click two keywords to select a range of keywords or ⌘+click to toggle the selection states of the keywords you click.)

As you might also expect, you can reorganize the button set groups in the far-left table. Your new organization will be reflected in the Button Sets pop-up menu in the Keyword Controls panel. You can also hide, but not remove, a button set by unchecking it.

Before we leave the Edit Button Sets panel, notice two buttons in the bottom-left corner labeled Import and Export. As you build button sets, especially if you have multiple computers and multiple copies of Aperture, you might choose to share these button sets between computers. When you click Export and choose a place to save a file, Aperture will create an XML file containing your button sets and keywords. You can copy this file to another computer and import it using the Import button. Aperture will replace your buttons with those stored in the file. You can also back up this file so that if something happens to your main computer, you can always recover your keywords.

Once you're ready, click OK to confirm your changes. Find your new Parade set in the Button Sets pop-up, and watch the buttons change to reflect the keywords you added into this set.

As you might expect, if you are in a Compare Viewing mode with two or more images up, you can apply keywords on the preset buttons to the compare image (the one with the yellow border) by pressing Option+keyword number. Similarly, to remove a keyword from the compare image, press Option+Shift+keyword number.

The Keywords HUD

When you want to add keywords to images, you don't have to use the keywords buttons or type the keyword. Bring up the Keywords HUD, available in both Windowed and Full Screen mode, by selecting Window > Show Keywords HUD or by pressing Shift+H.

The Keywords HUD, visible in Figure 4.12, contains controls identical to the Keywords Library portion of the Edit Button Sets panel from the previous section. In fact, the process for adding, rearranging, and removing keywords using the buttons in the HUD is the same as it was for adding, rearranging, and removing keywords using the buttons in the Edit Buttons Set panel.

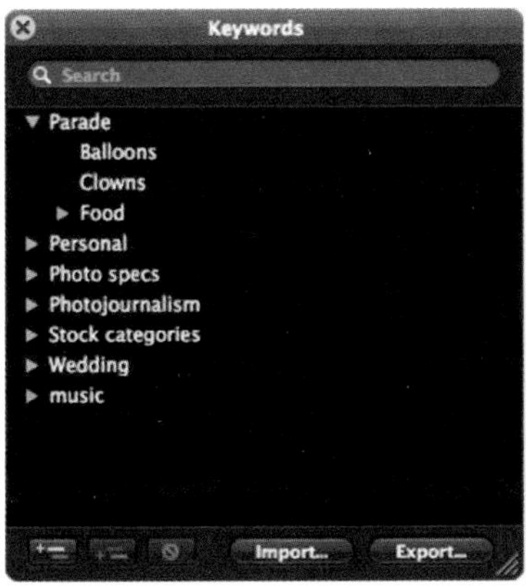

Figure 4.12:
The Keywords HUD

When the Keywords HUD is open, you can apply keywords to an image by dragging them from the HUD and dropping them onto the image or its thumbnail. To apply multiple keywords to an image, select multiple keywords and drop them onto an image. If your browser is in List mode, drag the keywords onto the image's row. Again, if you drag a group onto an image, Aperture will apply only one keyword, the group keyword, to the image. Similarly, if you drag a child onto an image, Aperture will apply only the child keyword. In other words, as we mentioned with the parade example earlier, if you drag "Parade" onto an image, Aperture will apply only "Parade" and not its child "food." If you drag "food" onto an image, Aperture will apply only "food" and not "Parade."

To remove keywords from an image, you can manually delete them in the Inspector or use the Metadata > Remove Keyword submenu to remove individual keywords. If the keyword you want to remove is part of the current Keywords button preset, pressing Shift+Keyword Number will also delete the keyword. Metadata > Remove Keyword > Remove All Keywords (Shift+9) will clear the image's keywords.

Note: If you remove a keyword from the HUD, Aperture does not remove it from the images.

Another way to remove keywords is to select a group of images (not all of them need not to have the keyword set), type the keyword into the text field in the keywords control, and press Shift+Return, instead of Return. Aperture will remove the keyword from the selected images.

Rating Images

Keywords help you locate images, but they don't help you edit them. Ratings, on the other hand, do. Aperture provides a seven-tiered rating system (one through five stars, unrated, and rejected) that you can apply to each image to help you pick your best images and delete your worst images.

The simplest way to rate an image is to select it, decide what rating (1–5 stars) you want to give the image, and choose that rating from the Metadata menu. If you have the Browser or Viewer set to show a metadata set that includes ratings, which we cover in detail in Chapter 3 and that you can access under View Options (View > View Options or ⌘-J), such as Grid View - Basic, you'll see your rating appear with the image.

If, after rating an image, you want to re-rate it, simply select it and pick the new rating from the Metadata menu. Use Metadata > Increase Rating (=) and Metadata > Decrease Rating (–) to adjust the rating. The control bar also contains increase and decrease rating buttons, which are indicated by up- and down-arrows in Figure 4.13. To clear the rating, select Metadata > Unrated (⌘+Option+0).

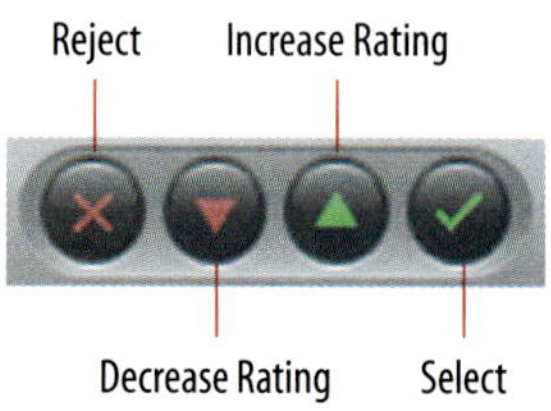

Figure 4.13: The rating buttons in the control bar

If you have an image that you really like, you can flag it as a *select*. A select is simply a way to quickly rate an image with five stars. Make an image a select by choosing Metadata > Select, pressing the backslash key (\), or clicking the Select button (the button with the green checkmark) in the control bar.

Similarly, if you have an image that you don't want to keep, you can flag it as a reject. To reject an image, choose Metadata > Reject, press O, or click the Reject button in the control bar (the button with the red X). Aperture will display a small X badge on the rejected image. Rejected images are not deleted, but they are temporarily removed from sight by default when, after rating an image as a reject, you move on to the next image. If you want to see all of your rejected images, choose the Rejected smart album under Library in the Projects panel. To permanently delete these images, select them and choose File > Delete Master Image And All Versions. To un-reject an image, select it and increase its rating.

In Chapter 3, we mentioned two useful viewing modes, Compare and Stack. Both of these viewing modes let you select a compare image and view other images at the same time in order to determine which is better. Aperture provides a set of keyboard shortcuts, which you can see by pausing the cursor over the buttons in the control bar so that you can apply ratings to either the select image or the compare image. In general, just as when you're applying keywords to the compare image (the one with the yellow border), the key commands that affect the compare image are the same as the ones that affect the alternative image, but you also hold down the Option key when you press them.

Again, as we covered before, Stack goes a bit further and lets you see images within only one stack. You can promote and demote images within that stack, using the Stack > Promote (⌘+ [) and Stack > Demote (⌘+]) commands.

In practice, use ratings to flag your best images in these viewing modes. For instance, if you have a large stack to sort, it might be tedious to keep flipping images. As you work through the stack, rate the images, and then promote your best images until they're on top. Sort those images to find your stack pick. If you have only one clear standout in the stack, you can automatically place it at the top of the stack by using Stack > Pick (⌘+\).

Changing Metadata on Multiple Images

Very often, you'll have a group of images with similar metadata or a group of images to which you want to make the same metadata changes. One option would be to manually go to each image, make your changes, and move onto the next. However, Aperture provides two useful ways to make bulk changes, helping you to avoid some of this tedious image-by-image editing.

Metadata Using Batch Change

You can access the Batch Change tool by selecting a few images and choosing Metadata > Batch Change (⌘+Shift+B). Aperture will bring up the window in Figure 4.14. In this window, you can adjust the metadata on multiple images at once. You can change the time zone, change the version naming format, and set values for fields within your metadata sets.

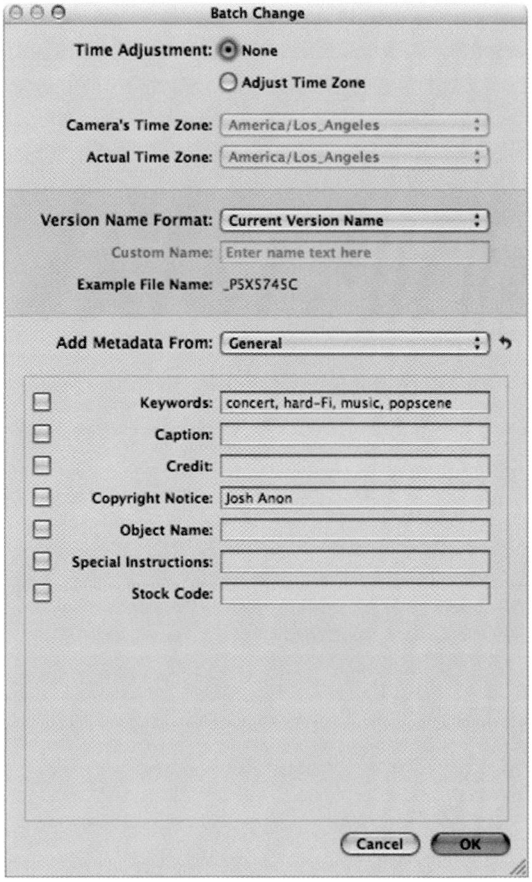

Figure 4.14:
The Batch Change window

Using this tool is fairly intuitive. For instance, if you want to adjust the time zone on a number of images, follow these steps.

1. Switch the radio button at the top so that Adjust Time Zone is active.
2. Just as you did in the Import window, select the time zone to which you had the camera set.
3. Select the time zone you were actually in when you captured the image.
4. Click OK.

If you select each image individually and look at its date in the Metadata Inspector, you'll see that Aperture has adjusted each image that you selected.

Metadata Using Lift and Stamp

Another common situation is when you've set up the metadata in one image and you'd like to copy that metadata to another image (or images). In this case, you'll want to open the Lift And Stamp tool by clicking the Lift button ( ) in the toolbar or by pressing O. Aperture will open a window similar to Figure 4.15.

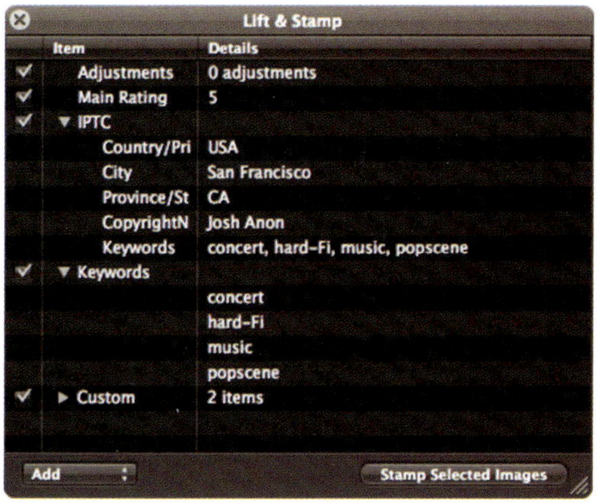

Figure 4.15:
The Lift And Stamp window

The Lift And Stamp tool allows you to take any changes you've made to an image, be they image adjustments (which we'll cover in Chapter 5) or metadata changes, and "stamp" those changes to another image. When it's first opened, the cursor changes to an up-arrow. Click an image to "lift" its information into the Lift And Stamp window.

Note: Selecting an image and then bringing up Lift And Stamp will not lift the metadata from the selected image. You must click the image you want to use as the source.

After you pick a source image, Aperture will populate the Lift And Stamp window with a list of every change you've made to the image, including Adjustments, Main Rating, Keywords, RAW Fine Tuning adjustments, and more. A check box appears to the left of each item. A checked item means that when you stamp these changes onto a new image, that item will be stamped. An unchecked item, conversely, means that Aperture will not copy this change to a new image. As an example, if you've set some IPTC metadata, such as a copyright and location, as well as a rating on one image and you only want to copy the IPTC data to the other images. In this case, you would only have IPTC checked and Rating unchecked.

If you're unsure about the contents of one adjustment item, you can see exactly what data Aperture will copy to your new image by looking in the Details column. Some items, such as IPTC, also have a disclosure triangle next to the item name indicating that you can open the item to see more detail.

When you open the disclosure triangle, you might want to stamp the overall group (e.g., keywords) onto a new image but not stamp a specific item (e.g., a specific keyword). To remove the specific item, select the item in the Lift And Stamp window and press the Delete key. The original metadata, on the image you lifted the contents of the Lift And Stamp tool from, will not be affected.

At the bottom-left corner of the Lift And Stamp window is a pop-up where you can choose between Add or Replace. When you choose Replace, if the images you're stamping onto already have values for the items you've picked to stamp, Aperture will replace the old values with the values that you're stamping. If you choose Add, Aperture will combine the existing values with the values that you're stamping for each destination image.

Once you've picked which items you want to copy to another image, move your cursor over the other image, perhaps in the Browser. Watch how the cursor changes to a down-arrow, indicating that you can stamp. Alternatively, if you selected the images you want to copy the data onto, before bringing up the Lift And Stamp window, you can use the Stamp Selected Images button in that window instead of stamping each image.

If you want to lift from a different image, you can click the Lift button in the toolbar again, or you can hold the Option key while clicking an image. To switch back to Stamp mode without picking a new image, click the Stamp button ( ) in the toolbar or release the Option key.

To review, the process for lifting and stamping image data, such as metadata or adjustments, is as follows.

1. Load the Lift And Stamp tool by clicking its button ( ) in the toolbar or by pressing O.
2. Click the image or thumbnail from which you want to lift metadata.
3. Configure the Lift And Stamp window so that you'll stamp only the data you want, such as IPTC metadata including keywords, but not image adjustments.
4. Click the image or thumbnail onto which you want to stamp the metadata.

As a shortcut, if you want to copy all of the metadata and adjustments from one image onto another, without bringing up the Lift And Stamp tool's window, simply:

1. Select the source image.
2. Choose Metadata > Lift (⌘+Shift+C).
3. Select the destination image.
4. Choose Metadata > Stamp (⌘+Shift+V).

Finding Your Images

One of the main reasons for using metadata, such as keywords and ratings, is to help you find your images later. Each browser allows you to search within the current collection by filtering the images you see in the Browser. In other words, you can search through the current images and restrict the Browser so that perhaps only five-star images containing the string "Disneyland" are visible. Your other images are still in the current project, album, or light table (whatever group the Browser is attached to), but they're temporarily hidden.

To help you find your images, Aperture provides a built-in Project Management layout. As we mentioned in Chapter 3, this layout hides the Viewer and the Inspector, shows the Projects Panel and Browser, and makes the Browser area as large as possible. To switch to this layout, select Window > Layouts > Project Management or press ⌘+Option+M.

Aperture has a search field, similar to the one in the Finder, at the top of the Browser, as indicated in Figure 4.16. If you enter some text into this field, Aperture will search each image in the current browser's metadata for that text string, and Aperture will hide any image for which it doesn't find that string. The fields that it searches through depends on the search scope you select. You can clear a search string by deleting the string you entered or by clicking the Cancel button ( ) that appears in the search field.

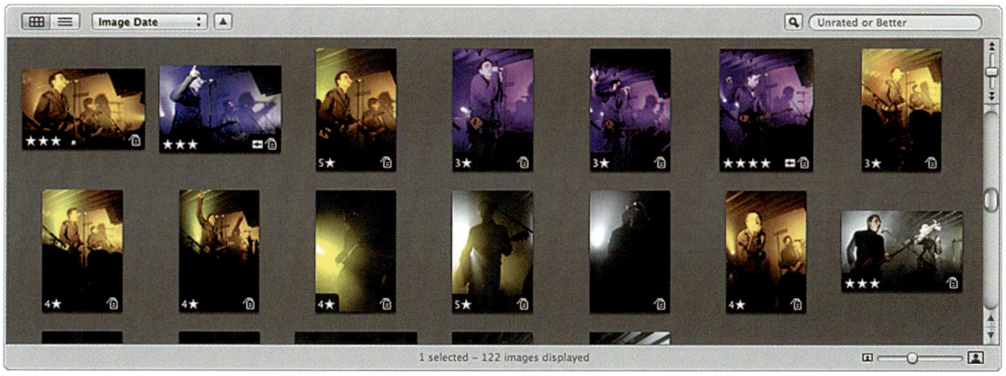

Figure 4.16: The Browser filter field

By default, when the search field is empty, a placeholder value saying "Unrated or Better" will appear. Each browser is automatically set to filter out rejected images. That's why when you reject an image, it's hidden, even though it hasn't been deleted yet.

In Aperture 1.1, it's possible to change the default search type. To do so, select the Search Scope pop-up menu in the search field. Aperture will open the menu in Figure 4.17, and to change your default search behavior, pick another option, such as "Show All."

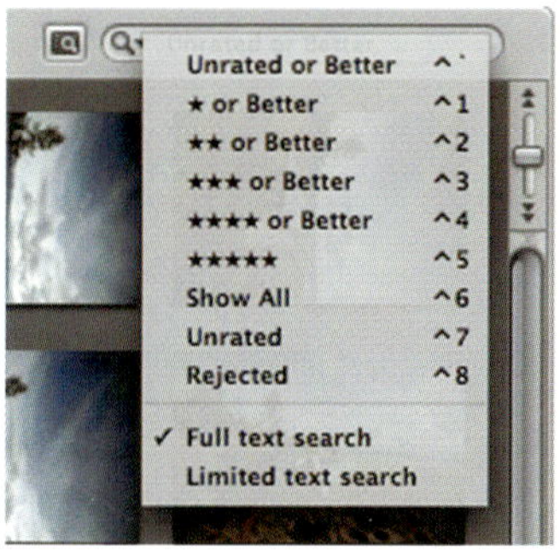

Figure 4.17: The Search pop-up menu

From that pop-up menu, you can also toggle between a full text search and a limited text search. A full text search will search every field in every image for the string you type into the search field. If you choose "Limited text search," Aperture will search through any data you've manually entered into an image as well as the image's aspect ration, filename, import group, master location, rating, orientation, pixel size, processed pixel size, and version name. There is also a pop-up menu under Preferences (Aperture > Preferences) where you can choose between full or limited text search.

If you click the Query HUD button ( ) to the left of the Filter field, Aperture will open a panel similar to Figure 4.18, where you can filter you images using more than just string searching. If you select Edit > Find, Aperture will automatically display the Query HUD for the currently selected browser.

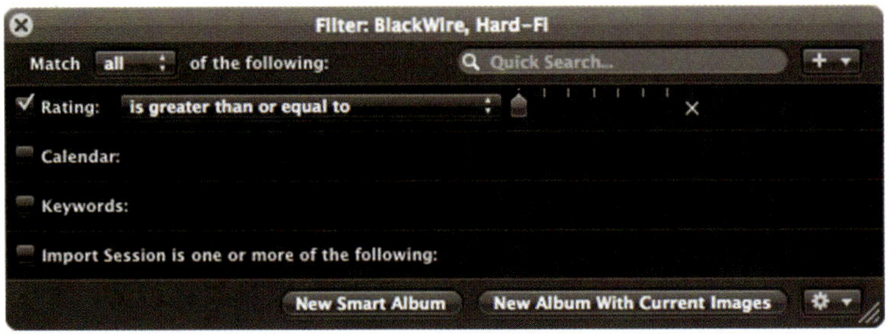

Figure 4.18: The Query HUD panel

When you open the filter's Query HUD panel, you'll see that it looks very similar to the smart album Query HUD panel we showed you in Chapter 2, "Importing and Organizing Your Images." In fact, many parts are identical. For instance, at the top-left, you'll see the same pop-up, where you can switch between using *all* criteria you specify (an image must be rated five stars *and* contain the keyword "California") and using *any* criteria that you specify (an image must be rated five stars *or* contain the keyword "California"). At the top-right, you'll find the same Add Criteria button ( ) you saw in the Smart Album panel. Here too, you can use it to add new criteria to use to determine which images to show.

The Query HUD also has a search field, set identically to the one in the Browser. If you type a value within the field in the panel, Aperture will update the field attached to the Browser and automatically start filtering the images for that string.

By default, the Rating criteria in the Filter panel is selected and set to show any image with a rating greater than or equal to unrated. In other words, show any image that isn't a rejected image. If you want to see every image, even if it's rejected, you can uncheck the rating criteria to deactivate it or use the slider so that the rating criteria is set to show any image with a rating greater than or equal to rejected. In Aperture 1.1, you could also click on the Search pop-up menu and set it to "Show All" instead of bringing up the Query HUD.

> **Note:** If the images in your stack have different ratings, the Browser filter looks at the stack pick—the image on top of the stack—to determine if the image passes the filter or not. In other words, if you reject the stack pick and the Browser is not set to show rejected images, Aperture will filter the entire stack out of the view, even if another image in the stack has a five-star rating.

In general, we recommend unchecking the rating criteria or setting the browser to Show All so that you always see all the images in your browser. That way, if you change your mind about a rejected image's rating, it's easy to find the image to change its rating. Plus, when you're done editing, deleting your rejected image is as simple as following these steps:

1. Sort your images by rating by setting the Sorting pop-up in the Browser to Rating.

2. Select the rejected images.
3. Choose File > Delete Master Image And All Versions.

As an example, if you want to filter your browser to see only landscape-oriented images, follow these steps:

1. Activate the Query HUD panel by pressing the Query HUD button ( ).
2. Select Other Metadata from the Add Criteria button ( ).
3. Set the first pop-up to Orientation and leave the second pop-up set to Contains.
4. In the text field, enter **landscape** and press Tab to confirm your changes.

Your Filter panel should appear similar to Figure 4.19. Aperture automatically will filter out any portrait-oriented images in the Browser. Click the Close button ( ) to close the Filter panel. When you're ready to see all your portrait-oriented images again, click the Clear Filter button ( ) in the Filter field and watch your images reappear.

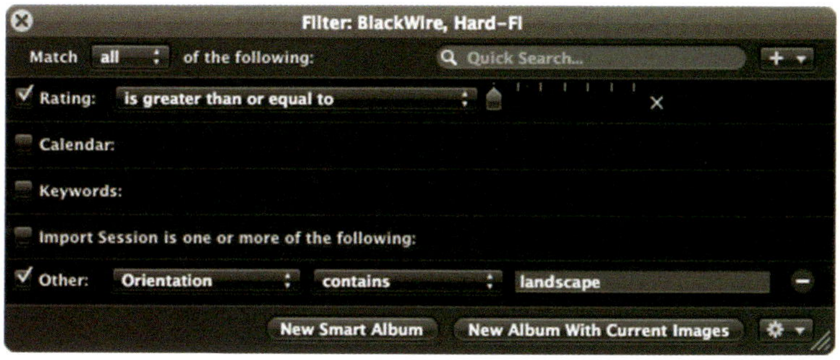

Figure 4.19: The Query HUD panel set to show landscape images only

Once you've set your criteria, while the Query HUD panel is still open, you'll notice a few extra buttons at the bottom of the panel. New Smart Album takes the criteria you're using to search and gives you a new smart album with that criterion. The difference between making a new smart album and filtering an existing one is that filters are somewhat temporary—you can quickly set and clear them, whereas smart albums are a bit more lasting. Plus, a filter simply restricts what you can see in the current collection of images, whereas a smart album creates a new collection with no filter (aside from Aperture's default Hide Rejected Images filter).

If you don't want a smart album, you can use a button to create a new, non-smart album with the current images. Furthermore, if you click the Action menu, you'll find commands to automatically create other items with the current set of filtered images, such as a light table.

Note: If you want to search all of your images in all of your projects for a particular image, select the All Images smart album from the library and use the Query HUD in that album's browser.

Smart Albums with Keywords

We covered smart albums in Chapter 2, but we skipped over one important possible criterion—keywords. Using this criterion is very straightforward, but it's worth mentioning because using keywords is a very easy way to view subsets of your images that you may want to use for a specific purpose, such as a stock submission or a presentation to a client.

Start by creating a smart album as you would normally. Select a project and choose File > New Smart > Album (⌘+Shift+L). Check the Keywords criteria, and set the pop-up to Contain One Or More Of The Following if you want your smart album to match any keyword you select, or choose Contain All Of The Following if you want your smart album to match every keyword you select.

When you checked the Keywords criteria, Aperture automatically expanded that field to show every keyword present in the current project. If you've set only a few keywords in the current project, this will be a small list, whereas if you've set many keywords, this list can get quite large. To pick keywords for the smart album, simply check each keyword. As an example, Figure 4.20 shows a smart album that is set to show every image that's been tagged with "abstract" and "flower."

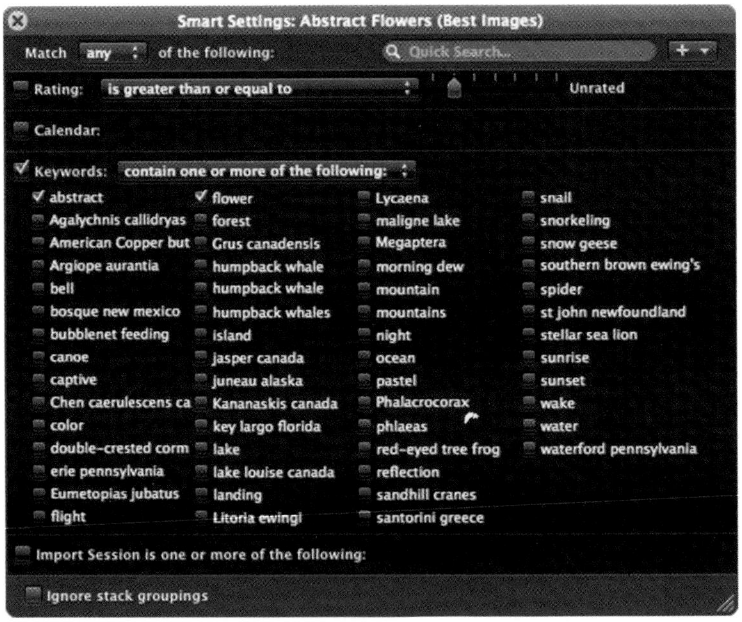

Figure 4.20: A smart album set to show images that have been tagged with "abstract" and "flower"

As with the other fields in a smart album, you can change later the keywords you want to use in your smart album. Click the Query HUD button ( ) next to the smart album to bring up the query HUD, and you can change the keywords you're using to define the smart album.

Backing Up Your Images

One of the biggest problems digital photographers face is how to safeguard their work. Thankfully, many systems administrators have been dealing with the backup problem for years, and digital photographers can take advantage of the tools and techniques they've created. First, we'll address vaults, the tool that Aperture provides to back up your work, and then we'll explain some of the general concepts that these systems administrators have developed.

Vaults

For this section, we're going to assume that you have an external hard drive, be it a RAID drive (we'll explain what a RAID setup is later on) or a single drive, for your backups. That way, you can continually update your backup, and the computer doesn't need special software to write to your backup device.

A vault is essentially a backup copy of all of your image files and the Aperture database. What's special is that Aperture can incrementally update a vault, meaning that rather than backing up gigabytes of data each time you need to back up your work, Aperture will update only the vault with any changes you've made since it was last updated. Furthermore, as opposed to just making duplicates of your master files, vaults store the other information you add to an image, such as keywords, and other files, such as light tables. Keep in mind that syncing a vault updates any changes you make, including deleted images.

At the bottom of the Projects panel, there's a small tab labeled Vaults. If you click the Show Or Hide Vaults button ( ), Aperture will open the Vault panel so that it looks like Figure 4.21. Once you've set up one or more vaults, this panel will list each vault. The three buttons (from left to right) are Update All Vaults ( ), Show Or Hide Vaults ( ), and the Action menu ( ). The commands in these buttons and the Action menu are also in File > Vault.

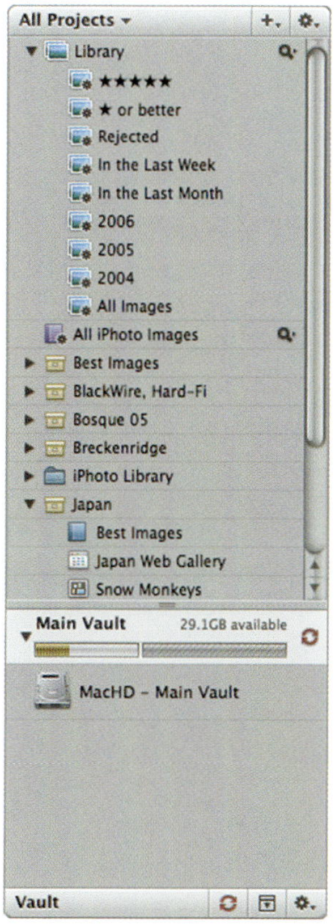

Figure 4.21:
The Vault panel with one vault

To add a vault, select Add Vault from the Action menu and pick a place on your external drive to save your vault. Aperture will update the Vault panel to show your vault. If you click the disclosure triangle to the left of the disk space indicator, Aperture will show you where your vault is. To start syncing the vault to your library, click the Sync button (⏏) to the right of the disk space indicator.

When Aperture is done syncing your vault, the Sync button will change from red to black, indicating that there are no changes to sync. If you make a change in your library, the Sync button will turn yellow to indicate that there are unsynced changes. To sync the changes, you can click the Sync button for the vault, select the vault, and choose Update Vault from the Action menu, or you can just click the Update All Vaults button to sync each vault.

If your vault is on an external hard drive, you need to do one of two things to safely eject the hard drive. In the Finder, you can select the hard drive and choose File > Eject. Alternatively, in Aperture, you can open the disclosure triangle next to the vault name and click the Eject icon (⏏) next to the vault's drive name.

When you're ready to remove a vault from Aperture, and not just the drive that contains the vault, select it and choose Remove Vault from the Action menu. Aperture will ask if you want to remove and delete the vault or just remove the vault. Removing a vault removes it from Aperture, but it does not delete it from the hard drive. For example, you would remove a vault if you had stored it on a DVD-R. In this case, you'll want to remove the vault from Aperture since you can't update the vault after you burn the disc, but you can still restore from it later on. As another example, if you decide to move a vault from one hard drive to another, and you want to use the original hard drive for something aside from your vault, remove the vault from the first drive and add a new vault on the second. By using Aperture to manage these vaults, instead of manually copying and removing files in the Finder, the vault's update feature will continue to work.

If you have multiple photo libraries that you switch between using the Aperture library path preference, you'll want to carefully track which vaults sync to which libraries or remove your vaults from Aperture before switching libraries so that you don't accidentally overwrite a vault.

Note: If you remove a vault, you can restore from it later, but you can't add it back into the Vault panel to sync to your library.

At some point, you may want or need to restore your Photo library from a vault. To start, select File > Vault > Restore Library. Aperture will open the window in Figure 4.22. Here, you'll need to make two decisions: from which vault do you want to restore and to where do you want to restore it. Oddly enough, Aperture doesn't list your known, existing vaults in the Source pop-up. You must choose Select Source Vault and locate the vault you want to use.

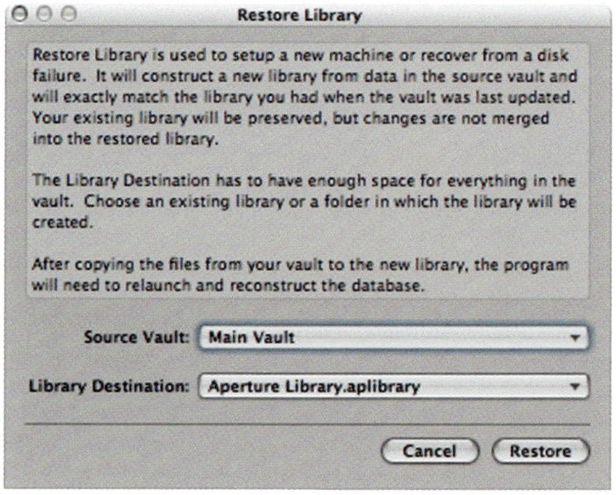

Figure 4.22:
The Restore Library window

For the library destination, if you select a folder with an existing library, Aperture will replace that library with the backup stored in the vault, and it will preserve your existing library by renaming it. If you select a folder without a library, Aperture will expand the vault into a new library stored in that folder. You can switch to that restored, new library by selecting its folder under the Aperture preferences and relaunching Aperture.

Note: When you restore an existing library from a vault, Aperture replaces your library with the contents of the vault. It does not append the two.

Make sure you have sufficient disk space to expand the vault. If you don't, Aperture will warn you, and it won't let you restore the vault into the specified location.

General Backup Concepts

The idea behind a backup is simple. Keep an up-to-date duplicate copy of your work so that if your main copy has a problem, you can replace it with the backup. However, there are multiple potential issues to consider.

A naïve solution would be to make a duplicate copy of every photo and store it on your computer's hard drive. However, if your hard drive crashes, you will lose both your primary and backup copy. You could install two hard drives in your computer and put your backups on the second hard drive. This is better than placing them both on the same hard drive, but what if there's a power surge and your computer isn't on a surge strip? In that case, you'll still loose both your primary and backup copies

Continuing along this line of thinking, you might decide to buy an external hard drive. This is a bit better because you would have a separate drive, but what if there's a fire in your office? Your computer and backup drive could melt. You could solve this situation by storing the drive in another location, such as your house.

RAID

However, what if you go to use your backup copy and discover that the external drive has gone bad? Well, ideally you'll have another copy of your work or you'll have a RAID (Redundant Array of Inexpensive Disks) setup.

The idea behind RAID is that you take two or more hard drives, which are relatively cheap, and connect them together in various ways so that they appear as one hard drive to the computer. RAID 0 is the simplest method, but it is also the least useful for backup. Here, the disks are simply chained together so that your computer sees one hard drive that's the size of the all the drives combined. The benefit to RAID 0 is that the data is spread over the drives so that the computer often will be using both drives at once. Because disk access is often one of the slowest parts of any application, programs that have to read a lot of data from disk very quickly, such as Final Cut Pro, benefit from keeping each project on a RAID 0 drive. However, given that photographers tend to pull up images separately and that although digital images are large, they are still relatively small compared to video, RAID 0 isn't very useful to digital photographers.

However, RAID 1 is useful for backup. The idea here is that you have two identical disks, and each disk automatically copies the other one. If you back up your work onto a RAID 1 setup, you can still retrieve your work if your main copy and one of the backup drives go bad. The downside is that the total available storage space is limited to the size of one drive, because the other drive is used to duplicate the first.

RAID 2 is not normally seen commercially, but RAID 3 sometimes is. RAID 3 is similar to RAID 0, but it requires at least three drives, and it can also perform some basic error correction. RAID 3 is mainly useful for times when you need to access a lot of data quickly but still want some basic error correction in case one drive goes bad. RAID 4 is also not commonly seen and not worthy of discussion.

RAID 5 is another common setup, providing a reasonable balance of performance plus error correction. You need at least three identical drives, but unlike RAID 1, the total available disk space is slightly greater than one drive. RAID 5 works by storing its data among the disks while keeping what are called *parity bits* so that it can correct any errors in your data files when needed. Another benefit to RAID 5 is that it has the fastest read rate setup.

There are additional types of RAID, but they often are beyond the cost and usefulness to the average consumer. On the contrary, RAID 0 and RAID 1 systems are accessible enough that Mac OS X's built-in Disk Utility tool contains a feature to let you set up either a RAID 0 or RAID 1 system, perhaps with two external hard drives. You can find more information by going to http://www.apple.com/support/.

The disadvantage to using the Disk Utility tool to set up a RAID array is that you're relying on the computer to control the disks. This is called using software RAID. If you were to take those disks and plug them into another computer, such as a PC, they wouldn't function as a RAID array. Furthermore, the drives are separate meaning that you have to plug them both in, taking up two ports, to use your RAID array.

As an alternative, companies such as Kano Technologies sell desktop, hardware RAID 1 and RAID 5 units (Figure 4.23). Available in FireWire and USB models, these hardware units are all-in-one solutions with no setup required. You literally plug these drives in and use them as you would any other hard drive. You can take the whole unit offsite to store it safely, and if one of the drives fails, you can replace it without losing your data.

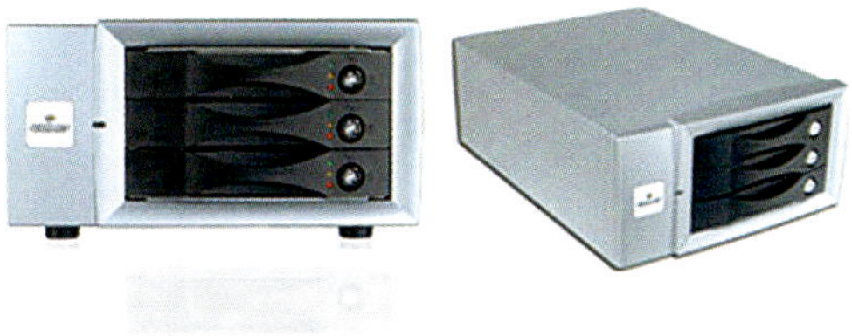

Figure 4.23: Kano Technologies' SureVAULT 800 RAID-5 product

Burning Media

Another option, which is a bit cheaper than keeping multiple hard drives, is to burn a backup copy of your work to a DVD or CD. In Chapter 6, for example, we'll show you how to export projects. To back up a project, you could burn an exported project to a DVD.

This method is one of the cheapest solutions available, but there are two main issues. The first is that often, you want to back up more data than can fit onto a DVD. Double-layer DVDs (DVD+R DL) that can hold over 8GB of data might be an answer, but they're not as common. If you are backing up individual images, it's tedious but easier to spread your files out over multiple disks. If you're trying to back up a project to a DVD, you can't manually spread it over multiple discs. However, some third-party software, such as Roxio Toast 7, include special features to spread files across multiple DVDs.

The second main problem with using burned media as a backup is its longevity. Stamped media, such as your Aperture DVD, has a longer expected lifespan than a DVD-R you burn yourself since the creation process is different. Commercial disc creation involves actually shaping the media so that the only way to lose the data is by damaging the DVD or CD. However, this technique is too costly for consumers. Instead, most computers now include either combo drives (DVD reading and CD writing) or SuperDrives (DVD writing and CD writing). These drives use lasers to burn holes in the media to which they're writing.

In general, one-time burnable media (CD-R as opposed to CD-RW) has an expected lifetime on the order of decades (however their longevity depends on a variety of factors including the original quality of the disc and the way it's been stored) and is far more stable than rewritable media. This is logical since it's not designed to be erasable and overwritable. There are a few things that you can do to extend your disc's lifetime. For one, the dyes on a given disc that your drive burns are similar to film in that to create the best image, you need the correct exposure. Sometimes, burning at your drive's fastest setting doesn't allow the lasers to spend enough time creating each hole. However, burning a disc at 1x can overexpose the dye. Burning at the fastest speed can sometimes lead to more movement in the drive, jittering the disc, and affecting its longevity. Burning at a medium speed will provide the best longevity.

When DVDs start to fail, they tend to fail from the outside edge toward the center. If you only use 75 percent of the disc's capacity, you'll limit the amount of data you lose because drives write from the inside toward the outer edge. Flexing DVDs, even minor flexing, can also cause significant damage.

Labeling can also destroy data because the chemicals in the ink or adhesive labels wear through the disk. If you really need to label your disc, you can safely label the clear, inner portion of the disc or use special labeling pens, such as one sold by Delkin that is guaranteed to be safe for discs.

The quality of the discs you buy also affects their longevity. In fact, cheaply made CDs that you burn as fast as possible and label might only last two years. On the other hand, companies such as Delkin sell archival gold DVD-R and CD-R discs which they claim to have a storage life of 100 years for DVD-R discs, and 300 years for CD-R discs. If you choose to backup to burnable media, these archival-grade discs are your best choice.

Note: Burn two backup copies using discs that you purchased at different times or from different manufacturers. If one company accidentally has a bad run of discs, you'll still have a second, safe copy. This technique is also useful if you're using other removable media, such as tapes.

Tape Drives

Tape drives are an inexpensive way to store large quantities of data. With tapes that sometimes hold 40+ gigabytes of data, you can back up your entire library. Some of the newer drives use FireWire and USB 2 and can back up 5GB of data in about half an hour. Tapes can have a shelf life of between 30 to 100 years, and they typically don't have any special storage requirements.

Note: If you don't have offsite storage available, tapes, CDs, and DVDs can easily be stored in a fireproof safe.

The downside to tapes is that you have to use special software to read and write to them. A tape drive won't appear as a hard drive onto which you can drop files. Meaning you can't use Aperture's Vault feature with tape drives. However, the special backup software for tapes often provide incremental backup, just like Vaults. Experts continue to predict tape's demise, and although it hasn't happened yet, it could happen in the near future.

One thing to keep in mind with all of these backup techniques is that you'll periodically want to update your backup medium. For instance, if you're still storing data on a SCSI hard drive, you'll probably want to transfer the data to a FireWire hard drive because SCSI interfaces aren't very common now. If you need your backup five years from now, you'll be more likely to find a computer with a FireWire port than one with a SCSI port. Another benefit to switching to newer backup formats is that the drives are larger; you can consolidate the number of drives or discs you need for backup by upgrading formats.

By now, you should be comfortable importing, organizing, viewing, and finding your images. In the next chapter, we'll show you how to adjust your images so that you can turn a three-star image into a five-star image.

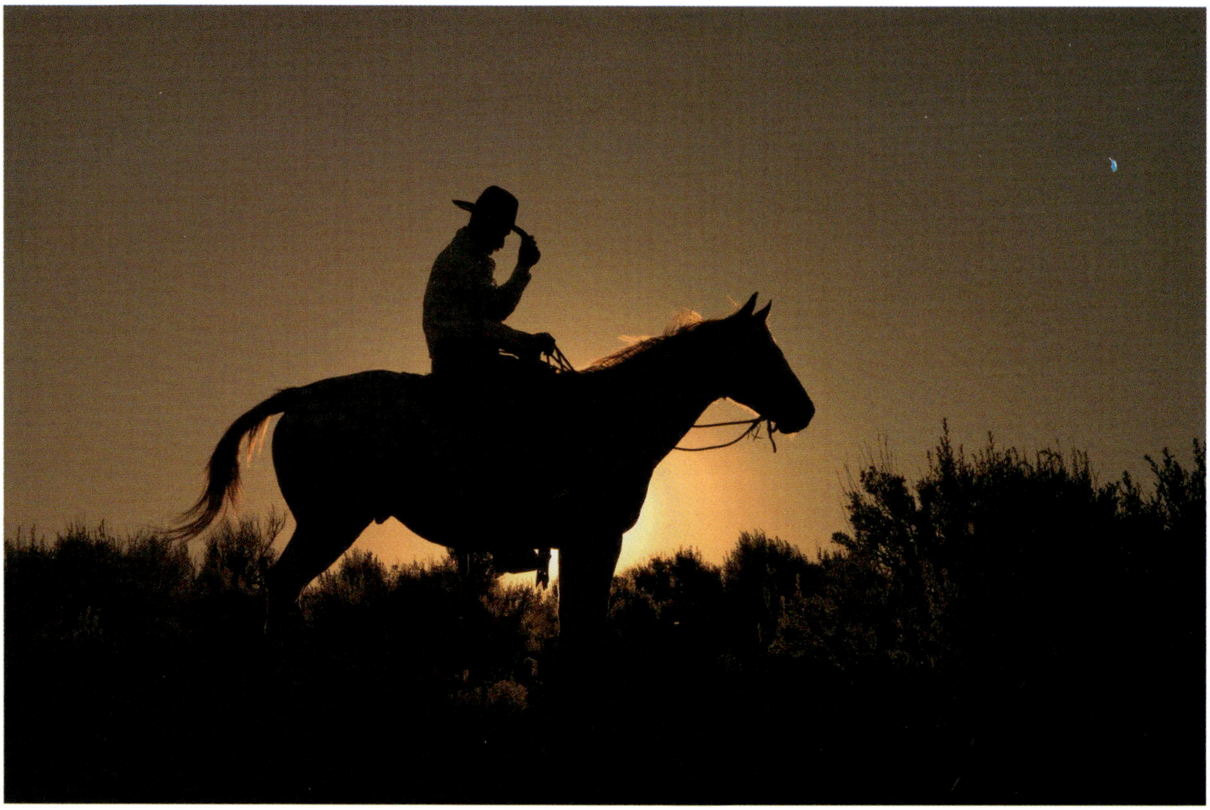

Nondestructive Image Processing

One of Aperture's most exciting features is the ability to make changes to your images that are forever nondestructive and reversible within Aperture. These changes are recorded as a series of instructions for each version of your master file and take up minimal file space on your hard drive. Therefore, you can create, compare, and even save multiple versions of an image without needing terabytes of storage.

Aperture offers a variety of image-processing tools so that for many images you can make all your global adjustments completely within Aperture. In this chapter, we'll cover how to use each of the image processing tools.

5

Chapter Contents

Overview of the Tools

Before you start to use the various tools, it's helpful to have an understanding of the various image processing tools as a whole, including where to find them and how they're set up. We'll go into detail about how to use each tool later in this chapter in the "Using the Image Processing Tools" section.

The image processing tools are available in three locations. If you have set your view to show the toolbar (View > Toolbar or Shift+T), the basic tools as shown in Figure 5.1 will be at the top of your monitor. The toolbar contains the Selection, Rotate Right/Left, Straighten, Crop, Spot & Patch, Red Eye, Lift, and Stamp tools. You can access the toolbar while using any view, as well as when you're in Full Screen mode. These same tools are also accessible via the Adjustments Inspector and the Adjustments HUD along with many more adjustment filters.

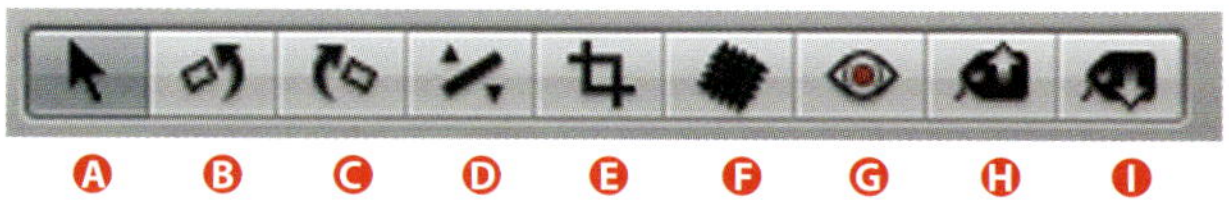

- A Selection
- B Rotate Left
- C Rotate Right
- D Straighten
- E Crop
- F Spot & Patch
- G Red Eye
- H Lift
- I Stamp

Figure 5.1: The Aperture toolbar

> **Note:** When you're in Full Screen mode, the toolbar will be hidden but will appear when you hover the cursor near the top of your monitor.

To access the Adjustments Inspector, click the Inspector button ( ) or click the Adjustments And Filters View button ( ). In this view, the Adjustments Inspector will appear along the right of your image, as shown in Figure 5.2.

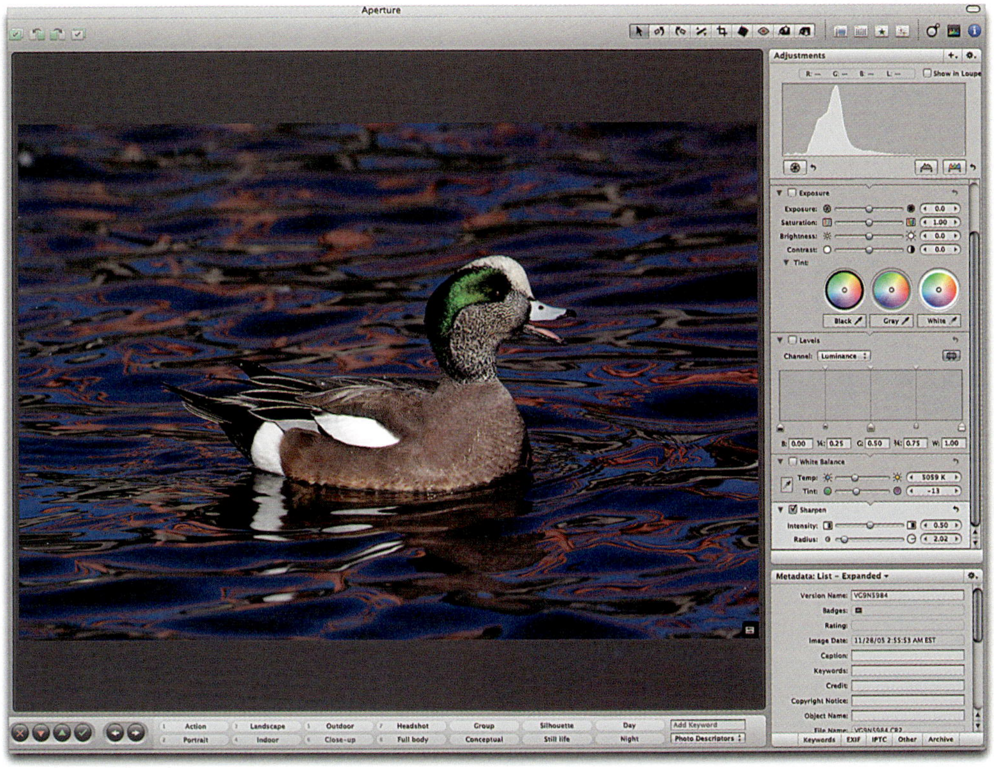

Figure 5.2: The Adjustments Inspector will appear on the right when the Adjustments and Filters view is used.

If you prefer to work in one of the other views, including Full Screen mode (which is accessible by pressing F for Full Screen view), you can access the same tools by using the Adjustments heads-up display (Adjustments HUD). To access the Adjustments HUD, do *one* of the following:

- Click the Adjustments HUD button ( ) in the toolbar.
- Press the H key.
- Choose Window > Show Adjustments HUD.

The Adjustments HUD (Figure 5.3) is identical in function to the Adjustments Inspector, but you can control the size and placement of the HUD. By making the HUD wider, making accurate adjustments with the various sliders can be easier, and because it's free floating, you can position it on the screen wherever it's most convenient to you. In addition, you can use whichever view you prefer. We generally prefer to use the Adjustments HUD in conjunction with Full Screen mode.

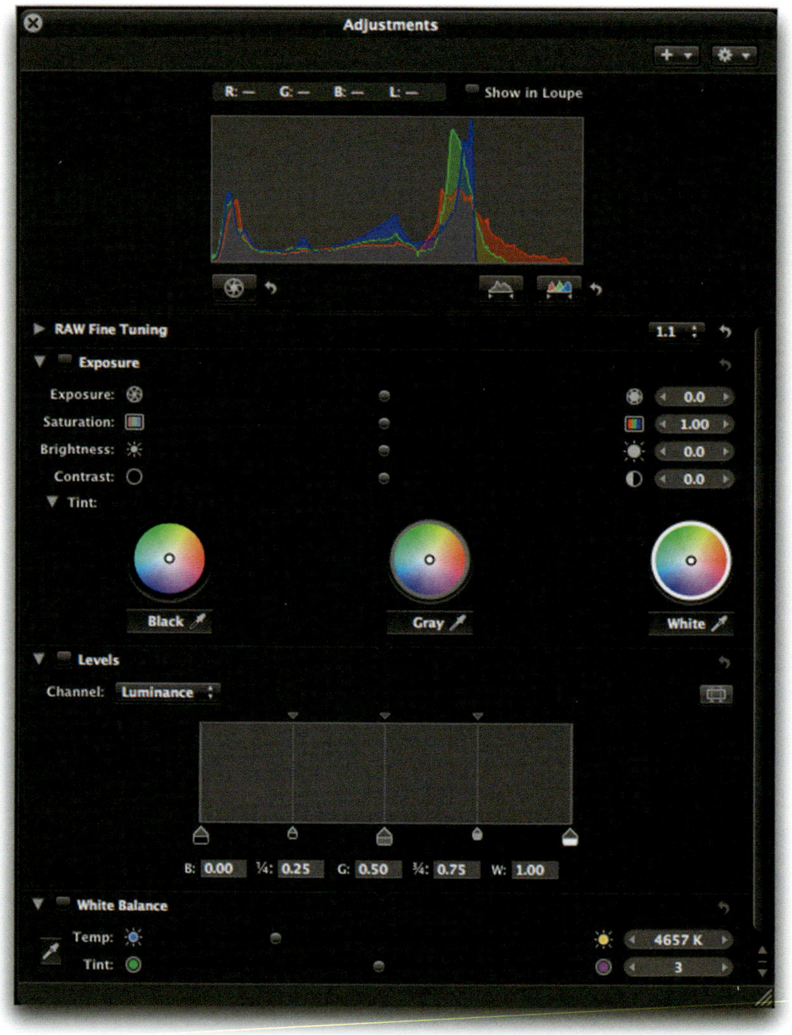

Figure 5.3: The Adjustments HUD contains the same controls as the Adjustments Inspector, but it is free floating so you can place and size it for convenience.

The RAW Fine Tuning controls, as well as the Auto commands, Exposure, Levels, and White Balance, appear in the Adjustments Inspector and HUD by default. By clicking the Add Adjustments pop-up menu button (+ ▾) in the upper right of this dialog box (Figure 5.4), you can access the tools that reside in the toolbar as well as the Highlight/Shadow, Monochrome Mixer, Color Monochrome, Sepia Mixer, Noise Reduction, and Sharpen filters.

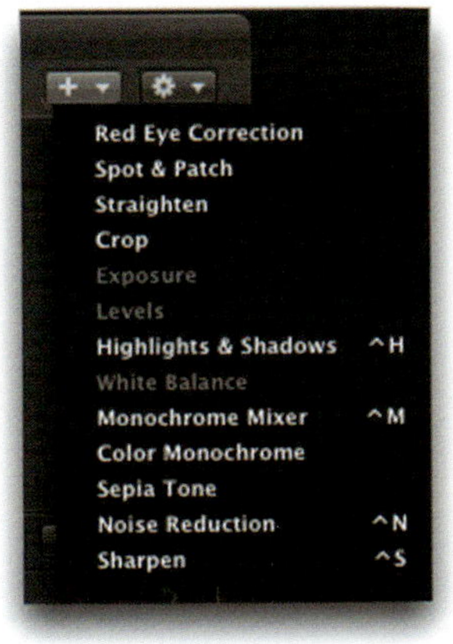

Figure 5.4:
To access additional adjustment tools, click the Add Adjustments pop-up menu in the Adjustments Inspector.

Many of the adjustment tools share a similar structure, as shown in Figure 5.5. The disclosure arrow ( ) on the left reveals the controls for each adjustment, and a check box ( ) indicates whether that tool is being applied to the image. Use the check box to toggle effects on and off as you work. Click the Reset button ( ) on the right to reset all the parameters for that specific tool.

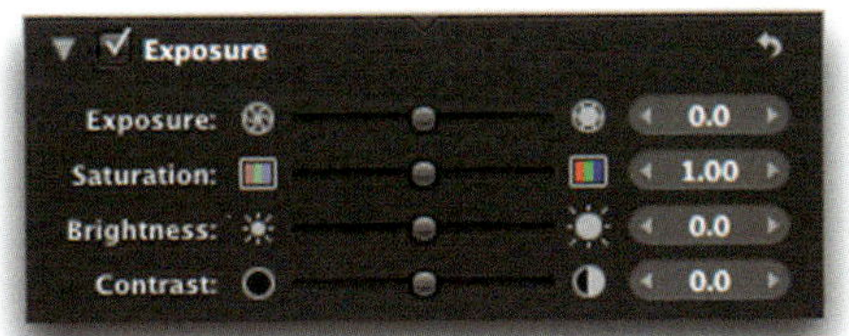

Figure 5.5:
The image-processing tools share similar controls.

To remove the effects of all the tools from a single image, click the Adjustment Action pop-up menu button ( ) in the upper right of both the Adjustments Inspector and HUD. Select Remove All Adjustments from the menu. To remove all the adjustments from a group of images, first select the images, then, in the main menu bar, choose Images > Remove All Adjustments From Selection.

The Image Processing tools contain two types of sliders, as shown in Figure 5.6. One is the familiar slider with which you adjust parameters by dragging left or right. Aperture conveniently places an icon at both extremes to help identify the effect of the adjustment. The other is a value slider, also known as a *scrubber,* which can be set three different ways: double-click the number and type in the desired value, click the left or right arrows to increase or decrease the value, or drag within the value field. By typing a number and/or clicking the right and left arrows, you can use much higher values than are available from the basic slider with many of the tools. For example, the Exposure slider extends between +/– 2.0 stops, but by using the value slider you can make adjustments between +/– 9.99 stops.

Figure 5.6: Make adjustments by dragging the slider or by using the value slider/scrubber.

Note: Hold down the Option key while dragging the slider to make adjustments in smaller increments, and hold the Shift key to make adjustments in larger increments.

Aperture provides two ways to sample the color values in an image. The first is to place the cursor over the desired part of the image or thumbnail. The Color Meter, located above the histogram in the Adjustments HUD and Inspector, will display the color values of the pixel(s), as shown in Figure 5.7. The meter will display not only the R, G, and B values for the pixel, but also the luminosity value.

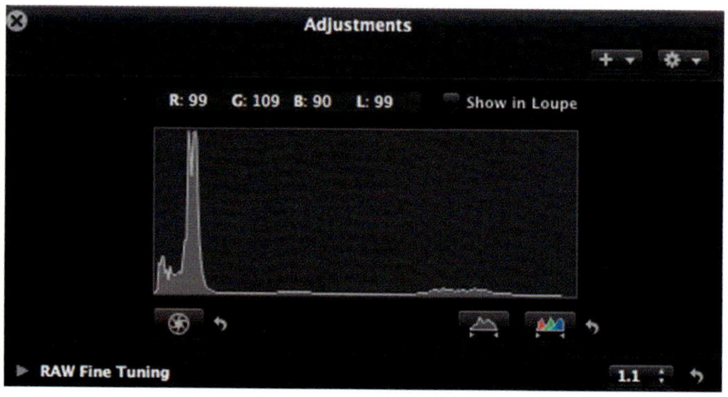

Figure 5.7: The Color Meter readout is located above the histogram in the Adjustments HUD and Inspector.

The second way to sample color values is to use the Loupe. The Loupe will accurately show precisely which pixel(s) are being sampled. To use the Loupe to sample colors, follow these steps:

1. In the Adjustments HUD or Inspector, select the Show in Loupe check box.
2. Click the Loupe icon ( ) in the toolbar or press the tilde key (~).
3. Place the crosshair target area of the Loupe over the desired pixels. The color values will appear in the Loupe, as shown in Figure 5.8.

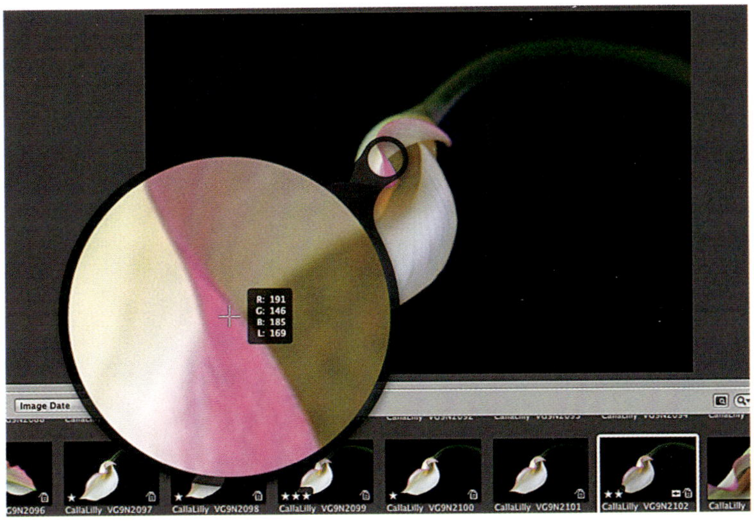

Figure 5.8:
A readout of the pixel color values appears within the Loupe.

Use the Adjustment Action pop-up menu, shown in Figure 5.9, to set the Color Meter to display RGB, Lab, or CMYK color values and to specify the number of pixels to be sampled. We leave our default sample size set to 3 × 3.

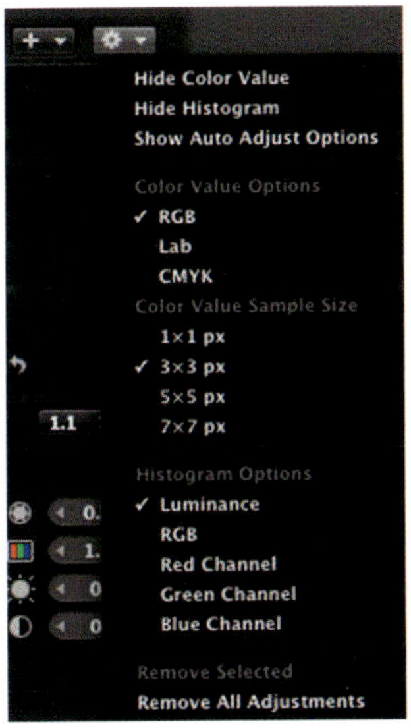

Figure 5.9:
Set the desired color mode and sample size from the Adjustment Action pop-up menu.

Using the RAW Fine Tuning Controls

The RAW Fine Tuning controls enable you to modify how Aperture initially decodes RAW files. In fact, the decoding is individualized for each camera model, but the four controls shown in Figure 5.10 (Boost, Sharpening, ChromaBlur, and Auto Noise Compensation) allow you to further adjust the process to reflect your preferences and needs. You can modify these controls on an individual image and/or save the settings as defaults so that they are applied to newly imported images.

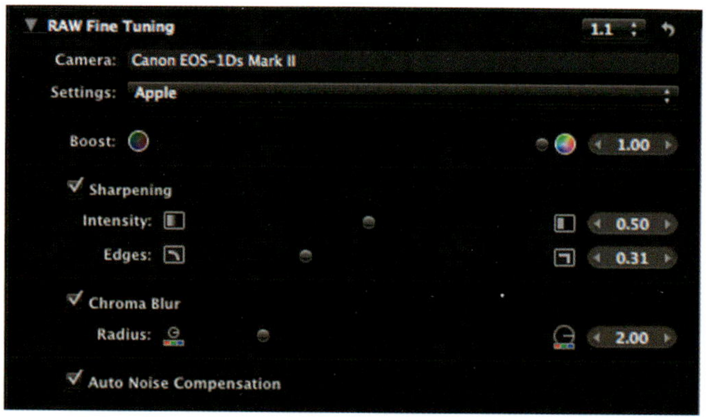

Figure 5.10:
The RAW Fine Tuning controls offer additional control over the initial RAW decoding algorithms.

Note: Some of the controls may not be available for all camera models.

Adjusting the Boost Parameters

The Boost controls enable you to modify the initial contrast in the RAW file. The Mac operating system uses algorithms calculated for each digital camera's RAW file format to establish what it thinks are the optimal contrast settings. By using the Boost controls, you can decrease this contrast. When the slider is set all the way to 0, no contrast adjustment is applied, whereas the default value of 1.0 uses the full recommended contrast adjustment.

Rather than drag the slider, you can click the left or right arrow in the Boost value slider to adjust the contrast in 5 percent increments.

Adjusting the Sharpening Parameters

The digital process slightly softens images. To counteract that effect, you can opt to apply some sharpening during the decoding process. This is akin to first pass sharpening. The Mac operating system has calculated default recommended sharpening values for each camera type. However, if the Sharpening check box is not selected, Aperture applies no sharpening during the RAW decoding process.

To apply sharpening during the decoding process, do the following:

1. Select the Sharpening check box. The recommended default values are set for both the Intensity and Edge sliders.
2. Drag the Intensity slider to the right to increase the strength of the sharpening and to the left to decrease it. Clicking the right or left arrows in the value slider field will increase or decrease the sharpening in 5 percent increments.
3. Drag the Edges slider to the right to intensify the sharpening that occurs at hard edges and to the left to decrease it. Clicking the right or left arrows in the value slider field will increase or decrease the sharpening in 5 percent increments.

Setting the Chroma Blur Parameters

The Chroma Blur controls are used to correct color noise. Color noise is unexpected color blobs that may occur with long exposures and/or high ISOs. It's more common in shadow areas but may occur in midtones or even light areas and is readily apparent when you zoom in on an image to 200 or 300 percent magnification. Some camera models are more prone to color noise than others. The Mac operating systems has calculated default values for each camera model.

The Chroma Blur works by slightly smearing or blurring the colors. To use it, do *one* of the following:

- Select the Chroma Blur check box and drag the Radius slider to the right to increase the chroma blur effect and to the left to decrease it.
- Click the right and left arrows in the value slider box to increase or decrease the amount of chroma blur in increments of one tenth of a pixel.
- Double-click the number in the value slider field, to specify a value between 0.10 and 10.00 and then press Return.

Using Auto Noise Compensation

By default, the Mac operating system assesses the noise characteristics of each camera and uses this information to calculate settings for other parameters such as sharpening. If you prefer *not* to have this automatic adjustment, deselect the Auto Noise Compensation check box. Unchecking this box removes the Auto Noise compensation.

Default RAW Fine Tuning Settings

If you regularly prefer using certain Aperture settings when decoding your RAW images, you can save these settings and establish them as the default settings for that particular camera. To set new default values for the RAW Fine Tuning settings, follow these steps:

1. Set each of the parameters as desired.
2. Click the Settings pop-up menu and choose Save as Camera Default. The Settings pop-up menu will change from Custom to Camera Default.

To restore the previous default camera settings, choose Clear Camera Raw Default from the Settings pop-up menu. The display will read Former Camera Default. Choose Apple to restore Apple's default settings.

Migrating Your Images to Aperture 1.1

The RAW Fine Tuning controls are available only for images imported using Aperture 1.1 or those images that you migrate to version 1.1. Images that you previously imported using Aperture 1.0 will retain the original version 1.0 RAW decoding algorithms even though you have upgraded to version 1.1. This prevents any unexpected changes in their appearances. You can migrate these older images to version 1.1 either individually or as a group.

To migrate a single image, select 1.1 from the pop-up menu by the RAW Fine Tuning controls Version pop-up menu.

To migrate a group of images, follow these steps:

1. Select one or more images.
2. Choose File > Migrate Images.
3. Aperture will open a dialog box where you can set your migration options, as shown in Figure 5.11.

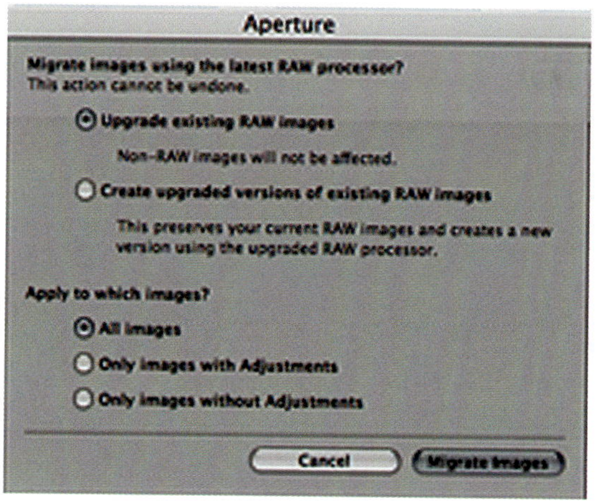

Figure 5.11:
The Migrate Images dialog box

Note: Migrating your images can be slow. Try to migrate your images as you need them, such as for a book or for a web gallery, instead of all at once.

- The first radio button lets you choose to have both a 1.0 and a 1.1 version of your image (Create upgraded version of existing RAW images) or just one version (Upgrade existing RAW images).
- The second radio button allows you to pick between upgrading all images, any image with an adjustment, or images without adjustments.

Once you've migrated your images, Aperture will show the RAW Fine Tuning controls for these images. However, should you want to switch back to a 1.0 version, you can't simply undo the migrate command. Instead, follow these steps:

1. Select the RAW image and open the Adjustments HUD (press H) or Inspector (press I).
2. Using the Version pop-up menu, select 1.0 to have your image use the Aperture 1.0 converter.

Using the Histograms

At the top of the Adjustments HUD and Inspector is a histogram that reflects the distribution of the tonalities of the pixels from pure black on the left to pure white on the right. Aperture updates the histogram in real time as you make changes. By keeping an eye on the histogram, you can judge when an adjustment is introducing clipping, which could mean losing some important details in the image.

By default, the histogram is set to show the luminance values. These values are determined by combining the brightness values from each of the three channels (R, G, and B) for each pixel. The resulting histogram shows a single set of data, as shown in Figure 5.12.

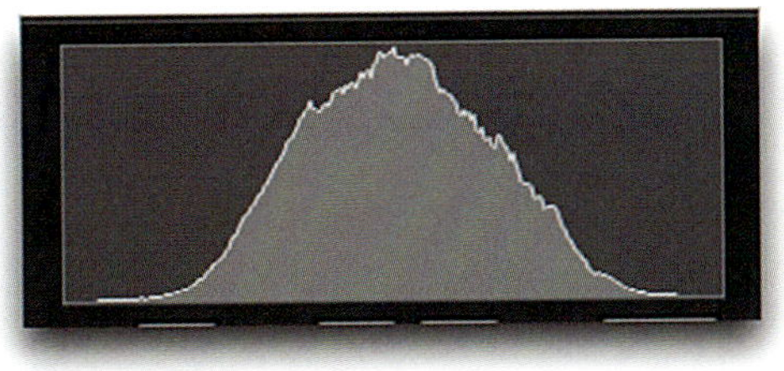

Figure 5.12: A histogram showing luminance values

You can opt to set the histogram to show RGB data by clicking the Adjustment Action pop-up menu shown earlier in Figure 5.6 and selecting RGB. Three histograms, one for each channel, will be displayed superimposed over one another, as shown in Figure 5.13. This can be helpful when you're making color adjustments by enabling you to see the effect of the adjustment on each color channel. If you are specifically interested in the histogram for a particular channel, you can opt to set the histogram to display data for that channel alone by choosing the corresponding channel from the Adjustment Action pop-up menu.

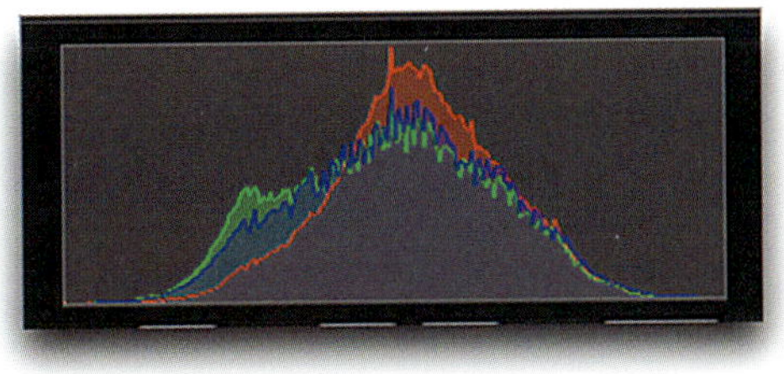

Figure 5.13: A histogram showing the RGB values

The Levels Adjustment Filter also contains a histogram that by default is set to show luminance values, but it can be changed to show an RGB histogram or a histogram for a single channel. Then the changes that you make will apply only to a specific channel. That way you can make Levels adjustments to modify colors and color casts. We'll cover this in more detail later in the chapter when we talk about using Levels adjustments.

Using the Image Processing Tools

Aperture has placed the basic tools in the toolbar and the more advanced adjustment filters in the Adjustments Inspector and HUD. You can use these tools while in any view, even if you are in the midst of compiling a book, web page, slideshow, etc. We'll begin by covering the tools available in the toolbar and then we'll cover those in the Adjustments Inspector and HUD.

Using the Toolbar Tools

By default the toolbar is set to the Selection tool so that when you click an image, the image will be selected. The Rotate Left ( ) and Rotate Right ( ) buttons are intuitive. Click them to rotate your image 90 degrees. Clicking them a second time rotates the image 180 degrees, etc.

Using the Crop Tool

The Crop tool ( ) allows you to crop your image to a custom size you visually determine or to a predetermined aspect ratio. When you first click the Crop tool, a small dialog box appears (see Figure 5.14). You can select a predetermined size, which defines an aspect ratio for your crop, by clicking the Constrain Cropping Tool To check box and then choosing the desired size from the pop-up menu. Alternatively, you can enter any numbers in the Height and Width boxes you desire. By clicking the double-arrow between the Height and Width boxes, you can rotate the crop 90 degrees.

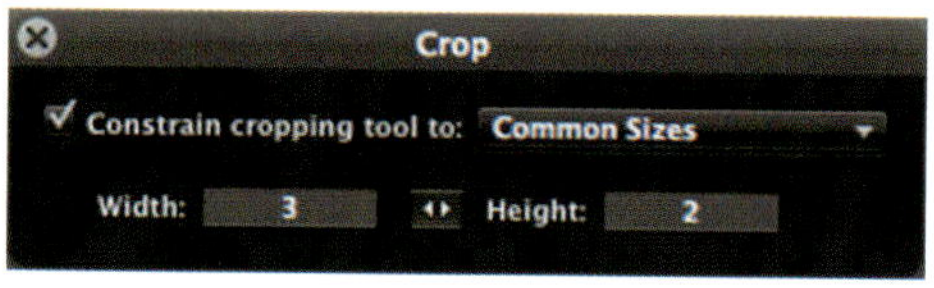

Figure 5.14:
The Crop dialog box allows you to select among numerous common crop sizes and to create a specific crop ratio for an image.

To use the crop tool click in one corner of your image where you wish the crop to begin and drag diagonally across the image to the end point as shown in Figure 5.15. The area that will be removed will be shaded. You can move the crop by clicking anywhere within the cropped image and dragging the crop to a new area. This way you can refine the position while maintaining the same size crop.

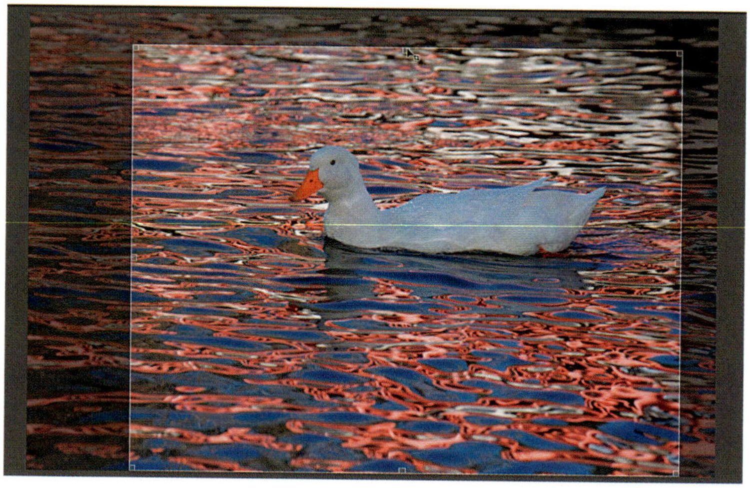

Figure 5.15:
After drawing your initial crop, you can refine the size and position to best present your image.

You can also change the size of the crop. If you have chosen a specific crop ratio, you can click the handles on the cropped image preview and drag them larger or smaller. Because the same aspect ratio will be maintained, the horizontal and vertical sides of your image will increase and decrease together. If you have drawn a custom-sized crop, you can adjust any side individually by clicking a handle on that side and dragging it inward or outward. If you click a corner handle, both the horizontal and vertical side will adjust together, maintaining the same aspect ratio.

When you are happy with the crop, press Return to apply it. Your image preview will change to reflect the crop. However, if you ever want to change the crop, all the original information is still there. All you have to do is click the Crop tool, and you can modify the crop. Nondestructive cropping is one of Aperture's significant benefits.

To replace a crop, click and drag a new crop. To remove a crop entirely, uncheck Crop in the Adjustments HUD or Inspector.

Using the Straighten Tool

Although there are some photographers who always carefully manage to have straight horizons, many of us find that in the heat of the moment when trying to capture a breathtaking image, the camera wasn't exactly level. Aperture's Straighten tool () offers an easy way to remedy the problem.

To use the Straighten tool, click it in the toolbar and then click and drag slightly on your image. As shown in Figure 5.16, a grid will appear that you can use to align with some portion of your image that should be horizontal or vertical. By dragging farther, the image will be rotated progressively further. To rotate the image in the opposite direction, drag the cursor the opposite way. Click closer to the edge of the image to make the tool rotate in smaller, more easily controlled increments.

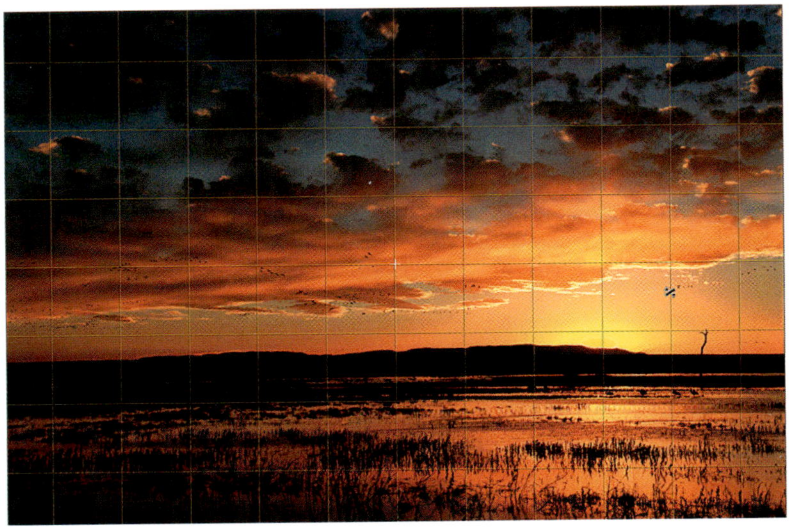

Figure 5.16: Align the grid with a horizontal or vertical element in your image to straighten it.

Once you use the Straighten tool, it appears in the Adjustments Inspector and HUD. The value field window to the right of the slider displays the degree of rotation (see Figure 5.17). You could highlight that number and fill in a specific number if you know the exact degree of rotation you need. However, most of the time it's easier to click the right or left arrows and rotate the image in one-degree increments and then use the slider to fine-tune the rotation. You may find the sliders easier and more precise to use than simply clicking and dragging on the image to straighten the image. If so, access the Straighten tool from the Adjustments HUD Add Adjustments pop-up menu ( ).

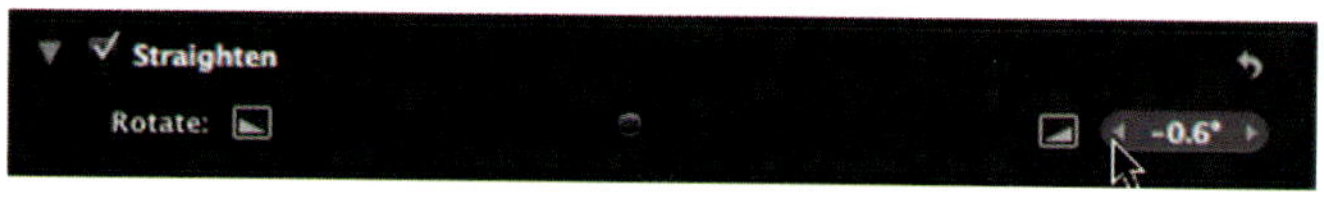

Figure 5.17: By clicking the small arrows, you can adjust the rotation of the image in one-degree increments and then fine-tune it with the slider.

As you rotate the image, it is automatically cropped. The more extensive the rotation, the greater the crop.

Note: If you don't want to crop the image, but would rather add canvas in the missing areas, you'll need to use an external editor such as Photoshop. We'll cover how to do that in Chapter 6, "Exporting Images."

To reset the image to the original rotation, click the Reset arrow ( ) in the upper right of the Straighten portion of the Inspector or HUD.

Using the Spot & Patch Tool

In most image editors, cloning and healing are permanent changes. Although in Photoshop you can perform both functions using layers, you can't later change your mind about a specific cloning or healing act you did in the midst of a major clean up. Rather you'd have to delete the layer and begin anew or go back in history to the step reflecting that particular change. The remaining cleanup you did after that step would be lost.

Aperture allows you to perform similar dust cleanup using the Spot & Patch tool and enables you to later revise any of those changes without losing any cleanup that you may have done since. The Spot aspect of the tool is similar to the Spot Healing Brush in Photoshop CS2. It analyzes surrounding pixels and uses that information to replace the problem area. Details are blended in a radial pattern when the Spot tool is used. The Patch aspect of the tool is similar to Photoshop's Clone Stamp tool. It replaces pixels in a problematic area with an exact copy of those from a designated area.

Before using the Spot & Patch tool for dust cleanup, it's best to zoom in to a 100 percent view. To do this, press Z. The image preview will zoom to 100 percent and a small box with an even smaller red box within it will appear. The red box shows you where you are within the image. It's akin to the Navigator in Photoshop. To begin, set the red box in the upper-right corner by clicking it and dragging it. Slowly and sequentially drag the red box within the little box. When you find a dust spot, stop and use the Spot & Patch tool as described in the following text. When you reach the other side, carefully navigate down and then across the image the other way. Continue until you have checked and removed dust from the entire image.

Initially, when you click the Spot & Patch tool ( ), a small dialog box with a Radius slider will appear (see Figure 5.18). Use this slider to select the size of your Spot tool. The Spot tool appears as circle with a target within it before you click the dust. (You can adjust the size after the fact by accessing the Spot & Patch tool from the

Inspector or HUD.) Click the problematic area. After you click, a yellow circle will appear indicating that the area inside has been spotted. In many cases, the dust will be gone with one click. If not, access the Spot tool from the Adjustments HUD or Inspector and adjust the parameters such as radius and opacity, which we'll describe shortly.

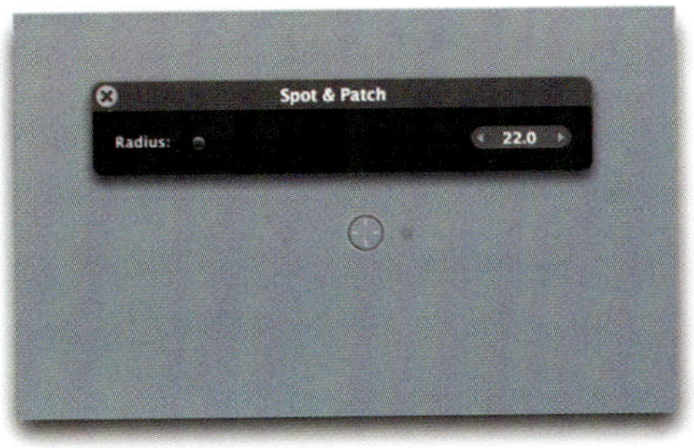

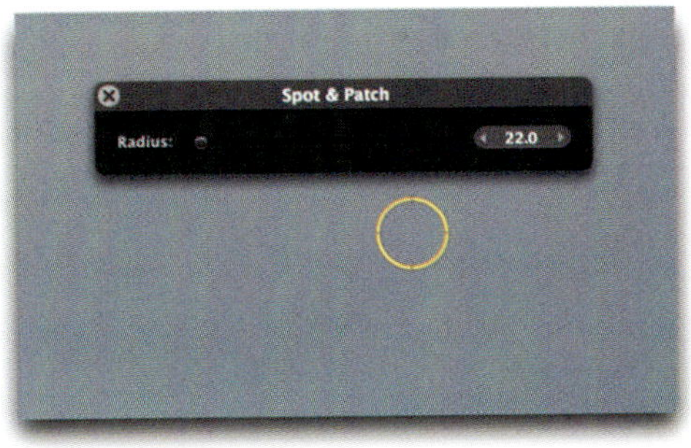

Figure 5.18: Use the Radius slider to set the size of the spot before you click the problematic pixels.

If you prefer to clone from one area to another, you will need to use the Patch tool. You begin the same way as with the Spot tool. Select the size of the tool and then click the problematic area. Next, hold down the Option key and click an area that you would like to use as a replacement. A white circle will appear with a line connecting it to your spot, which appears as a yellow circle as shown in Figure 5.19. The contents of your spot are replaced with the pixels of the area you select. You can click in the white circle and drag it elsewhere in your image, and the contents of the spot will reflect whatever pixels are under the white circle.

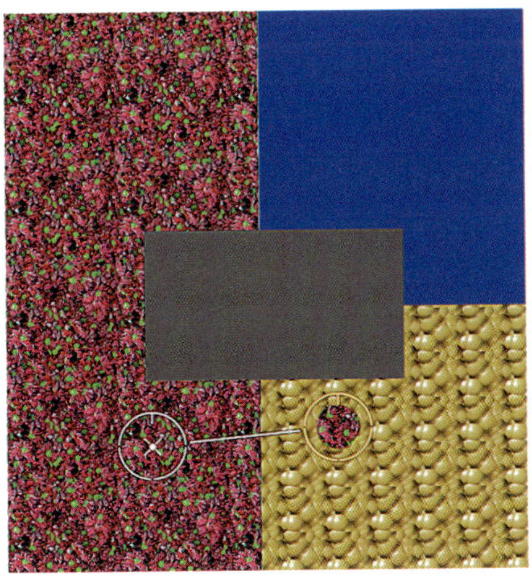

Figure 5.19: When you use the Patch tool, a white circle will appear. Drag the white circle to define the good pixels to be used to replace the problematic pixels.

Alternatively, to clone the area, click the problem area and then check the Patch box within the Spot & Patch pane of the Adjustment Inspector or HUD. This will cause a white circle to appear. To select the replacement pixels, drag the white circle to the desired area. You can also use this approach if you decide to later convert a Spot to a Patch.

Once you use the Spot & Patch tool, its settings are visible within the Adjustments Inspector and HUD. In addition, more options appear (see Figure 5.20). You can modify the radius of the Spot by using the Radius slider inside the Spot & Patch pane. This slider is different from the one that appeared initially when you selected the Spot tool. This slider adjusts the radius of the spot after the fact, whereas the first slider adjusts the radius of the tool before you use it. If your first attempt to fix the spot wasn't completely successful, being able to adjust the radius after the fact eliminates the need to start all over with a different-sized tool. This way you can select precisely the size you need and see the effects of the different sizes in real time.

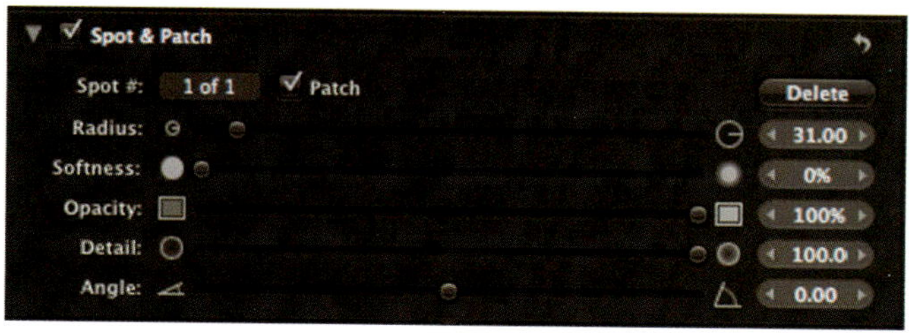

Figure 5.20: Additional controls appear within the Adjustments Inspector and HUD after the Spot tool is used to refine the effect.

The second slider adjusts the softness or feathering of the tool. By default it is hard (0 percent soft). To make it softer and have a more feathered edge, adjust the slider to the right.

The third slider adjusts the opacity of the Spot & Patch tool. By default, it's at 100 percent. Reducing the opacity makes the change more transparent. This can be useful to help blend the changes.

The next slider is the Detail slider, which by default is at 100 percent. If you are using the Spot tool, reducing the Detail reduces the blending effect so that more of the original texture is visible. If you have used the Patch tool, reducing the detail slider increasingly restores the original texture of the area while using color from the sampled area.

If you have used the Patch tool, you can also use the Angle slider. The Angle slider rotates the replacement pixels so you can select a source that has an angle that is different from what you need. We find this feature to be quite helpful in making sure our repairs look natural.

Note: The best way to get comfortable with the Spot & Patch tool is to experiment with it. We have provided a practice demo image, SpotPatch.tiff, on the companion website for you to use. Go to www.sybex.com/go/apertureexposed to download the file. Try copying the various textures and colors to other areas in the image. Use it to see the differences in the Spot & Patch tools, as well as the effects of the various sliders. By taking time to do this, it will be easier for you to use the Spot & Patch tool quickly and effectively on your own images.

The Spot & Patch tool is well suited to removing dust from digital images; however, if you want to remove objects from your image, you may prefer to open the image in an external editor, such as Photoshop, and use its various cloning and healing tools. We'll cover how to do this in Chapter 6.

Using the Red Eye Tool

Although many cameras use flashes with "red-eye reduction" features, sometimes we still wind up with pictures of people and animals that look more like demons due to their red eyes. Aperture has a very quick and easy-to-use tool to eliminate the red and make the eyes appear human.

To remove red eyes quickly, select the Red Eye tool () and follow these steps:

1. A small dialog box will appear with a Radius slider. Adjust the radius so that the circle will be just slightly larger than the eye, as shown in Figure 5.21.

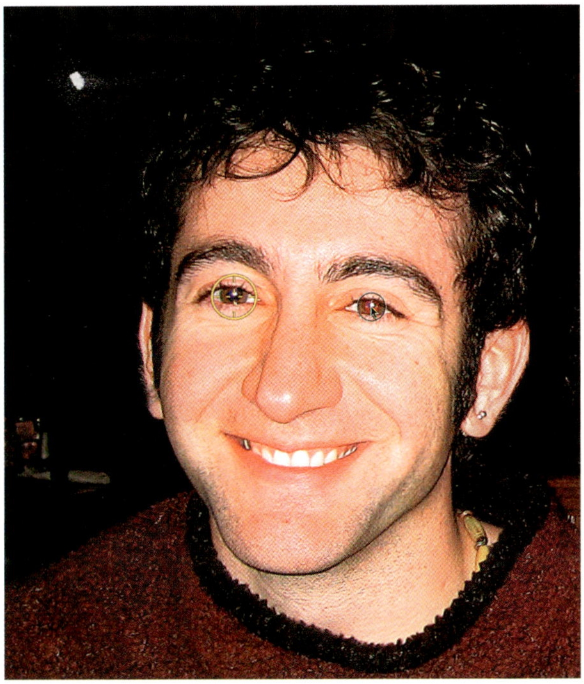

Figure 5.21: Adjust the Red Eye tool so that it is slightly larger than the red eye and click to create a more normal eye.

2. Click the red eye, and the red will be replaced by black.
3. If you need to adjust the size of the Red Eye tool after the fact, you can use the Radius slider that appears in the Red Eye Correction portion of the Adjustments Inspector or HUD. You can also adjust the sensitivity to remove more or less of the red.

The Red Eye tool is impressively proficient at removing red eyes. Take a moment and download the red eye sample image named JoshRedEyes.tiff from our companion website (www.sybex.com/go/apertureexposed). Use the Red Eye tool to make Josh look more human. We think you'll be impressed.

Using the Adjustment Filters

Aperture offers multiple adjustments to modify the tonalities and colors within your images. Some are more automatic, relying on the software to make decisions for you, whereas others offer you more control over how you want the image to appear. As you become more familiar with these options, you'll soon discover your favorites. Most images do not require you to use all the adjustments that are available. Depending on the circumstances of the image, a particular type of adjustment may be more or less helpful.

All these features are found in both the Adjustments Inspector and the Adjustments HUD. Access them from whichever one you prefer.

Note: After making an adjustment, you can compare the image with and without the change by toggling the check box in the left-upper part of each adjustment filter. To reset any of the filters to the default values, click the Reset arrow in the upper-right corner of the corresponding pane.

Using the Automatic Adjustments

Immediately under the histogram in the Adjustments palette are three small buttons, as shown in Figure 5.22.

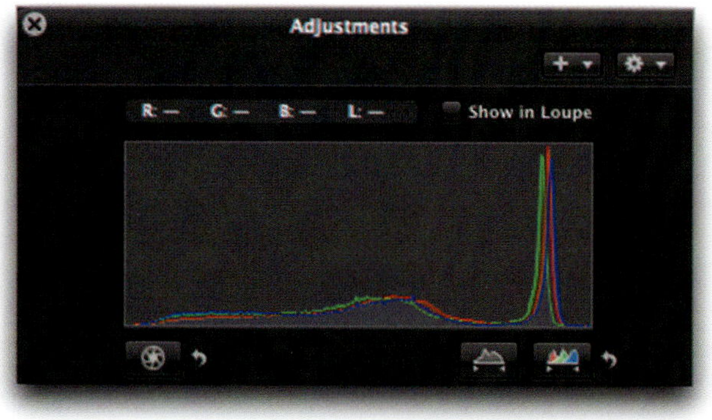

Figure 5.22: Several automatic tools are located just under the histogram in the Adjustments Inspector and HUD.

Note: If the histogram is not visible, click Adjustment Action pop-up menu ( ) at the top right of the dialog box and select Show Histogram.

The Auto Exposure button ( ) will modify the Exposure setting in the Exposure Filter according to how bright it thinks your image should appear based on an algorithm. After you click this auto adjustment, you will see the Exposure slider move. The Reset arrow next to this button is used to remove the auto adjustment. If the auto adjustment isn't quite perfect, you can fine-tune the adjustment by adjusting the Exposure slider manually.

Note: The Auto Exposure button works only with RAW files.

The middle button ( ) is the Automatic Levels Combined button. It will adjust both the black and white points to maximize contrast within the image based on the combined luminance value of each pixel. Each channel is adjusted identically based on the total luminance value of each pixel.

The next button (), Auto Levels Separate, is also an automatic Levels adjustment, but it adjusts the black and white points separately in the Red, Blue, and Green channels. The results you get will often differ significantly from the results of using the previous (combined levels) auto adjustment. If you want to quickly correct a color cast as well as the contrast within an image, this is the adjustment to use.

To set the clipping values for the Auto controls, choose Show Auto Adjust Options from the Adjustment Action pop-up menu, as shown in Figure 5.23.

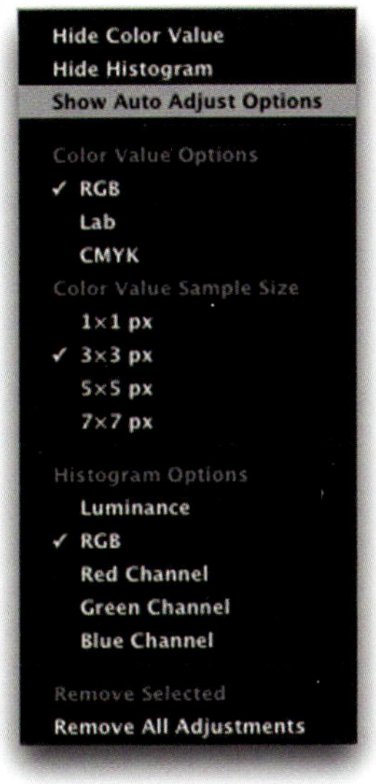

Figure 5.23: The Adjustment Action pop-up menu

Sliders for the Black Clip point and the White Clip point will appear under the Auto Adjust icons, as shown in Figure 5.24. We normally leave the clip options set to 0, but some photographers prefer a very small amount of clipping.

Figure 5.24: The Clip Options sliders

Although auto adjustments appear seductively fast and easy to use, we prefer to use some of the other adjustment options so that we retain more control over the appearance of our images.

Using the Exposure Filter

Whenever you open the Adjustments Inspector or HUD, the Exposure controls appear by default. The Exposure filter automatically becomes active as soon as you change any of the sliders within it. At first glance, there appears to be a considerable overlap between some of these controls, as well as with the Levels controls, and knowing where to begin in order to achieve the best results might be difficult. By following our suggestions for using these various adjustments, you will be able to effectively and efficiently optimize your image.

Setting the Exposure Slider

The first slider within the Exposure filter is the Exposure slider. As you adjust this slider, the entire histogram shifts to the left or right. The entire image becomes darker or lighter accordingly, as shown in Figure 5.25. Use this slider to set a white point and adjust the brightness of the image between +/– 2.0 stops.

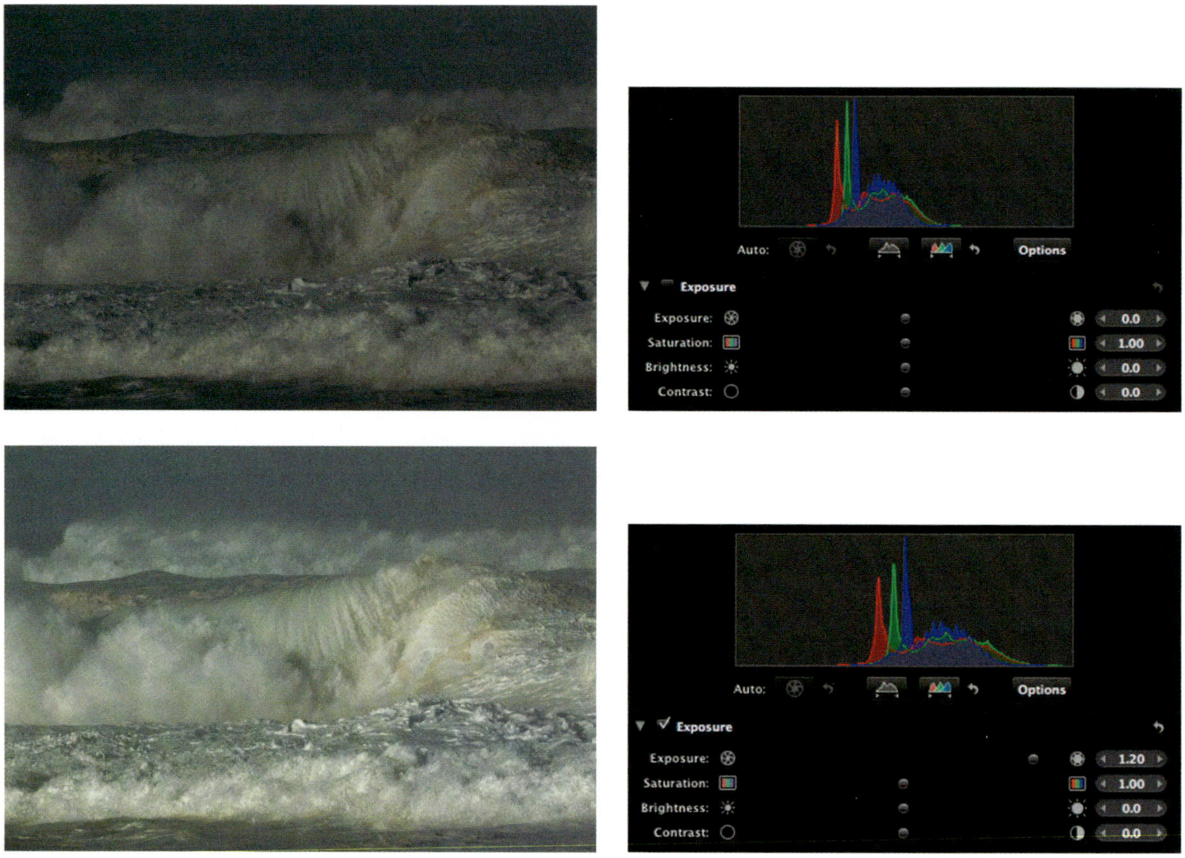

Figure 5.25: When the Exposure slider was adjusted, the entire image became brighter and the histogram moved to the right.

Click the right and left arrows in the value slider window to adjust the exposure in 1/10 stop increments. By using the value slider field, you can make more extreme brightness adjustments from +/– 9.99 stops. Of course, information that was not captured by the sensor still won't be there, but you can reveal all the information that was captured.

It's a good idea to have the highlight warning turned on so you don't accidentally lose any information as you set the Exposure slider. The warning causes blown-out pixels to appear bright red. To turn on the highlight warning, choose View > Highlight Hot Areas from the top menu bar. We leave this setting on for most of our work. That way we can readily see if we make an adjustment that would clip any pixels.

Note: Although it might be tempting to slightly underexpose your pictures while shooting to ensure that you don't clip the highlights in the RAW file, doing so is not a good idea. Having to lighten a dark image often reveals more noise in the darker tonalities than would have been there if the image had been properly exposed. It's best to capture the image as bright as possible without burning out/clipping any of the highlights.

Setting the Brightness Slider

The Brightness slider also adjusts the brightness of your image, but it primarily affects the middle tones. It also sets the black point (Figure 5.26). You can watch the histogram to help determine where to set this slider. You can also use both the Exposure and Brightness sliders in conjunction with Levels, which we'll do with this image. Setting the black point with the Brightness slider will result in an image that's too dark. We'll lighten the middle tones in Levels.

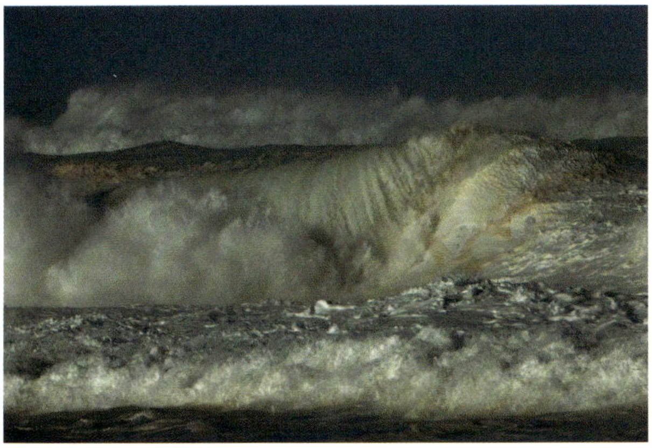

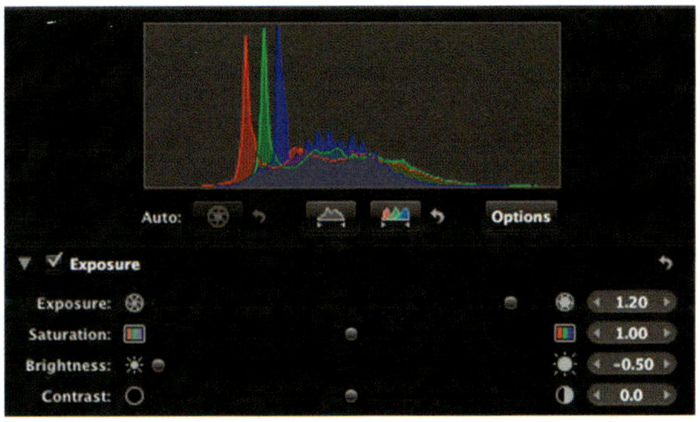

Figure 5.26: Use the Brightness slider to set the black point.

Note: Levels Adjustment controls allow more precision in determining the range of tonalities to be brightened or darkened. We prefer to use Levels adjustments to set the white and black points for most of our images. We use the Exposure slider to modify the overall range of the exposure of the image and then fine-tune it with Levels.

Setting the Contrast Slider

Moving the Contrast slider to the right shifts the bulk of the pixels toward the extremes of the histogram, which increases contrast as shown in Figure 5.27. Similarly, moving the slider to the left shifts the majority of the pixels toward the center of the histogram, which reduces the contrast. Clicking the right or left arrows in the value slider field will change the contrast in 5 percent increments.

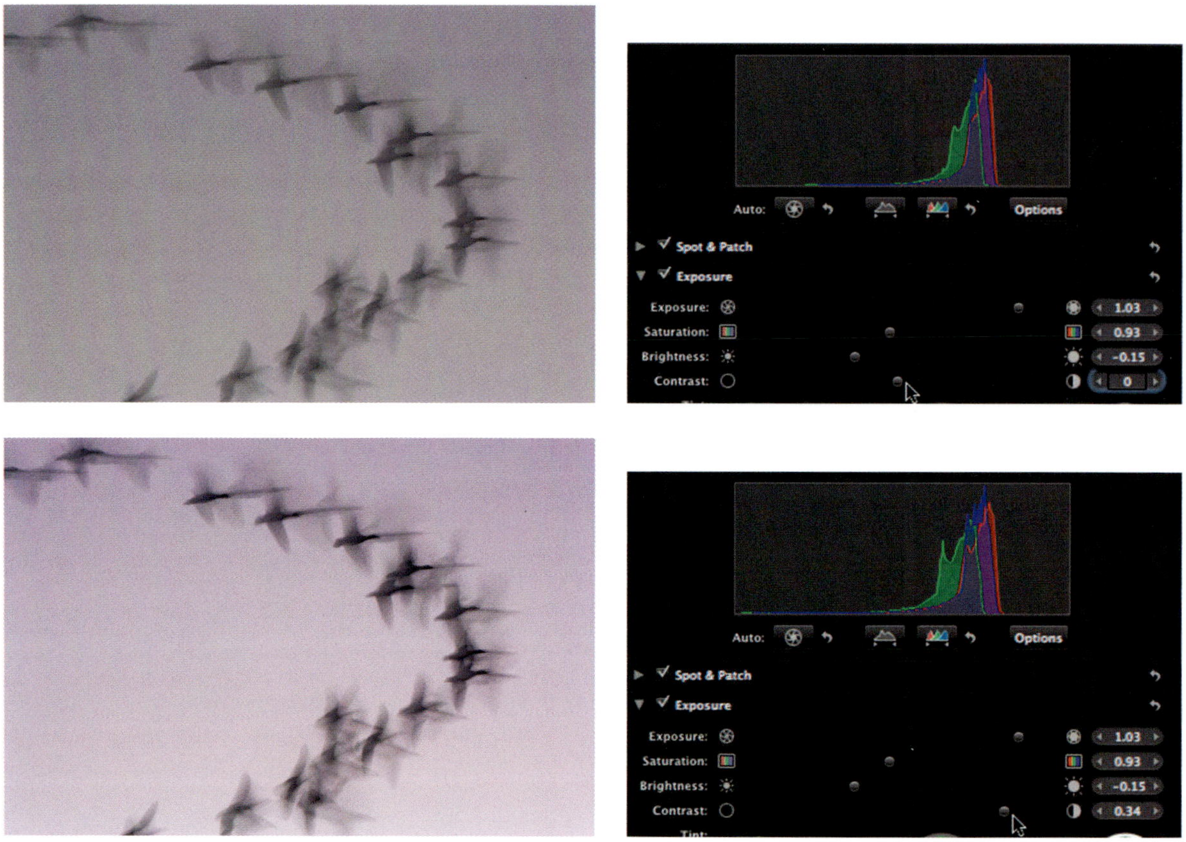

Figure 5.27: Moving the Contrast slider to the right increases the contrast.

At times, you may need to tweak the Exposure and/or Brightness settings after adjusting the contrast.

Note: To reveal highlight and shadow detail in images with high contrast, use the Highlight & Shadows adjustment.

Setting the Saturation Slider

Moving the Saturation slider to the right increases saturation, and moving it to the left decreases it. If you move it all the way to the left, you can desaturate the image completely and turn it into a black-and-white image. However, a better approach to creating a black-and-white image would be to use the Monochrome Mixer filter that we'll cover later in this chapter.

Adjust the Saturation slider to your taste. As a general rule, it's best to use a light hand because oversaturated images often look gaudy and fake.

Setting the Black, Gray, and White Tints

Setting the Black, Gray, and White tints can be used to neutralize a color cast or to create a color cast within a range of tonalities in your image. This differs from White

Balance in that you can differentially modify a range of tonalities rather than the color cast of the entire image. This can be particularly helpful when there have been mixed lighting conditions in a photo. Some types of lighting affect the colors in specific tonal ranges. Therefore, you might need to reduce a color cast that is pronounced in the darkest tones but negligible in the light tones and so forth.

You can use the White, Gray, and Black eyedroppers to have Aperture automatically neutralize a color cast by selecting an eyedropper and clicking on a corresponding tone in the image. Alternatively, you can make the adjustment manually using the color wheels.

When you select an eyedropper, a loupe appears over your image preview. Position it so that the small square in the center is over the desired pixels and click. Aperture will remove the color cast in that tonal range.

Note: When using the Black and White eyedroppers, make sure that the pixels in the target area of the Loupe are not from the opposite tonal range. Bright pixels in the target range of the Black eyedropper, or very dark pixels in the target range for the White eyedropper, may lead to aberrant results.

To manually change the color cast within approximately the lightest 20 percent of the pixels in your image, click the circle in the color tint wheel above the White eyedropper and drag (Figure 5.28). You'll see that the farther you go from the center, the stronger the color tint is that is introduced into the whites in your picture. The particular color that is introduced (or removed) depends on the point you select on the color wheel. If you are trying to remove a color cast, move the color wheel the opposite direction from the offending color.

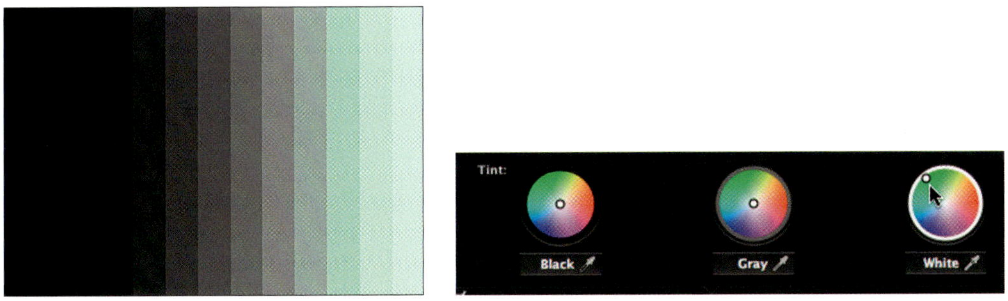

Figure 5.28: Adjusting the color wheel above the White eyedropper alters the color cast of the lightest pixels.

Note: To reset a color wheel, double-click it.

Similarly, if you click the color wheel above the Black eyedropper (Figure 5.29), you can alter the tint of the darkest pixels within your image. Adjusting this color wheel has a significant effect on the darkest half of the tonal range—from the blacks through the midtones, with the strongest effect occurring to the darkest pixels.

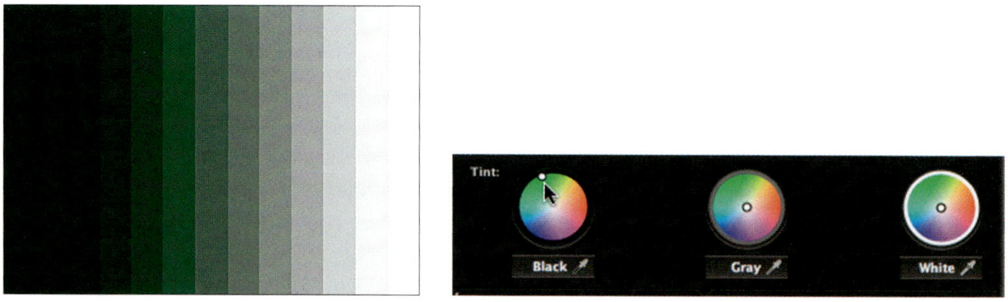

Figure 5.29: Adjusting the color wheel above the Black eyedropper alters the color cast of the darkest half of the tonalities.

Adjusting the color wheel above the Gray eyedropper changes the colors of all the pixels except the whites and blacks, as shown in Figure 5.30.

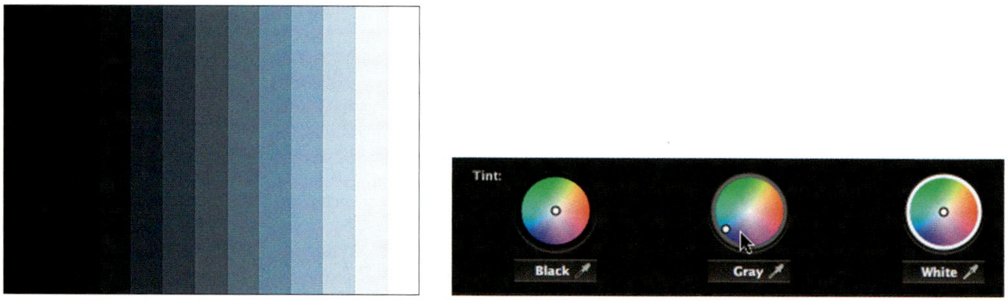

Figure 5.30: Adjusting the color wheel above the Gray eyedropper alters the color cast of everything except the lightest and darkest tones in the image.

To neutralize an image, use the White eyedropper to click a pixel that should be neutral white, the Black eyedropper to click a pixel that should be neutral black, and the Gray eyedropper to click something that should be a neutral shade of gray. If having a neutral image is important to you, it would be helpful to include a neutral gray card in one of the images shot under the same lighting conditions. That way you can click the card in the picture using the Gray eyedropper and stamp the other pictures with this adjustment. We'll talk more about batch changes later in this chapter.

By adjusting the three different color wheels individually, you can correct and/or create different color casts in the various tones in your picture. This is something that may be beneficial to some of your images, but is unlikely to be necessary on all of them.

Note: To become more familiar with the tint controls, go to our companion website and download the file named `graybars.tiff`. Then try adjusting each of the tint color wheels while noting the various effects.

Using the Levels Controls

The Levels controls in Aperture are more sophisticated than the Levels controls currently offered in most other image-editing programs. Not only are there controls to adjust the endpoints and the midpoint of the histogram, you can add Quarter Tone controls as well. The Quarter Tone controls enable you to more accurately control the lightening or darkening you apply to different tonal ranges.

You can adjust Levels using just Luminance or the combined RGB channels or within any individual Red, Green, or Blue channel. Set the histogram to Luminance when you want to modify the overall brightness and/or contrast of an image but not affect the color cast.

To increase the contrast within the image, drag the endpoints of the histogram inward. Remember to make sure the Highlight Hot Areas alert is on. If you used the Exposure, Brightness, and/or Contrast sliders, you may not need to adjust the endpoint sliders.

Even when you are happy with the black and white points in your image, you may feel that the midtones are too bright or too dark. You can move the middle slider to make the bulk of the image lighter or darker, as shown in Figure 5.31.

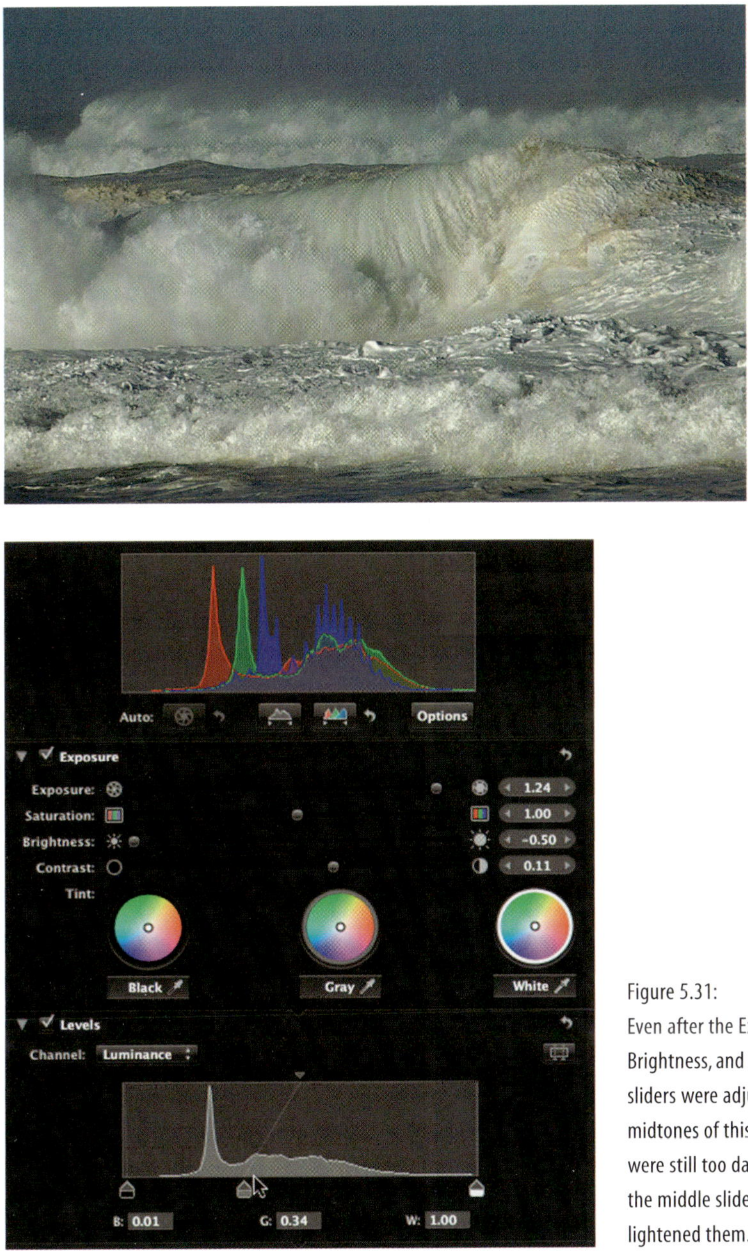

Figure 5.31: Even after the Exposure, Brightness, and Contrast sliders were adjusted, the midtones of this picture were still too dark. Moving the middle slider in Levels lightened them.

Sometimes moving the middle slider improves some areas but makes others too light or too dark or conversely, not light or dark enough. That's when the Quarter Tone controls come in handy. To access the Quarter Tone controls, click the Quarter Tone Controls button ( ) in the Levels controls. Two new sliders that can be adjusted independently of the others will appear. They will enable you to lighten or darken the dark quarter tones and light quarter tones separately.

Note: The dark Quarter Tone controls, also called the Shadow Brightness Levels slider, affect the shadows to midtones. The light Quarter Tone controls, also called the Highlight Brightness Levels slider, affect the midtones to highlights.

There are two ways to adjust the Quarter Tone controls. You can move them from the top and/or from the bottom. We're going to explain the effects of moving these controls using a diagram, and then later in this section we'll apply the controls to an image.

The easiest way to understand the effect of the top control is to leave the bottom control alone initially. As shown in Figure 5.32, when you move the top control on the dark Quarter Tone control, you are in effect instructing Aperture to take the quarter tone values and make them closer to the half tone values or closer to black, thereby lightening or darkening them. If you are using the light Quarter Tone control, moving the top instructs Aperture to make the light quarter tones closer to midtone values or closer to white, again darkening or lightening these tones. Figure 5.32 shows the changes that result from adjusting the top dark and light Quarter Tone controls dramatically to the right and left.

Moving the top of the Quarter Tone sliders is in effect an instruction to take the quarter tones and make them lighter or darker. Similarly, adjusting the top of the Three Quarter Tone slider is an instruction to modify the three-quarter tone range and make it lighter or darker.

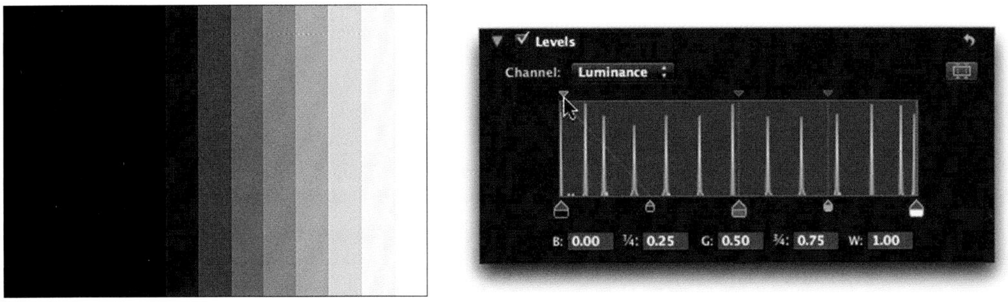

Darkening the dark quarter tones (top-left control)

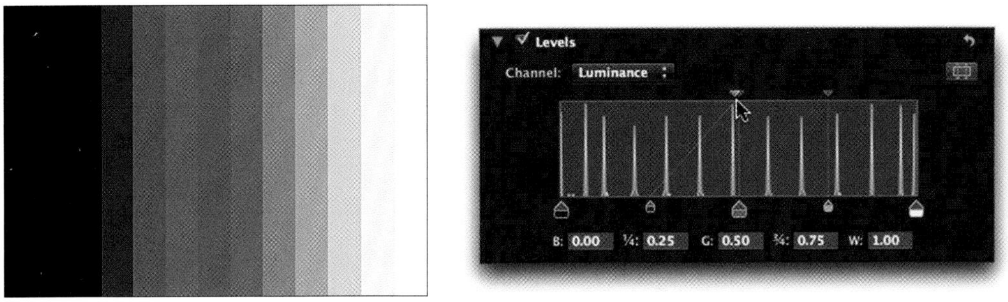

Lightening the dark quarter tones (top-left control)

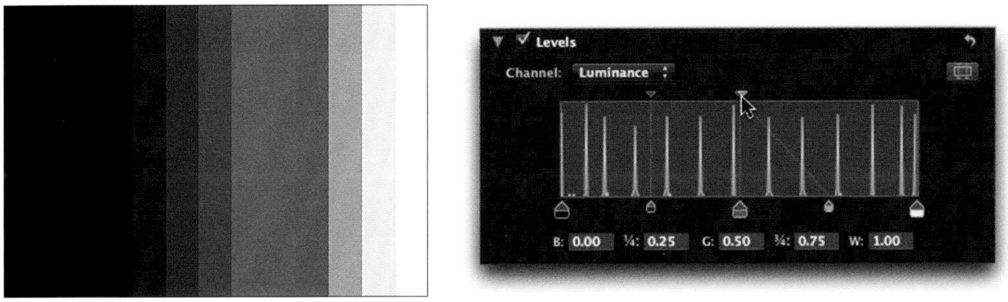

Darkening the light quarter tones (top-right control)

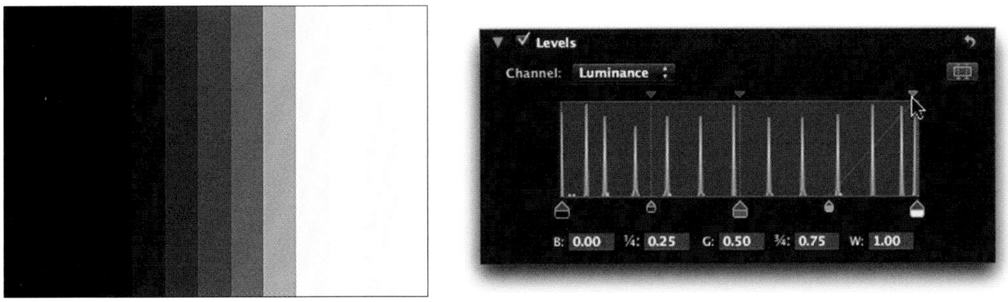

Lightening the light quarter tones (top-right control)

Figure 5.32: Adjusting the top Quarter Tone control to the left darkens that tonal range; moving it to the right lightens those same tonalities. Similarly, moving the top Three Quarter Tone control to the left darkens those tonalities, and moving it to the right lightens those tonalities.

You can also choose to adjust these controls from the bottom. Moving them to the left lightens the associated values and to the right darkens them. This gives the same type of instruction as when you adjust the top sliders. However, the specific commands differ slightly. You are modifying the range of tonalities to be changed, and you are instructing Aperture to make those tones closer to black or quarter tones for the Shadow Brightness Levels slider or to make them closer to white or three-quarter tones for the Highlight Brightness Levels slider.

For example, if you take the Shadow Brightness Levels slider and move it to the left halfway toward black, as shown in Figure 5.33, you are in effect saying, "Take the darkest one-eighth tone values and make them quarter tone values," thereby lightening some of the darker tones in the picture. Similarly, moving that Quarter Tone control to the right, halfway toward the middle tone control in effect says, "Make the three-eighths tones like the quarter tones," which would darken them.

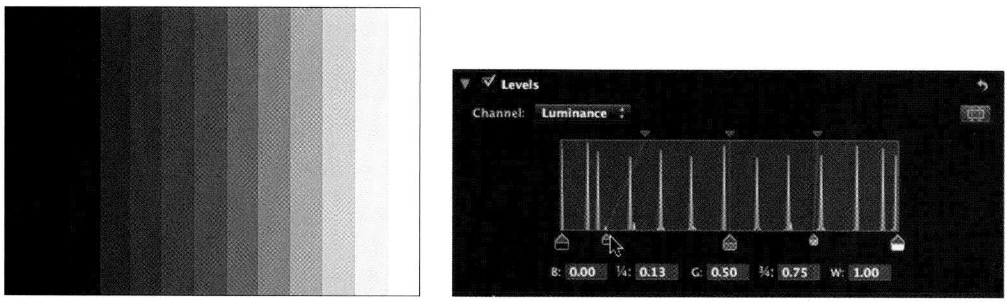

Lightening the one-eighth tones (bottom-left control to the left)

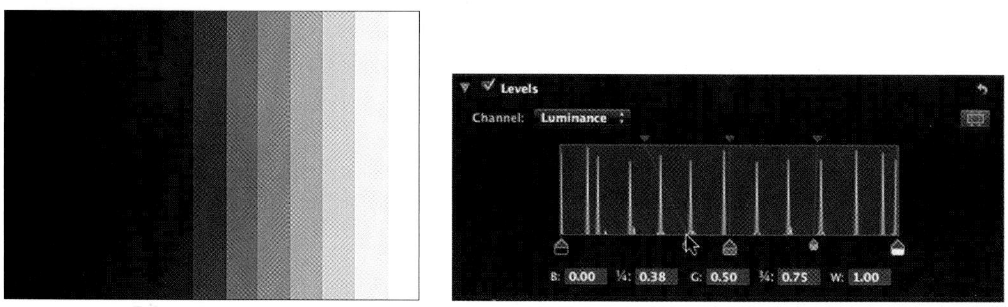

Darkening the three-eighth tones (bottom-left control to the right)

Figure 5.33: Adjusting the Quarter Tone control to the left from the bottom is giving the instruction to modify the one-eighth tone values to make them quarter tone values. Moving the bottom Quarter Tone slider halfway to the right will darken the three-eighths tones.

As shown in Figure 5.34, if you take the Highlight Brightness Levels slider and move it left from the bottom halfway toward the half tones, you are instructing Aperture to take the five-eighths tones and make them three-quarter tones, which would lighten them. If you move the control halfway toward white, you are saying make the seven-eighths tones appear as quarter tones, which would darken them.

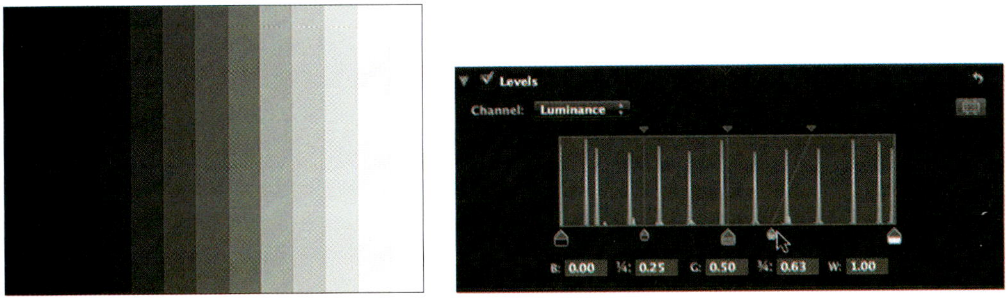

Lightening the five-eighth tones (bottom-right control to the left)

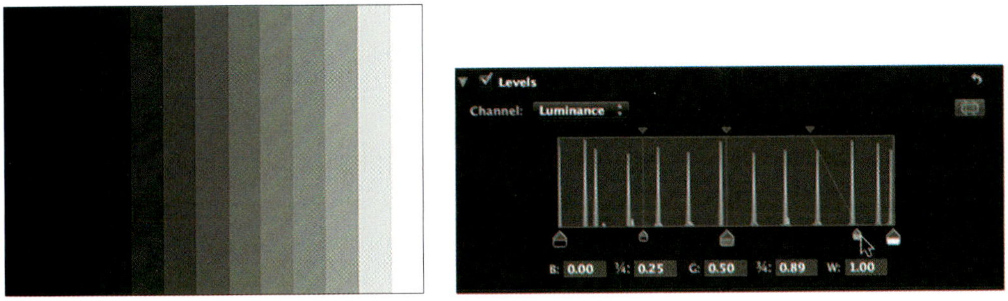

Darkening the seven-eighth tone (bottom-right control to the right)

Figure 5.34: Adjusting the Three-Quarter Tone control to the left from the bottom lightens the five-eighths tones while moving it to the right darkens the seven-eighths tones.

If you move the top and bottom controls so that the Quarter Tone control is a perfectly vertical line, it will have no effect on the image. Option+Click on a Quarter Tone control to reposition the entire slider.

> **Note:** The actual algorithm used for the Levels controls appears to create a curve within the selected tonal range, so this explanation is slightly simplified. However, following the concepts in this section will help you effectively use this advanced Levels interface.

Clicking the middle Levels Brightness control will move the Shadow Brightness Levels slider and the Highlight Brightness Levels slider with it, however, you can adjust the latter independently. This enables you to increase or decrease the contrast within certain tonal ranges. While this isn't quite as much control as Photoshop Curves offer, it is significantly more control than most Levels adjustments offer.

Let's put this information to practical use. To increase the contrast in the midtones of your image without affecting the darkest and lightest tones, move the tops of the Shadow Brightness Levels slider and the Highlight Brightness Levels slider away from the center. This is akin to creating an "S" curve in Photoshop Curves, as shown in Figure 5.35. If you move the top controls toward the center, you will decrease the contrast in the middle tones, akin to a "reverse S" curve. Alternatively, you can adjust the bottom controls and modify the range of tonalities in which you increase or decrease the contrast.

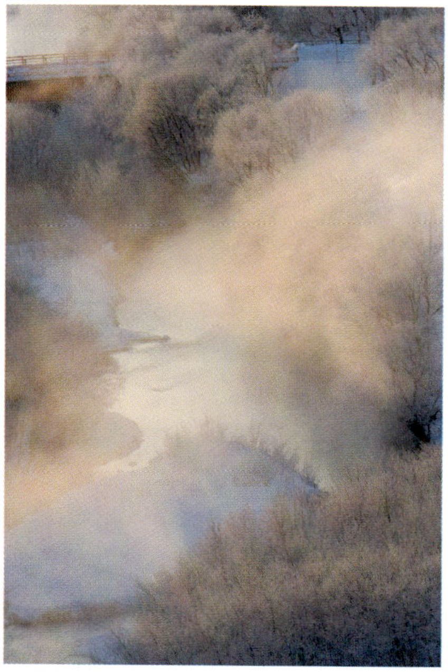

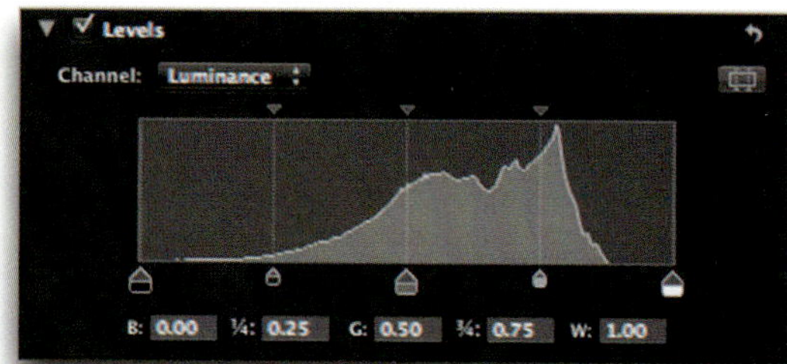

Original Image

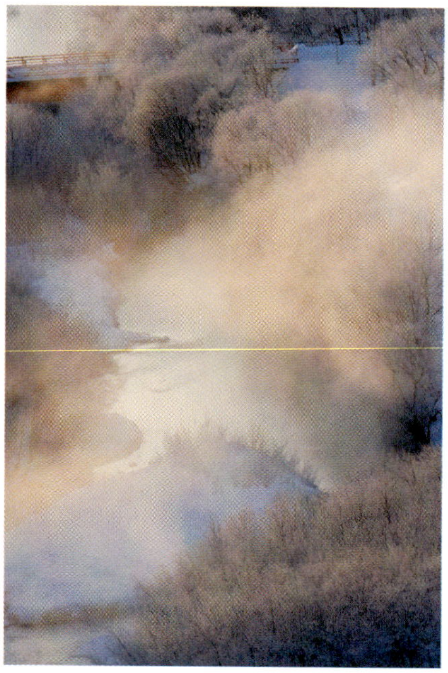

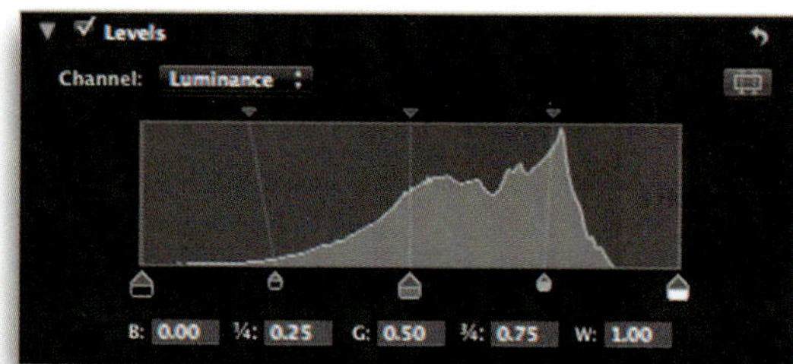

Increased Contrast

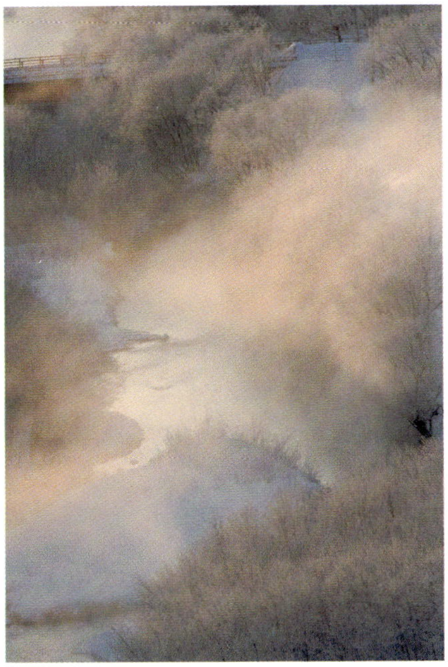

Reduced Contrast

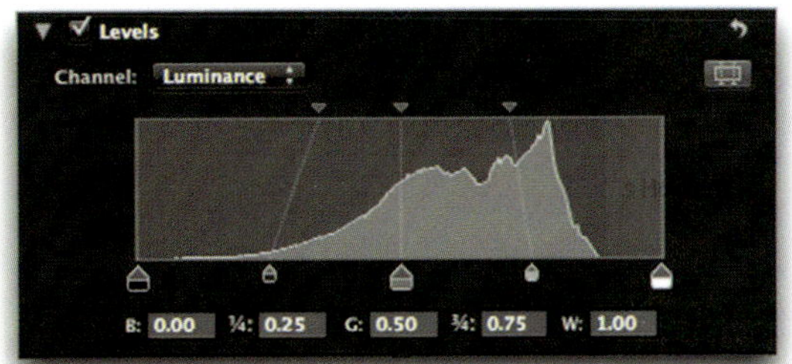

Figure 5.35: Adjusting the Quarter Tone controls away from the center increases the contrast within the midtones.

You can also use the Shadow and Highlight Brightness Levels sliders to lighten or darken a range of tones more or less than neighboring tones.

Note: Just reading about this can make the Quarter Tone controls sound very confusing. In reality, they're fairly easy to use. We've created a demo called `graybars.tiff` on the accompanying website (`www.sybex.com/go/apertureexposed`) that contains the same file we used for the demo figures in this section. Open the file and experiment with the Quarter Tone controls in Aperture. We think you'll be comfortable with this powerful version of Levels after you've used it a short time.

By carefully using the Exposure, Brightness, and Levels tools together, you can make some very impressive exposure modifications, even in cases where the contrast range of the scene appeared to be more than what a digital camera could capture. Figure 5.36 shows the initial digital capture of a volcano and the same image after using the three Tonal Adjustment filters. The detail that is visible within the image is impressive, and it took very little effort to dramatically improve the image.

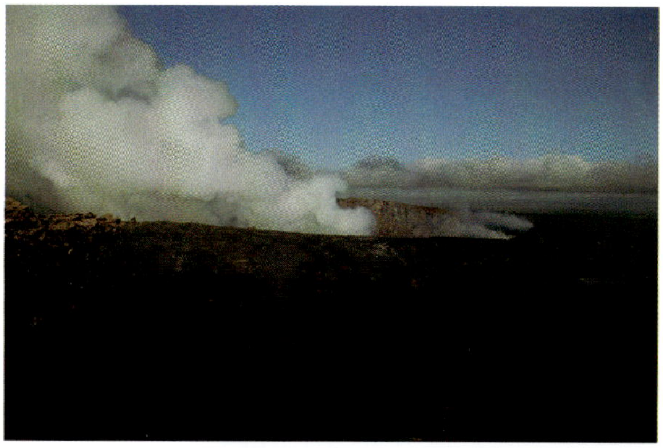

Before

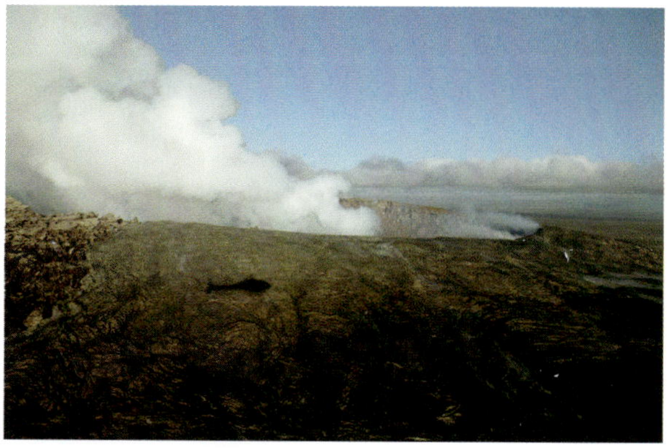

After

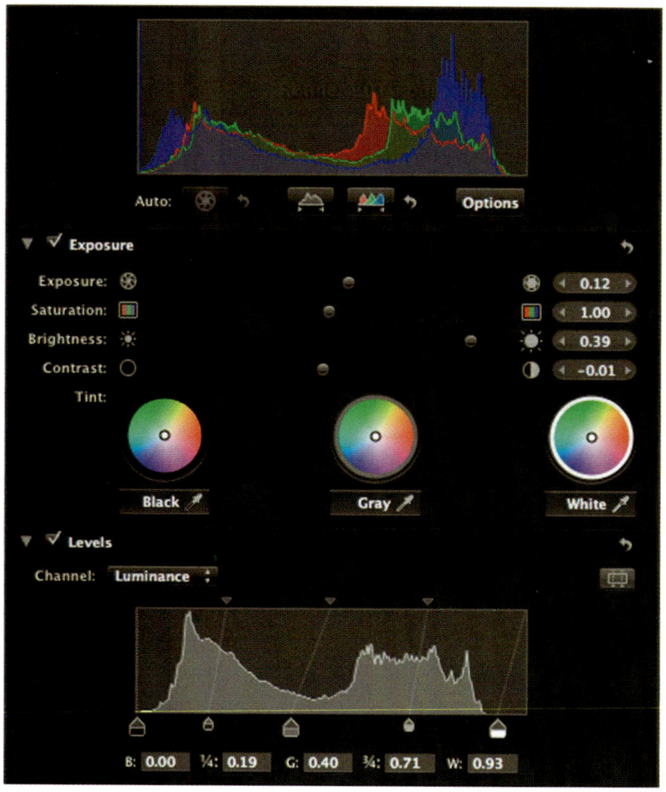

Figure 5.36: This picture came to life after using the Exposure, Brightness, and Levels tools in conjunction with one another.

Note: The volcano picture is also an excellent candidate for the Highlights & Shadows adjustment. In such cases, you can make corrections using one set of tools, such as we did here, and then create a second version and use other tools, such as Highlights & Shadows. Doing so will help you get a feel for the subtle differences among the tools and the results.

Adjusting Color Using Levels

To adjust color via the Levels controls, select a particular color channel from the pop-up menu. The controls work in the RGB space, so selecting a color channel means you will affect that color and its opposite. Therefore, adjusting the Red channel will affect the red and cyan tones; in the Green channel, green and magenta tones are altered; and in the blue channel, blue and yellow tones are affected.

With the Red channel selected, moving the Black Levels slider to the right will decrease the red and add cyan to the shadows. Moving the middle slider to the left will add red to the midtones, and moving it to the right will add cyan. Moving the White Levels slider to the left will add red to the highlights.

Note: Be aware that moving the end sliders can affect the contrast within the image.

Similarly, with the Green channel selected, moving the Black Levels slider to the right decreases green and adds magenta to the shadows. Moving the middle slider to the left will add green to the midtones and to the right will add magenta. Adjusting the White Levels slider to the left will add green to the highlights.

With the Blue channel selected, adjusting the Black Levels slider to the right will add yellow to the shadows and decrease blue. Moving the middle slider to the left will add blue to the midtones and to the right will add yellow. Moving the White Levels slider to the left will add blue to the highlights.

Using the White Balance Controls

You can use the White Balance controls to neutralize a color cast or to create a more pleasing color cast. If there is anything in your picture that you know should be neutral—that is the Red, Green, and Blue channel values should all be equal—select the Eyedropper tool in the White Balance pane and then click that part of your image. The point that you clicked will be remapped to be neutral and the remaining pixels in the image will be remapped accordingly, as shown in Figure 5.37. If you know you want a neutral image, it makes sense to shoot one frame with a neutral gray card in the picture. Then click the card with the eyedropper. Any color cast will be removed.

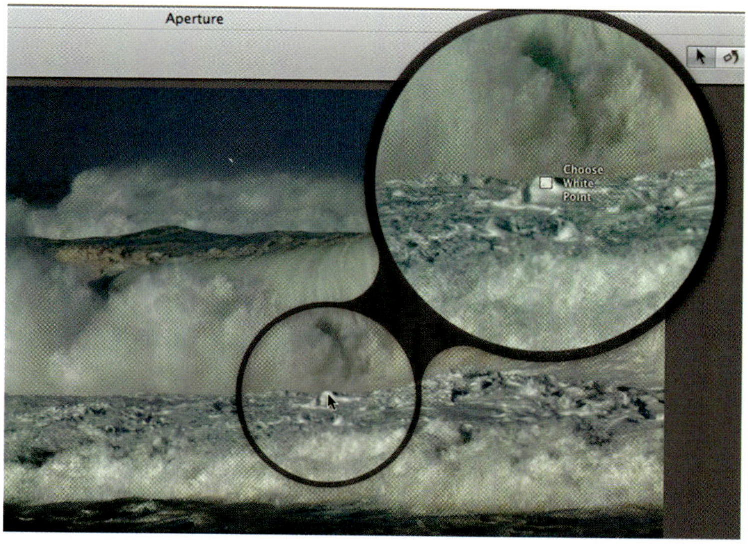

Before

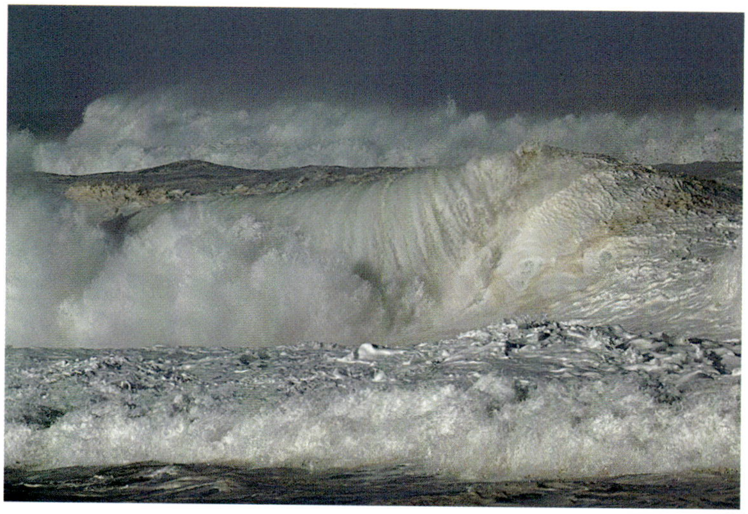

After

Figure 5.37: The White Balance eyedropper automatically opens the Loupe with a small square indicating the target pixels to use for the white point. Clicking the white foam with the White Balance eyedropper removed the color cast from this image.

While certain types of photography require neutral images, other types such as nature and travel photography often prefer to have a warm color cast to their images. You can subjectively alter the color cast by adjusting the Blue/Yellow and/or Green/Magenta sliders to alter the color cast within the picture. Although normally you will be making subtle changes this way, it's also possible to make dramatic changes as shown in Figure 5.38.

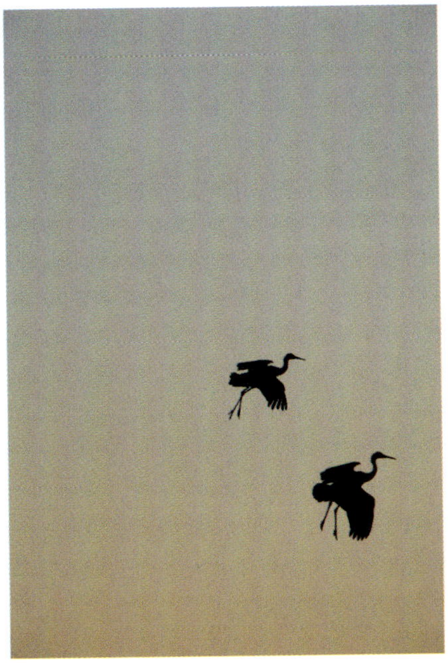

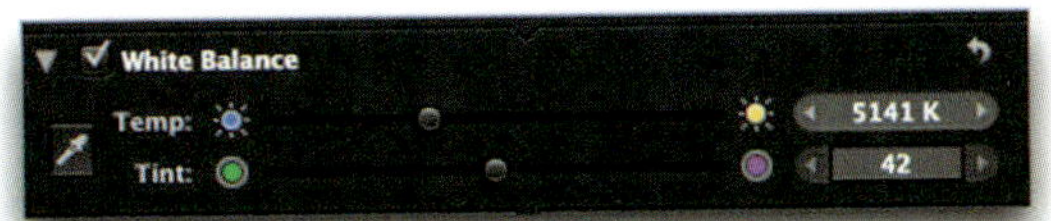

Before

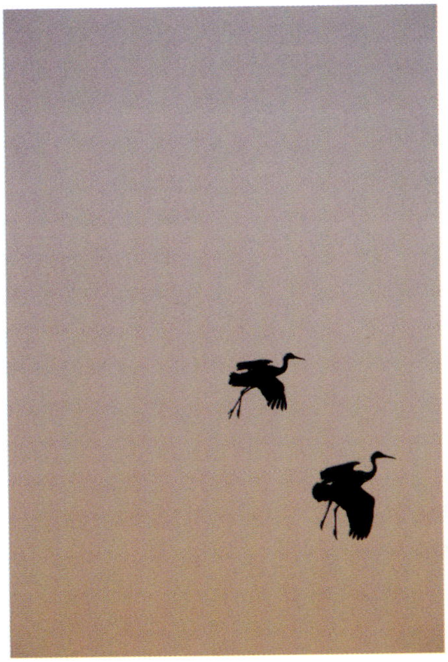

After

Figure 5.38: By adjusting the White Balance sliders, the colors of the sunset sky were dramatically changed in this picture.

The White Balance tool differs from the Tint adjustments in the Exposure pane in that each Tint adjustment affects only a subset of the tonalities; White Balance changes affect all pixels.

Using the Highlights & Shadows Filter

The Highlights & Shadows filter is a powerful tool for restoring detail in blocked-up shadow areas (areas that are so dark you can't discern details although they are there) or extremely light areas of images. It yields impressive results when used correctly, but it's not a panacea for every picture. It works by lightening dark areas and reducing the contrast among those tonalities and/or darkening excessively light areas and reducing the contrast in those tonalities. If used carelessly, this reduction in contrast has the potential to ruin a picture.

If you have an image that has blocked-up shadows, or very light but not completely blown-out light areas, try using the Highlights & Shadows filter before making other tonal adjustments in Levels.

To access the Highlights & Shadows filter click the Add Adjustments pop-up menu in the upper right corner of the Adjustments HUD or Inspector. Initially you'll see sliders for Highlights & Shadows that control the amount of lightening or darkening that will be applied to your image.

Click the Advanced expansion arrow to reveal more controls. High Tonal Width enables you to determine the range of light tones that will be darkened, beginning with the tone next to pure white. Pure whites will not be darkened. The Low Tonal Width control allows you to determine the range of dark tones to be lightened, beginning at the darkest tone after black. Pure black tones will not be lightened. By default these two sliders are set to a value of 40.0. It's a good idea to set these sliders to affect only those tonalities that need to be lightened or darkened in your image. Don't adjust pixels unnecessarily.

There is also a Radius slider. You adjust this slider in conjunction with the Amount slider. The lower the radius, the more noticeable the effect of the Highlights & Shadows adjustment, but also the greater the loss of contrast within the affected tones. The higher the Radius setting, the more contrast that is retained, but the effect of the adjustment will be less noticeable. In many ways, this is a visual adjustment that must be individually determined for each image, as shown in Figure 5.39. The Radius setting specifies how large an area around each pixel that Aperture will use to determine a pixel's tonality.

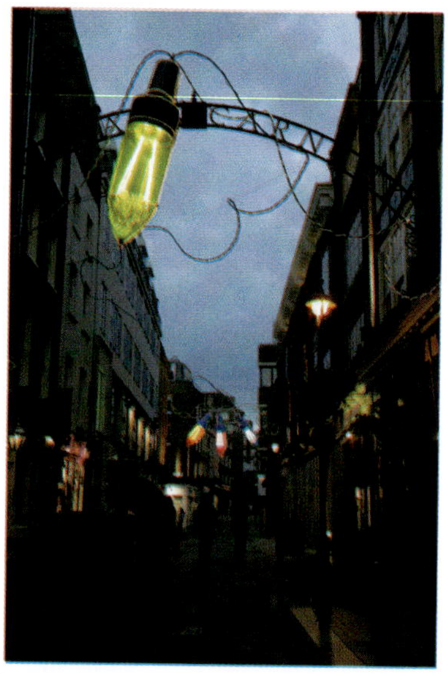

Original image

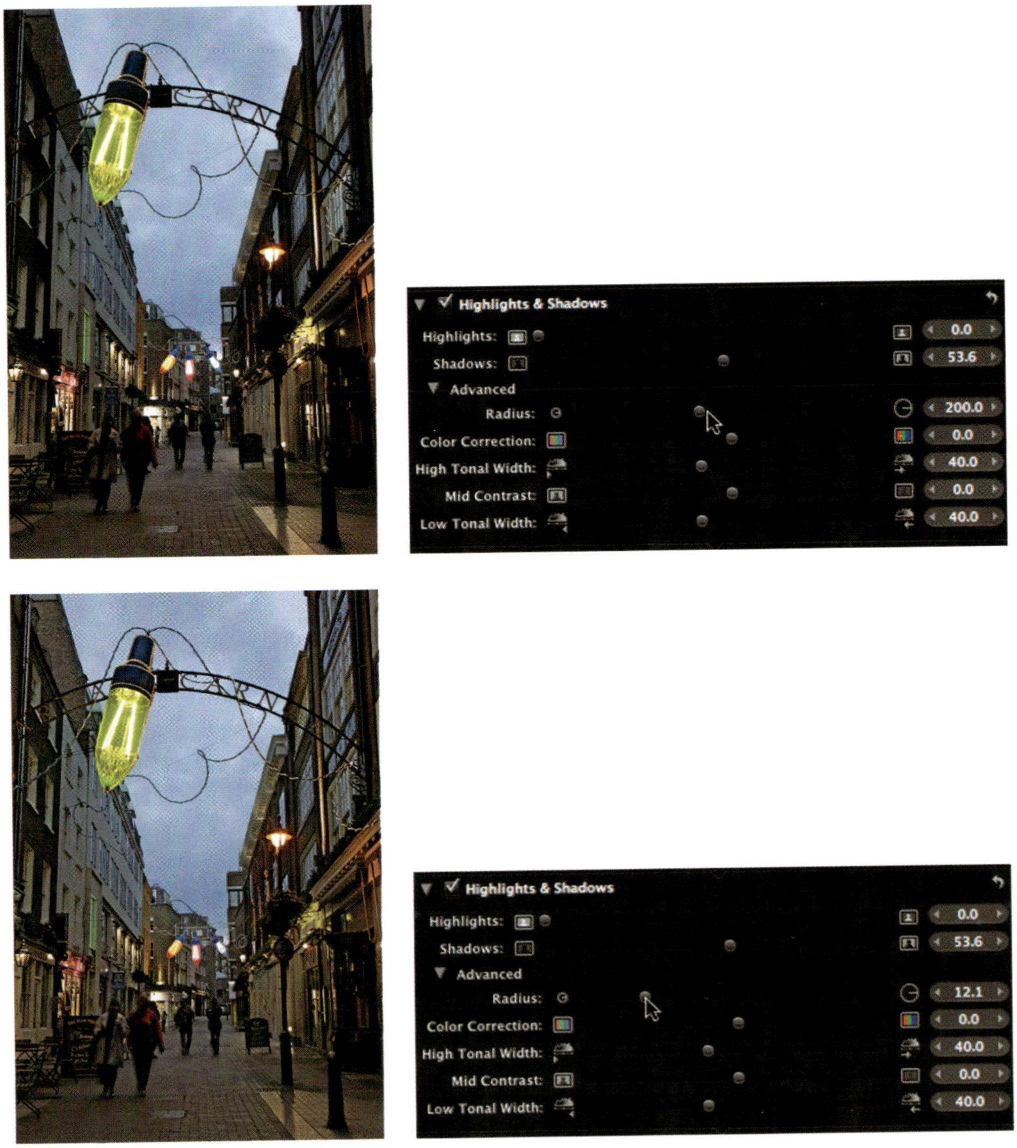

Figure 5.39: Varying the Radius setting in Highlights & Shadows can yield very different results in an image.

Note: Readers who are more technically inclined may be interested to know that Aperture converts the image from RGB color space to YIQ. It then uses the Radius setting to make a blurred version. Aperture then takes the Y, luminance, component from the blurred version to determine the amount of lightening or darkening to apply.

Use the Color Correction slider to adjust the amount of saturation applied via the Highlights & Shadows controls. The change is usually most noticeable in the saturation of the dark areas.

The last slider, Midtone Contrast, increases the contrast in the midtones by forcing more values toward the extremes. If you have adjusted only the shadows (or just the highlights) and then increase the midtone contrast, you may find that you have unintentionally overlightened or overdarkened values you were not planning to adjust. Try using the Quarter Tone controls in Levels instead. In some cases, it may be helpful to open the image in an external editor, such as Photoshop, and apply a curves adjustment.

Note: Once again, experimenting with these controls can be helpful. The file `graybars.tiff` on the accompanying website can be used to help visualize the effects of the sliders in the Highlights & Shadows adjustment. Note which tonalities change with each adjustment and the interactions among the sliders.

As you make your Highlights & Shadows adjustments, keep in mind that the goal is to enhance the visibility of detail in the deep shadows and the very lightest tonalities. You're not trying to adjust the exposure of the entire image. You can make Levels adjustments after Highlights & Shadows, as well as finessing the Brightness and Exposure sliders.

The Highlights & Shadows adjustment only works with RAW images.

Using the Monochrome Mixer

Aperture contains three filters that can quickly change the entire appearance of your image. The Monochrome Mixer enables you to convert the image to black and white, while the Sepia and Color Monochrome filters add an overall color wash to the image.

To access the Monochrome Mixer, click the Add Adjustments pop-up menu in the upper-right corner of the Adjustments Inspector or HUD. As shown in Figure 5.40, the default settings for the mixer are Red 30%, Green 59%, and Blue 11%. These settings refer to the percentage of information contributed by each channel to the final image. You can adjust the three sliders to whatever yields a striking black-and-white image. By varying the contribution from each channel, you can alter the contrast and draw attention to different parts of the image.

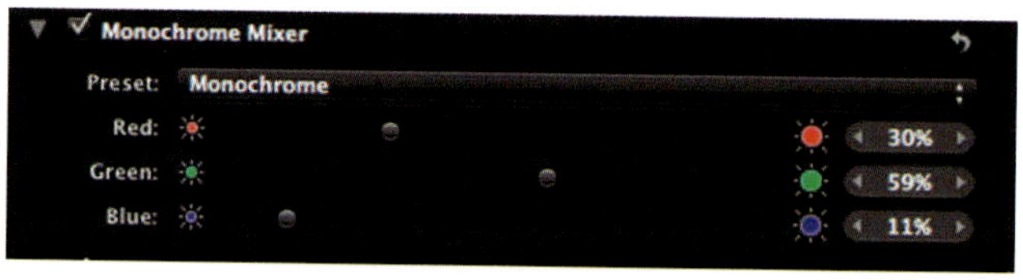

Figure 5.40: The Monochrome Mixer enables you to determine the percentage of information contributed by each color channel.

Aperture provides some preset combinations in a pop-up window that provide an easy starting place. Each filter sets the R, G, and B channels as shown in Table 5.1.

Table 5.1: Balance of the Monochrome Mixer Filters

Filter	Red	Green	Blue
Red Filter	100%	0	0
Orange Filter	50%	50%	0
Yellow Filter	34%	66%	0
Green Filter	0	100%	0
Blue Filter	0	0	100%

You can accept any of these presets as is, or you can select the one that comes closest to creating the look you want for your image and then modify it by further adjusting the sliders. If your image uses the full range of tonalities from black to white, it's likely that you'll want your Monochrome Mixer settings to add up to roughly 100 percent. However, if your image does not use the full tonal range, it's quite possible you may want to have the total be greater than 100 percent.

In some cases, you may need to tweak the Exposure and Brightness settings or the Levels adjustment because the color version may work best with one group of settings and a black-and-white version with a slightly different group of settings. It's a good idea to make certain the View > Highlight Hot Areas command is on to warn you if your settings are causing you to lose detail in any areas.

As shown in Figure 5.41, the results obtained by using the Monochrome Mixer are more dramatic than those obtained by simply desaturating the image. If your goal is to create a black-and-white image, the Monochrome Mixer is a fast way to achieve striking results.

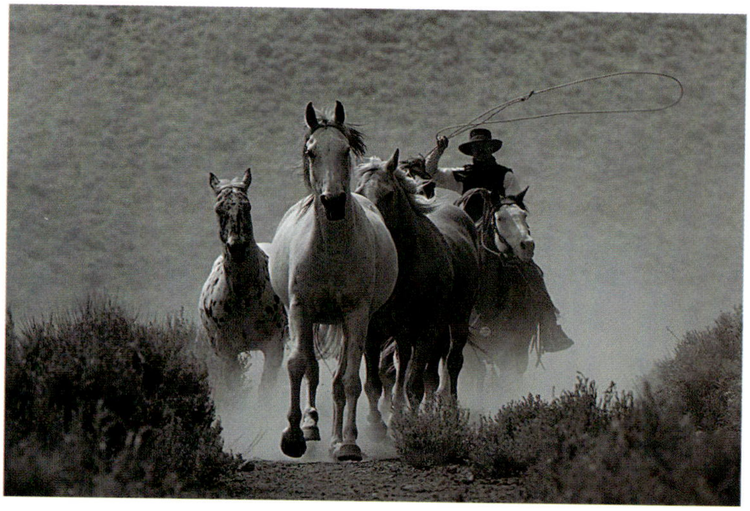

a

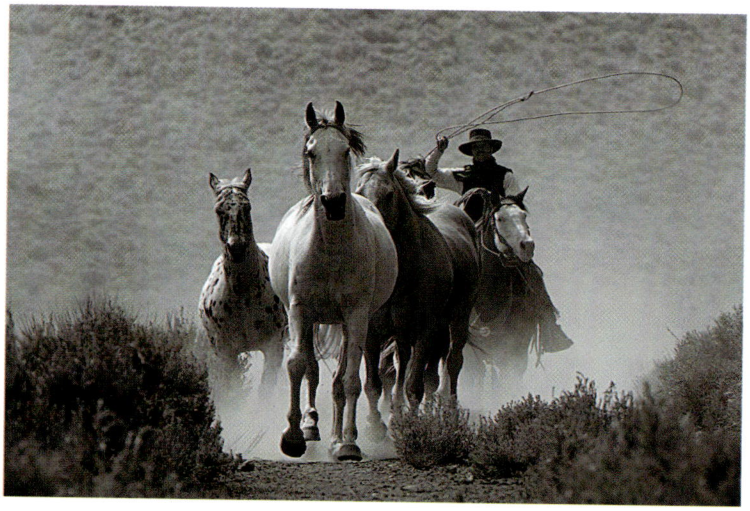

b

Figure 5.41:
Compare the bland results obtained by simply desaturating an image (a) with a version created using the Monochrome Mixer (b). For creating black-and-white pictures, the Monochrome Mixer is far superior.

Using the Sepia and Color Monochrome Filters

Both of these filters apply a color wash to your image. As shown in Figure 5.42, the Sepia filter is a preset color, whereas the Color Monochrome filter initially uses a default color but enables you to customize the color.

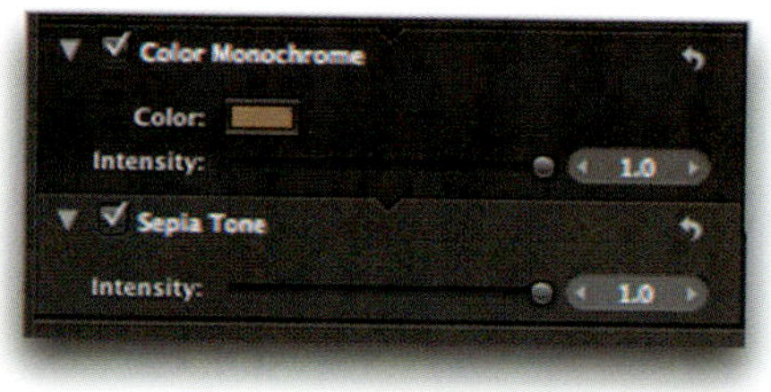

Figure 5.42:
The Sepia and Color Monochrome filters share similar controls.

The Sepia filter can be accessed through the Add Adjustments pop-up menu in the Adjustment Inspectors or HUD. With one click, you can convert your color image into a sepia-toned image. The Intensity slider enables you to reduce the effect, allowing some of the original color to come through.

You can use the Sepia filter without first converting the image to black and white, but you will get slightly different results if you do. Try using the Monochrome Mixer in conjunction with the Sepia filter. Then uncheck the box by the Monochrome filter. That will allow you to decide which version you prefer.

The Color Monochrome filter is accessed from the same pop-up menu. It also has an Intensity slider that can be used to allow some of the original color to show through. If you have also used the Monochrome mixer, then reducing the Intensity slider will result in a more black-and-white appearance.

The default color choice used by the Color Monochrome filter is slightly less harsh than the Sepia filter and yields very appealing results, as shown in Figure 5.43.

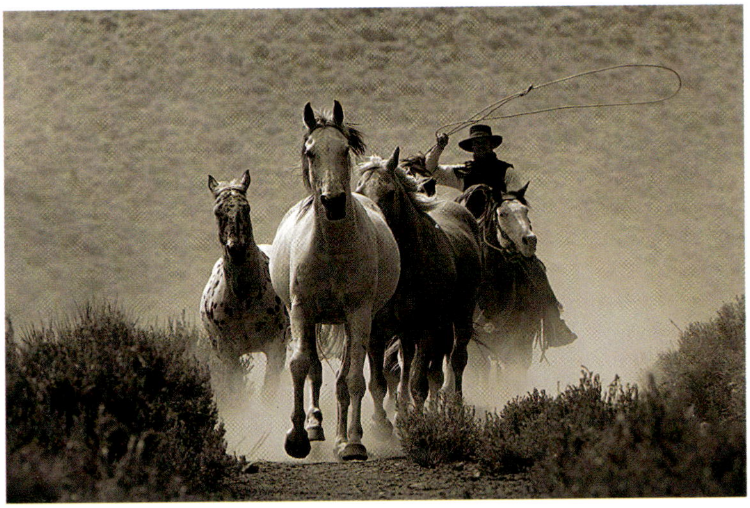

Figure 5.43: Using the default color, the Color Monochrome filter creates a very pleasing wash over your image.

If you want to create a unique look for your image, you may want to specify a custom color to use for the color wash. To do so, click the little color swatch by the word "color." A Colors dialog box, as shown in Figure 5.44, will appear.

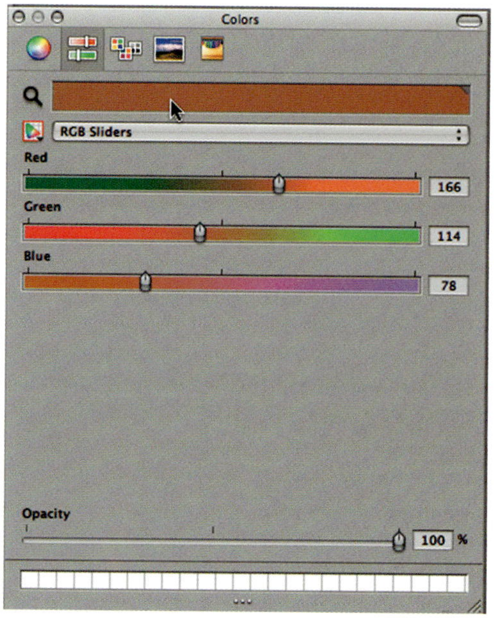

Figure 5.44: Using the Colors dialog box in the Color Monochrome filter, you can specify the exact color to use. The color appears in the sample next to the magnifying glass.

You can select the color by adjusting the RGB sliders until you find the desired color. If the color you want to use is in a different image or elsewhere on your computer, click the magnifying glass by the sample of the current selected color. Then place the magnifying glass on the target color and click. This color will then be set as the color to use for the wash.

By clicking the color sample in the Colors panel a small swatch will appear filled with the color. You can save this custom created color for future use by dragging the swatch to one of the white boxes at the bottom of the color dialog box as shown in Figure 5.45. To delete a color swatch, click a white box and drag it on top of the one you wish to delete.

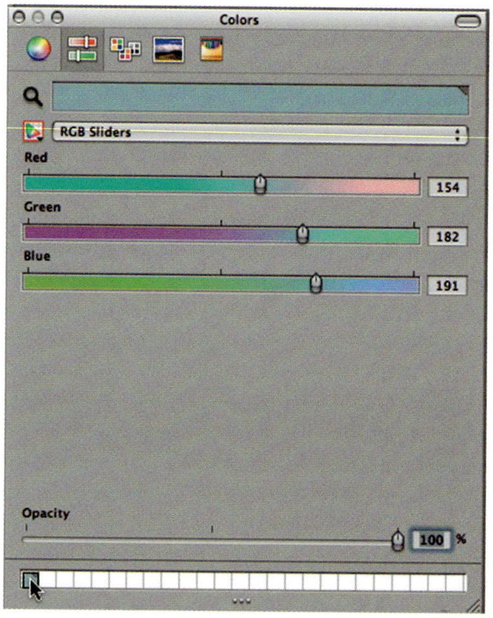

Figure 5.45: To save a custom color, drag a swatch to the squares at the bottom of the Colors panel. You can then use it with other images at any time.

Using Noise Reduction

As digital cameras continue to evolve, noise is becoming less of a problem than it used to be. However, even with the best of the newest cameras, very long exposures and/or high ISOs, as well as underexposed images that must be lightened extensively, can lead to noise in the images. Further, some camera bodies are more prone to noise than others. For most of our images, we leave the Auto Noise Compensation checked in the RAW Fine Tuning controls described earlier. However, noise can still be an issue in some images. To check whether noise is a problem in an image, use the Loupe tool as shown in Figure 5.46.

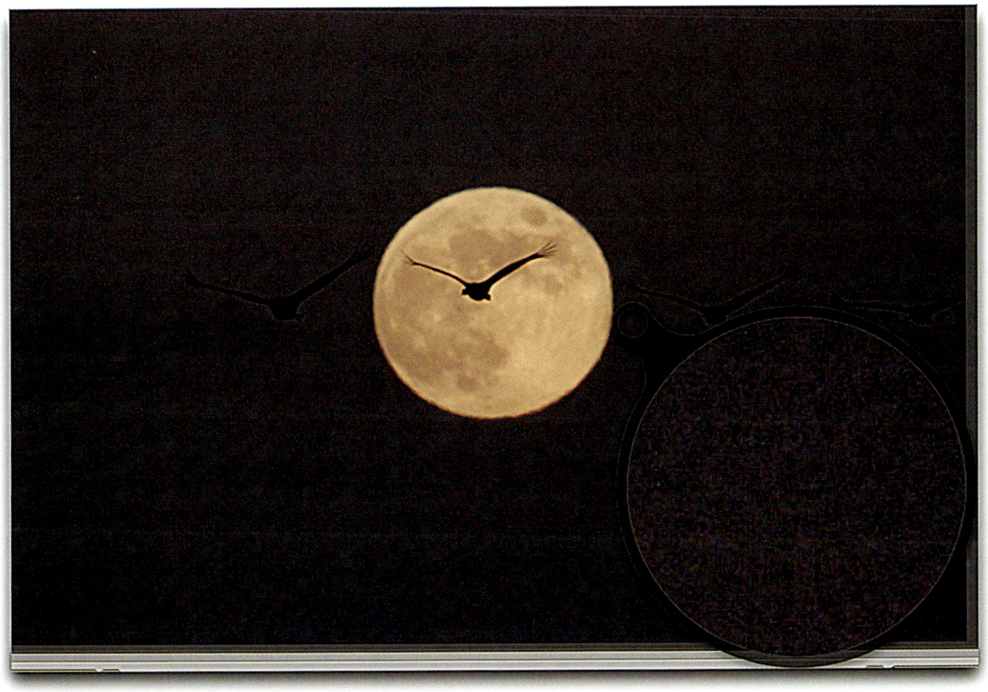

Figure 5.46: Noise can sometimes be a problem even with the best of the most modern cameras due to long shutter speeds, high ISOs, and/or underexposed images that must be lightened.

There are two types of noise. One is color noise, which leads to unexpected magenta, green, or blue pixels in areas that should have smooth colors. The other is luminance noise, which refers to unexpected dark and light areas in areas that should be tonally smooth. An image may suffer from one or the other or both. Color noise can be reduced by using the Chroma Blur controls in the RAW Fine Tuning controls, as described earlier in this chapter; luminance noise can be addressed via the Noise Reduction filter.

To access the Noise Reduction filter, click the Add Adjustments pop-up menu in the upper-right corner of the Adjustment pane. There are two sliders, a Radius slider and an Edge Detail slider. The greater the Radius setting, the more noise reduction you are applying. The higher the Edge Detail setting, the less noticeable the effect will be. There is a trade-off between the two because reducing noise means losing detail. Noise reduction is done by blurring certain pixels, and obviously when pixels are blurred, detail will be lost. Instructing Aperture to retain edge detail means that less noise reduction will be apparent. By clicking and dragging in the Value field, or clicking the right arrow, you can extend the range to 2.0.

The algorithm that Aperture uses for noise reduction determines a threshold value to define what to consider as noise. Small changes in luminance below that value are considered noise and are blurred to reduce the tonal variation. Changes above the threshold value are assumed to be an important part of your image—a detail or edge—and are sharpened. The greater the radius, the larger the local blur for the noise reduction. The greater the Edge Detail, the more sharpening that's applied. By clicking and dragging in the Value field you can extend the range of the effect. Figure 5.47 shows the image after noise reduction has been applied with a Radius setting of 2.10 and Edge Detail setting of 0.50.

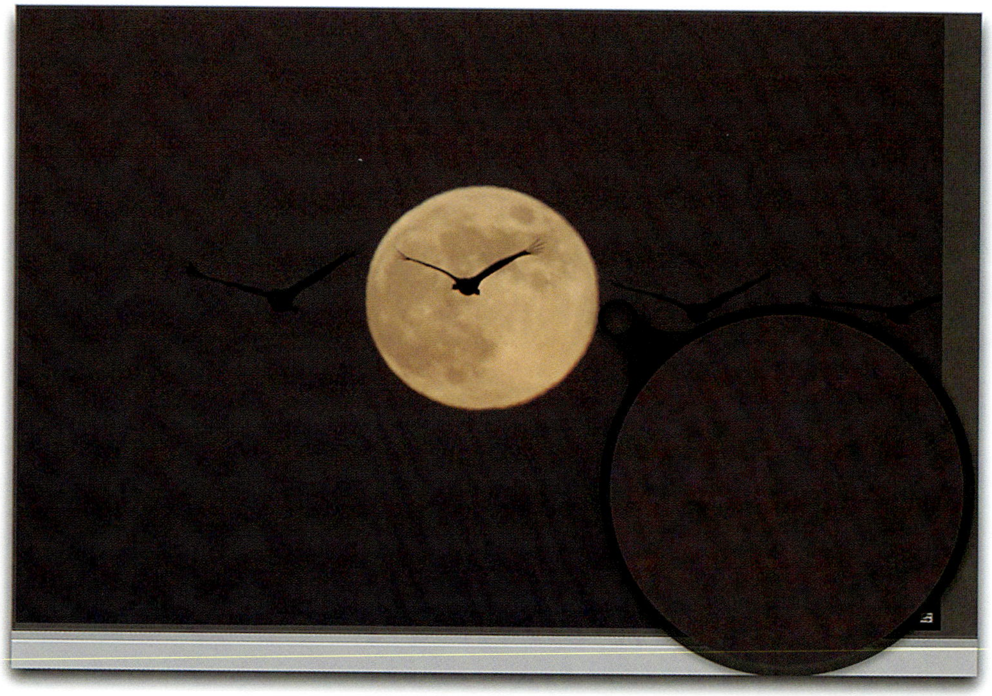

Figure 5.47: The Noise filter significantly reduced the noise in this image.

Many images have bothersome noise primarily in the darker portions of the image or in areas such as skies where the tonal and color variations are more obvious. In addition, the noise may occur primarily in one channel. With such images, it can be beneficial to open them in Photoshop and use a layer mask along with Photoshop's Noise Reduction filter to limit any potential loss of detail to areas where detail is less important. In addition, the Photoshop Noise Reduction filter enables you to apply the noise reduction on a per channel as-needed basis, which also helps to preserve detail. Alternatively, you may want to use a software program or plug-in specifically designed for noise reduction in particularly troublesome images

Using the Sharpen Filter

The sharpening done in the RAW Fine Tuning controls is essentially first pass sharpening to correct for softness introduced in the digital process. The Sharpen filter is used to further sharpen an image. However, it doesn't actually refocus the image to compensate for inadequate focusing or for camera or subject motion while the picture was taken. The Sharpen filter adds contrast to the edges within the image to give the illusion of increased sharpness. The contrast takes the form of the opposite color and tonal value, as shown in Figure 5.48. As a result, a white edge gets a black contrasting edge and a black edge gets a white contrasting edge. A light gray edge gets a dark gray edge applied, and so forth. Further, a red edge gets a cyan contrast, a green edge gets a magenta contrast, and a blue edge gets a yellow contrast. Nonpure tones also get their opposite color applied as a contrast.

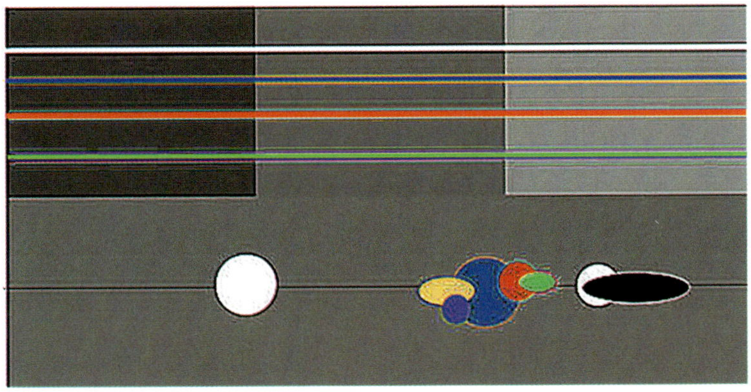

Figure 5.48: To create the illusion of increased sharpness, the Sharpen filter adds contrast to edges within the image.

The Sharpen filter is accessed from the Add Adjustments pop-up menu in the upper-right corner of the Adjustments pane. It has two controls. The first is an Intensity control that by default is set to 0.5 and extends from 0 to 1.0. By double-clicking in the Value field, or clicking the right arrow, you can extend the range to 2.0.

The second slider is the Radius slider. It controls how far out the contrast edge extends. By default, it is set to 1.0, although it extends from 0 to 20. By double-clicking in the Value field, you can extend the range all the way to 200, although it is unlikely you will ever need to do so. We prefer to use larger amounts and smaller Radius settings. However, the specific settings need to be determined according to the needs of the particular image. If overdone, digital sharpening leads to obvious halos and excessive contrast that can make the picture look grainy or bumpy.

The Sharpen filter in Aperture does a good job of applying small amounts of sharpening to an image when desired, as shown in Figure 5.49. Often we prefer to open our images in an external editor to apply sharpening because the actual amount of sharpening necessary will vary according to the file size. A large file of an image will require more sharpening than a small JPEG of the identical file. In addition, it can be beneficial to apply sharpening to only a portion of your image and not the background. You can do that by using advanced sharpening techniques in Photoshop. However, when speed is an issue, such as when you're generating a slideshow to show clients the images from a shoot, files can be very reasonably sharpened in Aperture.

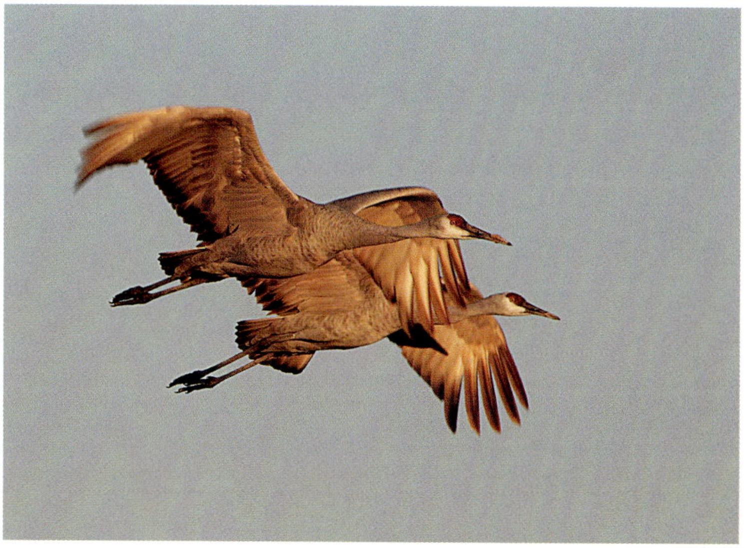

Before

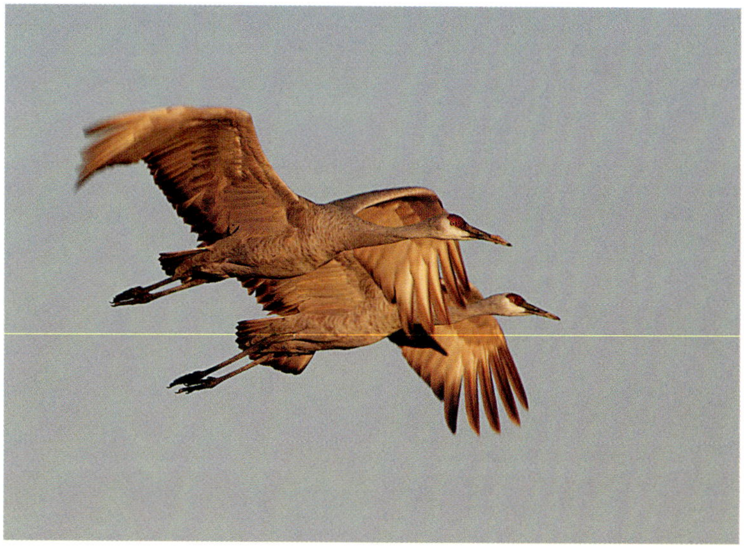

After

Figure 5.49: Using an Intensity setting of 0.77 and a radius of 1.37 visually sharpened and improved this image.

Batch Processing

Once you have set the various adjustments to optimize an image, Aperture makes it easy to repeat those adjustments on other images using the Lift and Stamp tools ( ).

To use the Lift and Stamp tools, first select the image that you have already adjusted. Next, click the Lift tool. A new dialog box will appear, as shown in Figure 5.50.

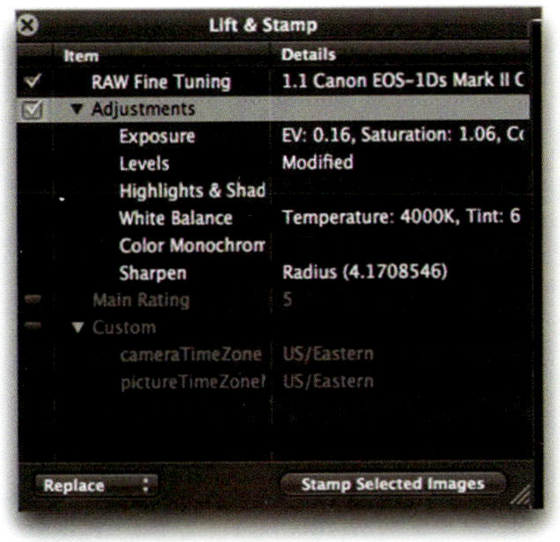

Figure 5.50: After you click the Lift tool, a dialog box appears listing the adjustments and custom metadata that are currently selected.

A check box and an expansion arrow appear by the words "Adjustments" and "Custom" in the Lift dialog box. To view the adjustments currently set within the Lift tool, click the Adjustments expansion arrow. If you don't want to copy the metadata and the RAW Fine Tuning adjustments, you can uncheck the Custom and RAW Fine Tuning boxes. (See Chapter 4, "Finding the Keepers," for more information on batch processing metadata.)

If you haven't used the Lift tool previously, it will contain the adjustments that are being used for the selected image. However, if you have used it previously, it will contain whatever adjustments were last used. To update the adjustments shown in the Lift dialog box, follow these steps:

1. Click the pop-up window at the bottom-left and choose Replace.

2. Click the selected image. The adjustments listed in the dialog box will be updated to reflect those in the selected image.

Note: If you Lift from one image and realize you lifted from the wrong image or simply change your mind, there's no need to start over and switch back to the Lift tool. Just press and hold the Option key while lifting from another image, and you can stamp the new adjustments

You can choose to copy all these adjustments to other images or just one or more of them. To delete those that you don't want to copy, choose the specific adjustment in the Lift dialog box and click Delete. To copy adjustments but not apply them, uncheck the corresponding box.

Note: The Crop and Straighten adjustments cannot be lifted and stamped. They must be applied individually to images.

Once you have the desired adjustments listed in the Lift dialog box, simply click the target image(s) to copy the adjustments to them. The Lift tool automatically switches to the Stamp tool. You'll notice a downward-pointing arrow, as shown in Figure 5.51, when you hover the cursor over the target image. After you click, the image thumbnail will be updated to reflect the new adjustments.

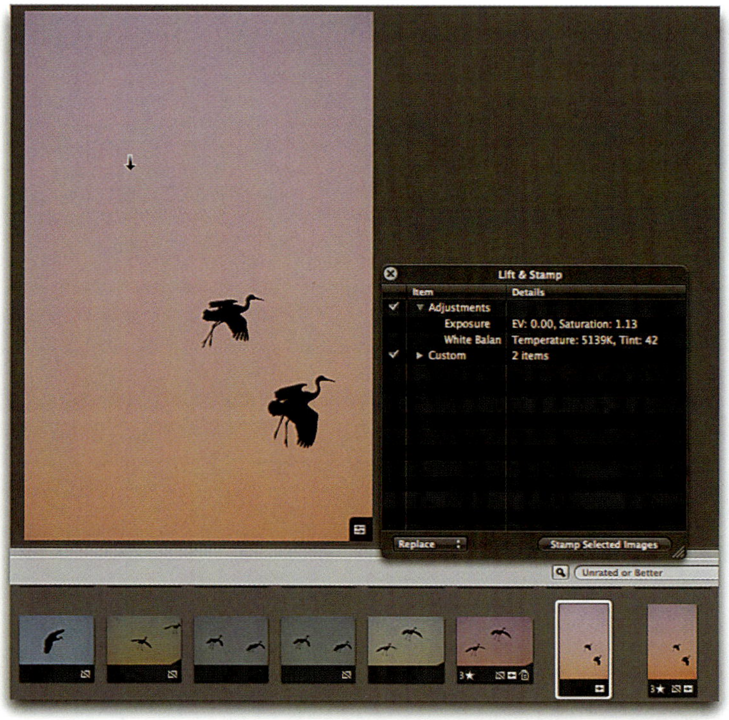

Figure 5.51: The Lift tool automatically becomes the Stamp tool and is indicted by a downward-pointing arrow as the cursor hovers over the target image.

If Add is selected in the Lift dialog box, these adjustments will be added to those already on the image, whereas if you choose Replace, the current adjustments will replace those that were already on the image.

Note: After you have batch-processed as many images as desired, be sure to click the Select tool in the toolbar. Otherwise, you might accidentally apply the adjustments to other images as you go on to your next task.

Understanding Masters and Versions

One of Aperture's major strengths is the ability to create and group multiple versions of your images. There are two types of versions in Aperture: versions that are tied to a master file and versions that are associated with a master file. For example, when you first import a file, Aperture automatically creates a version that is tied to the master file. As you might expect, when you modify this version, you do not actually modify the master. However, if you delete the version, Aperture will also delete the master file.

At the same time, you can manually make a new version that is associated with, but not tied to, the master. If you delete this version, Aperture will *not* delete the master file because this version is merely associated, and not tied to, the master. To make this type of new version, you have two options. If you want to start with a new version from the master image, with no adjustments applied, select any version of the image and choose Image > New Version From Master (Option+G) or click the New Version From Master icon ( ) in the toolbar. You would use this command if you were making two versions of an image, one in color and one in black and white, because each version would have different adjustments. If you have already made some adjustments to a version and want to use that version as the starting point for a new version, select that version and choose Image > Duplicate Version (Option+V) or the Duplicate Version icon ( ). You could use this command to experiment with an image after you had it adjusted to a point that you're happy with it, or you could use it to do before/after comparisons, as shown in Figure 5.52.

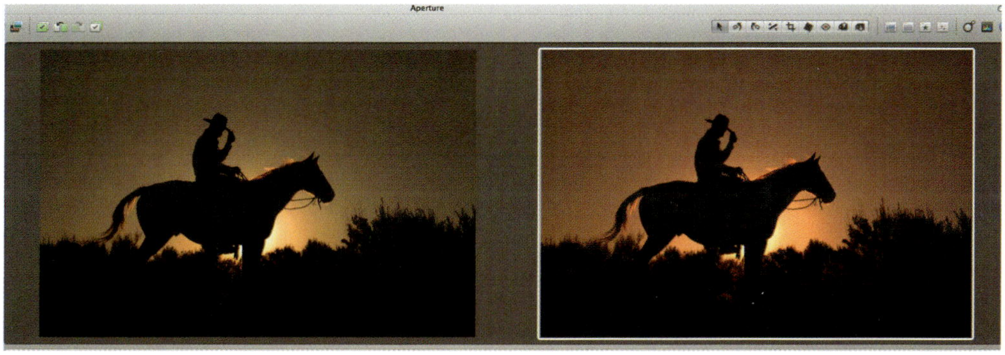

Figure 5.52: Viewing two or more versions of the same image simultaneously makes it easy to compare the effects of various adjustments.

When you open an image in an external editor, which we will cover in Chapter 6, Aperture will create a new version of your image that is tied to a new master file. It does so because external editors, such as Photoshop, can't understand Aperture's internal representation of its image adjustments. Aperture has to make a new version, tied to either a PSD or TIFF file, for your editor to read. If you try to delete this version, Aperture will remove the new master file.

One other issue with versions is how they relate to stacks. By default, when you make a new version of an image (either by making a new version from the master, duplicating a version, or opening the version in an external editor), Aperture stacks it with the original version. Similarly, when you first import an image, as we covered in Chapter 2, "Importing and Organizing Your Images," you have the option to *autostack* your images. With this option, Aperture automatically makes stacks of similar versions (based on the time the images were taken) of an image. The benefit to keeping your versions stacked is that all of your versions are grouped together. It is possible to extract an individual version from a stack, even if it is associated with but not tied to a master image, but generally there is no reason to do so.

You might be wondering what happens if you have a stack of images and the stack contains a black-and-white version plus a color version of your image. The color version is the stack pick, and you want to place the black-and-white version onto a Light Table. Aperture only allows you to place the stack pick onto a Light Table, book, web gallery, etc. Your first impulse might be to extract the black-and-white version from the stack and to place that version onto the Light Table. However, there is a better way.

Album picks let you override a stack pick for a particular album. Each stack can have its own album pick, and the album pick varies per album. In this example, you would make the black-and-white version the album pick in the Light Table. To do so:

1. Switch to the Light Table.
2. Expand the stack (select it and press Shift+K).
3. Select the black-and-white version.
4. Choose Stacks > Set Album Pick (⌘+|).

When you drag the image to the Light Table, Aperture will place the black-and-white version instead of the color version. One important point to note is that if you want to place the black-and-white version as well as the color version, two versions, in the same stack, you will need to extract one of those versions from the stack because Aperture won't let you place two or more versions from a stack onto a Light Table, book, etc. To place another version from a stack, in addition to the stack pick or album pick, follow these steps:

1. Switch to the Light Table or other document in which you want to use multiple versions.
2. Expand the stack (select it and press Shift+K).
3. Select the second (or higher) version that you want to place.
4. Choose Images > Duplicate Version (Option+V).
5. Select the duplicate version that you just selected, and make sure that only that version is selected (if the Viewer is set to Multi, you'll see only one image in the Viewer).
6. Choose Stacks > Extract Item (Option+Shift+K).

You will have a separate nonstacked version in this album that you can place onto your document.

Aside from the previous case, you will want to leave your versions stacked whenever possible to keep your versions grouped together. Unfortunately, working with stacked images can be somewhat confusing. Follow these guidelines when you're working with stacks:

- To move a stack of images to another album or project, the stack can be open or closed. If the stack is open, select the entire stack and drag and drop it to its destination. If the stack is open, and you select a version and drag and drop it to its destination, Aperture will still move the entire stack. You cannot move an individual version that is part of a stack to another album. As you might expect, holding down Option will toggle between Move and Copy.

- To delete a particular version permanently, expand the stack and select only that version (make sure no other image has a white selection rectangle around it). Choose File > Delete Version (⌘+Delete). If the version has a master file tied to it, Aperture will ask if you're sure that you want to remove this version.
- To delete a stack and all versions permanently, close the stack and choose File > Delete Master Image And All Versions.
- To remove a stack from an album, close the stack, select it, and either press Delete or choose Images > Remove From Album. This will remove the stack from that particular album, but it will not delete the stack and versions from the project, nor will it affect any other albums.

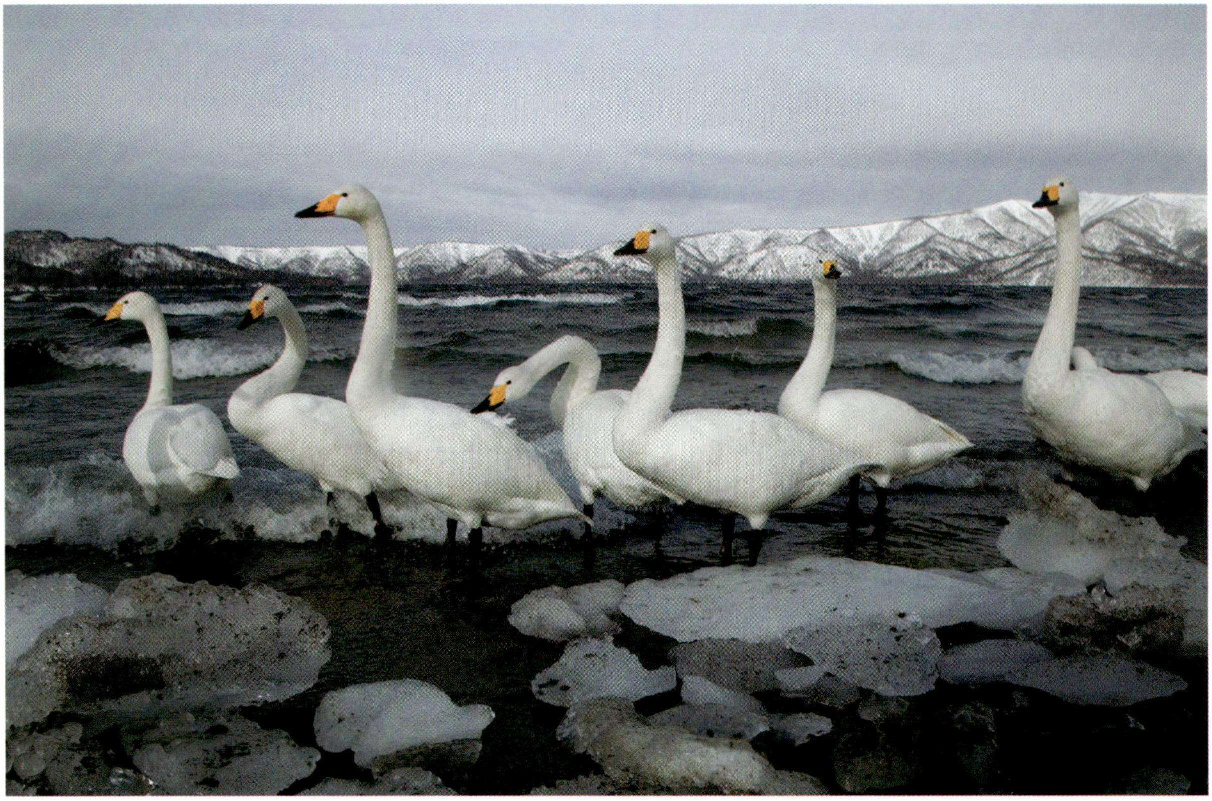

Exporting Images

Aperture is a feature-rich program; nonetheless, there will be times when you'll want to export your images. For instance, you might want to send images to a client, email them, add them to a Keynote presentation, or use an application other than Aperture to print them. At other times, you may need to open your images in an external editor such as Photoshop to perform advanced editing and/or compositing. When you complete a project, you may want to export the project itself and store it offline. Aperture makes it easy to move your images in and out of its library.

6

Chapter Contents

Opening Images in an External Editor (Photoshop)

Although you can make many image adjustments within Aperture, there are times when you need to make more advanced adjustments or perhaps make a composite. Aperture enables you to smoothly transition between the two programs, and it seamlessly integrates the changes you make in an external editor into a new full-size version of your image.

Specifying the External Editor

To open an image in Photoshop, or any other external editor, you must first establish that program as your external editor. To do so, follow these steps:

1. Go to Aperture > Preferences.
2. In the Preferences dialog box, click the Choose button under the External Editor box, as shown in Figure 6.1.

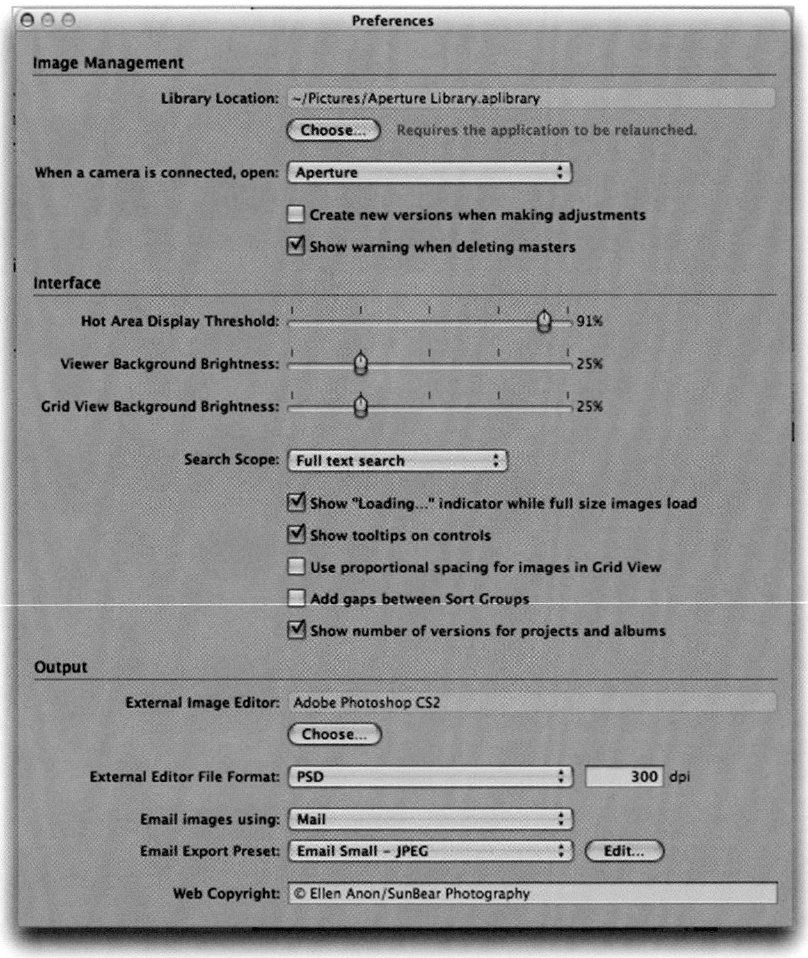

Figure 6.1: Open the Preferences dialog to set the external editor from your applications folder.

3. A new dialog box will appear listing all the applications on your computer. Navigate to the desired program.
4. Click Select.
5. Select the file type for these images, generally TIFF or PSD. The file type you choose is largely a matter of personal preference.
6. Specify the dots per inch resolution to use. Typically we use 300 since that's the resolution we use for printing.

The file that's generated when you open an image with an external editor will have the same name as the master file, but it will have a different extension.

Note: If you shoot with an original Canon 1Ds, you should specify PSD as the file format to use when opening files with an external editor. Choosing PSD rather than TIFF will avoid confusion since the Canon 1Ds uses TIFF extensions for the RAW files.

If you have opted to use the PSD format, make certain that in the Photoshop Preferences > File Handling you check Always in the box by "Maximize PSD And PSB File Compatibility." If you don't Aperture may use only one layer from the Photoshop file or none at all.

Note: If the Open With External Editor command does not appear in the contextual menus and is grayed out in the Images menu, you haven't specified your external editor.

You can't request to open the image in RAW format in another RAW converter, such as Adobe Camera Raw. You must have Aperture convert the RAW file and then further modify the TIFF or PSD version of it in the external editor. You can export the master file and then open it using another RAW converter, which we'll discuss later in this chapter; however, doing so will create two copies of the file, thereby doubling the storage requirements.

Note: For convenience, we'll often refer to opening images in Photoshop in this section, but the concepts and procedures apply to whatever external editor you set.

Opening Images in Photoshop

Once you have established the program to use as the external editor, going back and forth between Aperture and Photoshop is easy. To open an image in Photoshop, select the image and do one of the following. (We list the various ways to access this command since different readers will prefer one approach over another.)

- Press Shift+⌘+O.

- From the main menu, choose Images > Open With External Editor.
- Right-click/Control-click the image, and choose Open With External Editor.

Aperture will convert and create a new version of your image and open it in Photoshop. This new version is actually a new master file linked to the original.

Note: Because Aperture converts the image when it opens it in an external editor, it generates a new file, either a TIFF or a PSD. These are master files that are linked to the original master file. Due to the fact that they are complete files, they take up considerably more room in your Aperture library than versions that are made using only Aperture-based tools.

We prefer to set the Main Viewer to Multi, as discussed in Chapter 3, "Viewing Images." That way Aperture will display the Photoshop version of the image next to the Aperture version so you can compare the results, as shown in Figure 6.2. In this particular image, we used Photoshop to remove some of the branches in front of the owl and used a layer mask to apply more midtone contrast to just the owl.

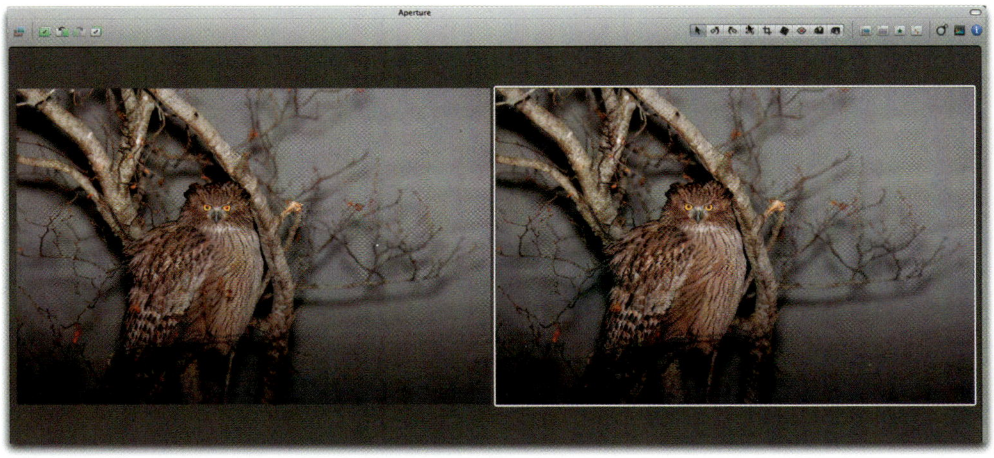

Figure 6.2: Aperture creates a new version of your image that you then modify in Photoshop. By setting the Main Viewer to Multi, you can readily compare before and after versions of your image.

Note: If you are in Full Screen mode when you tell Aperture to open the image in Photoshop, Aperture will automatically switch to the standard layout view.

Edit the image in Photoshop as desired. You can, and should in most cases, use layers for your adjustments. When you are happy with the results, click Save. Aperture will automatically update the version to reflect the changes you made in Photoshop. It may take a minute or so for the image preview to update.

Note: If you click Save As instead of Save when you save a file in your external editor, your new file will not exist within your Aperture library. To view it in your Aperture library, you'll have to import it.

If you have more than one version of an image that you open in Photoshop, you might want to rename one or both of them for ease of identification. You can do so by using the Metadata Inspector. Follow these steps to manually rename a file:

1. After opening the image in Photoshop, click Save when you have finished modifying the image.
2. Wait until Aperture has updated the version, then select it in the Browser.
3. If the Inspectors are not visible, press I.
4. Rename the file as desired.
5. Press Return.

While you are working within Aperture, you won't have access to the layers you created in Photoshop. However, if you reopen that version in Photoshop, all the layers will be intact! But if you make additional changes in Aperture on that version and then open it in an external editor, the layers will be gone because Aperture will generate a new version to send to Photoshop.

Understanding when Aperture will let you access a layered file and when it won't can be confusing.

- If your original master file was a layered file from Photoshop, and you have not made any adjustments to it within Aperture and its file format matches the file format selected in the External Editor File Format pop-up menu in the Preferences window, Aperture will send the layers to Photoshop. But if you've applied any adjustments to the file in Aperture, or the file format doesn't match what you've specified in the Preferences, then Aperture will send a flattened version of the file to Photoshop.
- If you use the Export Master command on either a master or a previously externally edited layered version, the version that Aperture exports will have layers.
- If you opt to use Export Version, the version that is exported will be flattened.

Note: If you open a file using Photoshop more than once, it's a good idea to unstack your files; otherwise Aperture creates a new version each time you try to use Photoshop on the file. You can quickly become inundated with versions. Even if the versions are unstacked, and you make adjustments in Aperture after the modifications you made in Photoshop, and then seek to do more in Photoshop, Aperture will create a new version.

Common Situations When Using Photoshop Is Beneficial

Aperture contains the tools you need for most basic image adjustments, but when you need to make more extensive or targeted adjustments, you'll want to open the image in a program, such as Photoshop.

For example, removing small dust spots in smooth toned areas is easy with Aperture; however, you'll probably want to use Photoshop for more complex cloning and healing techniques, such as removing an object. Similarly, you may want to take advantage of the chromatic aberration, vignetting, and perspective corrections available within the Lens Correction filter in Photoshop. In fact you might want to use any of the tools, filters, transformations, adjustments, and masking capabilities that are not available within Aperture.

All the adjustments made within Aperture are global adjustments, meaning that they are applied to the entire image. When you want to make adjustments targeted to just portions of your image, you'll need to open the image in Photoshop and use layer masks.

As we'll discuss in Chapter 7, "Printing," you may want to use Photoshop to prepare your image for printing. By using Photoshop, you can apply targeted sharpening to only those areas you want to sharpen rather than the entire image. That way your subject can be sharpened but the background can remain slightly softer to help it recede. With targeted sharpening there is also less chance of sharpening background noise in large areas that should be smooth such as skies.

Of course, any time you want to create composites or apply more artistic, creative effects, you'll want to use an external editor too.

Fortunately, Aperture makes it easy to use an external editor and still keep track of your files within your Aperture library. Just remember that every time you send an image to Photoshop, you pay a price. That price is the significant increase in storage space required to hold all your full-sized Photoshop versions.

Exporting Images

When you want to further modify your images using programs other than your external editor, use them in other applications such as Keynote, or present them to clients, you'll need to export your images. In addition, Aperture provides an easy way to email your images using export presets that we'll cover shortly.

When exporting an image, you can export either the master file or a version. Exporting the master file creates a copy of the original unmodified file outside the Aperture library, whereas exporting a version generates a copy reflecting all the modifications you applied in Aperture. The original master and/or version remain within Aperture. You can specify the file format for the copy, resize the file, apply profiles, add a watermark, and include metadata such as IPTC captions, keywords, and copyright information.

Note: It's important to use Mac OS X 10.4.4 or later, because earlier versions did not provide support for keywords upon export.

To simplify the export process, Aperture includes a set of export presets to use when exporting versions.

Using Export Presets with Versions

Export presets are groups of commonly used combinations of export settings such as resolution, file format, bit-depth, metadata, and watermark. Using the presets saves you the time required to specify every variable every time you export an image. Aperture ships with some default presets, but you can easily create your own. For example, if you commonly send images to a stock agency, you can create a preset containing the appropriate settings for those images. Then, each time you want to export images to send to your stock agency, you can simply select that preset.

Establishing the Export Settings

To access the export presets, go to Aperture > Presets > Image Export. A dialog box as shown in Figure 6.3 appears containing all the presets. You can click any of the presets and see what settings each contains and modify them as desired using the options in the right half of the box.

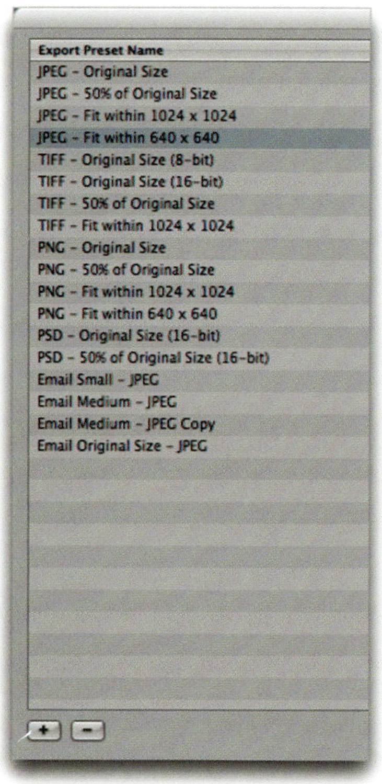

Figure 6.3: Aperture contains a variety of preset options to use when exporting images.

To customize a preset, use the pop-up menus in the right side of the dialog box. For example, you may want to specify Adobe RGB 1998 or ProPhoto as your ColorSync Profile for TIFF – Original Size 16-bit. This pop-up menu contains all the profiles on your computer. Scroll through them to select the one you want to use. In Figure 6.4, we have selected ProPhoto to be associated with the TIFF – Original Size (16-bit) export preset. We usually prefer to use Black Point Compensation, so we leave that checked.

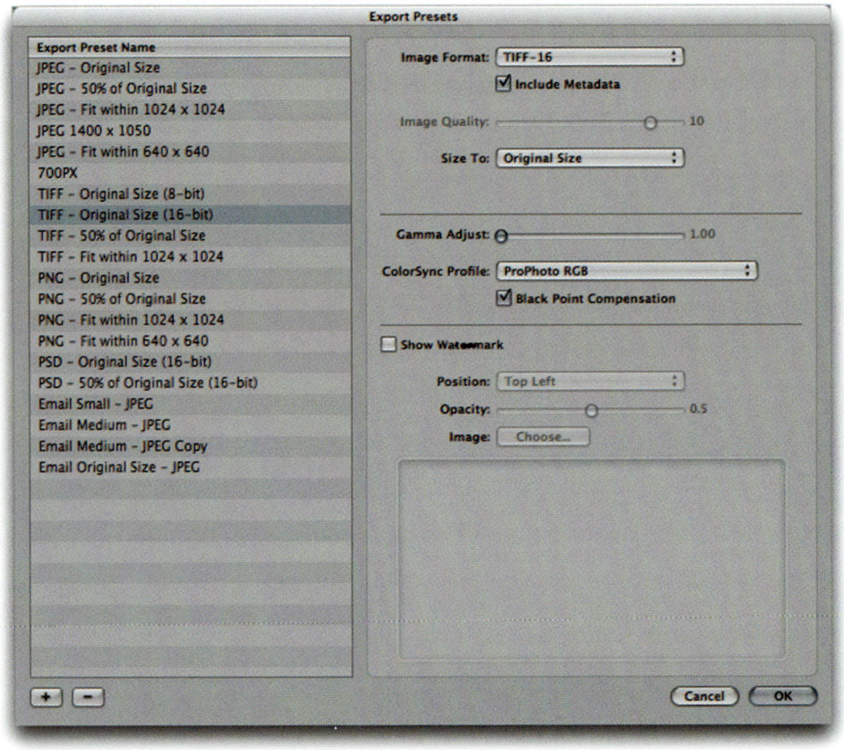

Figure 6.4: You can customize any of the presets for the file format, size, color sync profile, and watermark of your choice.

Because we usually prefer our small email images to be 500 pixels rather than 640, we modified the Email Small – JPEG setting to specify 500 for width and height in the Size To options, rather than the default values of 640. You can specify whatever values you prefer.

Note: Setting the height and width values to 500 × 500 will not change the actual aspect ratio of your image. Rather, it determines the maximum height or width for your image and the other dimension will automatically be adjusted accordingly.

You may want to create variations of these settings for specific clients or frequent usages. To create additional presets, take these steps:

1. Click the + button at the bottom left of the dialog box. This will duplicate the highlighted preset.
2. While the name box is highlighted, rename the preset.
3. Modify the settings as desired. You can specify sizes for any of the file formats, not just JPEGs. You could, for example, create a preset that saves files at 1000 × 1000, but in TIFF format. You can resize in inches, pixels, or as a percentage of the original size.
4. Specify the dots per inch (dpi) resolution: We typically use 300 dpi for our images that we'll print and 96 for images used in emails and/or slideshows.
5. Click OK.

In Figure 6.5, we have created a new JPEG setting to correspond to the resolution of our projector that is 1400 × 1050. We named the preset JPEG 1400 × 1050. We unchecked the metadata box and modified the width and height in the Size To options to 1400 × 1050. Now when we export images for use with this projector, the files will be the correct size, resolution, and color sync profile.

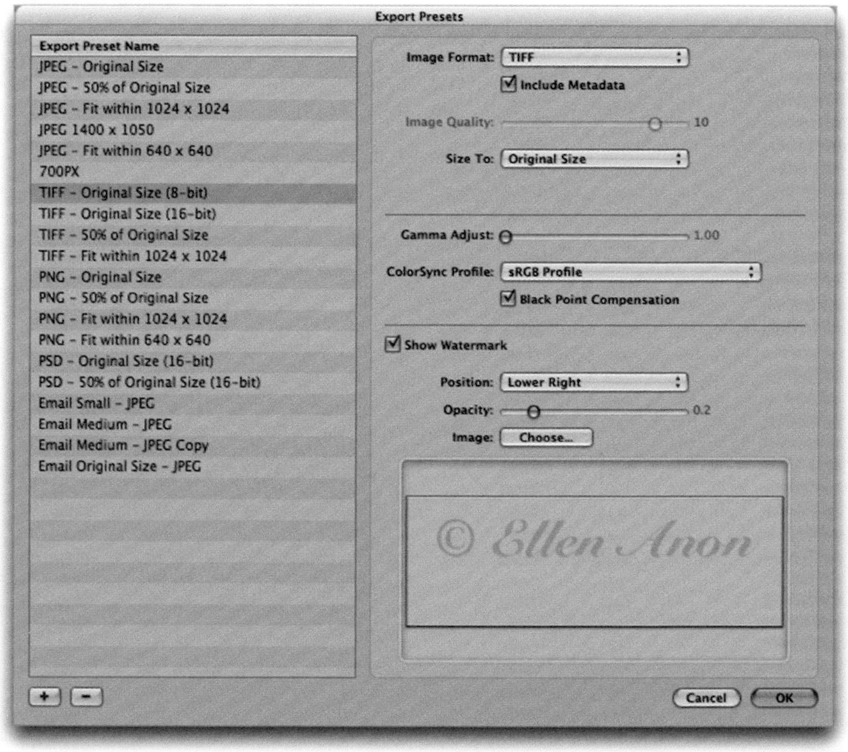

Figure 6.5: You can create and save new presets with settings you commonly use such as settings for projection.

Although there is an option to adjust the Gamma settings, this is one we don't often use. We prefer to optimize the image using the various adjustments covered in Chapter 5, "Nondestructive Image Processing." However, if you discover that the midrange brightness of your images is consistently too low for a specific use, you may want to adjust the gamma.

Aperture makes it easy to add a watermark to your images to help reduce theft, as shown in Figure 6.6. To use a watermark, follow these steps:

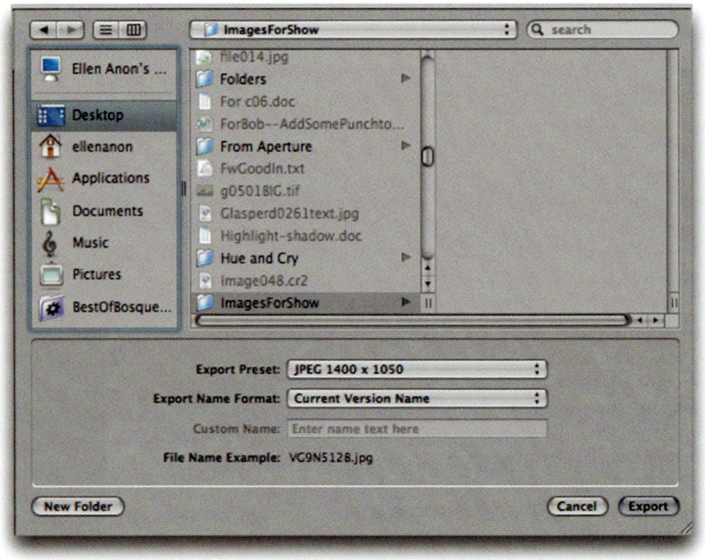

Figure 6.6: Adding a watermark to your image file can make it more difficult for people to use your image without your permission.

1. Create your watermark in Photoshop or other application, and save it.
2. Check the Show Watermark option in the Export Presets dialog box.
3. Use the Image Format pop-up menu to navigate to the image to use as your watermark. Note that you can save your watermark outside the Aperture library and still access it.
4. Set the Opacity slider as desired. If you want the watermark to appear as an obvious copyright notice, you'll want to set the opacity fairly high, toward 1.0. If you'd prefer a more subtle watermark, use a low opacity setting, such as 0.2 or 0.3. We used 0.3 in Figure 6.6.
5. Click OK.

Many people who use very translucent watermarks prefer the watermarks to be fairly large in relation to their image size so that the copyright can't be simply cropped out of an image. Those who use more opaque watermarks usually prefer them to be fairly small to not compete with the image. You'll need to determine what size watermark you prefer for various sizes of images. It can be helpful create a watermark folder containing several watermarks at varying sizes. That way you can choose the one that best fits a particular file.

Creating a Watermark

Creating a watermark to apply to your images is easy. To do so, follow these steps:

1. First open a new document in Photoshop. For small images, try a 650×200 pixel document at 300 dpi with a transparent background. For larger watermarks with long names, you'll need a larger document. It's important to choose Transparent for the background.

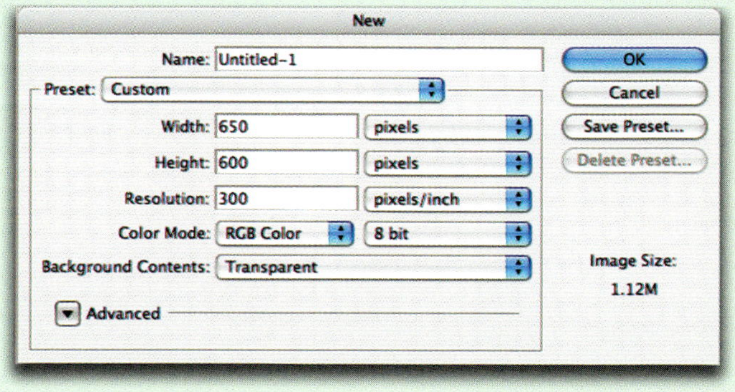

2. Select the Text tool. Choose the font, size, and color you prefer. We used Snell Roundhand in our example, but you can choose whatever font you prefer. For small files, try a font size of 14 or 18 point. You'll want to use a larger font size on larger images, so you may need to create several watermarks. Choose the color for your font. Usually, we prefer to use black, but on some images, you may prefer using a very light color. You'll adjust the final opacity of the watermark in the Export Presets dialog box.
3. Type the copyright symbol (Option+G) and then your name. Crop the image to a bit larger than your name. That way there will be some space below and to the side when the watermark is applied to your image.

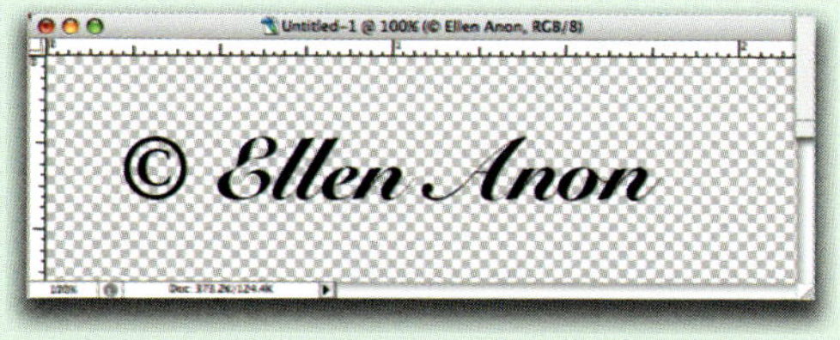

4. Save the watermark as a TIFF file, but make certain to save it with transparency. To do this, check Save Transparency in the TIFF Options Save dialog box.

You can even use the watermark feature to add a digital signature to your images. To do so, you'll need to make a scan of your signature and then open it in Photoshop. Unlock the background layer by double-clicking it and clicking OK in the dialog box that appears. Go to Image > Trim, and choose Bottom Right Pixel Color. Check all four boxes (top, bottom, left, and right) under Trim Away. Resize the image as necessary, and save it as described in Step 4.

To delete a preset you no longer need, highlight it and click the Delete button (–) at the bottom-left of the Export Presets dialog box.

Exporting with the Desired Preset

Once you've created the presets, follow these steps to export your files:

1. Select one or more images you want to export, and do one of the following:
    - Choose File > Export Versions.
    - Press Shift+⌘+E.
    - Right-click/Control-click the image, and choose Output > Export Versions.
2. A new dialog box appears, as shown in Figure 6.7.

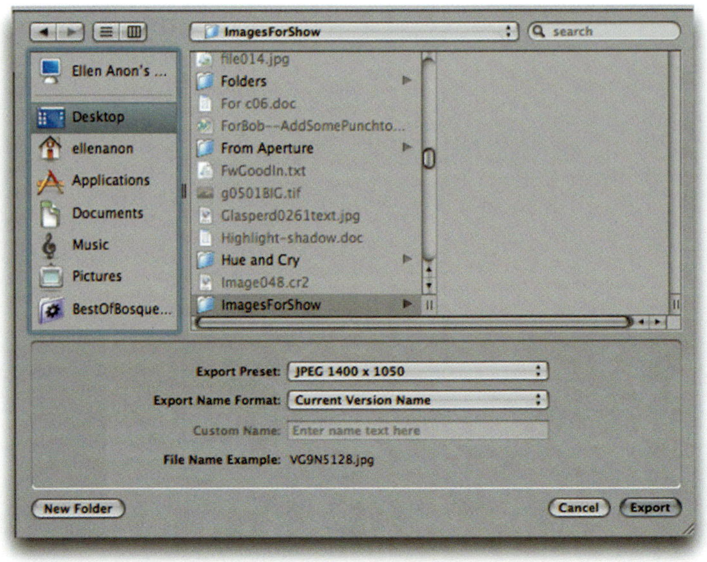

Figure 6.7: After you select File > Export Versions, a new dialog box appears. In it, you can choose where to export the file as well as the preset to use.

3. Specify where you want to store the exported files. You can create a new folder by clicking the New Folder option in the lower-left corner of the dialog box.
4. From the Export Preset pop-up menu, choose the export preset you want to use. In this example, we chose the JPEG 1400 × 1050 preset that we just created.

Note: To check the specifications of any preset in this menu, choose Edit, which is at the bottom of the Export Preset pop-up menu. This will return you to dialog box shown in Figure 6.3.

5. You can opt to use the Current Version Name for your images or rename them from the Export Name Format drop-down menu. Aperture enables you to create a custom name by selecting Custom Name With Index Or Counter and then typing the name in the appropriate box. Alternatively, you can opt to use the version name, the version name with the date and time the file was created, or simply the image, date, and time.
6. Click Export.

Note: To batch export, select multiple files and choose Export Versions. The preset you select will be applied to the files, and they will be exported to the location on your hard drive that you specify.

If you prefer to establish your own naming convention, click Edit at the bottom of the Export Name Format pop-up list. A dialog box will appear, as shown in Figure 6.8. Although we discussed this in Chapter 2, "Importing and Organizing Your Images," we'll review it here.

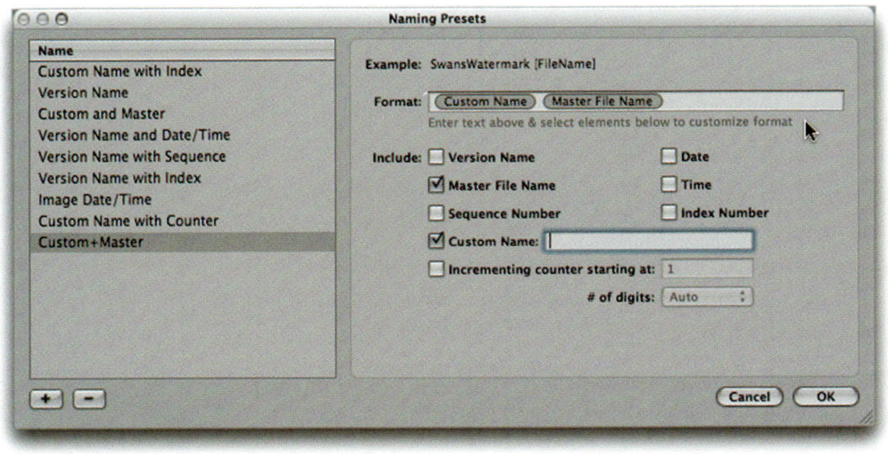

Figure 6.8: You can customize the naming convention to use by selecting Edit at the bottom of the Export Name drop-down list.

You easily can create completely new preset naming conventions. For example, if you want to use a custom name but you also want to include the master filename, follow these steps:

1. Click the + button at the bottom of the dialog box.
2. Assign a name to your new naming convention. In Figure 6.8, we used **Custom+Master**.
3. Check the appropriate boxes to indicate the information you want to include in the name. The item you check first will appear first in the name. Therefore, if you want custom text followed by the master name, check Custom Name and then check Master File Name. If you check the Master File Name first, it will appear first in the new name and you'll have to drag it elsewhere if you don't want it to be first.
4. Click OK.
5. In the original Export dialog box, enter the custom name you want to use, as shown in Figure 6.9. This way you can use the same preset in other situations and just type in a new custom name without having to create an additional custom name preset.

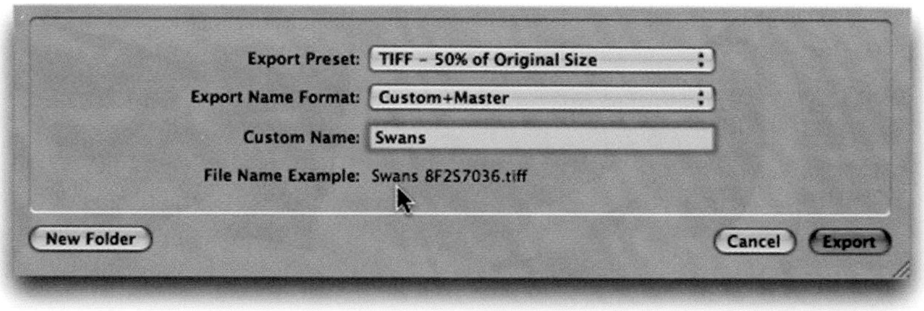

Figure 6.9: By creating a generic preset for custom name plus original, you can quickly customize the name for a file by typing the name in the text field in the Export dialog box.

After you select the location, preset, and naming format, click Export. Copies of your images will be ready for you to use as desired.

Exporting to Email

As you look through your images in the Viewer, you may realize that you'd really like to send a few pictures to friends or colleagues or even send samples to clients. Aperture has a sleek process to enable you to export your files directly to email.

To place images in an email, follow these steps:

1. Choose Preferences > Mail, and select the mail service you use, as shown in Figure 6.10.

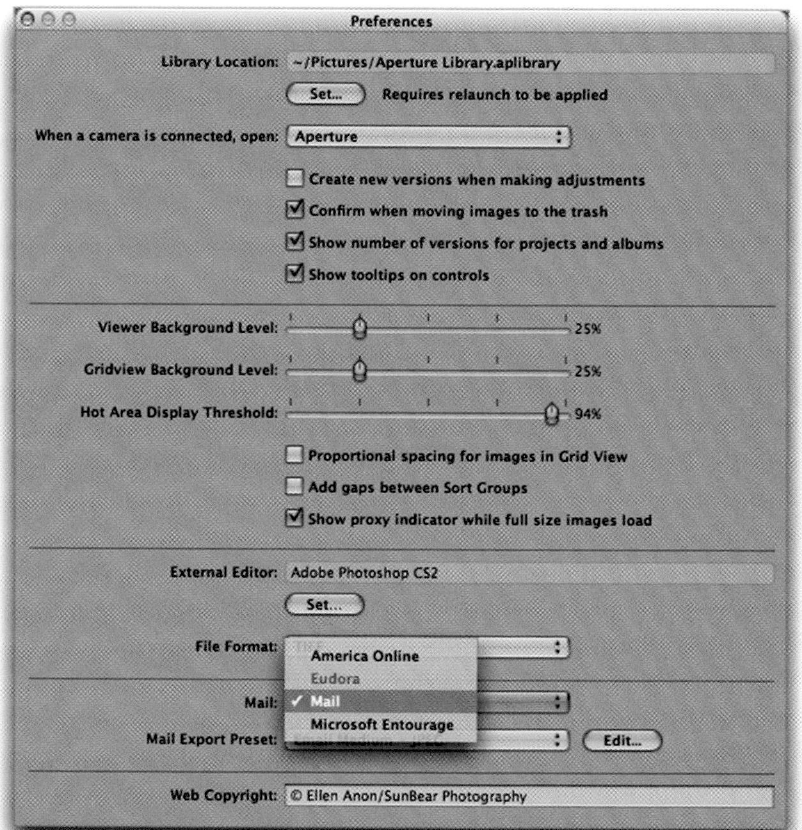

Figure 6.10: Select your mail service from the Mail pop-up menu in Preferences.

2. In the Mail Export Preset pop-up menu, select E Mail JPEG Small (or whatever size you prefer), and then click the Edit button.
3. In the Edit Presets menu, specify the size and color space, as shown in Figure 6.11:
    - Select the Image Quality using the slider. We usually choose 8.
    - Set the Size To pop-up menu to: "Fit Within Size" and then fill in the desired pixel dimensions. We usually use 500 pixels for the maximum height or width of pictures we want to email.
    - Set the Color Sync Profile to sRGB.
    - We recommend you use a watermark as we described earlier.

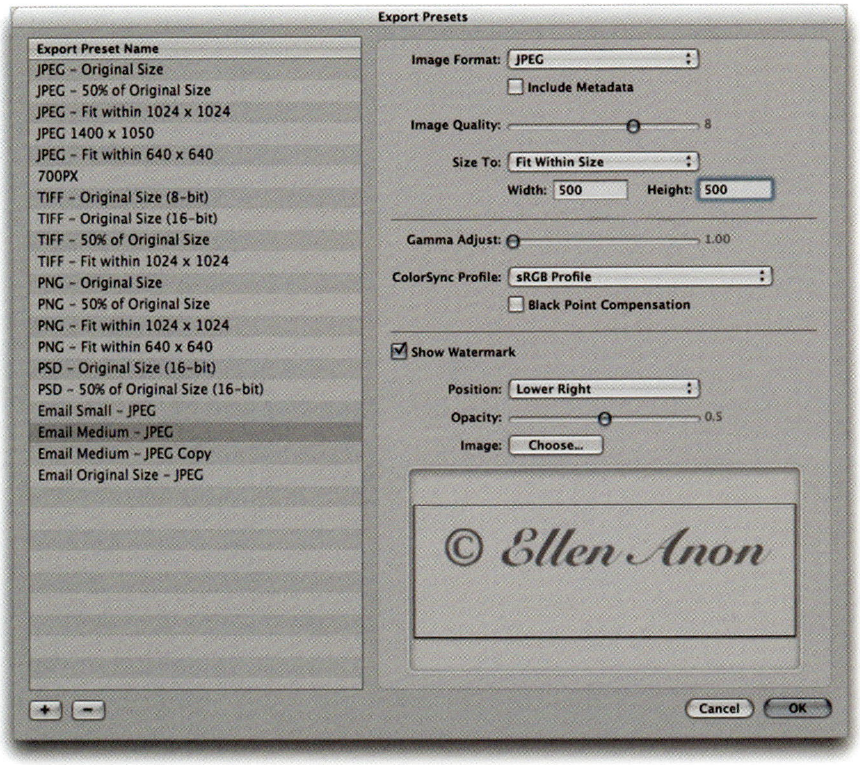

Figure 6.11: Specify the parameters to use for images you embed in emails.

Note: We choose 500 × 500 pixels for our emailed images so they're not overwhelmingly huge and will easily fit completely on someone else's monitor. Also they're small enough to discourage theft and major illegal usage.

4. Select the image or images you want to place in an email.
5. Go to the Main Menu bar and choose File > Email, or press Option+E. A progress bar will appear, and your image(s) will appear in an email, as shown in Figure 6.12. You can add text as desired.

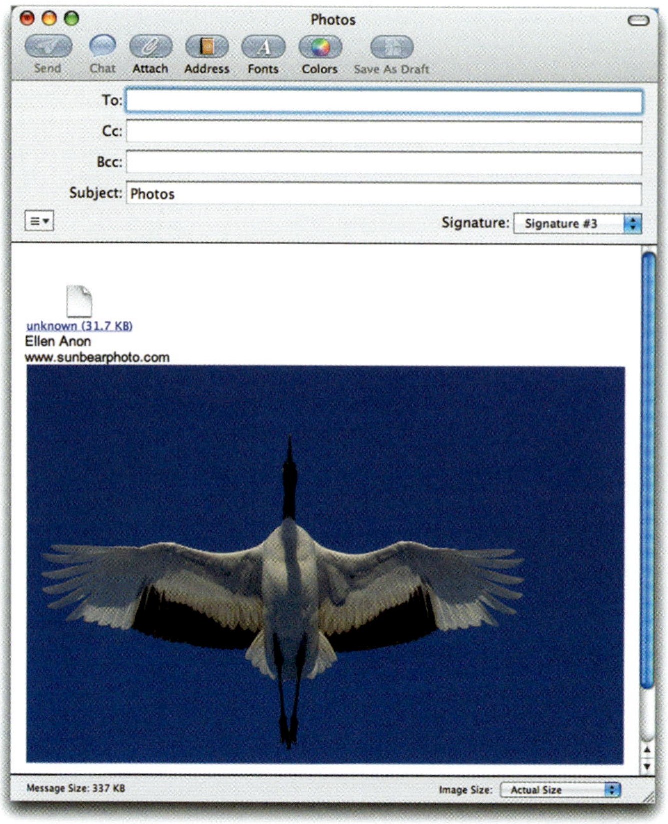

Figure 6.12: The images you select are automatically placed into an email using the parameters you determine.

Exporting Master Files

There may be times when you want to export your file as a RAW file. For instance, some contests and professional organizations require the original RAW file as verification that you didn't alter the image in ways that violate their rules. Further, each RAW converter offers slightly different capabilities, and with certain images you may prefer to use a different converter. For example, if you are using a lens that results in noticeable chromatic aberration or vignetting, you may prefer to correct these issues in the conversion process using Adobe Camera Raw.

Note: When you export a master file, it ends up being stored in two places on your hard drive. As a result, it takes up twice as much storage space. In Chapter 10, "Advanced Aperture," we'll show you how to use a different conversion program on a RAW file without exporting the file. That way you'll avoid the extra storage requirements, and the image will be maintained in your Aperture library.

Of course, you can export a master file even if it's not a RAW file. Whether it's a RAW file or another file format, you'll be exporting the unmodified original file.

To export the master file, take these steps:

1. Select the image, then press Shift+⌘+S or go to File > Export Master. Alternatively, you can right-click/Control-click the image and select Output > Export Master. A dialog box will appear, as shown in Figure 6.13.

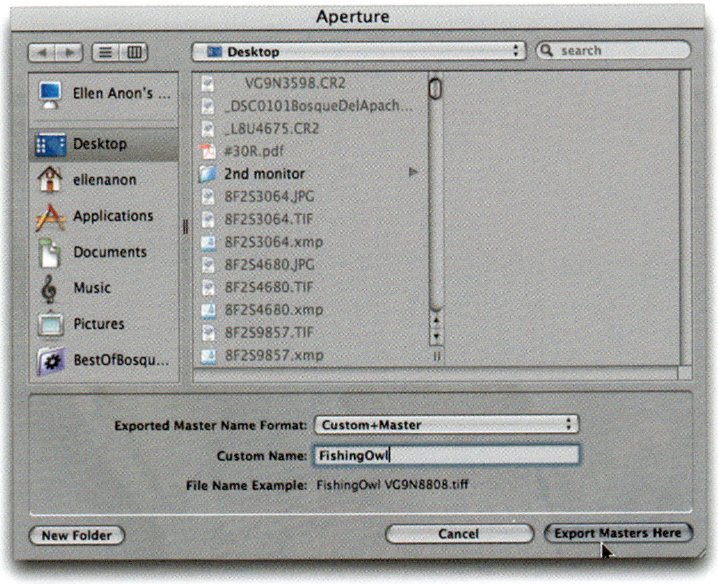

Figure 6.13: Use the Export Master dialog box to specify where to store the exported image and to create a new name for the file if desired.

2. Use the directory to specify where Aperture should send the file. You can select an existing folder or create a new one by clicking New Folder at the bottom-left of the dialog box.
3. Rename the file if you want. You can choose from the standard naming conventions just as when exporting versions, or you can create a custom name by selecting Edit at the bottom of the Exported Master Name Format pop-up menu.
4. Click Export.

As shown in Figure 6.14, a dialog box will appear in which you can create a new naming convention. Click the OK button (+) at the bottom-left of the dialog box, and then enter a name. In our example, we used **Custom+Master**. The Custom command enables us to add descriptive text, and the Master command provides the original filename generated in-camera. We left the Custom Name text field blank so that the naming convention is generic. Click OK in this box to return to the previous dialog box. To complete your filename, enter the desired descriptive text into the text field. In our example, we used **Bosque2005** to indicate that the file was taken in Bosque in 2005.

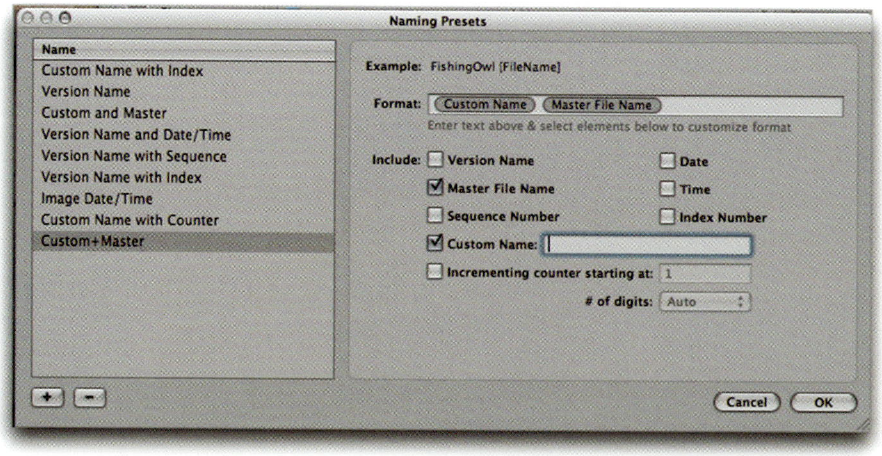

Figure 6.14: Creating a custom naming convention and saving it as a preset can save you time when you go to export files.

Exporting a Project

If you're working on a project and want to share it with coworkers, you might need to export your project to their computers. Similarly, some photographers create projects on their laptops while shooting on location and need to transfer these projects to their main computer at home. Further, some photographers need to export projects to store them offline when they're no longer current.

To transfer a project from one computer to another, follow these steps:

1. Select the project in the Projects panel.
2. Go to File > Export Project, or press Shift+⌘+E. Alternatively, you can right-click/Control-click the project in the Projects panel and select Export Project.
3. A dialog box will appear, as shown in Figure 6.15 in which you can specify a name for the project and select where to store it. You may need to temporarily store it on your desktop.

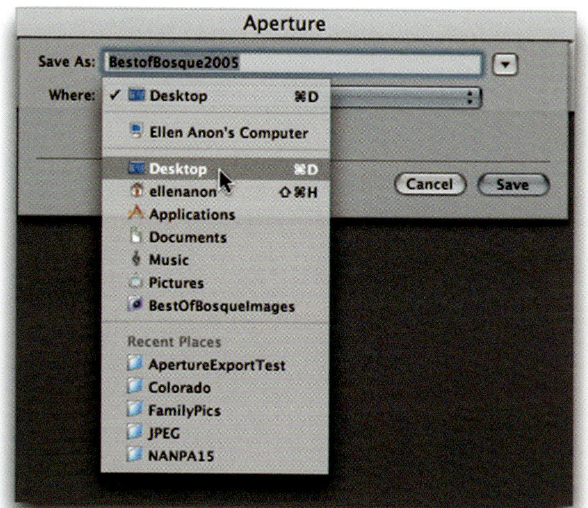

Figure 6.15: Specify a new name for the project and where to store it.

4. Click Save.
5. Network the computers together, or connect them using a FireWire cable in Target Disk mode.
6. Copy the exported project to the second computer.
7. If you connected the two computers in T mode, reboot the second computer normally.
8. Open Aperture on the second computer.
9. Select Library in the Projects panel.
10. Choose File > Import > Projects.
11. Navigate to the desired project, and click Open.

Using Two Macs in Target Disk Mode

Using two Macs in Target Disk Mode is easy. To do so, follow these steps:

1. Connect the two computers with a FireWire cable. The first computer should be On and the second should be Off.
2. Launch the second computer while holding down the T key on that computer. Continue to press T until the second computer's screen changes to a hard drive icon.
3. The second computer will appear as an external hard drive on the first computer. An icon for it will appear in the Finder of the first computer.
4. You can easily transfer files from one computer to another by navigating to the desired file or folder on the computer appearing as an external hard drive, and dragging it to the desired location on the main computer.
5. When done, you must "eject" the second computer from the first computer, as if it were a removable drive. To do so, drag its icon to the Trash/Eject icon.
6. Turn off the second computer and disconnect the cable.

Theoretically, it would be nice to be able to store all your images in your library, backed up to a vault. Many photographers shoot more images than their hard drives can hold. To create space for their new shoots, they must export their projects after completing them. For example, a wedding or portrait photographer may want to keep the images from the current year in the Aperture library, but those from previous years may need to be removed and archived elsewhere. Similarly, nature and travel photographers, particularly those who shoot stock, need room in their libraries to hold the most recent shoots so they can sort through their images, optimize them, and then send them to agencies. After that, they need to export the project.

To export a project for offline storage, take these steps:

1. Select the project in the Projects panel.
2. Go to File > Export Project, or press Shift+⌘+E. Alternatively, you can right-click/Control-click the project in the Projects panel, and select Export Project.

3. A dialog box will appear, as shown in Figure 6.16. Use it to specify a name for the project and select where to store it. Normally, you will want to store it on an external hard drive. Navigate to that drive.
4. Click Save.

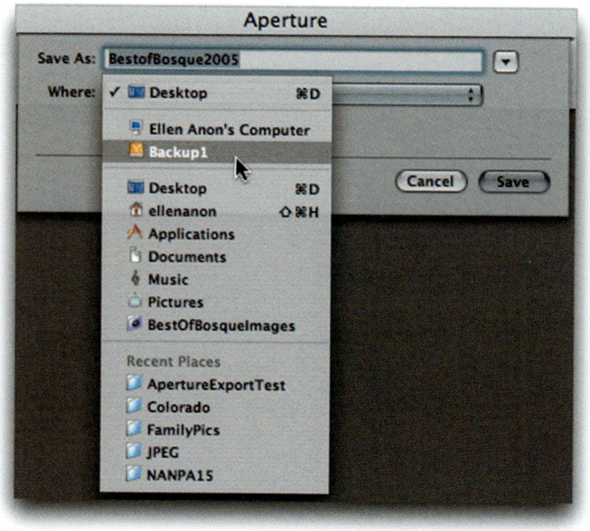

Figure 6.16: When you export a project offline, you can specify an external hard drive to store it.

Note: We prefer to use a RAID external hard drive system that provides a mirrored backup. Your projects (and libraries and vaults) must be stored on HFS+ formatted drives, which are Mac hard drives. You can't export a project to a drive formatted for Windows.

If your project is small enough, you may want to export it to a DVD. To copy it to a DVD, take these steps:

1. Select the project in the Projects panel.
2. Go to File > Export Project, or press Shift+⌘+E. Alternatively, you can right-click/Control-click the project in the Projects panel, and select Export Project.
3. The DVD will appear in the dialog box. Navigate to the DVD to select it.
4. Click Save.
5. Burn your DVD as usual.

Exporting a project does not remove it from your Aperture library. To remove it from the library and free up hard drive space, you must delete the project. Do not delete the project before you export it.

To delete a project, take these steps:

1. Select the project in the Projects panel.
2. Go to File > Delete Project, or press ⌘+Delete. Alternatively, you can right-click/Control-click the project in the Projects panel and select Delete Project. This will remove the project from your library.

Once you delete a project, the master files are moved into the Trash Can, and all versions and metadata are permanently deleted.

Importing a Project

You can reimport a project you moved offline by using the Projects panel and selecting File > Import > Projects. A dialog box will appear. Navigate to the project and click Open. Unfortunately, as of this writing, searching for images within projects that are no longer in the library is difficult.

Now that you know how to adjust your images, export them, and open them in an external editor, it's time to look at printing them.

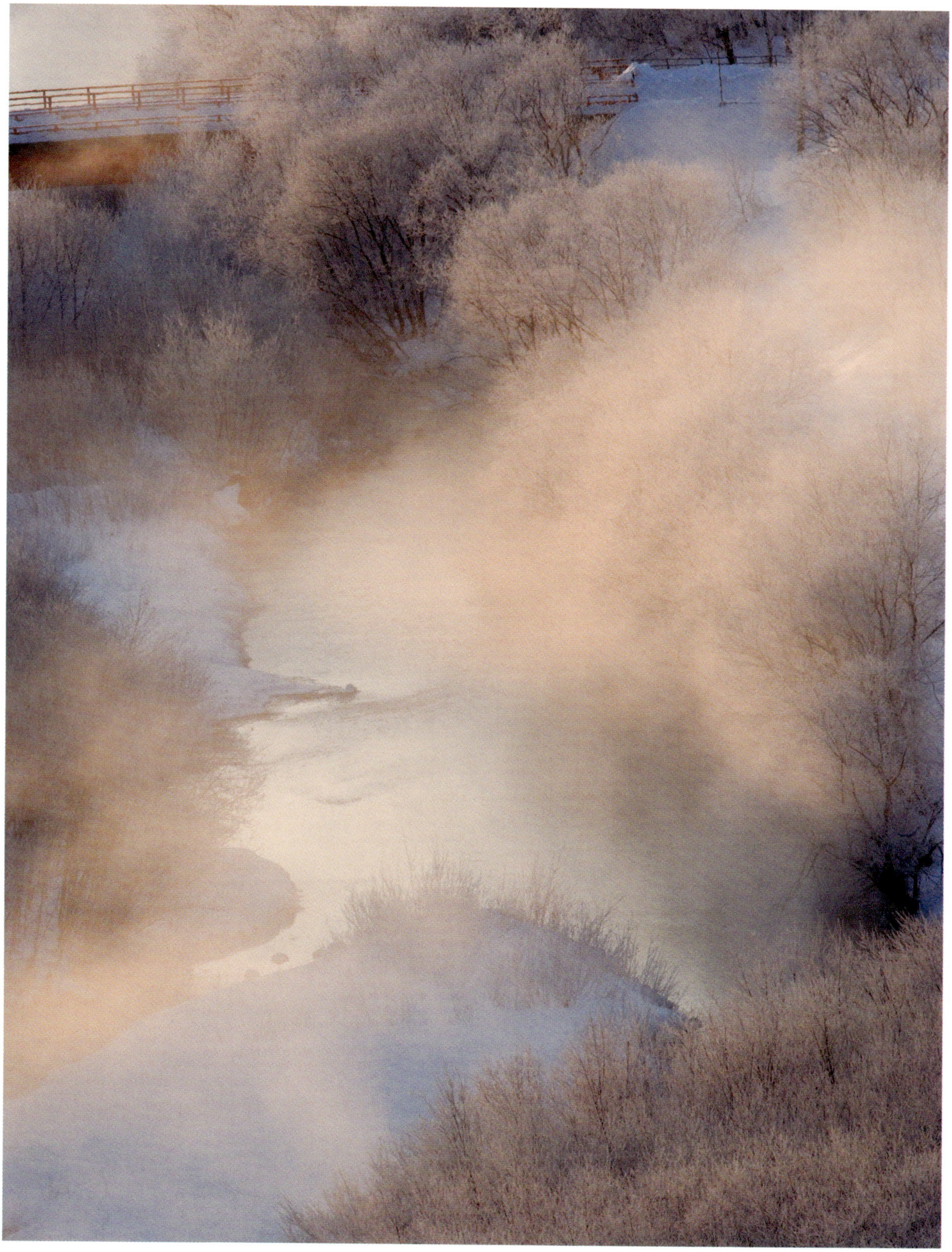

Printing

Ultimately, most photographers want to share their best images with others, either for commercial or personal reasons. To do so, we make prints, publish web pages, and even create custom books. Unfortunately, sometimes the output is not nearly as impressive as what we see on our monitors. In this chapter, we cover the steps to accurately prepare images for printing so that the results are as striking as the original image. (We'll cover creating web pages and custom books in Chapter 8, "Creating Web Content," and Chapter 9, "Creating a Book.")

7

Chapter Contents

Color-Managed Workflow

In an ideal world, every device—from our cameras to our monitors to our printers—would all automatically, accurately, and consistently reproduce exactly the same colors as what we see. However, in the real world our eyes acclimate to color casts that can cloud our subjective judgments about colors. To make things more complicated, each device is capable of capturing only a subset of colors and that subset varies according to the device. The crowning touch is that the colors we see on our monitors vary over time and lighting conditions, and the output from a printer varies by paper. All this can lead to great frustration when what you see on your monitor doesn't remotely resemble what you get as a print or, even worse, what someone receives in an email as an example of an image of which you're proud.

The solution is a color-managed workflow. A complete discussion of this topic is beyond the scope of his book. However, we will touch on several aspects of color management, including monitor calibration and soft proofing.

Note: For a practical guide to fully understanding color management, see Tim Grey's *Color Confidence* (Sybex, second edition 2006).

Monitor Calibration

One of the most crucial steps in a color-managed workflow is to calibrate and profile your monitor. The unfortunate reality is that not only does each individual monitor vary in the way it presents color and tone, but that same monitor will vary over time. Calibrating and profiling the monitor creates a mathematical description of how that particular monitor—in those specific lighting conditions—represents each color. The profile is the first step in creating files that will look similar on someone else's monitor (assuming it's also calibrated) and creating prints that will match what you see on your monitor. If you don't calibrate your monitor, the colors and tonalities in your output are almost guaranteed to differ from what you see on your monitor.

Note: Monitors need to be recalibrated at regular intervals. Although the recommendations vary for how often to calibrate a monitor, we recommend that most users recalibrate LCD monitors every three to six months and CRT monitors monthly.

To accurately calibrate your monitor, you'll need to purchase a calibration package that includes software and hardware. These packages do a far more accurate job of calibrating your monitor than software-only solutions that depend on subjective human judgments. The hardware is a colorimeter (a type of sensor, as shown in Figure 7.1) that measures the colors output by your monitor. Several different companies produce packages that are all quite good, including the Spyder2Pro packages from ColorVision (www.colorvision.com), EyeOne Display2 from GretagMacbeth (www.gretagmacbeth.com), and MonacoOPTIX from X-Rite (www.xrite.com).

Note: When calibrating an LCD monitor, be sure to carefully follow the manufacturer's instructions for using the colorimeter. When done correctly, it's easy and safe. However, if you attach the device incorrectly, you might accidentally suction it to the monitor, which could ruin the monitor.

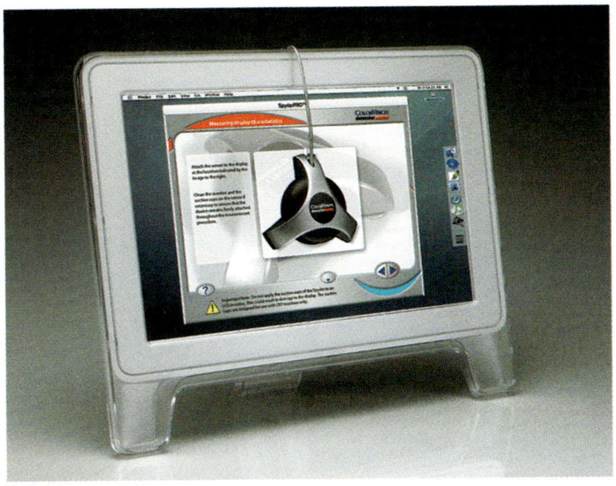

Figure 7.1:
Place the colorimeter on the monitor to measure different color samples supplied via the software. (Picture courtesy of ColorVision.)

Note: X-Rite recently announced it plans to buy GretagMacbeth.

One of the most economical and innovative calibration devices appears to be the Huey by GretagMacbeth. It not only enables you to calibrate your monitor, but automatically compensates for the ambient lighting in your room. We've not yet had a chance to test this device, but it certainly sounds promising.

Simply calibrating your monitor with one of the above packages is not enough; you must also consider the working conditions in your room. Although some extremists recommend painting the walls neutral gray, completely covering all windows, and even wearing black clothing and working in the dark, we don't go quite that far. The reality is that as the lighting varies in your studio, your perception of color and tonalities on your monitor will vary. Calibrating your monitor under the lighting conditions that you'll be using to work on your images is important. If you have a window near your monitor, it's a sure bet that bright sun shining in will vary your perception of tonalities. As the color temperature of the outdoor lighting changes, your perception of the colors on your monitor will vary. You might then adjust your images to be too warm or too cool, too bright or too dark.

For best results, the lighting conditions in your studio should be consistent and ideally slightly dim. In practical terms, this means that there should be blinds on the windows that are closed, and the artificial lighting in the room should be at a consistent level. Don't switch between a lamp with one type of light bulb and overhead lighting with another.

Soft Proofing Images

Even though you may have calibrated your monitor and you maintain consistent lighting in your working area, you may still notice differences between the image on your monitor and the output. Some of these differences result from differences in viewing something on a monitor with emitted light and a print that requires reflected light. However, there's more to it than that. Various types of paper such as glossy, luster, fine art matte, and water color papers, as well as the inks used with them, all reproduce colors differently. As a result, your print may look noticeably different than what you see on the monitor.

All of this may seem to indicate that what prints will look like is somewhat random. In fact, as long as you use printer/paper/ink profiles, you can soft proof your image. Soft proofing changes the onscreen image to simulate what it will look like using the output profile that you specify, as shown in Figure 7.2. You can further modify the soft proof version to make it look the way you had intended. Often, particularly with watercolor papers, there is a reduction in contrast and saturation.

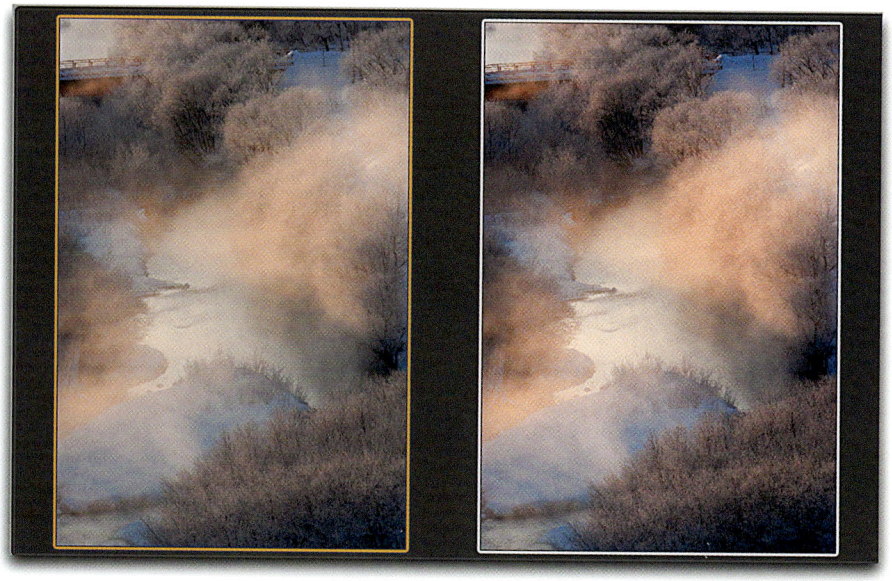

Figure 7.2: Soft proofing simulates how the image will appear when printed using the specific printer/paper profile. Differences may be subtle.

Custom Printer/Paper Profiles

Make sure that you previously have installed profiles for your printer and the particular paper and inks you'll be using. Most printers ship with profiles for commonly used papers and inks. Many companies, such as Epson, update these profiles on their websites as free downloads. Third-party paper companies often have profiles for their papers with popular printers available on their websites. These generic profiles meet the needs of many, or even most, photographers. However, some photographers notice enough deviation between prints made with these generic profiles and what they see on their monitors that they need custom profiles.

Continues

Custom Printer/Paper Profiles *(Continued)*

Both ColorVision (www.colorvision.com) and GretagMacbeth (www.gretagmacbeth.com), which we mentioned earlier, offer devices to calibrate printers. These devices are not inexpensive.

An alternative and more affordable solution is to have a company such as Cathy's Profiles (www.cathysprofiles.com) generate a profile for your printer and paper. Each profile costs $40 (at the time this book is being written), and you'll need a separate profile for each paper you want to use. Because most people find they primarily use two or three papers at the most, this can be a great solution providing both accuracy and affordability.

To soft proof an image in Aperture, follow these steps:

1. Duplicate the current version by choosing Images > Duplicate Version from the menu bar or pressing Option+G.
2. From the main menu bar, choose View > Proofing Profile and scroll through the list to the desired profile for your printer/paper combination, as shown in Figure 7.3.

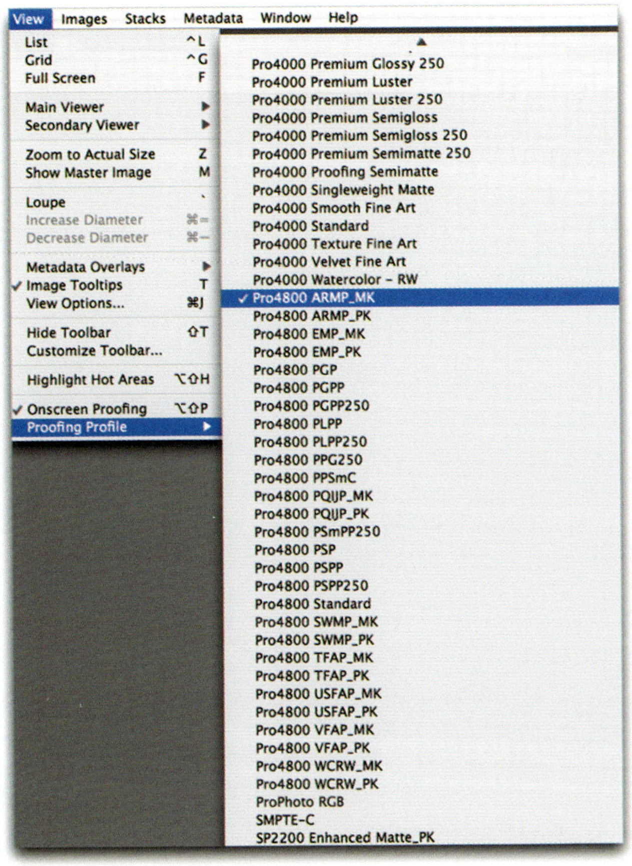

Figure 7.3: Choose your printer/paper profile from the list of all profiles in the computer.

3. Toggle the Onscreen Proofing option on and off by choosing View > Onscreen Proofing or by pressing ⌘+Shift+P to view the changes. If there are objectionable

differences in the Soft Proofed view, open the Adjustment Inspector or HUD by pressing H.

4. Adjust the proof version to make it appear closer to the optimized image. Often this will involve slightly increasing contrast, brightness, and/or saturation. The specific needs will vary according to the profile of the output.
5. Use the adjusted soft proof version as the basis for your print or email version.

Note: Unfortunately, all images in the viewer are shown using the same profile, so you have to toggle onscreen proofing on and off to see the changes rather than being able to compare soft proof versions side by side.

Printing Images

There are several types of printing you may want to do. You may want to print one or more images on individual pages, you may need to make a contact sheet with a number of images on it, or you may want to print a collage that you've assembled using the light table. You may even want to select a group of images and simply order prints from Apple. We'll begin by talking about printing single images on a page.

Printing Single Images

After you've finished adjusting your image, you can choose to sharpen and print it in Aperture or you can first open it in an external editor to resize and sharpen it. Although Aperture provides a sharpening tool (see Chapter 5, "Nondestructive Image Processing," for more details) the sharpening is applied to the image before it is resized according to your desired print size.

Many photographers making fine art prints for personal use, commercial use, or competitions prefer to first resize the image and then sharpen it according to its final size. The downside to this approach is that Aperture must create a new full file that gets sent to Photoshop, so it will take up more storage space.

Nonetheless, we recommend the following workflow when making fine art prints from Aperture:

1. Optimize the image using Aperture's adjustment tools.
2. Create a new soft proof version, if desired, and adjust it as needed.
3. Open the soft proof or the optimized version in Photoshop (or your external editor), and resize it to the desired output size (Image > Image Size).

Note: When sizing an image for print, we prefer to use 300 ppi for best quality. Although some people use 240 or even 180 ppi, there can be some slight loss of quality. The larger the print, the more likely the differences will be noticeable.

4. Currently, we prefer to use one of the sharpening filters in Photoshop such as Smart Sharpen. We may choose to apply targeted sharpening (see the sidebar for details).
5. Save the file in Photoshop—remember it's important to Save the file, and *not* do a Save As.
6. Choose File > Print Images from the menu bar.

If you want to make your prints without using your external editor, optimize and soft proof your image in Aperture. Then choose File > Print Images from the menu bar.

Targeted Sharpening

Many images have a primary subject that's central to the image and background objects that should be out of focus or even completely blurred. In such cases, it can be quite useful to sharpen the subject but not the background. We refer to this process as *targeted sharpening.*

To apply targeted sharpening in Photoshop, we follow these steps:

1. Duplicate the background layer by selecting the background layer and dragging it to the New Layer icon. If the image has numerous layers, we create a Stamp Visible layer by selecting the topmost layer and then holding down the Option key while going to the menu bar and selecting Merge Visible. It's important to continue to hold the Option key until the new layer appears; otherwise the image will simply flatten.
2. We apply sharpening on this new layer using Filter > Sharpen > Smart Sharpen and click the options for More Accurate and Lens Blur. Our settings vary according to the image, but we tend to prefer smaller radius settings (from 0.2 to 1.6) and larger amount settings (from 150 to 500). Larger more detailed files require higher settings than smaller less-detailed files.
3. We add a layer mask to that layer using the Add Layer Mask icon.
4. We hide the sharpening from areas where it's not needed by selecting the brush tool and painting with black in those areas on the layer mask. Sometimes it's easier to actually paint *in* where we do want the sharpening rather than paint *out* where we don't want it. In those cases, after we create the layer mask, we press ⌘+delete to fill the layer mask with black. Then we make white our foreground color in the Color Picker and paint with white on the layer mask where we want the sharpening to appear.

For more details about this, see *Photoshop for Nature Photographers: A Workshop in a Book* by Ellen Anon and Tim Grey (Sybex, 2005).

After Print Images is selected, the dialog box shown in Figure 7.4 appears. In the Preset Name panel, select the desired preset. When you're printing a single image, you will specify the number of copies you want and leave the pages setting to the default setting: All.

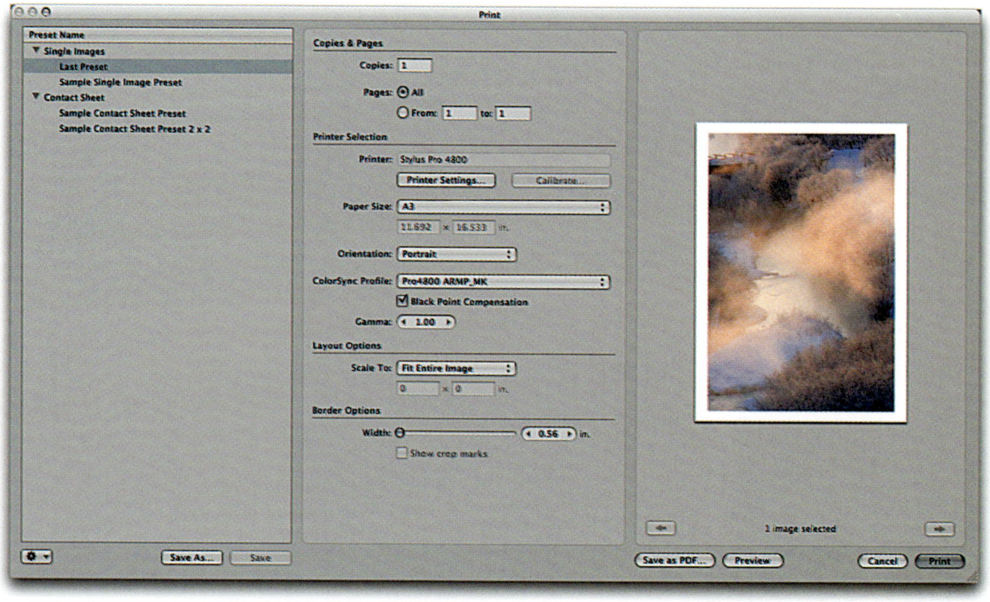

Figure 7.4: The Print dialog box

Under Printer Selection, click Printer Settings. This will bring up your standard printer dialog. First, make certain that the correct printer is selected. If it's not, use the first drop down to select it. Proceed through the menus in the third drop down box to the Print Settings interface, as shown on Figure 7.5. Make certain that all the options are correctly selected according to your feed method (tray, roller, manual, etc) and paper type, such as Velvet Fine Art or Luster, etc. Note that some of these settings and options vary according to the printer you're using. For the mode set, choose Advanced Settings and Print Quality 1440 dpi. We prefer to also check Finest Detail.

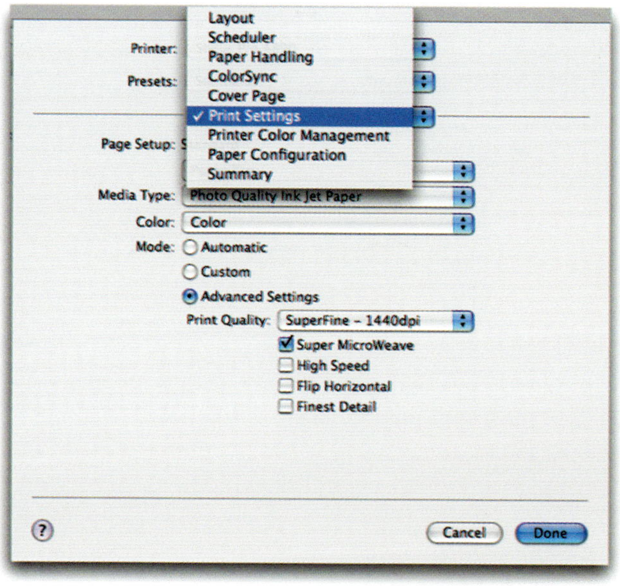

Figure 7.5:
The Print Settings dialog may vary according to the printer.

Note: Although you may be tempted to select 2880 dpi or higher for your printer resolution, most experts agree that there is little, if any, increase in quality, and it uses noticeably more ink.

The next menu from that same drop down box where you found Printer Settings is Printer Color Management. It is essential to set this correctly. This is the most common place people err, resulting in prints that don't match the monitor. *You must set this to Off (No Color Adjustment)*, as shown in Figure 7.6, as counterintuitive as it may feel. In fact this instruction is telling the printer to obey the color management that you specify in Aperture rather than having the printer apply its own adjustments. You can then click Done.

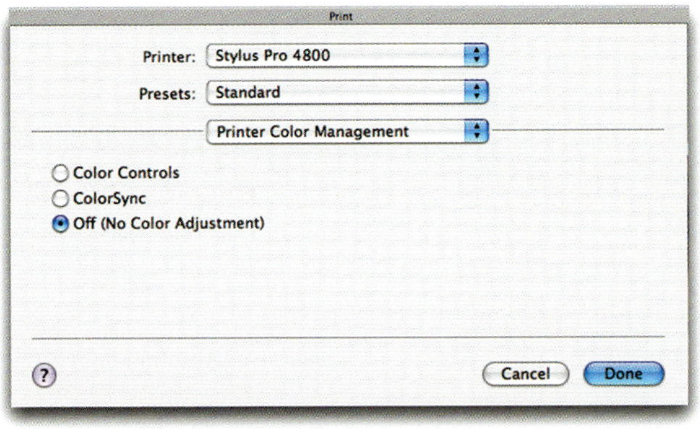

Figure 7.6:
For correct color output, you must specify No Color Adjustment.

The next step is to specify the Paper Size in the Aperture Print dialog box from the pop-up window. Choose from the numerous preset common values or enter a custom size.

To make a borderless full-bleed print, you should first calibrate your printer using the Calibrate button in the Print dialog box. The Calibrate button becomes active after you choose a borderless paper option in the paper size dialog and when you make a contact sheet. After you click the Calibrate button, a new dialog box appears as shown in Figure 7.7.

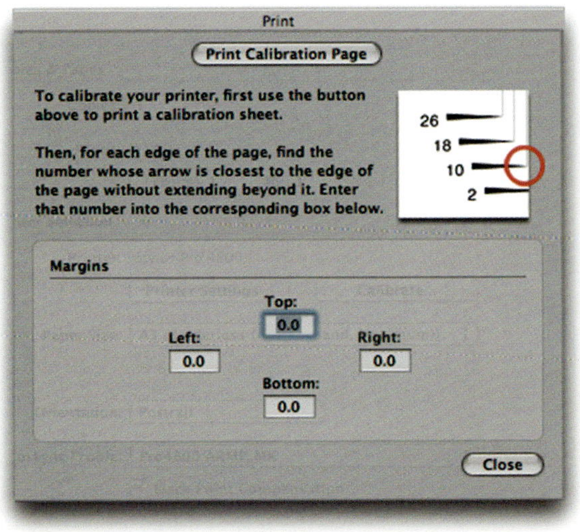

Figure 7.7:
The Print Calibration dialog box

Click Print Calibration Page to have your printer print a test sheet. You'll need to use the same size paper that you use for your prints or contact sheets, but you might prefer to use a cheaper paper because this is only used to establish the printing edges. On each edge of the paper, there will be a series of numbers with arrows associated with them. For each edge of the paper, determine which number's arrow is closest to the edge of the paper without going beyond it, and then fill that number into the corresponding spaces under Margins in the dialog box. By taking the time to calibrate your printer, you can ensure that the print appears centered on the page. Otherwise, one side might run slightly off the page.

The next choice is Orientation. Choose Landscape, Portrait, or Best Fit. Best Fit is useful if you're printing a series of images on several pages and some are horizontal and some are vertical.

Next, select the printer/paper profile from the pop-up window by Color Sync Profile. If you soft proofed your image, make certain to select the same profile. We prefer to leave Black Point Compensation checked (as shown back in Figure 7.4). If your midtones seem to be slightly too light or dark despite using the correct profile, you can adjust the gamma setting. Usually, we leave this at the default setting.

If you have resized your image in Photoshop, leave the Scale To pop-up window set to Fit Entire Image. However, if you prefer to have Aperture resize the image for you, then you can use one of the options in the pop-up window shown in Figure 7.8. Choosing Fill Entire Page often results in the image being cropped along one dimension unless the image aspect ratio matches that of the paper. You can choose one of the preset sizes such as 4 × 6 or 8 × 10, or you can specify a custom size.

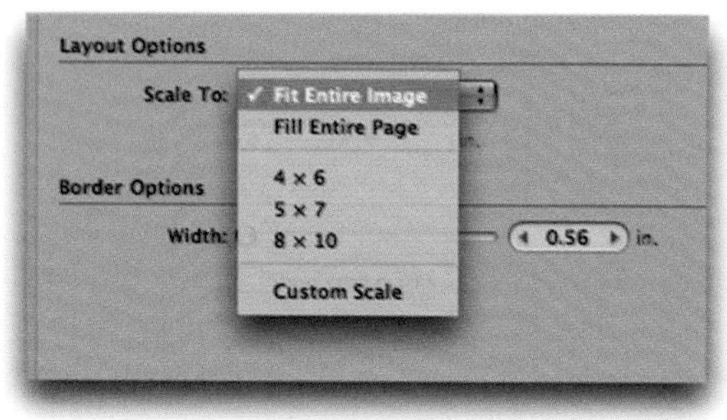

Figure 7.8: Aperture provides options for resizing an image in the Print dialog box.

After specifying the settings for these parameters, you can save your choices as a preset by clicking Save As from the bottom-left part of the Print dialog box. A new dialog box, in which you give the settings a name, will appear as shown in Figure 7.9. We suggest using a name related to image size, such as 10 × 15 Print That way whenever you want to make a print the same size on the same type paper, you can save time by using the preset.

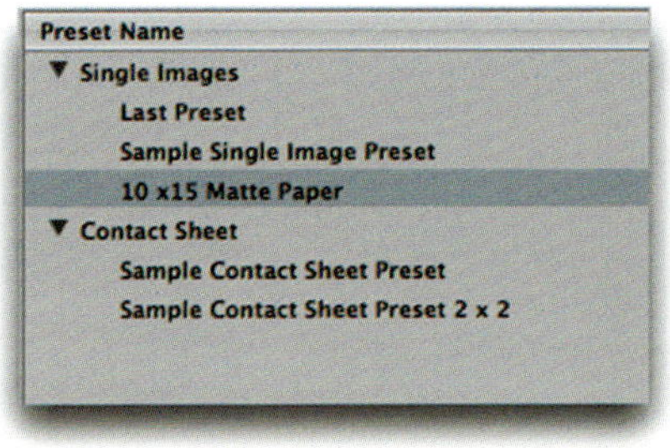

Figure 7.9:
Save commonly used settings as a preset to save time in the future.

Use the Preset Action pop-up menu ( ) to delete an existing preset you no longer need and to duplicate an existing one that you want to modify.

Note that when you're done, you can choose to print the image or save it as a PDF. You can also preview how the image will look. If you use the Preview option, check the option for soft proof.

If you want to make multiple different prints, you can prepare them all, select them, and then go to File > Print Images. Fill in the number of pages you want to print. To preview each image, use the arrow buttons ( ) to navigate to each page.

Ordering Prints through Aperture

Rather than make your own prints, you can easily order them through Aperture. This can be particularly handy if you need multiple small copies of an image. You can order prints in sizes ranging from wallet size to 20 × 30, as shown in Figure 7.10. The prices are pretty reasonable, but you have no control over the type of paper used or the settings.

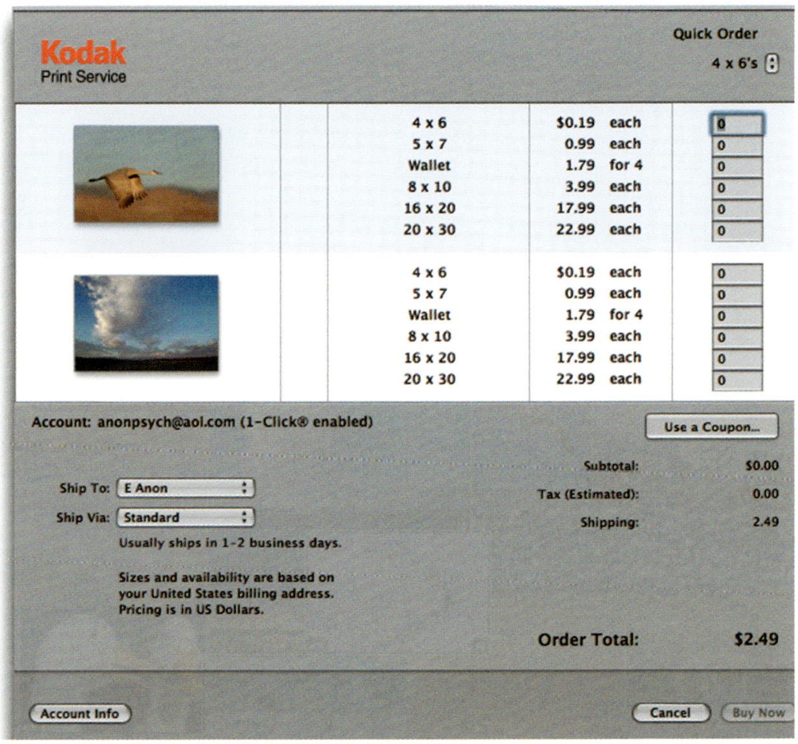

Figure 7.10:
The Order Prints dialog box

To order prints, first select as many images as desired and then go to File > Order Prints. You can specify different sizes and quantities for each picture in the same order.

Note: You may want to order some test prints at various sizes to get a feel for their character. While many people are quite happy with them, others notice some problems, particularly at larger sizes, and prefer to make the prints themselves.

Printing a Contact Sheet

Aperture's Print dialog box provides a flexible and fast way to create contact sheets. We find contact sheets particularly helpful on CD and DVD covers, where we include a sample of the images on the disc, as shown in Figure 7.11. That way we can quickly identify the one containing the images we're seeking. Many editors prefer to have contact sheets submitted along with digital images as a quick reference. Contact sheets can also serve as a double check to ensure that colors are reproduced accurately when files are sent to an agency that coverts them to CMYK space for press use.

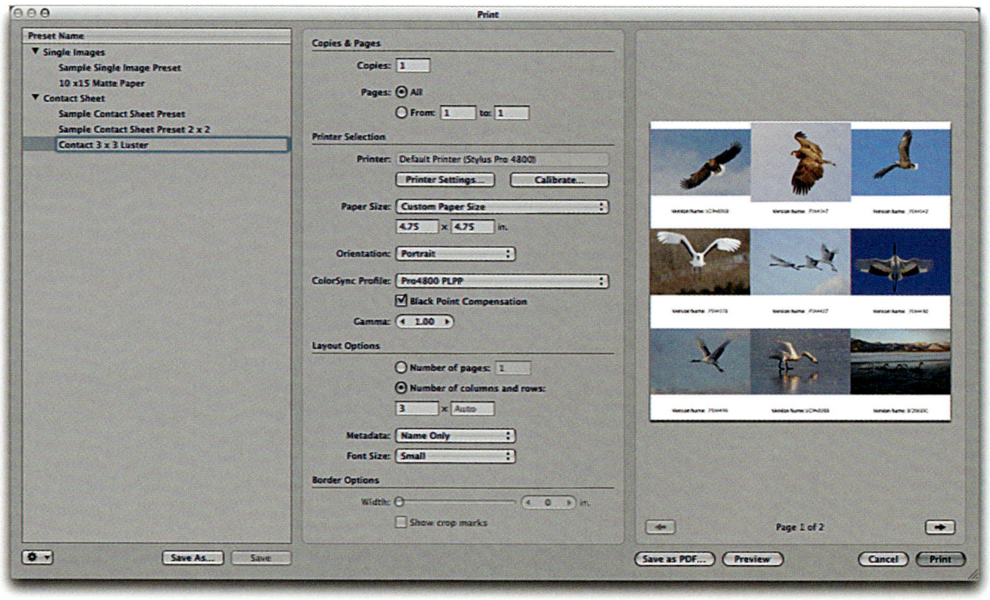

Figure 7.11: Contact sheets provide an easy reference for the contents of a CD or DVD.

Follow these steps to create a contact sheet.

1. Select the images you want to use for the contact sheet.
2. Choose File > Print Images.
3. Select one of the presets under Contact Sheet in the Presets panel on the left or New Contact Sheet from the Preset Action pop-up menu button ( ).
4. Specify the printer settings as described earlier, as well as the Paper Size, Orientation, Color Sync Profile, and Gamma.

5. Under Layout Options, specify the number of columns and rows.
6. If you want to have captions, such as the filename, appear beneath each image, select Metadata and the desired information from the pop-up menu.
7. If you elect to use metadata, also specify the Font Size. We normally use a small font size.
8. If this is a layout that you are likely to want to use repeatedly, save the settings as a preset by clicking the Save As button and giving the template a name such as CD cover. Then the next time you want to make a contact sheet for a CD or DVD, select that preset and you'll be ready to print.

Note: Often, it's better to select a few representative images, particularly from a DVD, rather than try to include all the images on a single contact sheet. If you include too many mages, they will be so small that they may defeat the purpose. Alternately you can create a series of contact sheets to place in the cover or include with the submission.

Printing a Collage from the Light Table

Sometimes, a collection of images presented together have greater impact and convey the essence of an experience better than the images do when viewed individually. In such cases (for example, photographs from a trip or an event), making a collage using the Light Table is a perfect solution. We covered using the Light Table in Chapter 3, "Viewing Images." We're going to assume that you're happy with the way you've arranged and sized a selection of your images, as shown in Figure 7.12.

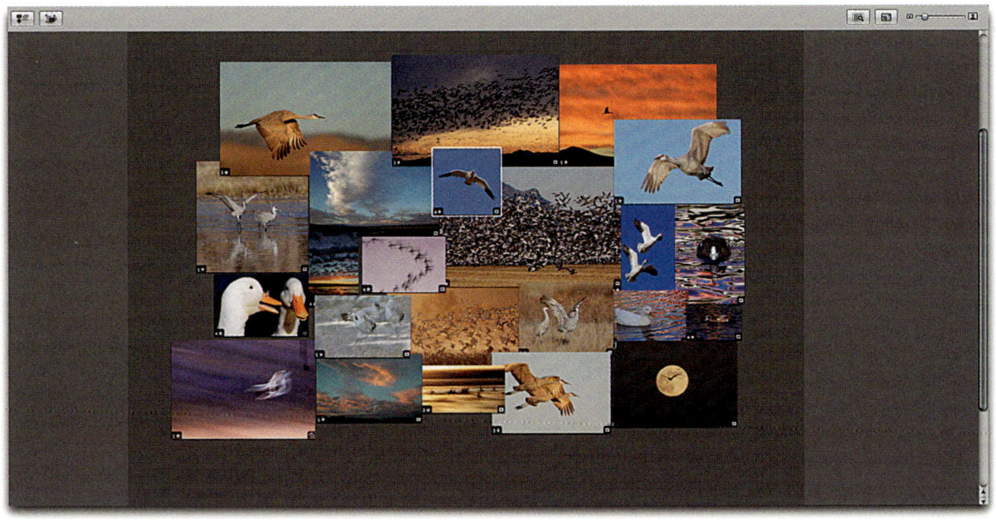

Figure 7.12: Use the Light Table to create a collage.

To print a collage, follow these steps:

1. Create the layout in the Light Table.
2. Click in the background of the Light Table to select the entire layout.
3. Choose File > Print Light Table from the main menu bar.
4. Double-check the preview for any unexpected spaces between images and return to the Light Table if necessary to adjust the layout.
5. Choose your settings as described earlier for printing a single image. Make certain to set not only the printer settings, but also the paper size and correct printer/paper profile, as shown in Figure 7.13.

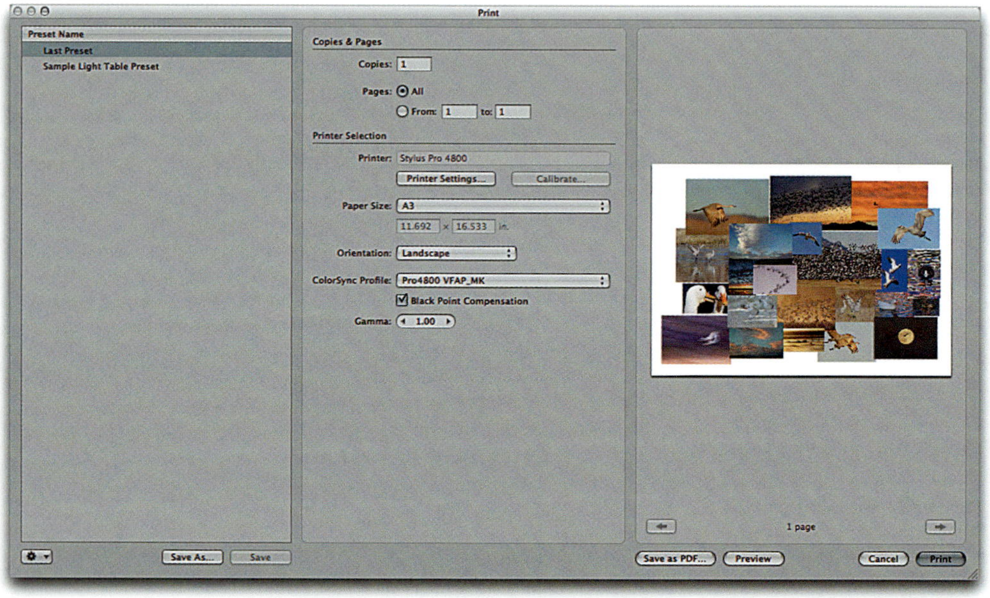

Figure 7.13: Choose the settings for a collage just as for an individual print.

6. Click Print.
7. If you want to post the collage to your website or email it to a friend, click Save as PDF. Then open the PDF in Preview and save it as a JPEG.

Creating Stylized Light Table Proofs

If you want to create proofs that are more stylized than the ones available in Contact Sheet mode, or if you just want to create comps that can easily be printed or saved as a PDF or JPEG, then Aperture's light table is for you.

1. Place some images on the Light Table
2. Drag-select over the images you want to print or save as a PDF. You can select some or all of the images; this trick works either way.

Continues

Creating Stylized Light Table Proofs *(Continued)*

3. Once you have your selection, choose File > Print Light Table. This command will print only the portion of the Light Table that you have selected. If you haven't selected any images, this command will print all of the images on the Light Table.
4. Aperture will automatically size the Light Table to the page size you specify using either one of Apple's presets or one that you create.
5. In the Print dialog box, you can choose between printing the Light Table layout to a printer or a PDF.
6. Although it's not an option in Aperture, you can also convert this layout to a JPEG for electronic publishing. To convert a PDF into a JPEG, open the PDF using the Preview software (included with your Mac) and then use the Save As option. Choose JPEG for the format. Saving it as a JPEG enables you to publish it on the Web or send it as an email attachment.

We thank our technical editor, Scott Bourne, for supplying this tip!

Now that we've shown you how to print your images, it's time to think about creating web pages to share your images.

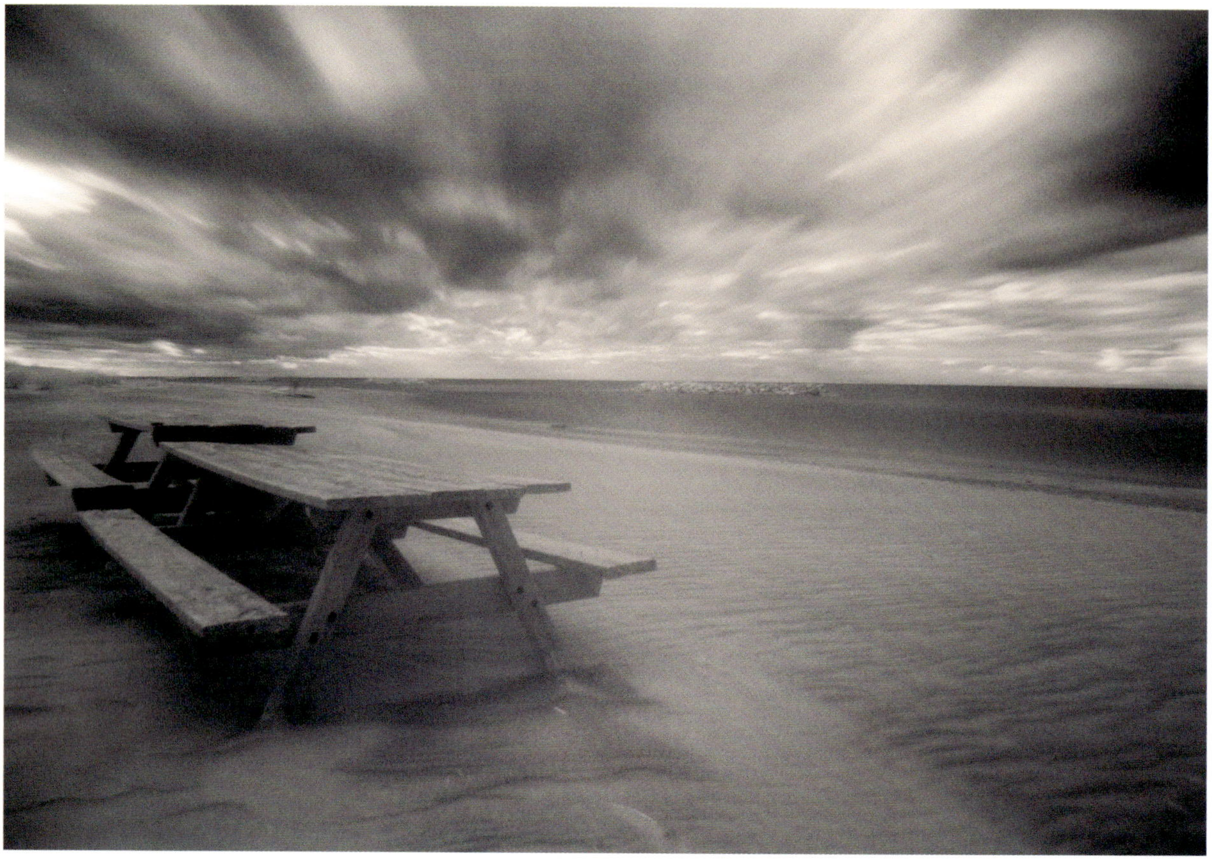

Creating Web Content

One of the most interesting parts of the Internet, to photographers, is how easily you can share your images using the World Wide Web. In Aperture, by rating your images and using smart web galleries, you can instantly create a professional-looking website containing your best images without ever having to see or write a single line of HTML. The entire process consists of picking the images you want in your site, picking a look for your site, and publishing your site. Combined with a .Mac account, you can even publish your site to the Web with a single button click. Here, we'll show you everything you need to know about web content in Aperture, including how to create your own web templates.

8

Chapter Contents

Creating Websites

The overall process for creating a website in Aperture is relatively simple. Step 1 is to pick which images you'd like to publish, and Step 2 is to determine what type of site you'd like.

You can set up two types of sites. The first type is a web gallery. This type of site is almost like a contact sheet for the Web. A web gallery contains index pages with thumbnails of your images and detail pages with a large version of your image and optional metadata. A web gallery would be useful for showing a client pictures from that shoot where the client already knows the context (such as a modeling session) for each image.

The other type, a web journal, has similar detail pages for each image, but the index page differs from a web gallery. With a web journal, you can add blocks of arbitrary images intermixed with blocks of text. Web journals are useful when you want to add a description to blocks of images or to have multiple rows with different numbers of images in each group. For example, if you take a photo tour and go to a variety of locations, you may want to add notes about the location below the thumbnails of your images from each location.

Once you've picked your images and site type, you can arrange them (or place them and add text in a web journal) on the page, choose a theme to customize your site's look (we'll cover the available themes and how to create your own later in this chapter), and publish them to the Web, including (but not limited) to your .Mac account.

Creating Web Galleries

Creating web galleries and web journals is similar, but we are going to focus on web galleries first. Make sure you're in the project where you want your website to be stored. To make an empty web gallery, select File > New > Web Gallery. Aperture will give you an empty website similar to Figure 8.1. Start by giving your website a name in the Projects panel, such as "My First Web Gallery." The gallery name is what will appear in the title bar in your browser.

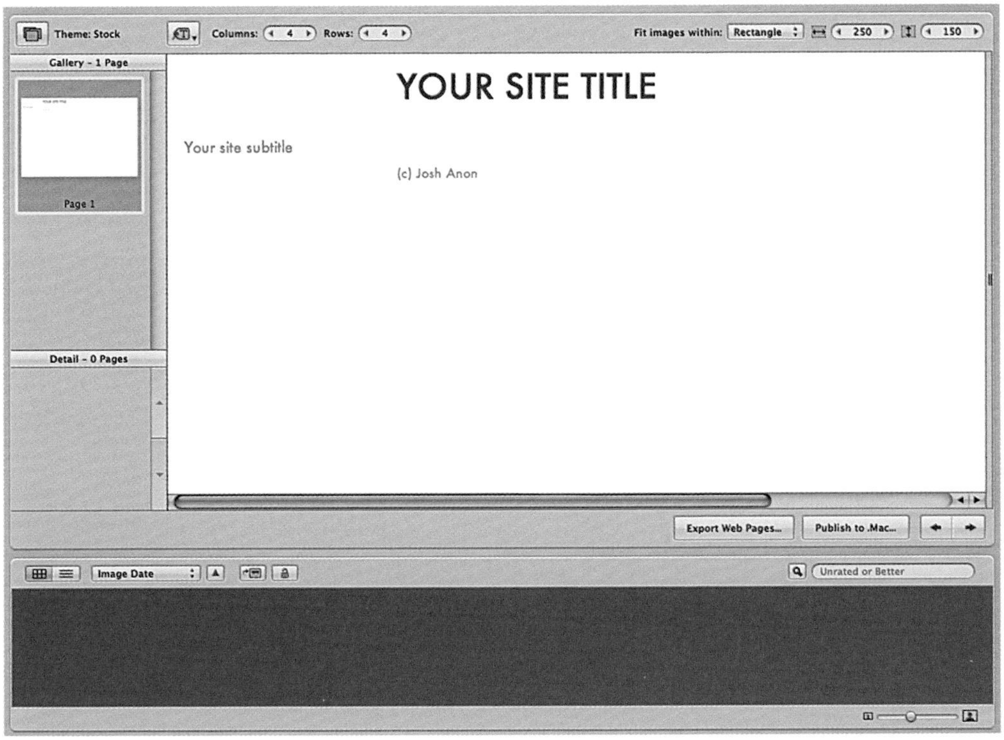

Figure 8.1: An empty web gallery

If, when you go to create your website, you have a rough idea as to what images you want to use in the site, you can create the site with those images right away. Select some images that you want to use to create a website. Then, select File > New From Selection > Web Gallery. You can also Control-click one of the selected images and choose New From Selection > Web Gallery.

At first glance, the website UI looks a bit confusing. However, it's actually quite similar to other views within Aperture. This view has three main parts, which are indicated in Figure 8.2. On the left, there is a view showing thumbnails for each page. The top of this part of the view is where you can see your site's index pages, the top-level pages with thumbnails of each image. The bottom of this view shows your detail pages. The detail pages are the pages for each individual image. Currently, the detail page is empty and only one page is in the index page portion. When you add images to your site, you'll see pages automatically appear in this area. You can move between pages by pressing the up- and down-arrows in this view.

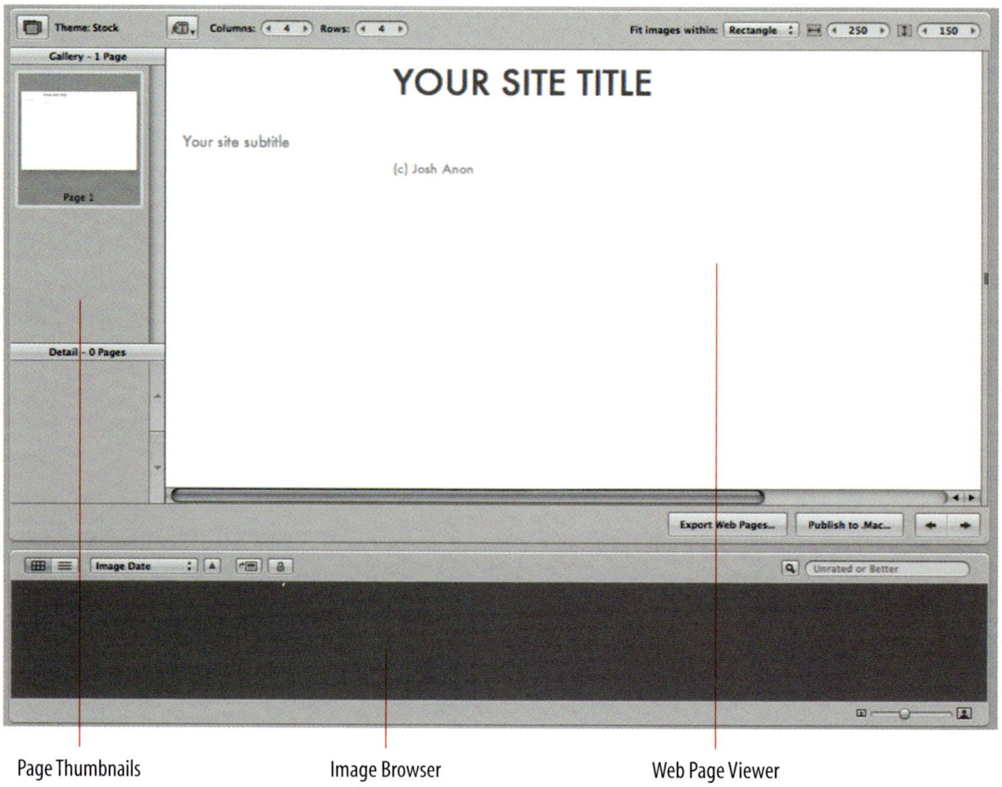

Figure 8.2: The three main parts of the web gallery

The second main part of the UI is the Browser, which, by default, is on the bottom. The Browser works exactly how you're used to its working elsewhere. You can sort it, filter it, resize it, and loupe images in it.

The last main area of the UI is the website viewer. This area shows the web page on which you are currently working. Plus, unlike other programs, this web view is live. In other words, if you click a link on the web page in this viewer, the Viewer will behave as a web browser and take you to that link's destination.

Note: Aperture, like Safari, uses Apple's WebKit technology, and what you see in Aperture is exactly what you will see in Safari.

Before we explain any of the other, new buttons in the view, we will add some images to the web gallery. The simplest way to do so is to switch to another album, select some images, and drag and drop them onto your web gallery in the Projects panel. You can also drag and drop images from other projects onto the web gallery. There are a few ways to add images from other projects:

- Drag from other projects onto the web gallery. Aperture will reference the images but not copy them to the web gallery's project.
- Drag images from other projects to the current project and then to the web gallery. Aperture will copy the image to the current project.

- Option-drag images from other projects to the current project and then to the web gallery. Aperture will move the image to the current project.

There is one more way to add images to your web gallery, combining a few tricks we discussed in earlier chapters. Start by selecting your web gallery. Press the Lock This Browser To The Viewer button ( ) so that as you select additional images, the Viewer stays locked to the Web view and doesn't switch to view each image that you select. Option-click the project or album containing the images you want to use in your website so that Aperture opens the new browser in a new tab (Figure 8.3). Then, select the images you want to add to your gallery and drag and drop them into the gallery's browser. This method is quite useful because it lets you see what images you've added to the web gallery, and you can quickly add images to the Browser because, by keeping the Browser locked to the Viewer, Aperture does not try to load the full version of each image that you select.

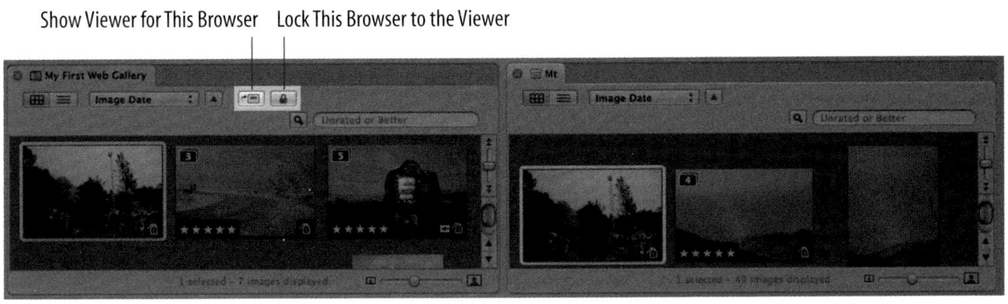

Figure 8.3: The Web Gallery view with two browsers open and the Lock This Browser To The Viewer button active

If you do want to see a viewer for your web gallery's selected images, press the Show Viewer For This Browser button ( ) to toggle between the Viewer and the Web Gallery view. As you would expect, to view each image in Full Screen mode, select the image and press F. When in full screen or when viewing the image in the Viewer, press H to access the Adjustments HUD to modify the image.

Customizing Web Galleries

As you add images to your gallery, Aperture automatically places them on your web page. The order of the images on the index page is the same as the order in the Browser. You can rearrange your images by moving them around (drag and drop them) in the Browser. If you filter your browser using the tools we covered in Chapter 4, "Finding the Keepers," Aperture will update the web gallery so that it displays only the filtered images.

When you add stacked images to your web gallery, Aperture automatically places the stack pick into the web gallery. Sometimes, though, you'll want to use an image that isn't the stack pick on your site. To do so, expand the stack (select the stack and choose Stacks > Open Stack) and select the image you want to use in your website. Next, select Stacks > Set Album Pick. Aperture will draw a small check box above that image, and your website will update to display that image instead of the stack pick. Each stack can have its own album pick, and you can think of album picks as a way to set an alternative stack pick without reordering your stack.

Note: To display more than one image from a stack on your website, you must extract the additional images from the stack. You cannot display both the stack and album picks when they're within the same stack.

Once you've added all of the images that you want to your site, you can make it easier to work with your web gallery. To do so, hide the Projects panel by selecting Window > Hide Projects. Then, move the Browser to the left and make it vertical by choosing Window > Rotate Workspace. Making these changes configures your workspace to look like Figure 8.4. The benefit to setting it up this way is that you can see more of your web page at once. Generally, once you've found the images you want to put on the site, you won't be switching to other projects and albums to find more images. If you remember the preset layouts from Chapter 3, "Viewing Images," you will recognize that this layout is Aperture's predefined Ratings and Keywords layout. You can quickly configure your workspace this way by choosing Window > Layouts > Ratings and Keywords.

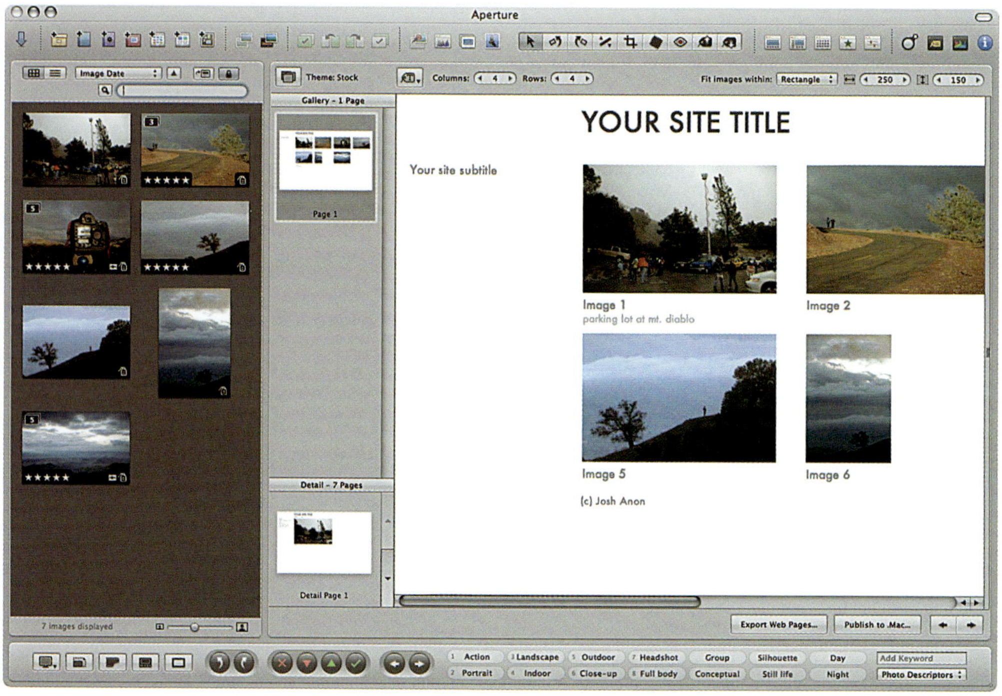

Figure 8.4: The Web Gallery view with the Projects panel hidden and the Browser rotated

After you have your images ordered however you'd like, it's time to start customizing the look of your site. Your first choice is what theme you'd like to use. Click the Choose Site Theme button (▣) at the top left of the Web Gallery view. Aperture will open a window (Figure 8.5) that lets you select from one of Aperture's built-in themes.

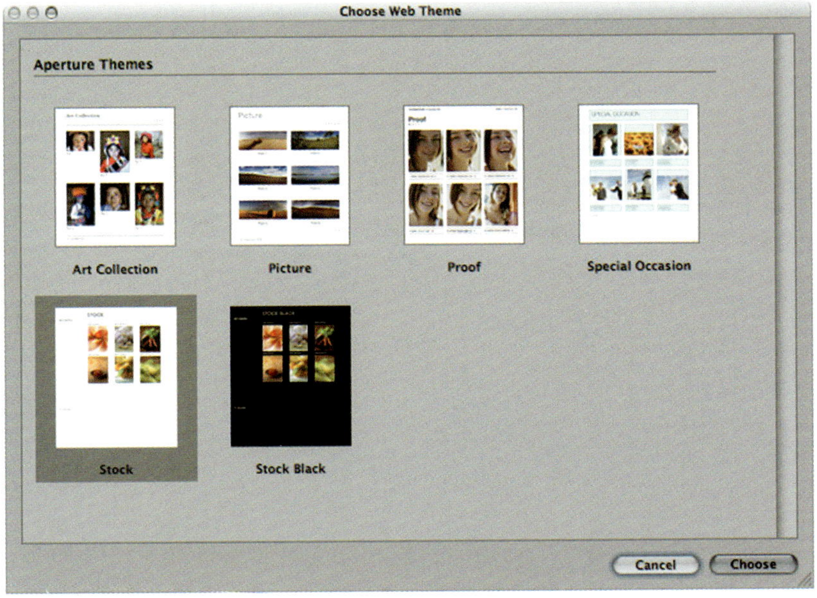

Figure 8.5: The Choose Site Theme window

Aperture has six existing themes: Art Collection, Picture, Proof, Special Occasion, Stock, and Stock Black. Each template has the same basic components, such as a title, thumbnail grid, copyright field, and image caption field. As you can tell from the thumbnails in Figure 8.5, Stock Black is the only theme with a black background, Special Occasion places a light blue background on each image and text field, and Picture places a gray background on each image. Pick each theme to see what it looks like. Later in this chapter, we'll show you how to make your own theme. For now, our screenshots will assume you've selected Proof.

At the very top of this page, you'll notice a field for your name that has the placeholder value "© Your document copyright here," next to the "Photographer:" text. Double-click this field to edit that text. (To make the copyright symbol, press Option+G.)

> **Note:** If all of your websites in Aperture are going to have the same copyright text, set your preferences so that each new web gallery automatically has your copyright. Open the Preferences window (Aperture > Preferences). The bottom field is labeled Web Copyright. Enter your copyright information in the text field to the right, and the next time you make a web gallery or journal, Aperture will automatically add this text.

The next field to edit is the site heading. Double-click the placeholder text "Your Site Heading" and type whatever you want to call your website. Some site themes also have a subheading that you can double-click and edit. At this point, there are no more fields that you can manually double-click and edit.

However, you'll see some text below each image. You can configure your web gallery to display a metadata set below the images. If you click the Metadata Set Displayed With Images button ( ), you'll get a list of all of your metadata sets. As you switch sets, Aperture automatically changes the text displayed below each image.

In general, it's better to set the detail pages to show the more complete metadata sets, such as General, and to have the index page show the smaller sets. Name & Caption is a good set for the index page, as it allows you to have both the image name and a short description of the image. Figure 8.6 shows these two different sets and pages. As usual, you can customize this text by opening the Metadata Inspector (Window > Show Inspectors) and entering values for the appropriate fields.

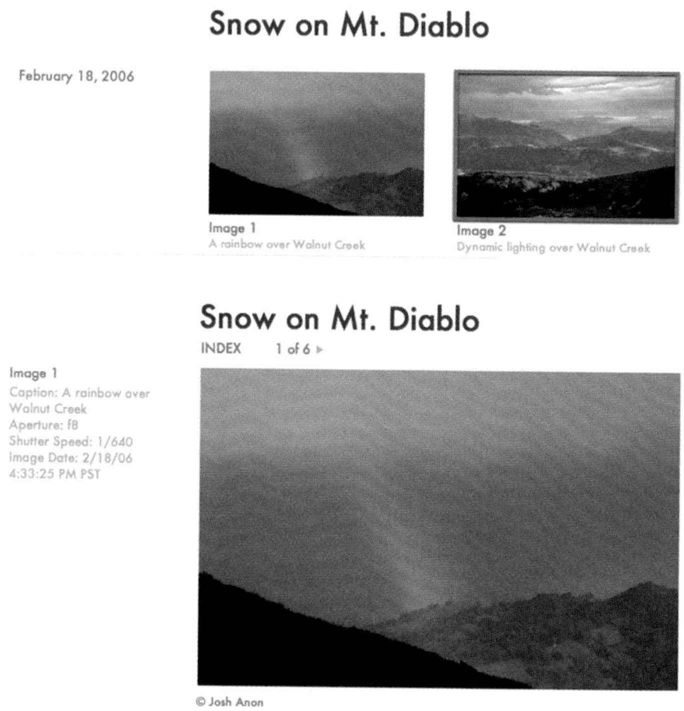

Figure 8.6: The Name & Caption metadata set is well-suited to the index page, whereas the General metadata set is well-suited to the detail pages.

Next to each image, you'll also see a number field that starts at 1 on the first image and ends at whatever number your last image has. The benefit to automatically numbering your images is that your clients can quickly say they'd like to purchase image 10, for example. Unfortunately, you cannot remove or edit this field within Aperture. Aperture automatically applies it as part of the theme. Later, we'll show you how to remove this field by modifying Aperture's web theme.

At the top of the window, you'll find controls, highlighted in Figure 8.7, for the layout and size of your gallery index's thumbnails. On the left, there are fields to control the number of rows and columns of images on each page. If you have more images than will fit on one page, Aperture will automatically make additional index pages and set up links between the index pages for you. To adjust the number in each field, you can use the arrows to the left and right of each field, double-click the field, and enter a number, or you can click and drag (scrub) the number in the field left or right. Your index page will update as you make your changes.

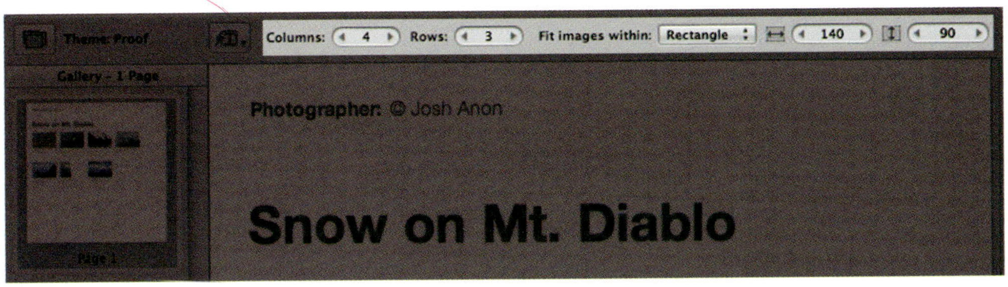

Figure 8.7: The controls across the top of the Web Page view let you lay out and resize your thumbnails.

On the right side of the controls, you'll find a pop-up menu to control the spacing of the thumbnails. Your options are Square, Rectangle, and Width. Square and Rectangle effectively say that you are going to define a box of a certain size, and your thumbnails will fit within that box, maintaining their aspect ratio. For instance, if you pick Square and set the size fields (to the right of the pop-up menu) to 140 × 140, any landscape images that you have will be 140 pixels wide and automatically sized to whatever height will let them fit within a 140 × 140 box. Similarly, for a portrait image, Aperture will set the thumbnail's height to 140 pixels, and it will automatically size the thumbnail's width to maintain the image's aspect ratio.

The difference between Square and Rectangle is that, with Rectangle, the thumbnail width and height fields can be different. If you have a gallery with a mix of landscape and portrait images, you'll notice that your images don't perfectly line up because the vertical images are taller than the horizontal ones (Figure 8.8). If you set the pop-up menu to Rectangle and set the height smaller, you can make the rows line up.

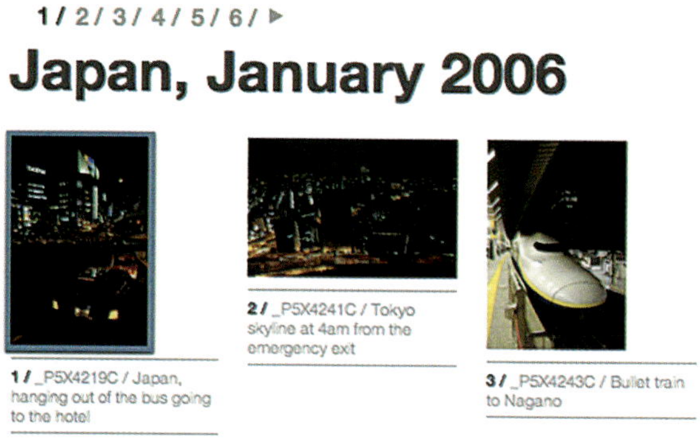

A

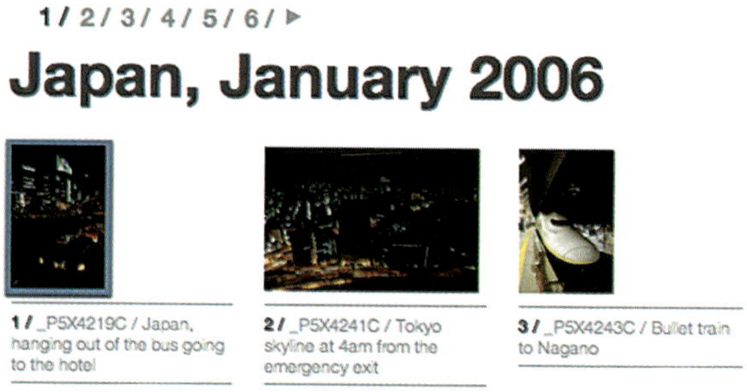

B

Figure 8.8: Image A shows the gallery thumbnail layout set to Rectangle at 140 × 140. Image B shows the thumbnail layout set to Rectangle at 140 × 90. Notice how the vertical and horizontal images don't line up in Image A but they do in Image B.

The third pop-up option, Width, lets you set the width of the image, and Aperture will automatically determine the correct height for each image. Keep in mind that portrait images will be significantly larger than landscape images due to their height being unconstrained. (Square and Rectangle let you set the maximum height for each image as well as the maximum width.)

Detail Pages

As you move your move your cursor over each image an arrow (➜) will appear. This arrow informs you that the image you're looking at is a hyperlink. When you click the arrow, Aperture will open the detail page for that image.

Within the detail page, the only field that you can customize is the metadata. To do so, as with the index page, click the Metadata Set Displayed With Images button (▾) and select which set Aperture should display below each image.

Although you won't find any controls at the top of the page for the rows and columns on each page (after all, you are showing only one image per page), you will find the image size controls. Here, just as on the index page, you can choose between Rectangle, Square, and Width settings. These settings are automatically applied to each detail page, giving you a consistent look for all of your detail pages. One setting that is easier to see with the larger images is how the Rectangle and Square settings preserve aspect ratio. Set the "Fit Images Within" Popup to Rectangle and start making the height larger and smaller. You'll notice that at some point, as you make the height field smaller (for a landscape image), the height constraint rather than the width constraint controls the image size. Similarly, as you make it larger, you'll get to a point where making height bigger has no effect because the width constrains the image size.

To move between detail pages, you can use the arrows on the left side of the Web view, next to the detail pages area, or you can use the arrows on the bottom-right side of the Web view. Earlier, we mentioned that the Web view is "live," meaning that you can click the buttons within the view and they'll act like real links. Within the Web view, you can use the buttons to go to the next and previous detail pages just as you would in a web browser. You can also click the index link on the detail page to jump back to the index page.

Smart Web Galleries

You can create a smart web gallery similarly to the way you created smart albums. To do so, choose File > New Smart > Web Gallery. Aperture will add a smart web gallery to the current project and bring up the Query HUD so that you can specify the smart album criteria. To edit the criteria at a later date, as you might expect, press the Query HUD button ( ) next to the smart web gallery in the Projects panel.

Creating Web Journals

The initial steps to create a web journal, either creating an empty journal or creating a journal from your selected images, are the same as the ones used to create a web gallery. Rather than selecting Web Gallery from the various menus, select Web Journal.

Once you have your desired images in the web journal's browser, you'll notice one very important difference between the web journal and a web gallery. Aperture does not automatically place images in the Browser in a web journal.

To place an image, select it in the Browser and drag it onto the web journal. Web journals contain blocks of text and images, starting at the top of the page. If you drag a second image onto the page and put it below the first image, you'll get a horizontal green bar (Figure 8.9) indicating that Aperture will create a new row for the image. If you drag the image to the right or left of the first image, you will see a vertical green line, meaning that Aperture will add this image to the same row as your existing image.

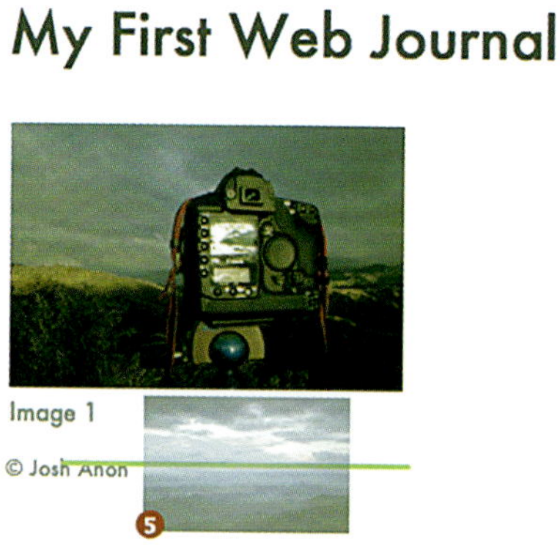

A

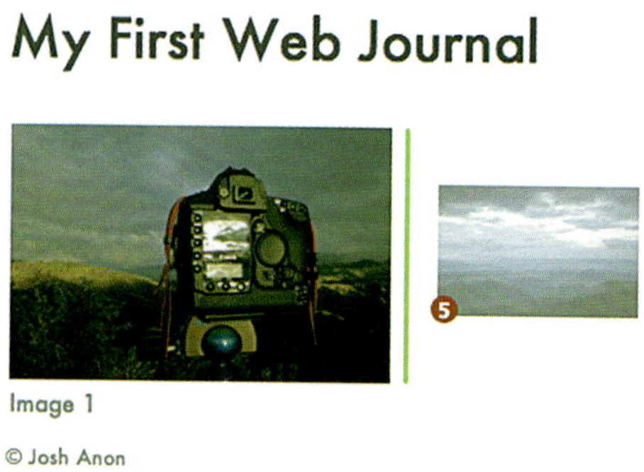

B

Figure 8.9:
When you drag an image to a web journal, you can create a new row (A) or add the image to an existing row (B).

At the top of the window, you'll notice a new button, Add Text Block ( ). If you press this button, Aperture will place a text block in a new row below your existing images. As expected, you can double-click this text block to edit it.

When you move your cursor over the text field, notice that Aperture draws a set of controls around the text field (Figure 8.10). The two controls on the left let you change the text format from a text block to a subheading. If you want to place multiple sets of images on the same page, use subheadings to divide each section. The next control switches the block back to a normal text block. The control on the far right will remove the text block. If you want to move the text block up or down, click and drag on the center area of the text block's top region, where there are three rows of four dots.

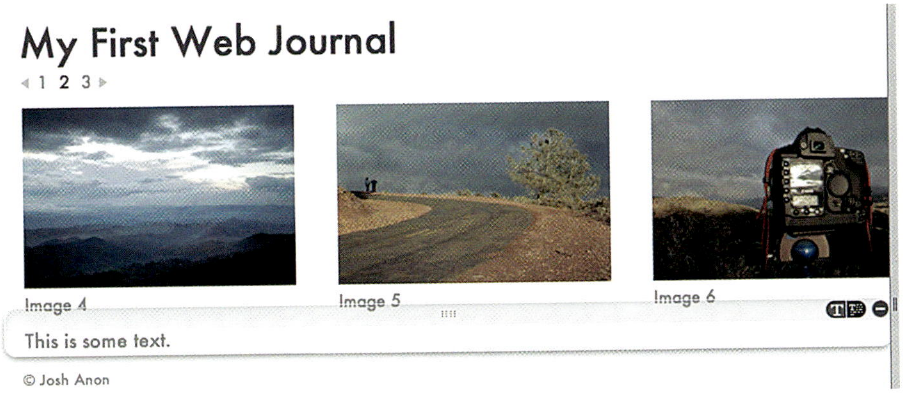

Figure 8.10: When you move your cursor over a text block, Aperture shows controls to change the format of the text block or to remove it.

When you move your cursor over a row of images, Aperture will reveal controls similar to those on the text block (Figure 8.11). There is a region in the center that you can click and drag to move the image row, and there is a control on the right that you can click to remove the row of images. As you move your cursor over each image, Aperture will reveal two controls. The button on top of the image will remove that individual image, and, like the web gallery index pages, the control on the bottom will take you to the image's detail page.

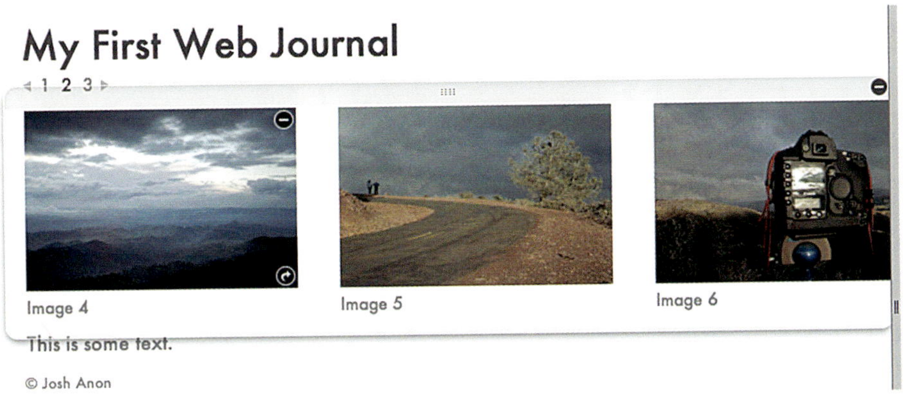

Figure 8.11: When you move your cursor over a row of images or a specific image, Aperture will reveal controls to move the row or delete the images.

You can continue to place images manually onto your web journal, or you can use some of Aperture's built-in commands to automatically make new index pages with specific sets of images. At the bottom of the Web view, above the Browser, you'll find an action menu ( ). Under this action menu are commands to make new pages based on your image's metadata. For instance, Aperture can automatically divide up your images based on rating, city, or date. Aperture will apply these commands to either the selected images or all images in your browser, if nothing is selected.

As an example, if you are keeping a photo blog of a trip, you can tell Aperture to create pages for each day, and it will group your images by day, making a new page for each day. Then, you can go to each page and add text describing what you were doing and what you took photos of on that day.

Note: To spell check any text you type into Aperture, Control-click the text and choose Check Spelling. Aperture will highlight each word that it considers to be misspelled.

If you want to manually make a blank page, press the Add Page button (+). To delete an index page, select it and press the Remove Page button (−).

After you place images onto your web journal, Aperture will display a small badge (1) on the image in the Browser, just as it did with books and light tables. Also as with books and light tables, you can toggle the Browser between showing all images ( ) and showing unplaced images only ( ). This browser also has the Lock This Browser To The Viewer button ( ) to help add images to your web journal.

You will find controls (similar to ones in the web gallery) at the top of the Web Journal view to adjust some of the page layout. The Columns control will adjust the number of columns in each image block. The Fit Images Within controls function the same way they do for the web gallery, as described in the previous section. Using the same buttons you use for web galleries, you can also set the site theme and change the metadata displayed with each image.

The web journal detail pages are also identical to those in the web gallery. You might expect to add text to individual journal image detail pages, but you can't. You can add text only to the journal index pages.

Exporting Your Site

In Aperture, when you are ready to publish your gallery or journal, you have two options for how to publish it. If you have a .Mac account, you can automatically export and upload your site in one step: click the Publish To .Mac button in the Web view. Aperture will check to make sure that you have a valid .Mac account (which you can set in your System Preferences under the .Mac pane) and that you can connect to your account. Then, Aperture will bring up the Publish To .Mac window (Figure 8.12), where you can set your gallery name and pick your thumbnail and image format. This window also displays your site's URL below the album name field. Click Publish to automatically export and upload your site. If you try to publish two sites with the same name, Aperture will prompt to see if you want to update or replace the existing site.

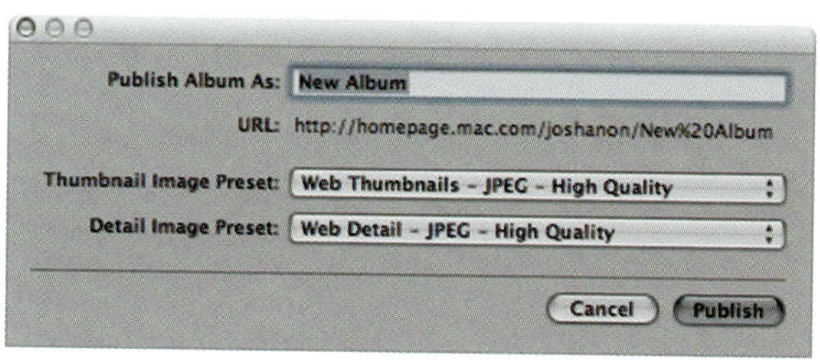

Figure 8.12: The Publish To .Mac window

Note: If you're publishing your sites to .Mac, create a site menu and add links for every photo gallery you want to be publicly accessible. By creating a site menu, you only need to provide clients with a link to the top level of your website (such as http://homepage.mac.com/joshanon) instead of numerous links to individual galleries.

Your second option is to use the Export Web Pages button to create a folder containing your website. When you click this button, Aperture will reveal the sheet in Figure 8.13. Here, you can pick which folder on your computer (or connected network volume) to use to store your album. There are also options at the bottom of the sheet to set thumbnail and image format—we will discuss those shortly. After you export your website, you can copy it to your web server using whatever means you normally do, such as file transfer protocol (FTP).

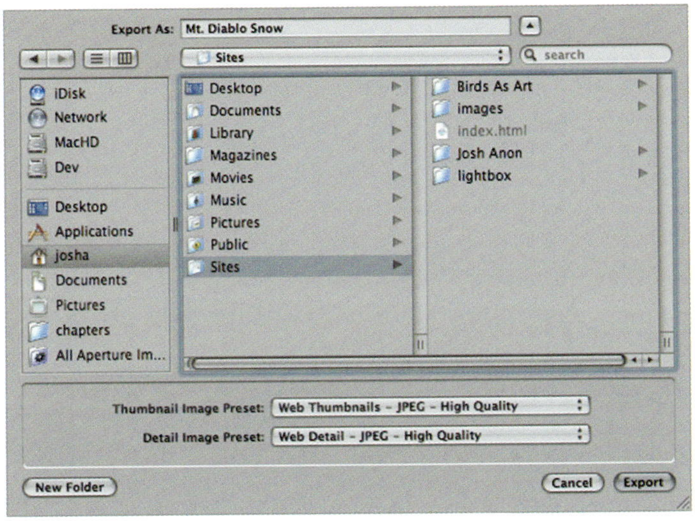

Figure 8.13:
The Export Web Pages sheet

Both windows have pop-ups to set your thumbnail and detail image formats. If you select Edit from the bottom of these pop-ups or choose Aperture > Presets > Web Export, Aperture will open a window (Figure 8.14) where you can see the details for these formats, modifying them as needed.

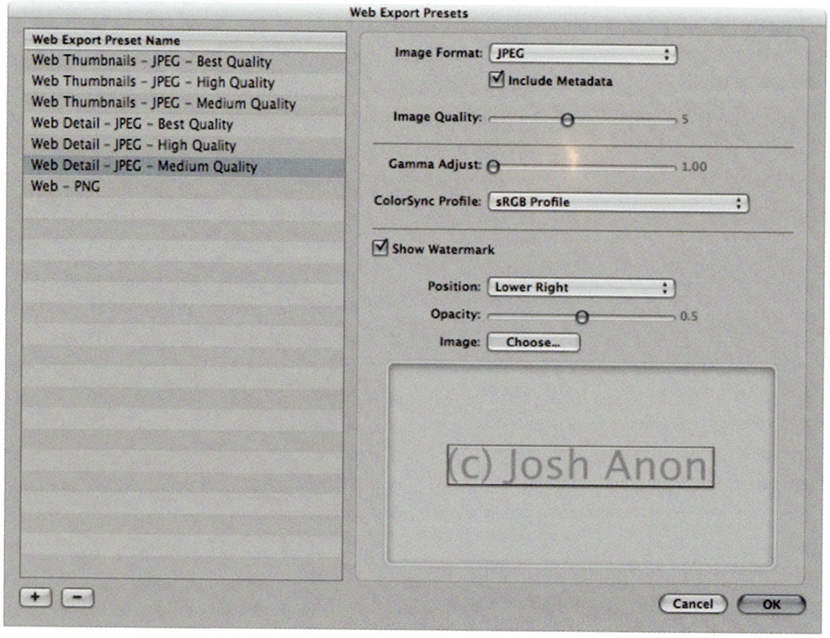

Figure 8.14: The Web Export Presets window

This window is identical to the Image Exports window we covered in Chapter 6, "Exporting Images." You can modify existing formats by selecting the format and changing its options, and you can add or remove preset formats by pressing the Add or Remove Preset buttons on the bottom left.

For each preset, the first option is which image format you want. For the Web, JPEG is usually the best option because JPEG images provide a good size-to-quality balance. You can use the Quality slider to set the image's quality, and higher quality images will be larger on disk. The Include Metadata button determines whether or not Aperture will embed your image's metadata into the image it generates.

The next set of options control the image's color. The gamma option is more useful for printing; however, if you want to boost the shadows in your image without significantly affecting your midtones or highlights, you can set a small gamma (1.1 at most). ColorSync profile determines which profile Aperture will embed into your images. In general, for the Web, you will want to pick sRGB. sRGB is designed to represent the average, uncalibrated computer monitor, and picking this profile will make sure that most people see roughly accurate colors when viewing your site.

The last option is whether or not you want a watermark. We highly recommend that you add a watermark to the detail version of your images. Given that anyone can Control-click your image and save it to their computer from their website, having a watermark on your image is your main defense against image theft.

We covered watermarks in detail in Chapter 6, but as a general reminder, make an image with a transparent background in a program such as Photoshop and add your watermark text in some visible color. You may want to have multiple watermarks and with varying colors. That way, if you have mostly dark images, you can pick a watermark with white text and vice versa. The size of your watermarks should be appropriate for your image size, which you set on the site's detail pages. If your images are 640 pixels wide, having a 1024-pixel watermark doesn't make sense, nor does having a 10-pixel watermark. A 150 or so pixel watermark on one of the bottom corners is probably sufficient to protect your image.

In general, select the medium-quality JPEG thumbnails preset (with no watermark) and the high-quality JPEG detail images preset (with a watermark). These settings work well because typically, you don't need very high-quality thumbnails, and you will not need to create the best-quality detail images unless you notice weird noise in your high-quality JPEGs. At the same time, medium-quality JPEGs are more likely to show JPEG compression artifacts, artifacts that won't be an issue with image thumbnails but that are not acceptable in the large versions of the image.

Using Other Tools to Make Websites with Aperture

Unfortunately, there is no way to create complete websites in Aperture. Its web creation ability is limited to galleries and journals. However, you can use the content you create in Aperture in other programs.

One way to use other programs is to make your web galleries within Aperture and then either edit the pages that Aperture outputs or to link to your Aperture gallery from a website that you make in another program. For example, you might use Aperture to make your galleries and use iWeb to make your site. Then, you might make a gallery index page in iWeb (take the Welcome template and delete the default content) where you place thumbnails from your web gallery, and make each thumbnail a link to your gallery. By creating your own custom Aperture template, you could even make your web galleries match the look and feel of the rest of your site.

An additional method is to export your images out of Aperture, as described in Chapter 6, and place them within your website-building program. The downside to this approach is that you lose Aperture's advanced gallery features, such as automatically displaying metadata (plus the ability to pick which metadata set your site uses) and smart galleries that automatically update.

A final option worth mentioning is a program from Lightbox Software called Aperture2iLife (www.lightboxsoftware.com). This program lets you use Aperture instead of iPhoto in your iApps, such as iWeb. Because it retains your albums, if you set up a smart album in Aperture with a given criteria, each time you run Aperture2iLife and open iWeb, you'll see an updated set of images in that album. You can use that updated album to determine what images you should add or remove from your page in iWeb.

Making Custom Web Themes

Before we dive into how to make your own web themes, we need to provide a warning. The information in this section of the chapter should be considered advanced material. The techniques we are going to show you are unofficial and unsupported, and they might change in future versions of Aperture. In other words, the information in this section could become outdated should Apple decide to change how Aperture's web tools work and your custom themes might break. However, because the ability to make web themes that blend with your existing website and the ability to customize Aperture's built-in themes is so useful, we are going to show you the secrets to making your own themes. For purposes of this discussion, we'll assume that you have a basic knowledge of HTML and Cascading Style Sheets (CSS).

Note: To learn about CSS, we recommend Virginia DeBolt's *Integrated HTML and CSS* (Sybex, 2005).

The first question you probably have is, Where are these web themes stored? Open a new Finder window, and find and select Aperture. Control-click Aperture and choose Show Package Contents. Drill down into Contents, into Resources, and into English.lproj (or whatever language you primarily use with Aperture). In the lproj folder, there is a WebThemes folder, and within that folder, there are folders for each theme.

For demonstrative purposes, throughout this chapter, we're going to make a gray version of the Stock theme, and we'll use the existing Stock Black theme as a starting point. Duplicate the Stock Black folder by selecting it in the Finder and choosing File > Duplicate. Rename the new folder from "Stock Black Copy" to "Stock Gray." When you open the Choose Theme sheet in Aperture, the folder's name will be the theme name.

Note: You can download the completed Stock Gray theme from this section from the book's companion website, www.sybex.com/go/apertureexposed.

We *highly* recommend that you do not modify a built-in theme. If you want to customize the theme, make a copy of it and modify the copy. This way, you will not accidentally corrupt Aperture's built-in themes. Also, keep a copy of any theme you modify or create outside of Aperture's WebThemes folder. That way, if you ever have to reinstall Aperture or if Apple modifies the WebThemes folder, you'll have a copy of your work.

Editing Your Themes in Website Editors

As we edit the various parts of the Aperture theme, we're going to open each page in a text editor such as BBEdit or TextMate. You can also use a website-creation program (such as Dreamweaver) to edit your theme. To do so, temporarily move your theme outside of the WebThemes folder, perhaps to your Desktop. Then, open up your web-editing program, make a new site, and set its root to be your theme's folder. You will see missing image tags where Aperture will insert your images and thumbnails, but editing your theme in a program such as Dreamweaver will give you instantaneous feedback for any CSS or HTML changes that you make.

What's in a Theme?

The contents of a web theme are rather simple. The albuminfo.plist file tells Aperture how the theme is set up and sets values for site parameters, such as the minimum and maximum number of columns. In general, unless you're creating a theme from scratch, you will not need to edit this file. Even if you are creating a site from scratch, we recommend copying the albuminfo.plist file from another theme and editing it as needed. To edit the file, you can either use the Property List Editor program, included free with Mac OS X as part of the developer tools, or you can open it in a text editor such as BBEdit. Generally, the fastest way to open files in your text editor is to drag the file onto the editor's dock icon.

Directly within the theme folder, there are between two and four HTML files. These are the template files that Aperture uses to generate your site. We'll show you how to modify these files. Their names describe their function. For example, detail.html is the template for the detail page, and journal-gallery.html is the shared journal and gallery index page.

The last two files are the icons that Aperture shows for your theme in the Choose Theme sheet. In general, the best way to create these icons for your revised theme is to finish your theme and create a sample gallery and journal using your theme. Take a screenshot of each of your sites and resize the screen captures to 90 pixels wide by 105 pixels tall. Then, replace the existing thumbnail.tiff and thumbnailJournal.tiff files in your theme's folder.

Within the Assets folder, there are two subfolders. The CSS folder contains the global.css file, which controls most of your site's appearance. We'll discuss how this file relates to your template HTML pages shortly, but suffice it to say that Aperture extensively uses Cascading Style Sheets (CSS) for each theme's appearance.

The Img folder, the second one, contains all the standard images, such as the next and previous arrows, on your site. Our template is going to include a small logo on it, and we'll store the logo image in the Img folder.

Editing the *global.css* File

Open the global.css file in the text editor of your choice. Assuming you're familiar with CSS, you'll notice that this file redefines several HTML tags, such as body (which controls the bulk of the page's formatting); defines some states, such as a:hover (what happens if you hover the cursor over a hyperlink); and defines several new classes such as .imageinfo (which Aperture uses around your image's number and metadata fields).

The first change we're going to make is to make the site background gray. Find the body block (it should be at the top), and look within there for the background-color style. Currently, the background is set to be black (#000). We're going to make it a dark gray by changing #000 to #444.

One side effect of changing our background color is that it might be hard to read some our text fields, such as the subheading. Let's modify our text fields' colors so that they're all reasonably bright.

As we look through the global.css file, h1 is the first text style we find. It's already set to white (#fff), which is plenty bright on gray. However, the next block, h2, has color set to #bbb (moderately bright gray). Make h2 a couple of shades closer to white by setting it to #ddd.

As we continue to read through the file, we eventually come to a style that Aperture uses for list items, links in general, and visited links. It's also set to a darker gray than we'd like (#bbb). Change the color entry for ul#nav li a, ul#nav li a:visited to #ddd.

The next block, ul#nav li a:hover, ul#nav li a:active, controls the color for unvisited links when we hover over them. Change its color from #ddd, which is now the color for our visited links, to #eee.

In this example, we are not going to modify our next and previous link images, but take note of how ul#nav .next a, ul#nav .next a:hover, ul#nav .previous a, and ul#nav .previous a:hover reference the arrow images. If you want to change the next and previous arrows, you can replace the existing files, giving your files the same name, or you can update the global.css file to point to your files instead.

The next block we're going to modify is the .imageinfo, .imageinfo a, .imageinfo a:visited, .imageinfo a:active, .imageinfo a:hover block. One place Aperture uses this style is for displaying image numbers. Change its color from #bbb to #ccc.

Because we'd like our web journal text to be readable, change the color for the .journaltitle and .journaltitle p blocks from #bbb to #ccc.

The final place we need to change text color in is the ul#metadata block, and Aperture applies this style to your image's metadata. Change its color from #999 to #bbb.

Editing the HTML Templates

Before we dive into HTML, let's make a new image in Photoshop to add to our site. For our demo, we made the image in Figure 8.15 by setting the color swatch to the same color as our site's background (#444444, which is red: 68, green: 68, and blue: 68 in decimal), adding some text and graphics, cropping the image to fit around our graphic, and saving the image as a JPEG. You can make any image you want, perhaps your studio's logo. Save it to the Desktop (if you're using the default OS save panel, Photoshop won't let you save inside a bundle, which is where our web theme is stored) and then move the image into the Img folder inside our Stock Gray theme. Do *not* embed an ICC profile when saving the image, as it will cause your background colors to not match in Aperture.

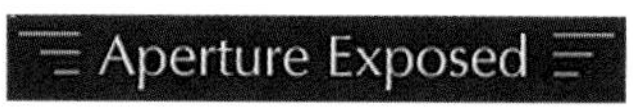

Figure 8.15: The demo image we created for the sample custom web theme

Editing the Index Pages

Now that we have our image together, let's open the journal-gallery.html page in our text editor. This page is the page that Aperture uses as the template for both web galleries and web journals. Some other web themes, such as Special Occasion, have separate templates for galleries and journals.

The key to sorting through this HTML is understanding that Aperture identifies sections of its HTML content using div tags that define a certain class, such as header and photo. Some parts, such as the pictureblock and navbar also have rkid values within a div tag, helping Aperture to determine what blocks of HTML represent what parts of the site. If you make your own template pages, make sure that you define areas for each rkid you see in the existing web themes. Otherwise, your custom theme might not behave properly in Aperture.

Throughout the page, you'll see special variables set apart because they begin and end with an underscore (_). Aperture replaces these variables, such as _TableWidth_, with values you define and values for each image.

Earlier, we mentioned how some templates (such as Stock and Stock Black) automatically display an image number below the image. If you want to get rid of this number, find the line that reads

```
<dt class="imageinfo">Image _PageNumber_ </dt>
```

and remove it. Instead of completely removing this line, you could also modify it, perhaps changing "Image" to "Photo," or you could move it.

Just to continue to explain the HTML template, notice that the images and web journal text are all contained within a table cell and set aside with a tag like this:

```
<div id="photo" rkid="content">
```

Within that block, there are three subblocks for each picture, web journal header, and web journal text block.

The pictureblock section contains the template that Aperture will use for each picture group, and the imageblock section contains the template for each image. To continue customizing our theme, let's put the image number above the thumbnail. Cut the line reading

```
<dt class="imageinfo">Image _PageNumber_ </dt>
```

and paste it before the <dd class="imagecell"> tag.

The next block on the page is the journaltitle block. As you might expect, this is the template that Aperture uses when you insert a web journal title block. Let's customize the style so that our titles are dark blue. Within the <h3> tag, add the text style="color:DarkBlue".

Note: CSS has a number of human-readable color names that you can use instead of hex values. You can find a complete list by searching the Web for "css color names."

The last content block is the journaltext block. It is similar to the other blocks we've seen already, but it contains a paragraph instead of a header or an image.

At the bottom of the page, you'll find a footer block. Let's add our image within this area. We called our sample image apertureExposed.jpg and saved it in our theme's Img folder. Insert the following:

```
<p align="center" contenteditable="false"><img
src="./assets/img/apertureExposed.jpg"></p>
```

immediately after the <div id="footer"> tag. To make the copyright text line up with our new image, add align="center" to the <p textid="copyright"> tag.

We've now finished customizing the index pages, and we'll continue to add our custom image to the detail pages.

Editing the Detail Pages

The content of the detail page template is very similar to the index page, but it does not have blocks for the journal header and text blocks. It only has the pictureblock. If you look at the bottom of the page, you'll find the same <div id="footer"> block from the index page. Make the same changes, inserting the following:

```
<p align="center" contenteditable="false"><img
src="./assets/img/apertureExposed.jpg"></p>
```

immediately after the <div id="footer"> tag and adding align="center" to the <p textid="copyright"> tag.

Trying It Out

After saving your changes, close and relaunch Aperture. Try making a new web journal, and set your theme to Stock Gray. Your website should look similar to Figure 8.16. If you have any errors, or something doesn't look quite the way you expected, double-check your typing. Even small, hard-to-find typos can cause chaos.

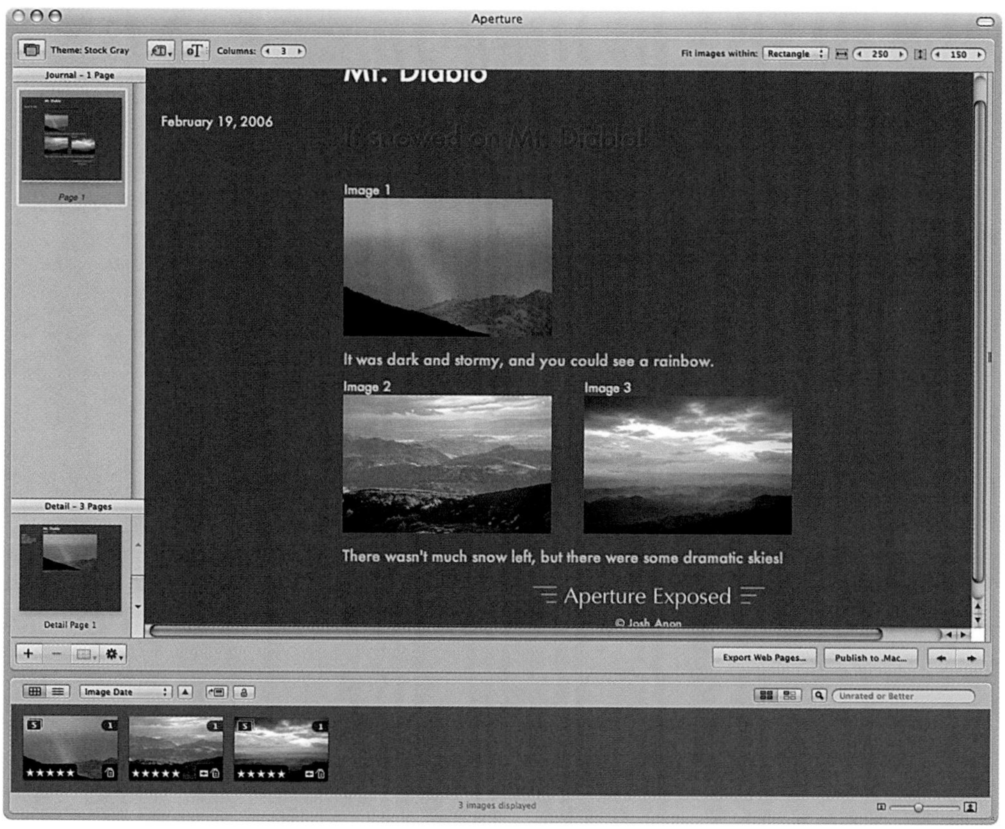

Figure 8.16: The completed Stock Gray theme with a sample web journal page

As you browse through your new theme, you'll notice that there are still a few details to finish. For one, the thumbnail icon in the Choose Theme sheet was the same as the Stock Black one. Additionally, the next and previous icons in the navigation bar have black backgrounds.

To fix your thumbnails, try creating a sample web gallery and web journal. Take a screen capture (use Grab, which you'll find in /Applications/Utilities) and resize the thumbnails to 90 pixels wide by 105 pixels tall. Copy those images into the theme folder, renaming them thumbnail.tiff and thumbnailJournal.tiff appropriately. When you restart Aperture, you'll see your new thumbnails.

To fix the navigation icons, open them in an image editor such as Photoshop (they're in the Assets/img folder) and change the background color to gray instead of black. Once you restart Aperture, you will see your new icons.

As we mentioned earlier, the completed theme is available on the Aperture Exposed companion website. To install it, download it and copy the Stock Gray folder into your WebThemes folder.

Now that you've learned how to make web pages, it's time to learn how to make books with your images. As you'll find in Chapter 9, "Creating a Book," the process is quite similar to making websites.

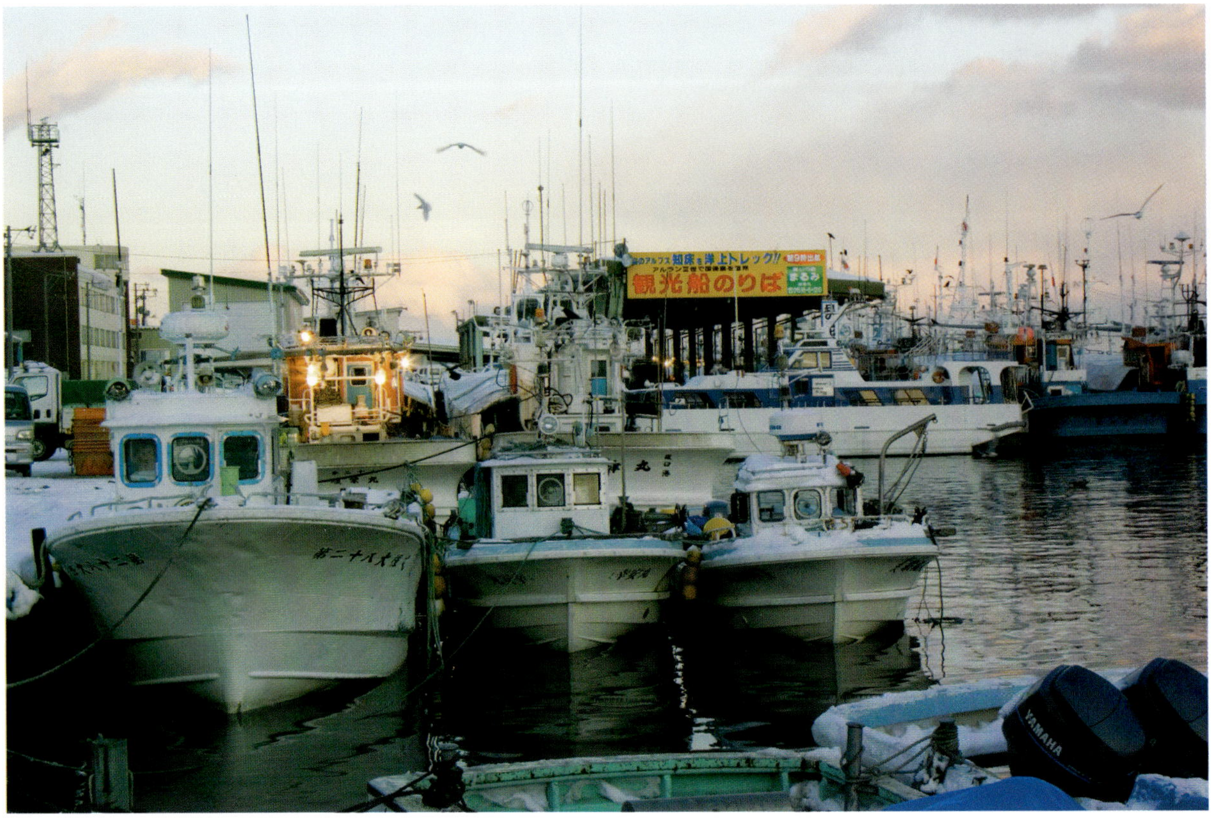
観光船のりば
まるみ
YAMAHA

Creating a Book

Creating a custom book is an ideal way to showcase your images for professional and personal uses. Aperture makes it easy to create a book featuring high-quality samples of your work as a promotional item to attract new clients or as a way to present proofs of a shoot to an existing client. Custom books also provide a great way to tangibly keep some of your personal images at hand so that they can be readily viewed and enjoyed by family and friends. They also serve as wonderful reminders of trips and special events.

9

Chapter Contents

Overview of the Book Creation Process

Before we delve into actually making a book, we're going to give you a global overview of the process. To start you'll need to select the images you want to include in your book, or begin with an empty book album and then add images. Later in this chapter, we'll cover both ways to create a book.

As you create the book album you also choose a size, mini or standard, and a theme for your book. The theme refers to the overall appearance, design, and layout of the book. Aperture provides different templates within each theme that you use to create each page. Of course you can easily modify the templates to fit your needs.

After you create a book album, the Book Layout Editor will appear. The Book Layout Editor (see Figure 9.1) contains several parts. On the left is the Pages panel, which shows a preview of each page in your book. Before you add images and/or text, placeholders are used on the pages so you have a feel for the overall flow of the book. As you add images the previews are updated. The Browser is at the bottom and contains all the images in your book album. The Viewer, which occupies the central portion, gives a larger preview of whatever page is selected in the Pages panel. To place images on a page, select the page so it appears in the Viewer and then click and drag the desired image from the Browser to the desired location on the page.

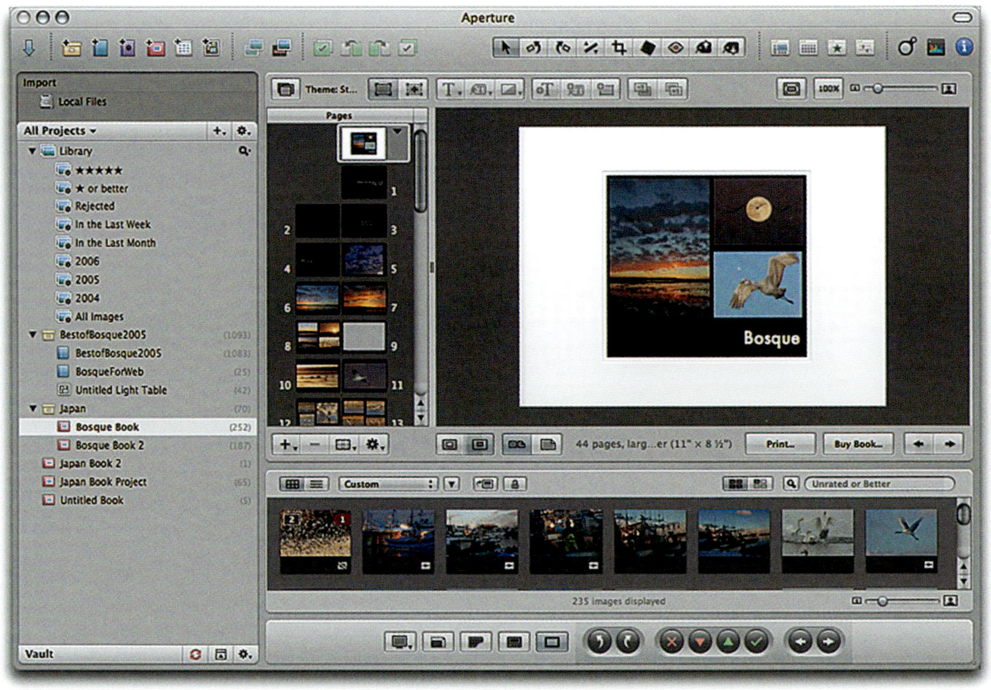

Figure 9.1: Aperture provides the Book Layout Editor to use when creating a book.

Aperture also enables you to readily add text, add or delete pages, and customize the templates. We'll show you how to do all of this later in the chapter. When you're done, you can print the book yourself or have it professionally printed and bound by Apple.

Tools in the Book Layout Editor

Before we go into the specifics of creating a book, we'll explain the various tools in the Book Layout Editor (Figure 9.2). We'll describe the buttons we commonly use; most are located above the Pages panel and the Viewer, but some are below them.

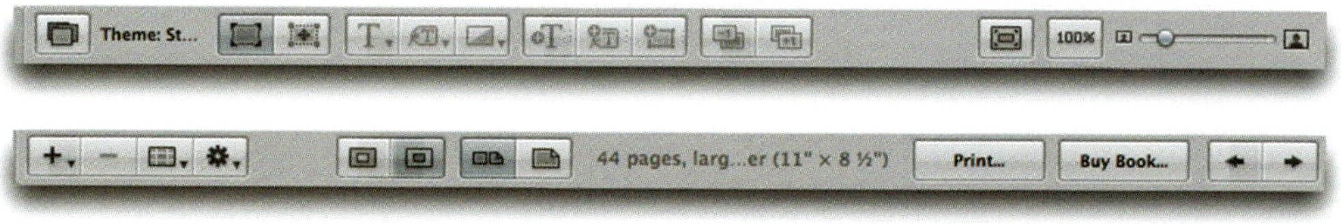

Figure 9.2: The Book Layout Editor contains a series of buttons above and below the Pages panel and the Viewer.

The Edit Content button ( ) is selected by default. It allows you to place images or text on a page according to the layout that exists on the page template. When this button is selected, the other buttons in the same row will be grayed out. You will only be able to place images into photo boxes already on the page and place text into text boxes already on the page.

The Edit Layout button ( ) allows you to modify the layout of the page, meaning that you can add or delete photo and/or text boxes, as well as modify their size and position. When this icon is selected, the other buttons in the row become active. (We'll cover those other buttons shortly.) To resize an image or text box, select that item, click the small handles on the sides of the box, and drag the box to the desired size. To delete a box, select it and press the Delete key.

With the Edit Layout button selected, you can add a place for an image by clicking the Add Photo Box button ( ) or add room for text by clicking the Add Text Box button ( ). Use the Text Style pop-Up menu button ( ) to select one of the default font sizes for your text. (We'll show you how to customize the text later.) To add a place for metadata, click the Add Metadata button ( ). The metadata boxes use information from the image's metadata. Use the Set Metadata Format pop-up menu button ( ) to choose what metadata appears in that box.

Note: See Chapter 4, "Finding the Keepers," for more details about using metadata.

You can apply a filter to a photo box before or after you place an image in that box by clicking the Photo Filter pop-up menu ( ). Filters enable you to change the image to black-and-white or sepia tones, as well as to fade the image to a wash so it can be used as a background for other text or images, as shown in Figure 9.3.

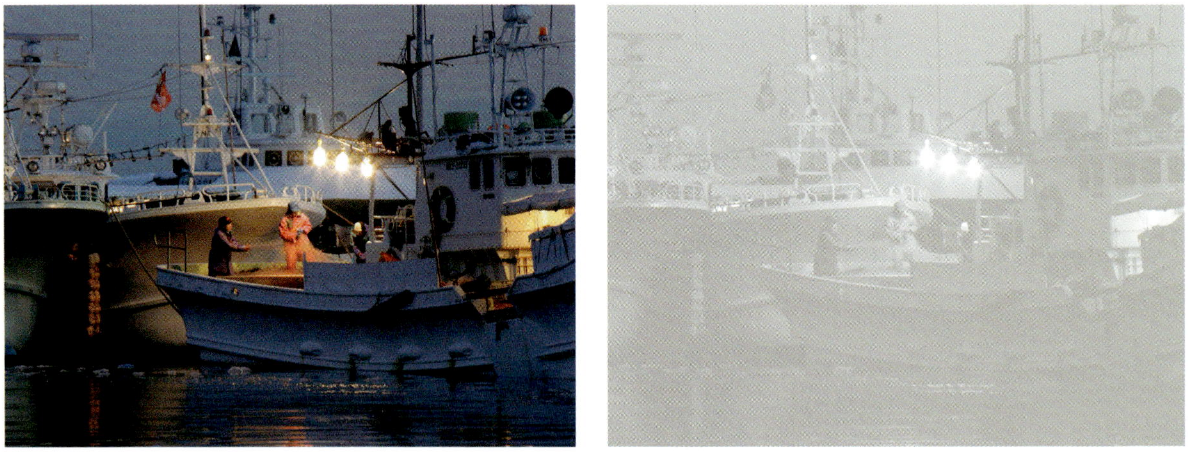

Figure 9.3: By using the Photo Filter to add a wash effect, an image can be faded for use as a subtle background.

As you design your pages, you might intentionally have some of the images overlap one another by resizing the photo boxes. When you do so, you can specify whether the selected image moves in front of another image or behind it by using the Bring Forward button ( ) or Send Backward button ( ), as shown in Figure 9.4.

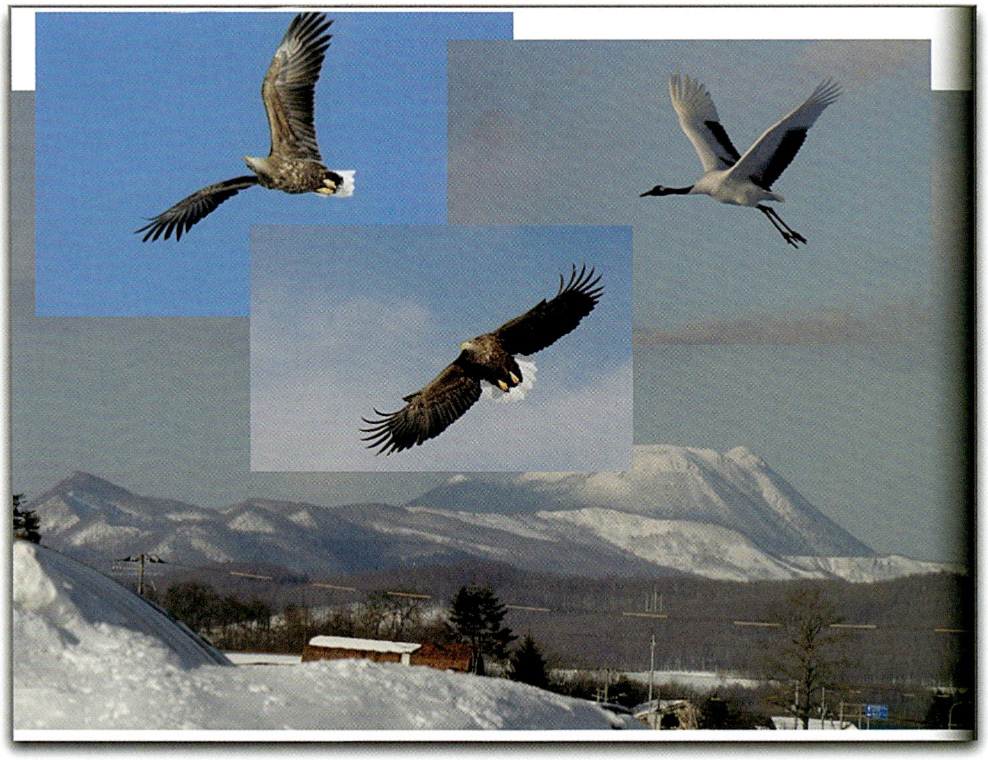

Figure 9.4: Overlapping images in your layout can be quite effective.

At the top-right of the Book Layout Editor are buttons that control the magnification of the page previews in the Viewer. The Scale To Fit button ( ) scales the preview of your pages to fit the Viewer window. Next to it is the Actual Size button ( ). Clicking it will display a page at its actual size. Next to the Actual Size button is the Display Size slider. Drag it to increase or decrease the size of the page preview in the Viewer.

Underneath the Viewer on the left side are the Show Full Spreads button ( ) and the Show Single Pages button ( ). Click these to show either a single page at a time or a two-page spread in the Viewer.

To the right of the Print and Buy Book buttons are the Previous Page button ( ) and the Next Page button ( ). Use them to navigate through your book.

Creating and Customizing a Book

Here's the fun part! We'll guide you through the steps to create a book.

Note: As you read this section, you might want to follow along on your computer using some of your own images.

Starting the Book Album

To begin you have to create a Book Album. You can select a group of images first or create an empty book album and later drag images into it one by one. Usually, we find it more efficient to select a group of images first. This can be as simple as selecting all the images within an existing project or album or selecting a subset of them, perhaps identified and sorted by ratings or keywords. You can always augment the selection of images later, and you aren't obligated to use all the pictures you bring into the book album in the book itself.

To create a new book album from a selection of images, follow these steps:

1. Select images from an existing album or project. It's a good idea to select more images than you're going to use in the book so you have choices and can use whichever images work best together.
2. Do *one* of the following:
   - From the main menu, choose File > New From Selection > Book.
   - Click the New Book from Selection icon ( ) in the toolbar.
   - From the Add To Library pop-up menu, choose New Book From Selection, as shown in Figure 9.5.

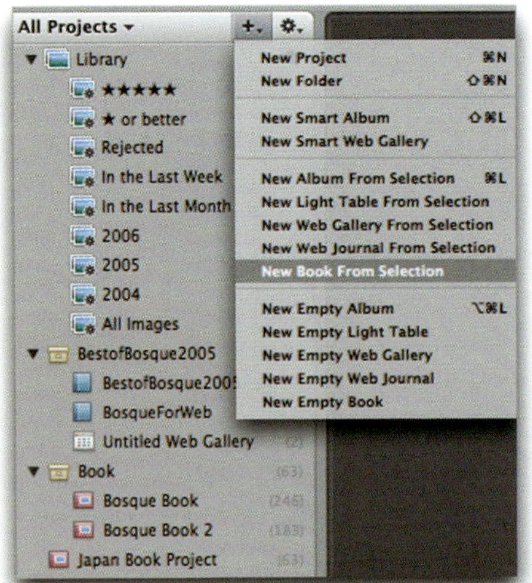

Figure 9.5: You can use the Add To Library pop-up menu to create new book albums.

3. Choose a size and a theme from the dialog box that appears in Figure 9.6. (We'll describe themes in detail in the next section.)

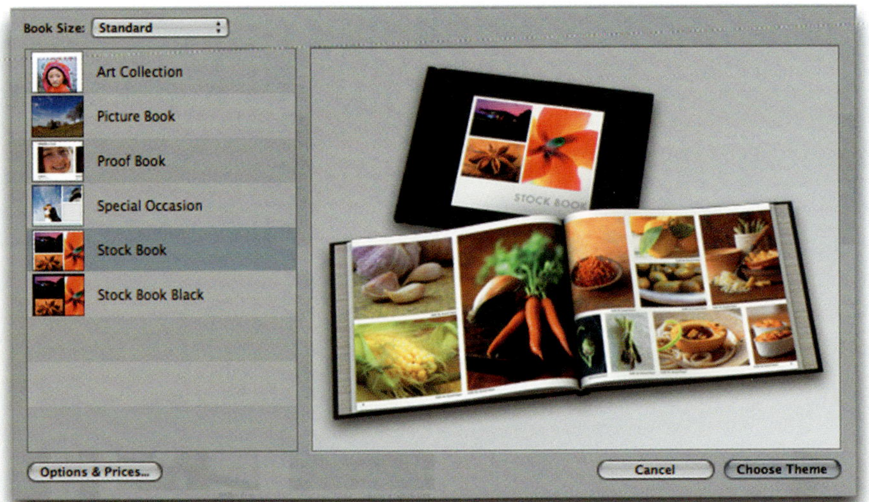

Figure 9.6: Choose a theme to determine the general appearance and layout of your book.

4. Click Choose Theme.

5. Name the book by immediately entering the desired name.

Some people prefer to create an empty book project and populate it with only the images they definitely want to use. To create an empty book album, follow these steps:

1. Do *one* of the following:

- From the main menu, choose File > New > Book.
- From the Add To Library pop-up menu, select New Empty Book.

2. Choose a size and a theme from the dialog box that appears.
3. Click Choose Theme.
4. Name the book by immediately entering the desired name.

To add images to an empty book album or to add additional images to a book album created from a selection, follow these steps:

1. Click the Lock this Browser to the View button ( ) located at the top of the Browser.
2. Option+click the project or album containing the images you want to use. This will cause the Browser at the bottom to divide into two parts. One will show the images in your book album, and the other will display the images in the source project or album.
3. Click and drag the desired images from the source album or project into the book album. The images will now appear in both places and you remain in the Book Layout Editor. This makes it easy to search for additional images while you're doing the actual layout of the book rather than check.

Choosing a Theme

You choose a theme for your book from the pop-up dialog that appears when you first create a book project. Each theme contains professionally designed templates for the pages. Although the pages within all the themes are quite customizable, it makes sense to choose the theme that comes closest to your vision of how you want your book to look.

The first option controls the size of the book: mini or standard. If you choose mini, the book is small—2.6 × 3.5 inches—and Aperture defaults the layout to one image per page. If you choose standard, the book will be 8.5 × 11 inches and you will have six theme choices: Art Collection, Picture Book, Proof Book, Special Occasion, Stock Book, and Stock Book Black. Each theme has a series of master pages/templates to choose among, as well as a default presentation of the number and order of pages.

Just because the theme is called one thing doesn't mean you have to use it for only that purpose (Proof Book with proofs, for instance). Feel free to choose whatever theme best suits your vision and purpose! And don't feel limited by the default themes because you can customize each page as desired. For example, we'll cover how to change the size, position, and aspect ratio of the picture templates to fit your images later in this chapter. Before we get to customization, let's take a look at each of the built-in themes.

The Art Collection theme includes a variety of text and image page choices, as shown in Figure 9.7. Most of the pages in this theme have pictures laid out as either full page, double spread, or two per page. Text pages can be in title, paragraph, or list format. This theme generally offers more text information about the images than does the Picture Book theme.

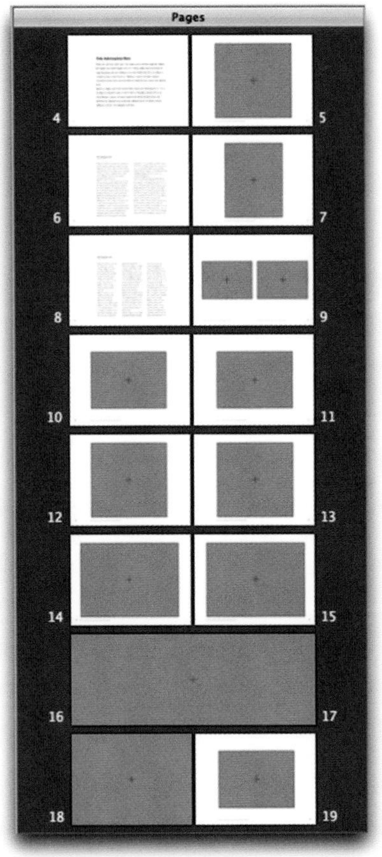

Figure 9.7:
The Art Collection templates are geared toward displaying images full-page or half-page along with text-oriented pages.

The Picture Book theme includes master pages for full-bleed pictures and double-spread full-bleed pictures, as shown in Figure 9.8. The only text pages available by default are title pages and table of contents. Blank pages are also available to customize as desired. The emphasis here is on each individual photo.

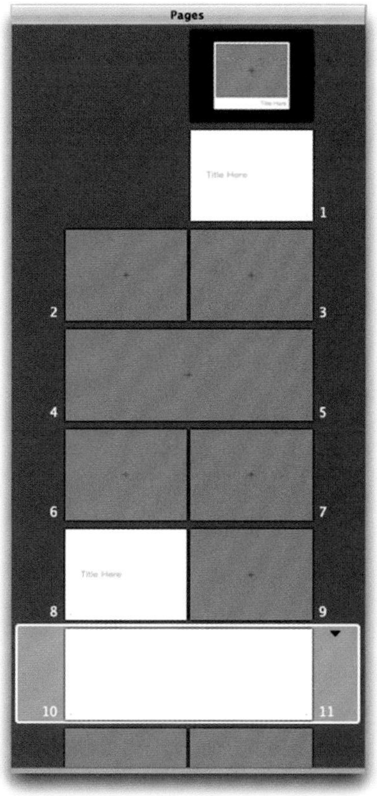

Figure 9.8:
The emphasis is on full-page and double-page spreads in the Picture Book theme.

Proof theme books have a variety of photo layout options, as seen in Figure 9.9. In addition, there is plenty of room for text to add information about the images, including captions and/or metadata. This format can be quite useful when presenting images to a client.

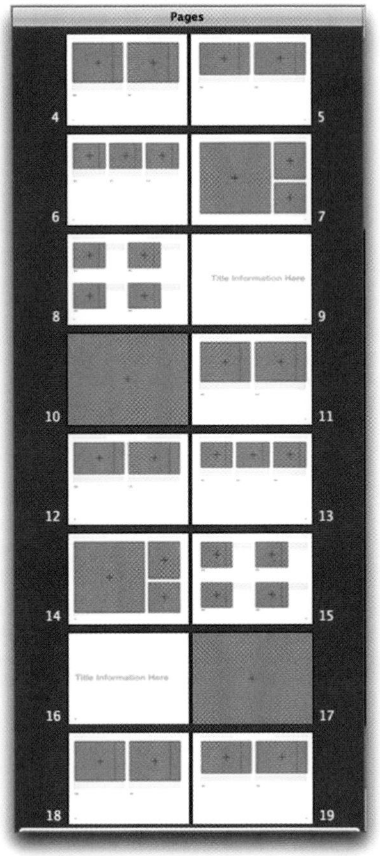

Figure 9.9: The Proof templates offer a wide variety of image layouts with room for text.

The Special Occasion theme is designed to tell the story of an event via pictures and text. As shown in Figure 9.10, the pages vary from double-spread images to pages with up to 12 different images per page, and there is room for explanatory text. In addition, there are text pages designed to list attendees, music selections, and more. If you have photographed an event and want to create a book to recapture the details and jog your memory, this is the theme to select.

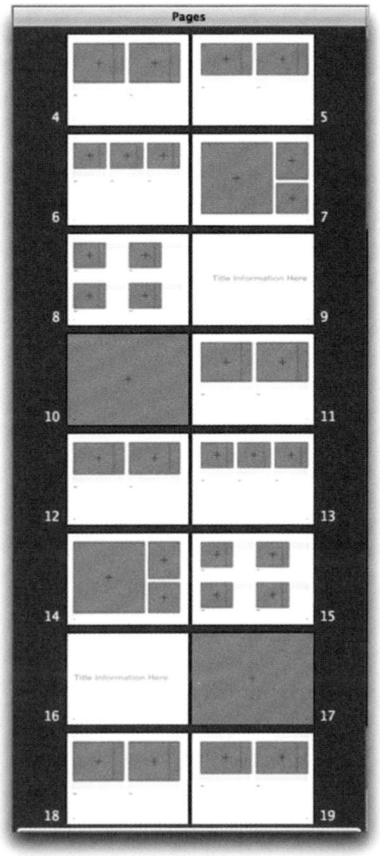

Figure 9.10: The Special Occasion theme contains a wide variety of templates to record the details of an event.

Stock theme books are designed to showcase your photography and present from one to eight images per page. They have places to add captions, or brief text, as well as page templates to use for a table of contents, title, and section titles to separate sections of pictures, as shown in Figure 9.11. You can choose the regular Stock theme or Stock Book Black that uses black backgrounds on each page rather than white.

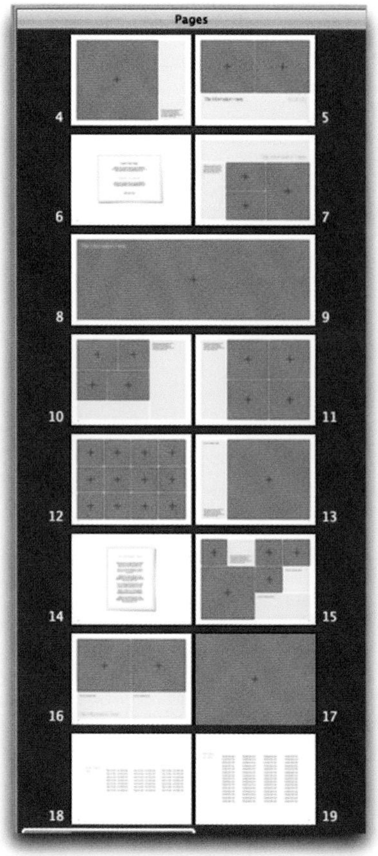

Figure 9.11: The Stock Book templates are designed to showcase your photography.

You can change the theme for a book at any time by clicking the Choose Theme button () at the top of the page layout preview in the Book Editor layout. However, if you've added text, some of it could be lost when you apply the new theme. Of course the pictures will be rearranged to fit the new templates.

Customizing the Theme

Although each theme has a specific number of pages with a specific template on each page, you can readily add, delete, or modify pages. You can alter the template used on any page within a theme via the buttons and pop-up menus found under the Pages panel, as shown in Figure 9.12.

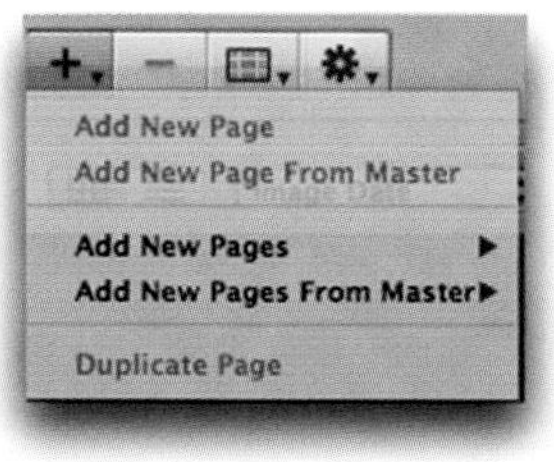

Figure 9.12: Adding or deleting pages is easy.

Use the Add Pages pop-up menu button ( ) to add additional pages to your book. Choose Duplicate Page to copy the layout and content of the currently selected page, and place the new page immediately after it. Choose Add New Page to have the new page appear at the end of the book and duplicate the layout of the currently selected page.

Use the Delete Pages button ( ) to remove the currently selected page. Use the Set Master Page pop-up menu button ( ) to change the layout template of the currently selected page. Click any of the master page templates to replace the template of the currently active page.

Note: Later in this chapter, we'll show you how to customize any of the individual templates.

If you selected a standard-size book in the initial dialog box, you can choose either a large hardcover book ( ) or a large softcover book ( ). These icons are below the page preview in the Book Layout Editor, and you can change between them at any time.

As of the time we are writing, the pricing structure for books ordered from Apple is as shown in Table 9.1 (all books have a maximum of 100 pages). You can check the pricing options by clicking the Theme button ( ) and clicking Options and Prices. This will connect you to a page on the Apple site with the most up to date information.

Table 9.1: Pricing for Aperture Books

Format	Size	Price per Book	Additional Pages
Mini softcover	2.6 × 3.5 inches	$3.99 up to 20 pages	$0.29 each
Large softcover (also called standard size)	8.5 × 11 inches	$19.99 up to 20 pages	$0.69 each
Keepsake books (also called large hardcover)	8.5 × 11 inches	$29.99 up to 20 pages	$0.99 each

Laying Out the Book

After you create a book album and select a theme, your next step is to place the photos and text in the book and alter the templates as necessary.

Placing Images in the Book

Some photographers, particularly those offering proofs of a shoot to a client, will appreciate Aperture's ability to quickly and automatically place images in a book. After creating the book album using one of the methods described earlier in this chapter, select Autoflow Unplaced Images from the Book Action pop-up menu, as shown in Figure 9.13. Choose Autoflow Selected Images to specify a subset of images to be automatically placed. Using the theme you specified, Aperture will create a book with as many pages as necessary.

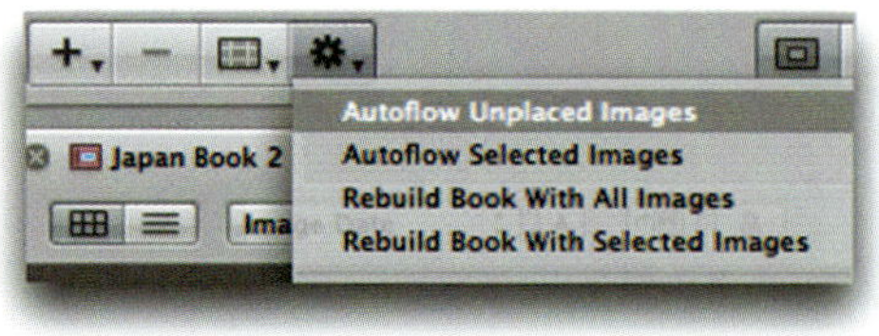

Figure 9.13: Using the Autoflow commands, Aperture can automatically place the images into your book.

Most photographers prefer to manually place their images in a book. To do so, make certain that the Edit Content button ( ) is selected; then click an image and drag it to the desired photo box.

We usually try to select landscape-oriented images to fit the horizontal photo boxes and verticals for the others. Nonetheless, the aspect ratio of an image often will be different from that of the photo box in the template. Aperture offers several choices as to how to proceed. Our preferred approach is to adjust the aspect ratio of the photo box to match that of the image by doing the following:

1. After dragging the image to the photo box, select the Edit Layout button ( ).
2. Right-click/Control-click the image and choose Photo Box Aspect Ratio > Photo Aspect Ratio, as shown in Figure 9.14. This slightly alters the photo box so that your entire image appears in a space as close as possible to the one appearing in the original template.

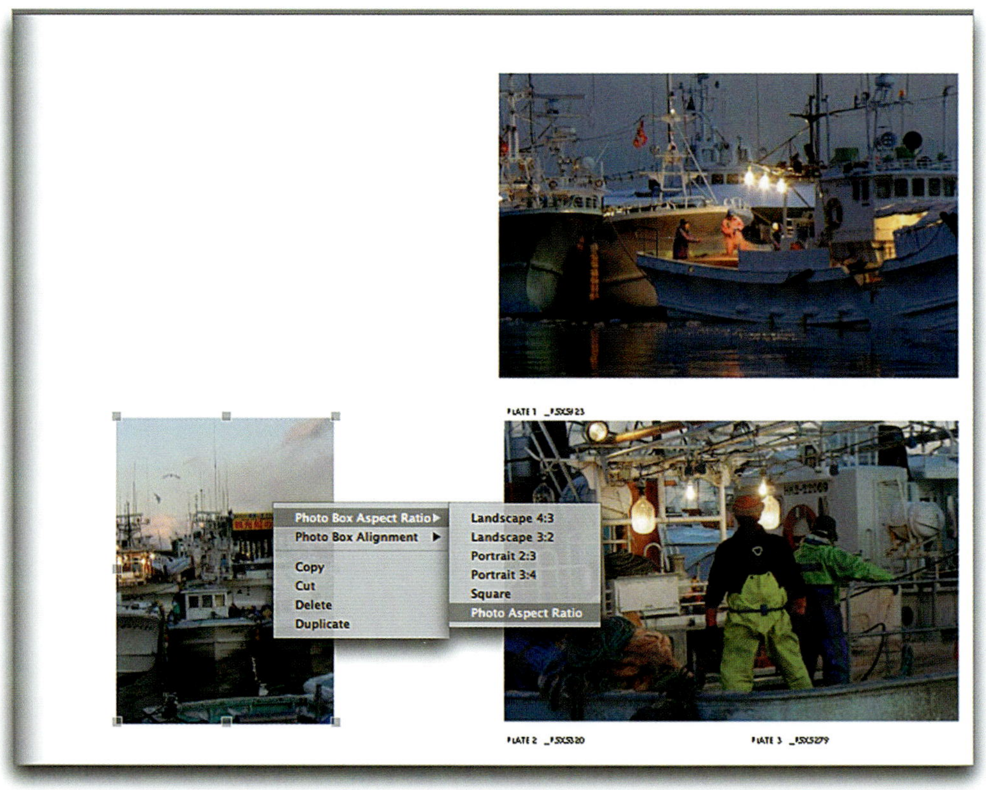

Figure 9.14: Adjust the Photo Box proportions to match your image's aspect ratio so your image is not cropped or distorted.

An alternative choice is to center the image within the space occupied by the photo box. To do this, right-click/Control-click the image after dragging it in place and choose Photo Box Alignment > Center. Of course, you could also choose Right or Left justify from the Photo Box Alignment pop-up menu.

If your image is larger than the Photo Box, you can also choose to show just part of the image. To do so, select the Edit Layout button and then double-click your image. The cursor will become a hand, and you will be able to drag the image around to show whatever part is desired.

Aperture places a badge with a number on each image after you have used it in the book. The number indicates how many times each image appears in the book. To see just the images that are still unplaced, check the Show Unplaced Images button ( ) in the Browser.

To remove an image from a photo box, right-click/Control-click the image and choose Delete Content from the context menu.

Adjusting Images in the Book

As you select images to place in the book, you may decide that they need some further adjustments. It's easy to make adjustments while creating a book.

To adjust an image, select it in the Browser and then press H or go to Window > Show Adjustments HUD. You may want to change to Full Screen mode by pressing F before making your adjustments. Adjust the image as you normally would. To return to the Book Layout Editor, press F again. The image will be updated in the book as well as in the Browser.

Creating Custom Page Templates

Although the templates have been professionally designed, there are many other ways to lay out your photos on a page. Aperture makes it easy for you to create your own page templates. Follow these steps to create a custom page template:

1. Select a master page using the pop-up menu from the Set Master Page button ( ) that comes close to what you need.
2. Adjust the size of each photo box by first selecting the Edit Layout button ( ). Click the photo box and drag it to the desired size using the small handles on the edges.
3. Click in the center of a photo box and drag to adjust its placement on the page. Yellow guide lines will appear, as shown in Figure 9.15, to help you center the photo box.

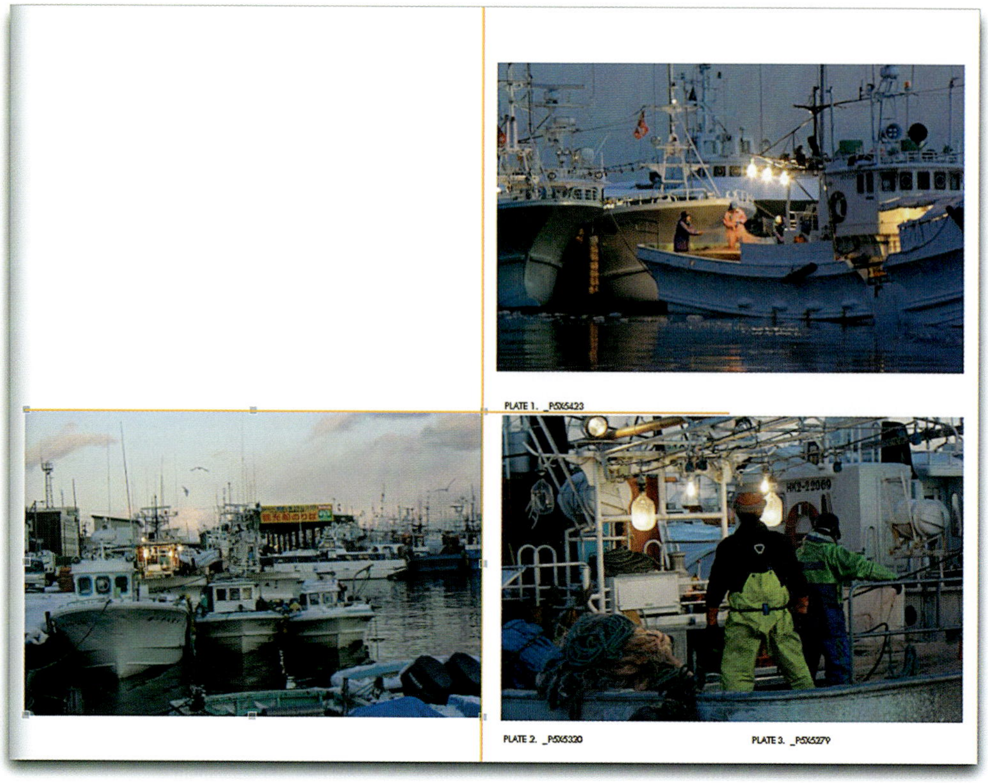

Figure 9.15: Use the yellow guide lines to align the new photo box.

4. To add additional photo boxes, with the Edit Layout button ( ) selected, click the Add Photo Box button ( ). Aperture will create a new photo box in the center of the page.

- Move the new photo box to the desired location by clicking in the center of the box and dragging.
- Adjust the size of the new photo box by dragging the handles on the edges accordingly.

5. Don't forget that you can have pictures overlap. To control which image is in front, use the pop-up menu from the Book Actions button and select Arrange, as shown in Figure 9.16.

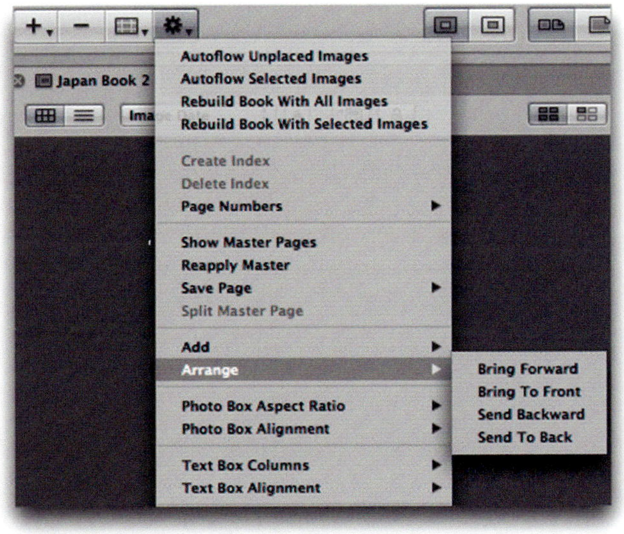

Figure 9.16: To place overlapping images, use the options in the Book Action pop-up menu.

6. You can save your custom layout for future use by selecting the Book Action pop up menu > Save Page > As New Document Master.

Note: By default Aperture is preset not to display plate numbers for images. To make the plate numbers visible, choose Enable Plate Metadata from the Book Action pop-up menu in the Book Layout Editor.

Third-party developers offer more options for layout styles. Silvery Stars Productions and mac:method offer two additional plug-ins with a variety of filters and templates to use with Aperture. To find them, go to:

`http://macmethod.com/ApertureBooks/Site/Signature%20Series.html`

Adding Text to a Page

Many themes include pages with default text boxes. When faced with a page with a default text box, such as for the title of a book, click within the text box. The placeholder text will be highlighted. Begin typing as desired. The font size and color will automatically be selected.

To make basic adjustments to your text including changing the font style, size and color, choose Edit > Show Fonts or press ⌘/T. Highlight your text and then specify your choices. The text will be updated to reflect the changes.

For more options to customize text, select the Edit Content button and then right-click/Control-click within the text box to reveal the pop-up menu shown in Figure 9.17. These choices will enable you to spellcheck and customize your text and even to hear it spoken aloud. If you select the text before Control-clicking, you will get three additional choices in the pop-up menu: Search In Spotlight, Search In Google, and Look Up In Dictionary.

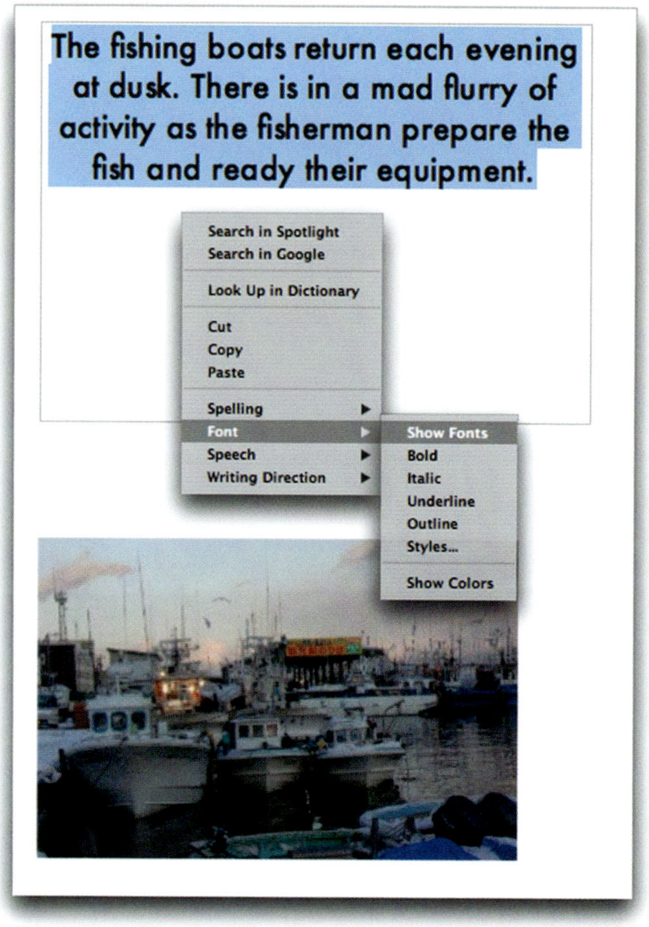

Figure 9.17: Numerous tools for enhancing your text are available by Control-clicking in the text box.

- Choose Font > Show Fonts.
    - To change fonts, highlight the text, and then select the desired font and size from the Show Fonts dialog box shown in Figure 9.18. The text will automatically update to reflect your selections.
    - Click the "T" button in the upper-left corner to add a drop shadow to the text.
    - Close the Show Fonts box.

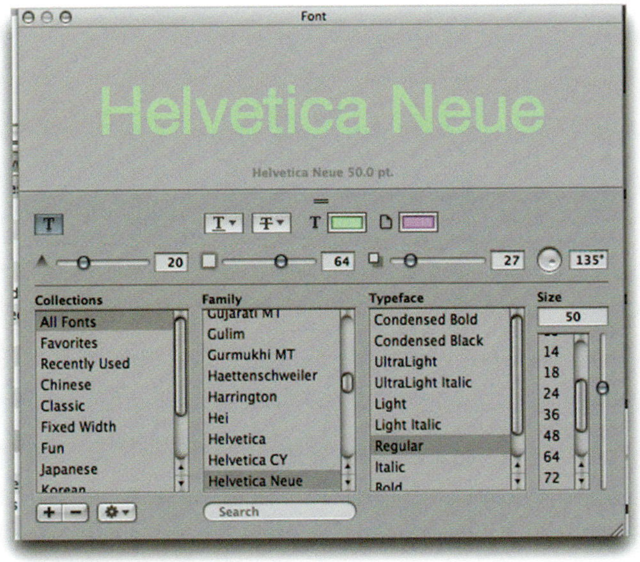

Figure 9.18:
Select your font from the
Show Fonts dialog box.

- Choose Font > Show Colors.
  - To change the font color, highlight the text and then select the desired color in the Color Picker shown in Figure 9.19.

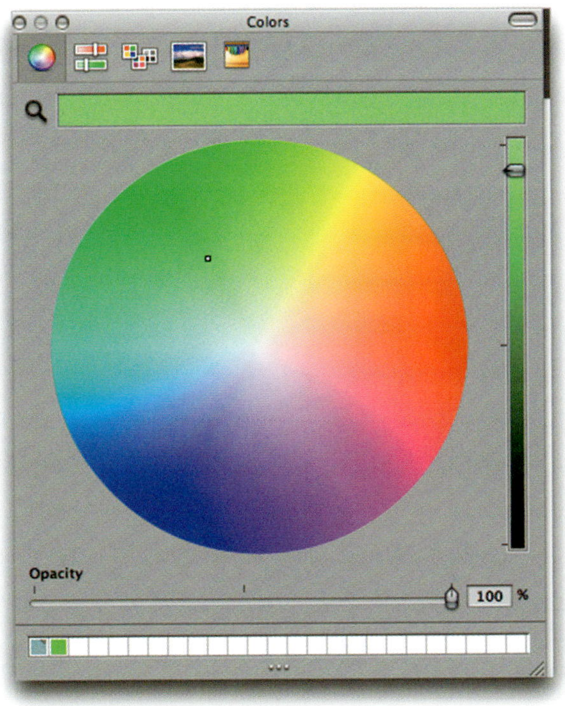

Figure 9.19:
Choose a color for the text
from the Color Picker.

  - Drag the sample of the new color to the highlighted text.
  - Close the Color Picker when you're done.

- Choose Spelling to see options for checking spelling.
  - Choose Spelling > Check Spelling As You Type.
  - Choose Spelling > Check Spelling to check the text after it has been typed.
  - Choose Spelling > Spelling to make a guess and have Aperture generate options for the correct word.
- Choose Speech > Start Speaking to have the computer read the selected text aloud. Make sure your speakers are turned on.

To add a text box to a page, select the Edit Layout button ( ), and then click the Add Text Box button ( ). A new text box will appear in the middle of the page.

- Click in the middle of the text box and drag it to the desired place on the page.
- Click the handles on the edge of the text box to adjust it to the desired size and shape.

When you are creating custom page templates as described earlier in this chapter, you can add custom text boxes to those pages as well. You can also create pages that are text only by taking the following steps:

1. Select a blank master page from the Set Master Page button ( ) pop-up menu.
2. Select the Edit Layout button ( ) and then the Add Text Box button ( ).
3. Right-click/Control-click within the Text Box. Two new options will appear: Text Box Columns and Text Box Alignment.
   - Choose Text Box Columns to set the number of columns you want to use for text on the page.
   - Choose Text Box Alignment to determine how the columns are spaced on the page.

Finishing the Book

After you have filled in all the pages, scroll back to the beginning and flip through the book page by page using the Next Page button. When you are happy you can click the Buy Book button or you can make a proof of the book by selecting Print to be sure you are pleased with the layout. You can also save the book as a PDF from the print menu.

When you click the Print button, the dialog box shown in Figure 9.20 appears. Click the Printer Settings button to access your normal printer control menus.

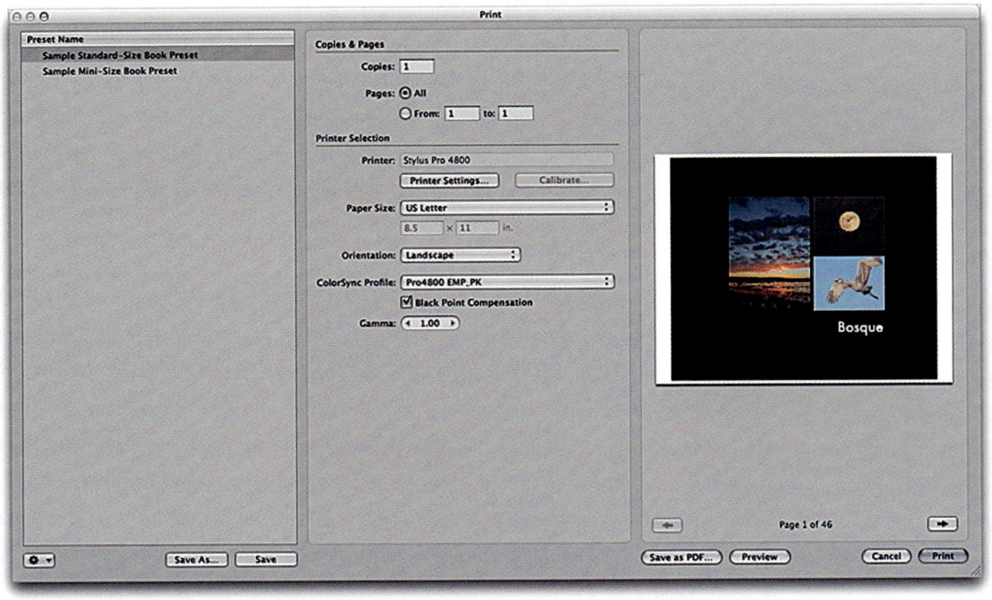

Figure 9.20: Aperture provides a print dialog in which you specify various parameters.

Specify your printer, as well as important parameters such as paper type and print quality, under the Print Settings dialog box. It is imperative to access the Printer Color Management dialog box (see Figure 9.21) and select Off (No Color Management). This allows you to specify the correct printer/paper profile for the printer to use. Failure to do this will result in a book with odd colors. Also specify the paper size and orientation in Aperture's Book Print dialog. You must select the correct printer/paper/ink profile from the pop-up window in the Color Sync Profile dialog box.

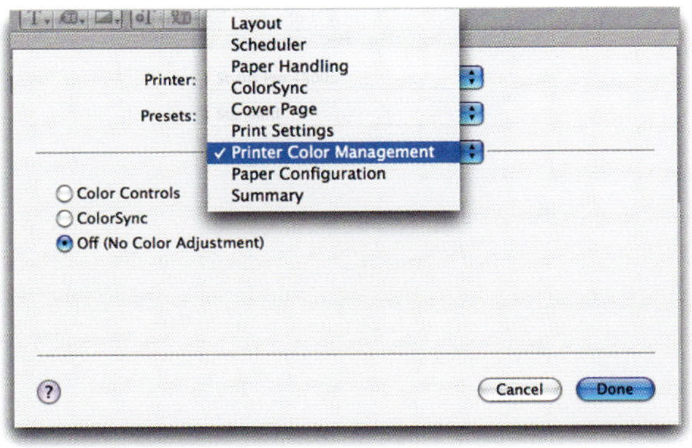

Figure 9.21: To maintain correct color management, you must access the Printer Color Management submenu in your Printer Controls submenus.

When you click the Buy Book button, Aperture makes a PDF of your book and uploads it to the Apple print servers. You'll see a progress bar while the PDF is being generated and a spinning indicator as it uploads. If there are problems, you'll get an error message. If everything works, you'll get a success message and an email confirmation.

So far, we're covered all the basics for using Aperture. In Chapter 10, "Advanced Aperture," we'll share some advanced tips and tricks for getting the most out of Aperture.

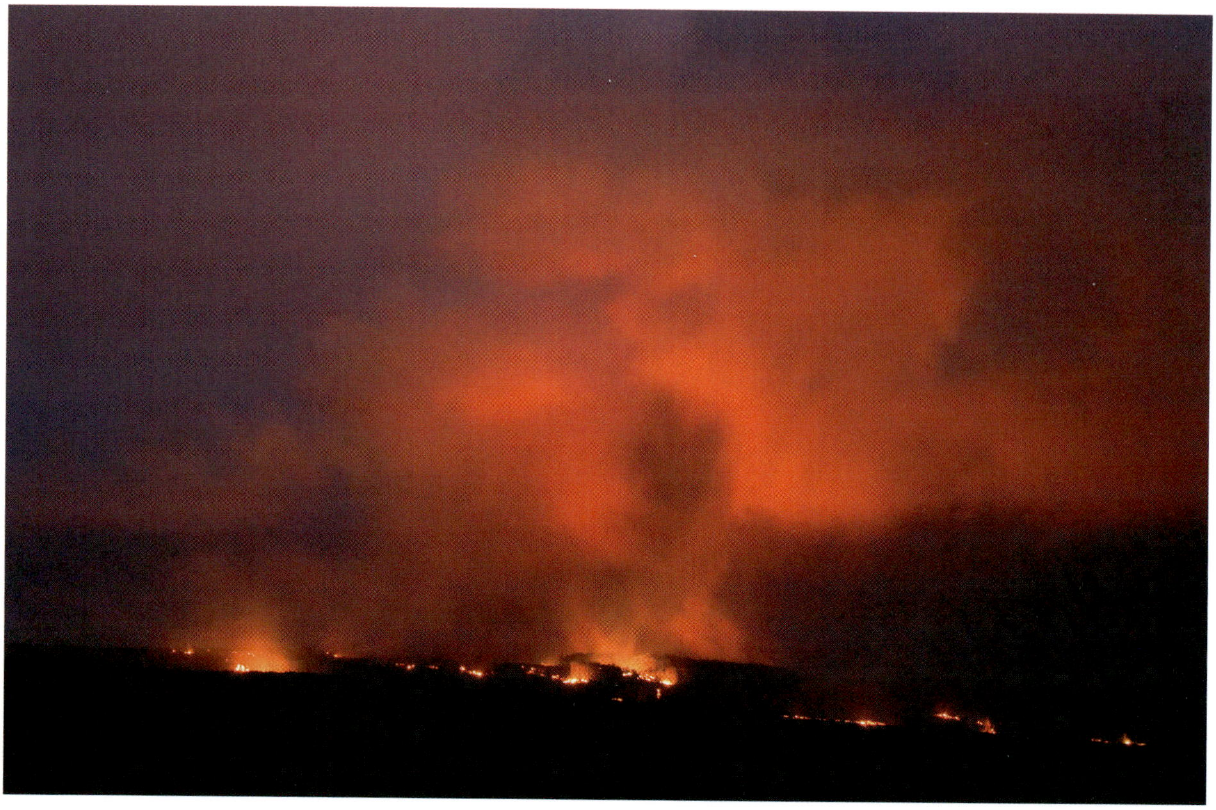

Advanced Aperture

By now, you've discovered all of the amazing tasks you can perform without leaving Aperture. However, as you will learn in this chapter, there are ways to make Aperture even more powerful and useful in your workflow, outside of Aperture. We'll show you how to use Apple's Automator program to create workflows for custom tasks. Furthermore, you'll learn how to explore your photo library directly to access your images so that you can use your images outside of Aperture without first exporting a master. Lastly, once in a while, something bad, such as an incorrect thumbnail, might happen to an image or your library, and it's important to know how to repair Aperture so that you can access your work. We'll explore all of these topics and more in the following pages.

10

Chapter Contents

Automator

Automator is a tool that Apple introduced in Mac OS X 10.4 Tiger to help people build workflows that accomplish their repetitive, manual tasks quickly and efficiently. Building on AppleScript and other technologies, the idea behind Automator is that certain actions, such as Assign Keywords to Images, can be steps in a workflow. By linking these actions together, you can quickly create complex workflows for various tasks. After you've set up the workflow, you need only press Run to execute the workflow, making the tasks easily reusable. Don't worry if any of this sounds confusing—creating workflows is really as simple as deciding what you want to do, determining what steps you need to take to do that task, and dragging and dropping the appropriate actions for each step within Automator.

When you launch Automator, which can be found in your Applications folder, you'll see an empty workflow with programs and their actions on the left (Figure 10.1). Click the different applications listed under the Library pane to see what actions are available. Some particular applications to look at are Aperture, Finder, iPhoto, and Image Capture. We'll be using actions from each of these applications throughout the chapter.

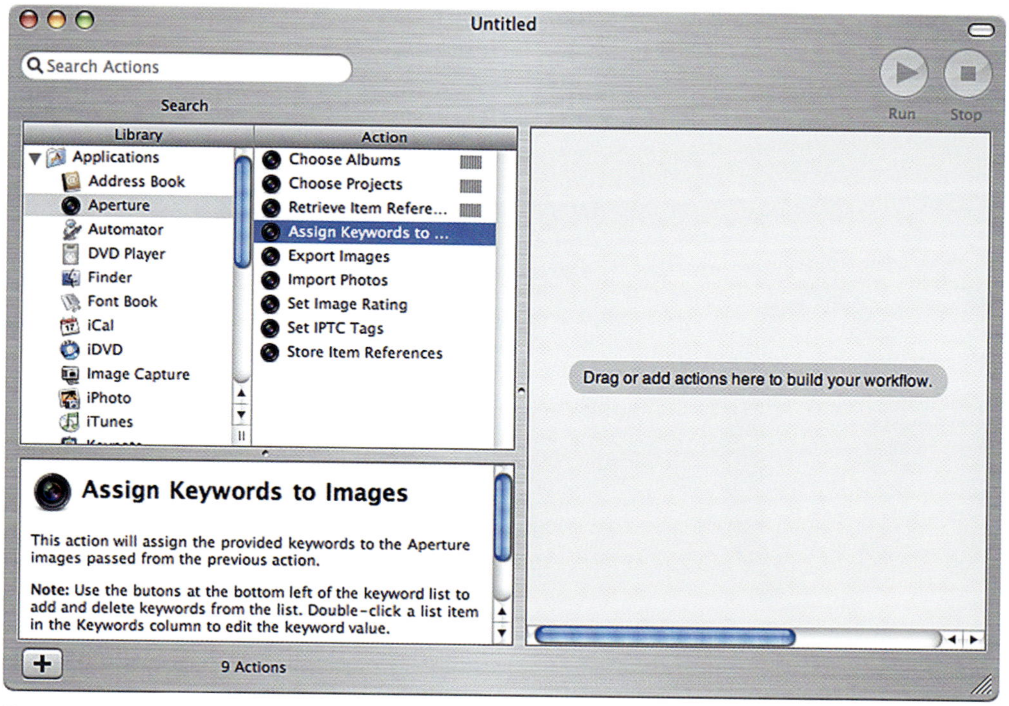

Figure 10.1: An empty Automator workflow

Note: The page http://www.apple.com/automator contains more information about Automator, including the latest available actions for Apple applications and third-party workflows.

Batch Rename

Before we try a more advanced Aperture workflow, let's make a simple Batch Rename action. When we're done, you will be able to select items in the Finder, Control-click them and choose Automator, and select this workflow. A special rename window will open, and when you press Continue, Automator will rename your selected files. If you have a lot of existing images that you want to rename before importing into Aperture, you could use this workflow to rename them.

Start by launching Automator (by opening it from your Applications folder), and in the blank window that appears, select Finder from the Library pane. The Action pane contains Finder actions, ranging from Eject Disk to Get Selected Finder Items. Select Get Selected Finder Items and drag it to the empty workflow area on the right. On the bottom of the action in the workflow, you'll see a small bit of text, as indicated in Figure 10.2 that says Files/Folders. This text tells you what type of information this Automator action will pass to the next action. Some actions also have a bit of text in their titles (such as the next action we're going to add), telling you what type of input the action takes.

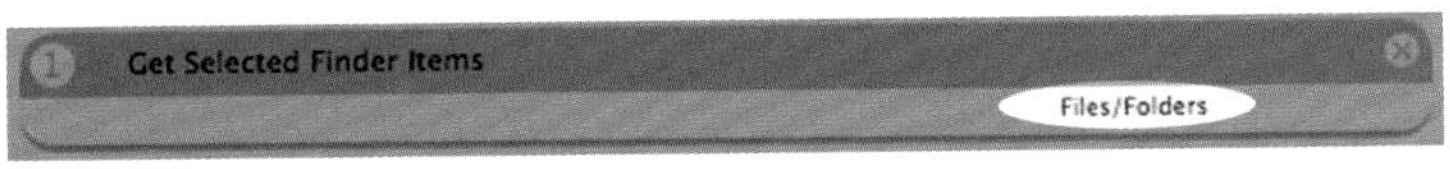

Figure 10.2: Each action will tell you what type of input and output it takes via small text labels.

The next step is to find and add the Rename Finder Items action to your workflow and to customize it. When you add this action, Automator will prompt you to add a Copy Files step. Because this workflow will modify the original files and not a copy of them, select Don't Add.

1. Change the type of rename from Add Date or Time to Make Sequential.
2. Change Add Number To to "new name" instead of "existing item name," and leave the new name field blank—we'll fill it in when we run the action.
3. Change the Separated By field to "underscore." At the bottom left of the action, Automator shows a preview of your new filename format.
4. Open up the Options box and check Show Action When Run. By checking this field, Automator will prompt for the rename format each time you run the action.

Your completed workflow will resemble Figure 10.3.

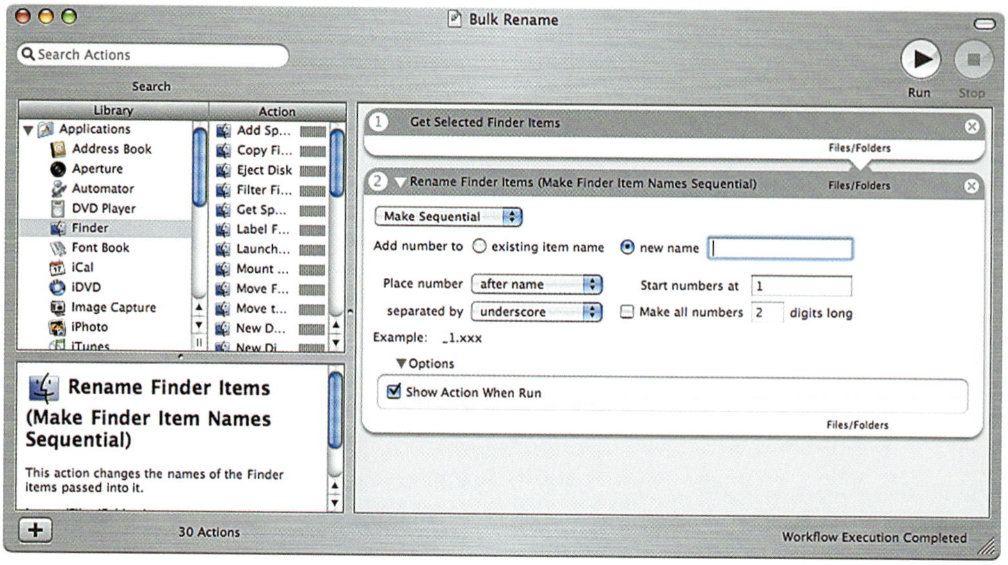

Figure 10.3: The completed Batch Rename workflow

The last step is to save this workflow. Save this workflow as a plug-in (File > Save As Plug-in) and name it "Batch Rename." Below the text field where you set the plug-in name, there's a pop-up menu where you set the plug-in type. For this plug-in, the default type Finder is the right type. By saving this workflow as a plug-in, you can select a group of files in the Finder, Control-click them, and select Automator > Batch Rename to run the action. When you run the plug-in, Aperture will open a window (Figure 10.4) where you can set up the name format.

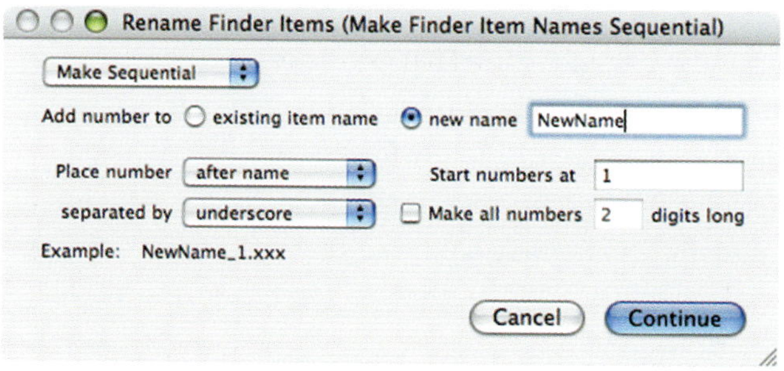

Figure 10.4: The running Batch Rename workflow will prompt you for the new filename format.

While the workflow is running, Automator will place a small status indicator in the menu bar (Figure 10.5). This indicator will tell you what the current running action is and give you a place to stop the action.

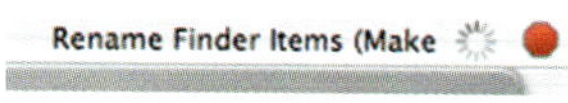

Figure 10.5: The Automator status indicator

As you can see, it is very easy to make powerful and reusable workflows. With a very small amount of work, you've set up a reusable Batch Rename command. Next, we're going to create an equally simple but more powerful Aperture workflow.

Aperture to iPhoto

Once in a while, you might want to do something with your images in iPhoto. For instance, you might want to make a calendar or card—services currently unavailable in Aperture—from your images. Or, you might want to add your images to iPhoto so that you can access them from Keynote or another application. Automator makes this process possible.

Start by making a new Automator document and selecting Aperture from the Library pane. In there, you'll find the actions in Figure 10.6. For this workflow, we're going to pick images from Aperture and then export them, giving us a list of files. Then, we'll add the iPhoto action to import photos, which takes a list of files. To create the workflow, follow these steps.

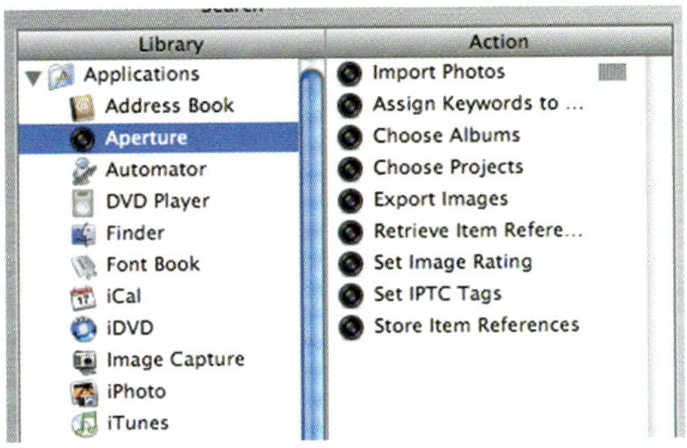

Figure 10.6: The Aperture Automator actions

1. Drag the Choose Albums action to the workflow area. You could drag out Choose Projects, but by using an album instead, it's easier to pick a smaller group of images to export.
2. Under Options, check Show Action When Run. That way, Automator will always ask which images you want to send to iPhoto.
3. Drag out the Export Images action. For most purposes, selecting JPEG - Fit Within 1024 × 1024 is fine for the Export Setting; however, if you're planning to make prints from these images, pick a higher-quality format such as TIFF - Original Size. Set the destination folder to Pictures so that you don't use your home directory as a temporary folder.
4. Select iPhoto from the Library pane and drag out the Import Photos into iPhoto action.
5. Check Delete the Source Images After Importing so that you don't end up with three copies of your images on your hard drive. This will not affect your original images. It will affect only the temporary images Automator creates from Step 3.
6. Under Options, check Show Action When Run and change the radio button to Show Selected Items. Check Add To, Choose Album, and New Album so that Automator will let you determine where in iPhoto to store your images.
7. Save your completed action as either a workflow (which you can edit later) or as a stand-alone application (choose Application from the pop-up at the bottom of the Save panel).

Your completed workflow should look like Figure 10.7. Run it and watch Automator send your Aperture images into iPhoto. If you select more than one album initially, your images from each of those Aperture albums will be combined into one iPhoto album. This action might take a few minutes to run, depending on how many photos you have to send to iPhoto, and Automator will display its progress in the top-right part of the menu bar, near the Spotlight icon (🔍).

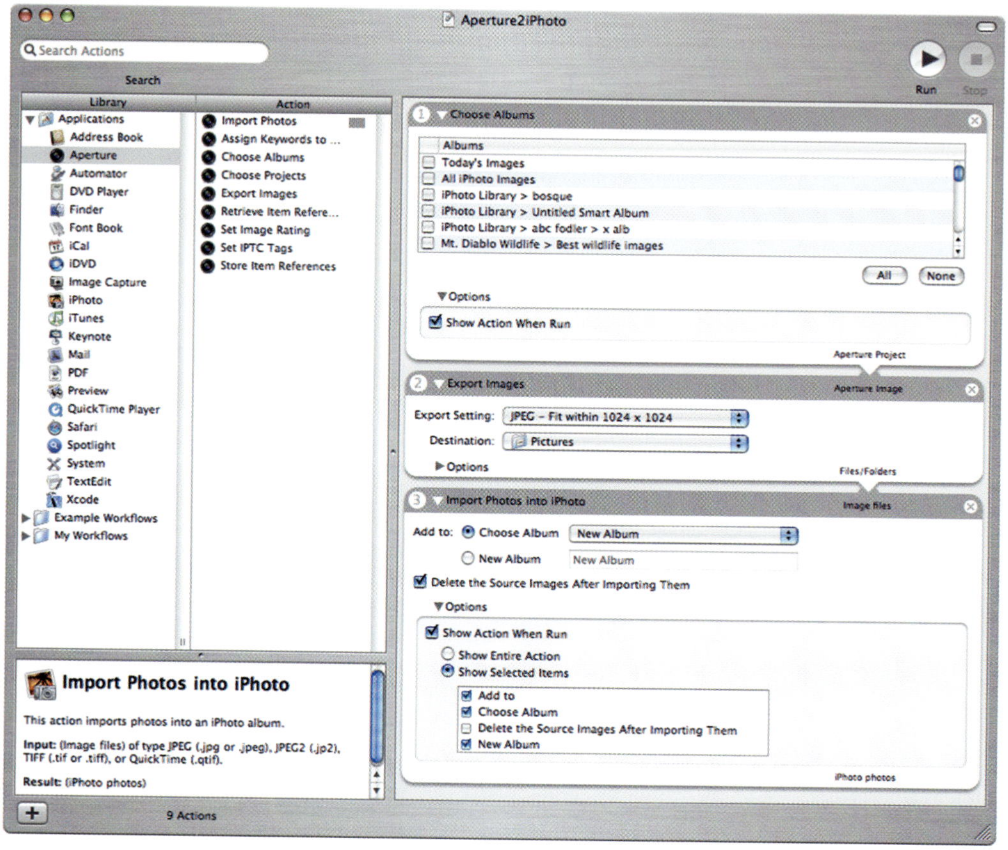

Figure 10.7: The completed Aperture-to-iPhoto workflow

Aperture2iLife

There are a few downsides to these Automator actions that let you send your files to your iApps. For one, you end up with multiple copies of your images. In our Aperture-to-iPhoto workflow, you end up with your images in Aperture and copies in your iPhoto library. Plus, if you add an image to your Aperture album, there is no straightforward way to just copy that new image to iPhoto. Also, exporting JPEGs can be slow.

Continues

Aperture2iLife *(Continued)*

Lightbox Software has a program called Aperture2iLife (www.lightboxsoftware.com) that allows you to temporarily replace iPhoto with Aperture. In other words, with one button click, you can use an Aperture project as your iPhoto library in your iApps (except for iPhoto), be it for adding images to a Keynote presentation or creating a web gallery in iWeb. One key benefit is that Aperture2iLife avoids making duplicate copies of your images. If you choose to generate JPEGs instead of using your master files, it generates them far faster than exporting your images. Plus, if you update an album in Aperture, simply restart Aperture2iLife to see your changes in your iLife application. However, it is shareware and not freeware. If you prefer a free solution, the Automator workflows we present in this chapter are more than adequate.

Aperture to an iDVD Slideshow

As another example of how to integrate Aperture, Automator, and iLife, the next workflow we're going to build will take images from Aperture and make an iDVD slideshow in the currently open iDVD project. As you build this workflow, notice how similar it is to the Aperture-to-iPhoto workflow from the previous example. Start by opening an iDVD project and navigating to a menu screen. Then, in Automator, make a new Automator document and select Aperture from the Library pane.

1. Drag the Choose Albums action to the workflow area. Again, you could drag out Choose Projects, but by using an album, it's easier to pick a smaller group of images to export.
2. Under Options, check Show Action When Run. That way, Automator will always prompt for which images you want to use in your slideshow.
3. Drag out the Export Images action. For most purposes, selecting JPEG - Fit Within 1024 × 1024 is fine for Export Setting. If you're making an HD DVD, make a custom Image Export preset in Aperture with the right HD size and select that format from the pop-up. Again, the destination pop-up is where you specify where Automator will store your exported images. Because Automator won't automatically delete these images with this workflow, use this pop-up to make a new folder to hold your exported images, perhaps under Pictures.
4. Under the iDVD actions, drag out New iDVD Slideshow. When you run this workflow, the options in this step allow you to configure your slideshow. Here, you can set a background audio file, the slide duration, and the slide transitions, all of which can be modified in iDVD. The name you give to your slideshow is how it will appear in the iDVD project's menu.
5. Under Options, check Show Action When Run. This way, Automator will always ask to set up your slide show when you run the action.
6. Save your workflow either as a workflow or as an application.

Your completed workflow should look like Figure 10.8. When you run it, your images should appear as an iDVD slideshow that you can burn to a DVD. This workflow will not automatically delete the temporary images that it makes in Step 3. You will have to find and delete those images when you are done with them.

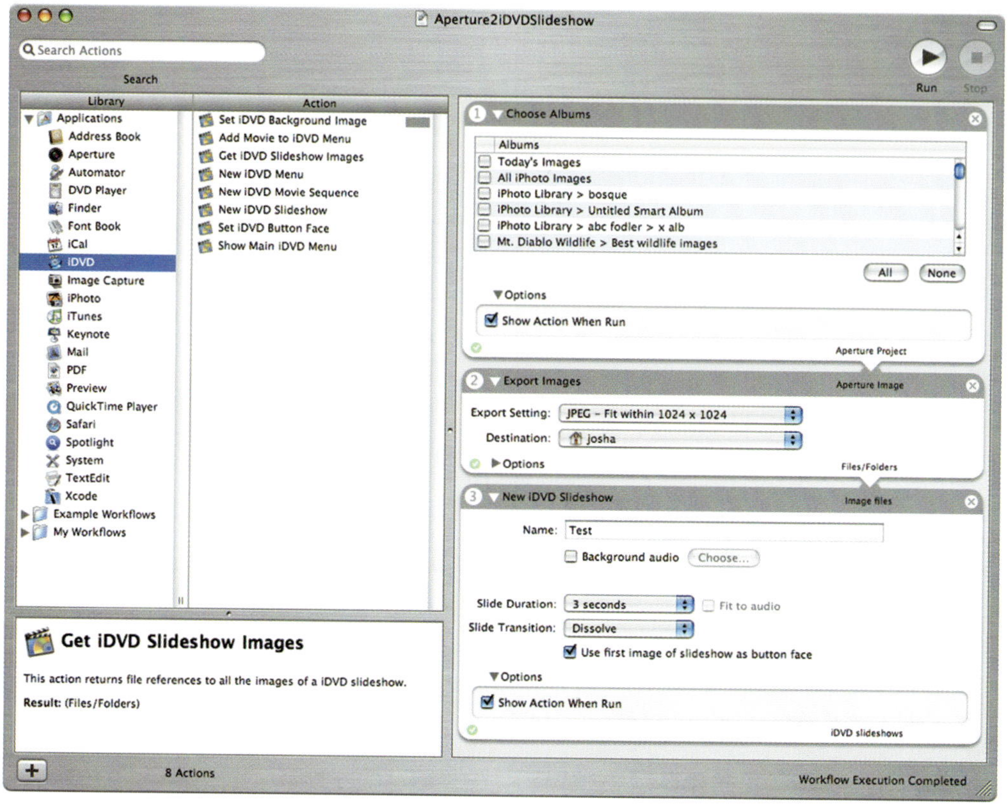

Figure 10.8: The completed Aperture-to-iDVD slideshow workflow

Automatically Import from a Folder to Aperture

Our next workflow will be to make a "hot" folder so that any image we place into it is automatically imported into Aperture. One reason to set up a hot folder is if you're using special software to take *tethered photos*, photos where the camera is directly connected to the computer while shooting, such as in a studio. Aperture itself doesn't support tethered shooting, but if you set another program to automatically save images you shoot into a hot folder, they'll automatically be imported to Aperture as you shoot. To set up a hot folder, take these steps:

1. Make a new folder somewhere, such as in your Pictures folder, called Aperture Hot Import.
2. In Aperture, make a new project called Hot Import.
3. In Automator, make a new workflow and drag out the Aperture Import Photos action.

4. You don't want Automator to pop up and prompt you to pick a project every time you put a new photo in your Import folder, and you'll use the Hot Import project from Step 2 as a staging area for your new photos. Select it from the Choose Project pop-up in Automator. If you instead set Automator to make a new project, each time you add an image to the Import folder, Automator will make a new Aperture project rather than adding to the existing one.
5. Check Delete the Source Images After Importing Them to avoid having multiple copies of your images.
6. Select File > Save As Plug-in and name the action **Import to Aperture**.
7. Set Plug-in For to Folder Actions.
8. Change Attached to Folder to Other, and browse for the folder you created in Step 1.
9. If Enable Folder Actions is visible and unchecked, check it.
10. Click Save.

Find some images and drag them into your Aperture Hot Import folder. Automator will automatically import them to the Hot Import project in Aperture. If you want to remove this folder action later, Control-click the Aperture Hot Import folder and select Remove A Folder Action > Import To Aperture.scpt. To disable folder actions, Control-click the Aperture Hot Import folder and select Disable Folder Actions. To edit your Import-to-Aperture workflow later, run Automator and open Home > Library > Workflows > Applications > Folder Actions > Import To Aperture.

Separate JPEGs and Import to Aperture

As we mentioned in Chapter 2, "Importing and Organizing Your Images," when you import RAW and JPEG files at the same time, Aperture shows you only the RAW files. However, it is often useful to have the JPEGs because they are far faster to work with for straight browsing. Ben Long created a donation-ware Automator action that separates JPEG files in a folder into a JPEGs subfolder. This action is available from our companion website, as well as from Ben's site at http://www.completedigitalphotography.com/. If you find this action useful, we're sure that he would appreciate a small donation.

Once you download the Separate JPEGs action, install it into Automator by selecting File > Import Actions and choose the Separate JPEGs.action file. This action will appear with the Finder actions.

The workflow we're going to set up will be a Finder plug-in. In the end, you will be able to Control-click a folder, select this workflow, separate your JPEGs, and have both your RAW files and JPEGs imported to Aperture in a project you specify. Then, in Aperture, you can use auto-stack to group your JPEG and RAW files together for easy browsing. To create this workflow, follow these steps.

1. Make a new Automator workflow and add the Separate JPEGs action. You can always make sure that you have the latest Separate JPEGs action by clicking the Check For Updates button within this action.

2. Add the Finder Get Folder Contents action and check Repeat For Each Subfolder. By default, if you pass the result from the Separate JPEGs action to the Aperture Import Photos action, Aperture will ignore the new JPEGs folder and import only the top-level RAW files. By adding this step, Aperture will import everything in the specified folder, including the subfolders.
3. Add the Aperture Import Photos action and under Options, check Show Action When Run. This will let you pick where you'll import these images to each time you run the action.
4. Select File > Save As Plug-in and name this Finder plug-in **Separate JPEGs and Import**.

Your completed workflow will resemble Figure 10.9. Try it out by Control-clicking a folder in the Finder that has both JPEG and RAW files and selecting Automator > Separate JPEGs And Import.

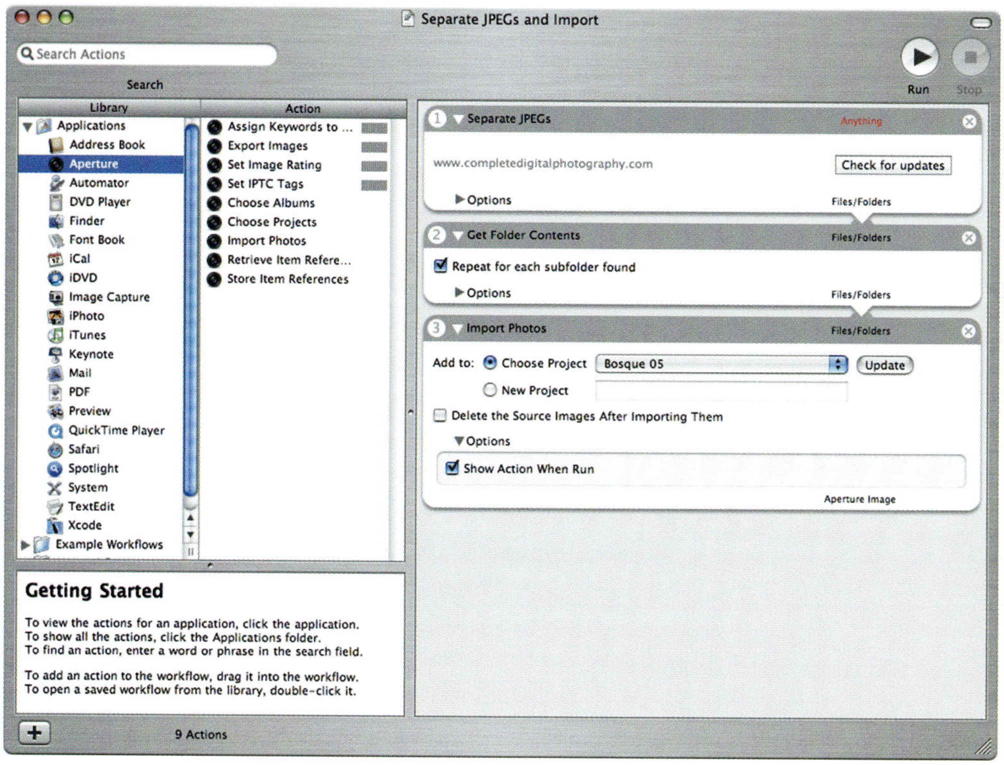

Figure 10.9: The completed Separate JPEGs And Import workflow

Note: To make it easier to determine which of your images are JPEGs, make a new metadata set using the Action menu on the Metadata Inspector. Open the Other panel at the bottom of the Inspector and add the File Name field to this set. Set your browser to show this set; by quickly glancing at your browser, you'll be able to tell which images are JPEGs. See Chapter 4, "Finding the Keepers," for more information about metadata and metadata sets.

When you switch to Aperture, notice that the RAW and JPEG files appear side by side. If you want to keep the JPEGs in their own folder, a simple solution would be to make a smart album within the project to search for JPEGs. To do so, add an Other criteria and set it to Filename. Set the text field to search for "jpg." The smart album will look like Figure 10.10, and it will give you all JPEGs within the project.

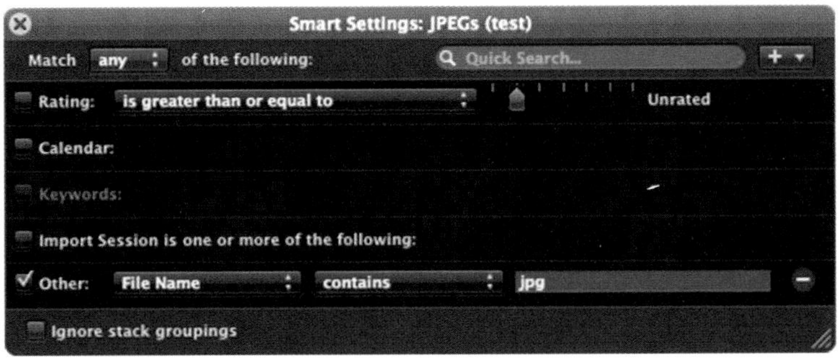

Figure 10.10: A smart album query to find all JPEGs within a project

Another way to keep your JPEG files separate within Aperture is to modify your Automator workflow so that it does not import to Aperture and it manually imports your images. When you manually drag the top-level folder containing your RAW files and the JPEGs folder into an existing Aperture project, Aperture will make a new folder within the project for your folder. This folder will contain two albums, one that has your top-level RAW files and another one named JPEGs that will contain the contents of your JPEGs folder. As expected, if you drag the folder onto an empty area within the Project panel instead of onto an existing project, Aperture will make a new project named after your folder containing the Images From Folder album and the JPEGs album.

Auto-Open in Adobe Camera RAW

Even though Apple's RAW converter is fairly good and getting better with each Aperture and OS release, there will be times when you want to use another RAW converter, such as Adobe Camera RAW. Throughout this chapter, we'll show you a few ways to access your RAW files directly. We actually mentioned the first way, exporting your master file, earlier in Chapter 6, "Exporting Images." This Automator action will help simplify your workflow by automatically opening that master file in Camera Raw for you. Just follow these steps.

1. Create a new folder somewhere called To Photoshop.
2. Make a new Automator workflow and add the Finder Open Finder Items action.
3. From the Applications pop-up within the action, select Other and then find and select your Photoshop application.
4. Select File > Save As Plug-in and save this workflow as a Folder Action plug-in attached to the folder from Step 1. Name this action **Open in Photoshop**. If needed, check the Enable Folder Actions button.

Your completed workflow should be very simple and look like Figure 10.11. To test it, open Aperture, select a RAW file, and choose File > Export Master. Browse to the folder you made in Step 1 and click Export Master Here. After Aperture finishes exporting, Photoshop will open the RAW file in its converter. Try taking this action further by combining it with a hot folder such as the one we made in the "Automatically Import from a Folder to Aperture" section so that you can save your new, converted file in that folder and have it automatically appear in Aperture.

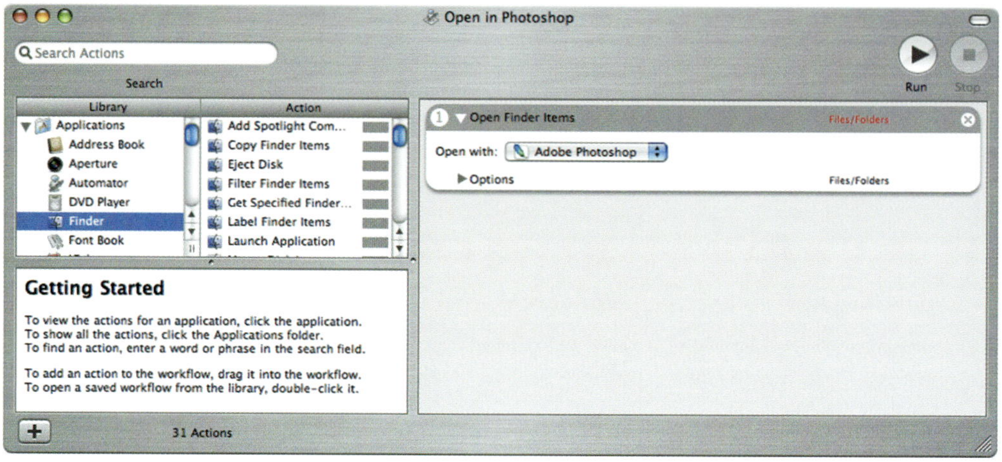

Figure 10.11: The completed Open In Photoshop workflow

Multiple Photo Libraries

As you use Aperture more and more, you might want to have more than one photo library. For example, you might have a library with images of your friends and family on your MacBook Pro's internal hard drive. Then, you might use an external hard drive when you're using MacBook Pro and Aperture for tethered studio shooting using the Automatically Import From A Folder action, as in the previous section. In Aperture, you can have only one library active at any given time, but you can switch between multiple libraries.

To make a new library:

1. Open the Aperture preferences.
2. Press the Set button under Library Location (see Figure 10.12).

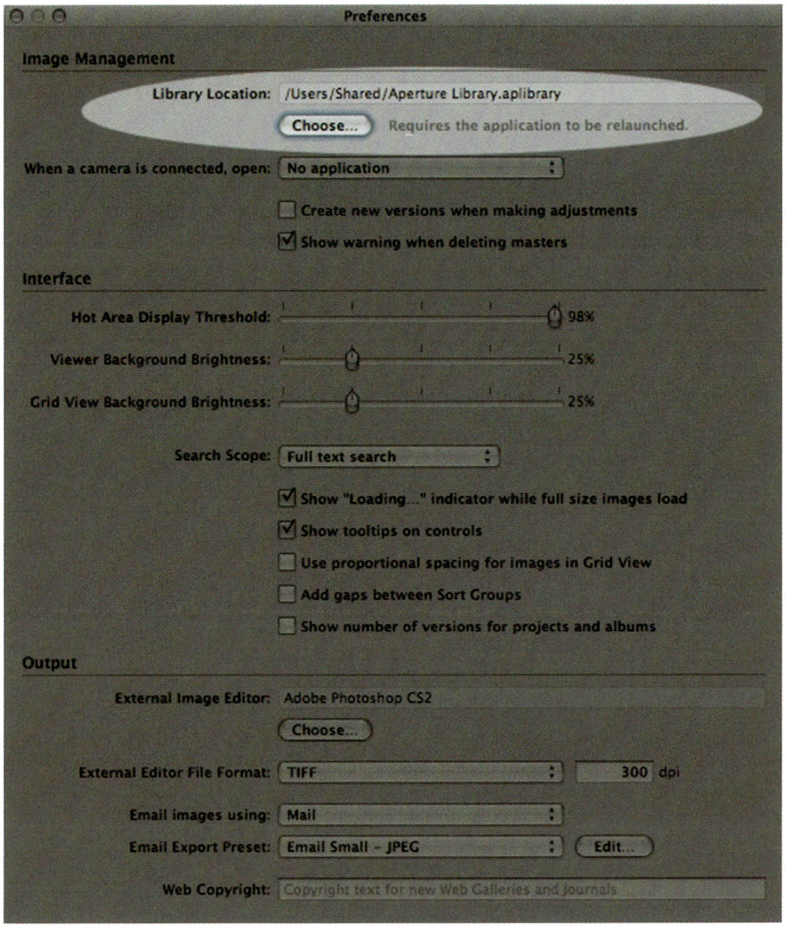

Figure 10.12: The Library Location section of Aperture's preferences

3. Select a folder that does not already have an Aperture Library.aplib file in it.

4. Quit and relaunch Aperture.

To switch to an existing library, follow the same steps; however, instead of browsing to a folder that does not have an existing Aperture Library.aplib file (Step 3), browse and select the existing Aperture Library.aplib file that you'd like to use.

Note: If you use Filevault to store your work, Aperture will run faster if you keep your photo libraries outside of your Filevaulted home directory (for example, in /Users/Shared). By keeping your images outside of your home directory, Aperture won't have to decrypt each image when you go to use it.

Aperture Library Spanner

Ben Long recently created a free script called the Aperture Library Spanner that allows you to extend your Aperture photo library to a second hard drive. When you run this script, it will create an Aperture Branch Library folder in your Aperture library. The script creates this folder outside your library and links it into your library (for the technically minded, it creates a symbolic link to a new folder). If you drag a project into this folder within Aperture, Aperture will move the project to wherever you stored your branch folder. Download Ben's script from

`http://www.completedigitalphotography.com/?p=417`

To set up the spanner, follow these steps.

1. Close Aperture and launch the Aperture Library Spanner, and you will see a window similar to Figure 10.13.

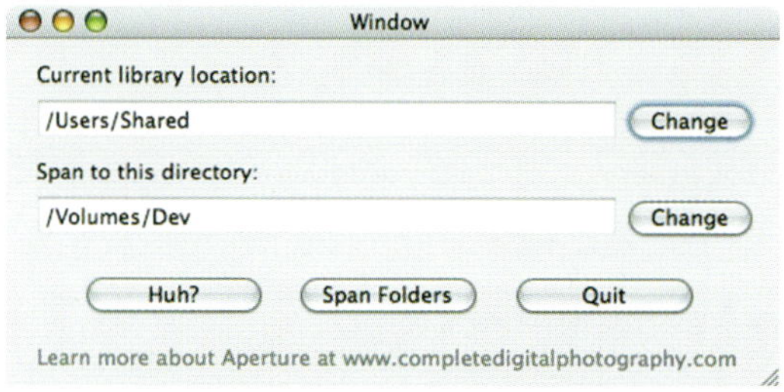

Figure 10.13: Ben Long's Aperture Library Spanner

2. Click the Change button next to the Current library location field, and browse to the folder containing your Aperture photo library (typically your Pictures folder).
3. Click the Change button next to the Span To This Directory field, and browse to the folder and drive you want to use to contain the external parts of your library.
4. Click Span Folders. The Aperture Library Spanner will make a folder named Aperture Branch Library wherever you set your span directory, and it will make a link to this folder in your Aperture library.
5. Quit the spanner and launch Aperture. You'll have an Aperture Branch Library folder beneath your Library. Move projects into it to move them to your external folder. Be warned that Aperture doesn't provide a progress indicator while moving projects, but you can see the progress by choosing Window > Show Task List.

Keep in mind that Apple does not officially support or sanction this script, and it might cause problems with your library. For example, if you've spanned your library to an external hard drive and launch Aperture without the drive attached, the Aperture Branch Library folder will be grayed out within Aperture. Furthermore, if you reattach the drive and restart Aperture, Aperture might not recognize the folder; you may be forced to rebuild your Aperture database by holding down ⌘+Option while starting Aperture. To switch back to a single-drive library, move your projects from the Aperture Branch Library folder elsewhere within your Aperture library, and then delete the Aperture Branch Library folder.

Note: If you have multiple photo libraries, you could set each of them to span to the same folder to share projects between libraries. However, be careful when you set metadata or make adjustments to the images in your shared projects, as the changes might get out of sync between photo libraries.

Exploring the Photo Library

Up until now, everything we've shown you in this chapter that involves accessing your Aperture images outside of Aperture has involved making a copy, be it an exported version or a master. This section is about how to dig into your photo libraries, explore Aperture's structure and files, and find your original images. Keep in mind that this is advanced and unofficial material that is unsupported by Apple. If you plan to change the contents of your library, we highly recommend that you make a backup copy of your library, perhaps using a vault, before making any such changes.

To start exploring, find your Aperture Library in the Finder. By default, it's inside the Pictures directory in your Home folder (Go > Home). As we mentioned in Chapter 1, "Welcome to Aperture," your photo library is a *bundle*. A bundle is a special type of folder that appears as a file in the Finder. If you double-click it, Mac OS X will treat the bundle as a file and try to open it in Aperture instead of opening a new Finder window. To look inside the bundle, Control-click the photo library and select Show Package Contents. A new window with files and folders that match the projects, folders, and albums you have within Aperture (Figure 10.14) will open.

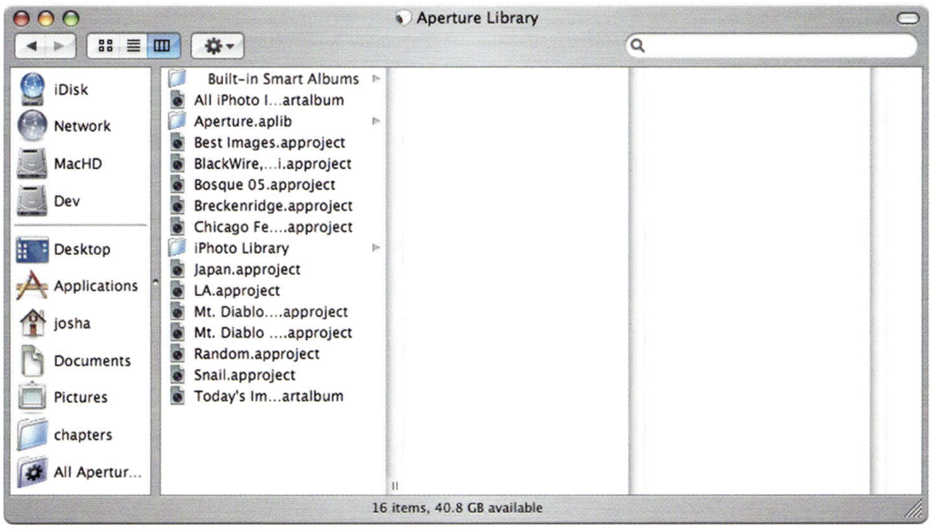

Figure 10.14: The top level of the Aperture Library

There are two folders that every Aperture library has, Built-in Smart Albums and Aperture.aplib. Built-in Smart Albums contains nine .apsmartalbum files, which correspond to the nine built-in albums under Library within Aperture. Each apsmartalbum file is a special type of property list file based on XML. Again, XML is a generic way to define specific keys and values, similar to HTML. If you want to see the contents of one of these apsmartalbum files, Control-click the file and select Open With. Select TextEdit from your Applications folder and click Open. Do not check the Always Open With box. You should have no need to open these files directly, and as such, we are not going to discuss their contents. If you do decide to change a file yourself, we highly recommend making a backup copy of any file first.

The second folder, Aperture.aplib, contains Aperture's database. The central database is called Library.apdb, and it is a SQLite database. If you're a very advanced user, you could open this file in SQLite and view or modify its contents. In fact, you can modify your Library.apdb file so that you can directly open your master files (such as RAW or layered-PSD files) in your external editor without first making a new version. We prefer to use a different, easier method that we'll discuss shortly when we explore projects to open master files. In the meantime, here's how to make your master files externally editable from within Aperture by modifying your database.

Note: Keep in mind that because this section refers to Aperture's internal database format, this technique could stop working in a future version of Aperture. One of the reasons we prefer the project-based method we'll discuss shortly is that technique is less likely to stop working in a future version.

1. Take note of the filename (or filenames) that you want to make externally editable and quit Aperture.
2. Open Terminal.
3. Type **sqlite3**.
4. Drag and drop the Library.apdb file into Terminal so that Terminal automatically inserts the full path to the Library.apdb file. Press Return to open SQLite.
5. There are two tables to update. First, to update the ZRKFILE table, type:

   ```
   update ZRKFILE set ZISEXTERNALLYEDITABLE = 1 where ZNAME =
   "YOURFILE.EXTENSION";
   ```

   Replace *YOURFILE.EXTENSION* with your file's name and extension. This text is case-sensitive, meaning that there is a difference between myfile.cr2 and MyFile.CR2. Make sure that what you type exactly matches the file's name in Aperture.
6. To update the ZRKVERSION, type this:

   ```
   update ZRKVERSION set ZISEXTERNALLYEDITABLE = 1 where ZNAME="YOURFILE";
   ```

   Again, replace *YOURFILE* with your filename, but do not include the file extension in this line.
7. Exit sqlite3 by typing Control+D.

When you relaunch Aperture, your file will have the Opened In External Editor badge (⊙). If you select the image and choose Images > Open With External Editor, your master file will open directly in your editor.

Exploring Project Bundles

Within your Library folder, you'll see an approject file for each of your Aperture projects. Each approject file is actually another bundle. Control-click one and select Show Package Contents. The Finder will open a new window showing the contents of that project. Figure 10.15 shows the contents of a sample project.

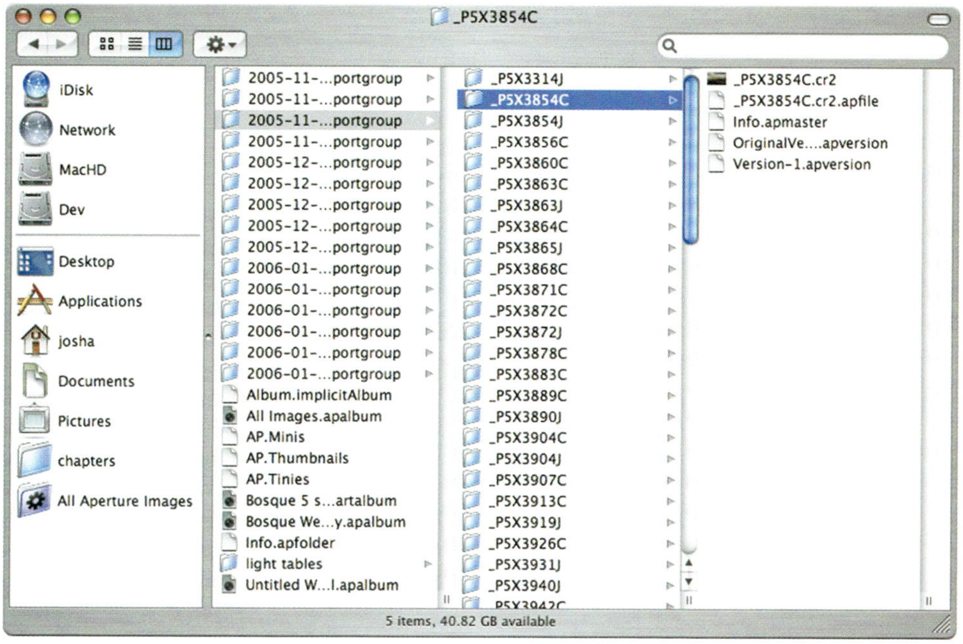

Figure 10.15: The contents of an approject file

Every project has a few similar files. At the top, there are importgroup folders; one for each time you imported images into this project. Next is an Album.implicitAlbum file. This property list file (which you can view in TextEdit) contains the implicit album that contains all of the images in the project. You should not need to edit this file.

Next, within your project, are the thumbnail files, AP.Minis, AP.Thumbnails, and AP.Tinies. These files contain multiple different versions of each of your images' thumbnails. Lastly, there is an Info.apfolder property list that contains basic information about the project, such as creation date.

Depending on what's in your project, you might have other files within the project. For instance, if you have albums in the project, you'll have apalbum property list files with information about each album (again, you should not need to edit these files). If your project has folders, you'll see the folder on the hard drive too. Each folder will have an Info.apfolder property list file containing basic information about the folder.

The part of the project folder that is interesting is the Importgroup folder (or folders). Each importgroup folder contains one folder for every image you've imported. As you can see in Figure 10.15, the image folders contain the image as well as at least four other property list files.

The apfile and apmaster contain Aperture-specific information, but the apversion files contain the image's metadata. The OriginalVersion.apversion file is for the master image, and the Version-1.apversion file is for the automatically created first version. If you open these property list files, you'll find a searchableProperties dictionary that contains keys and values for every bit of metadata set on the image. If you're an advanced user looking to write an Aperture-related program or script that uses Aperture metadata, we highly recommend that you use these apversion files instead of directly accessing the Aperture library.

As you have probably realized by now, because these image folders contain your master files, you can drag and drop each image into your editor, such as Photoshop, to open the master. You have to drag and drop the file into your editor because, unfortunately, most editors can't read inside a bundle, and you can't browse directly to your master file within your editor.

Note: If you're using Photoshop as your editor, within Photoshop's Open panel, click the Use Adobe Dialog and the Open panel will switch to an Open panel that allows you to browse the photo library and dive into the bundles (technically, we say that this dialog ignores the bundle bits).

If you open a RAW file to convert in another program, such as Adobe Camera Raw, do not save the converted file within the image folder. Instead, save it somewhere else and reimport it to Aperture, perhaps stacking it with the original image. If you open a non-RAW file, be careful when making changes. Aperture will not know that the image has changed, because you're modifying the file behind the scenes, and it will not update the image's thumbnail properly within Aperture.

Smart Folders to Find Your Aperture Images

By now, you are probably thinking to yourself, "Hey! This is great! You just unlocked my images for me. But do I really have to remember when I imported my images to find them?" Thankfully, Mac OS X has a great feature called smart folders that you can use to find all of the images in your project or library.

To make a smart folder that contains all of the image files within your library, follow these steps.

1. Control-click your Aperture Library and select Show Package Contents.
2. In the new window, select File > Find.
3. Change the Kind field at the top to Images, and the Find panel will show every image in your library. Your configured Find panel will look like Figure 10.16.

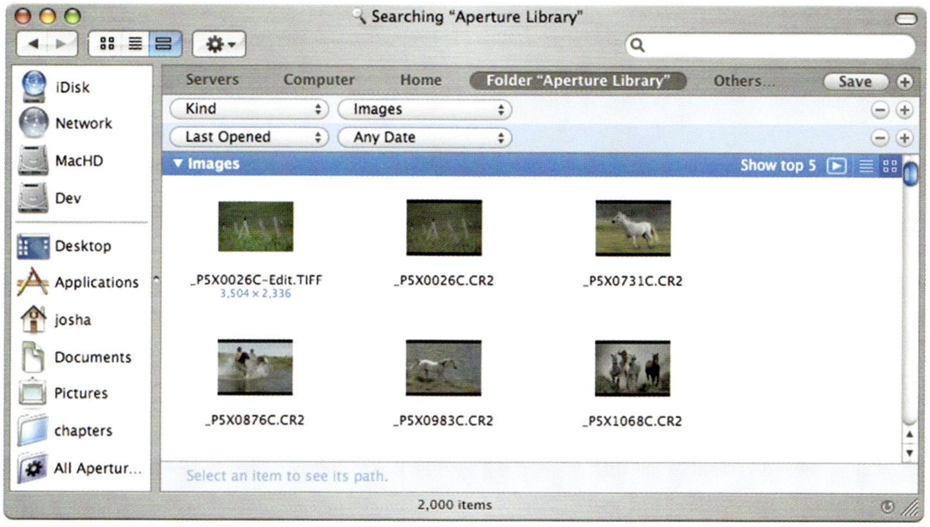

Figure 10.16: The Find panel configured to find all images within your Aperture photo library

4. Click the Save button at the top right and name your search **All Aperture Images**. Check the Add to Sidebar button and click Save.

From every Finder window, you will be able to quickly see all the images within your Aperture library by clicking the All Aperture Images smart folder. You can even access this smart folder from Open panels so that you can always get to your Aperture images.

However, as your Aperture library grows, your All Aperture Images smart folder could potentially contain tens of thousands of images. The solution is to make a smart album folder for your various projects.

1. Control-click your Aperture Library and select Show Package Contents.
2. Find the project for which you want to make a smart folder. Control-click it and select Show Package Contents.
3. In the new window, select File > Find.
4. Change the Kind field at the top to Images. The Find panel will show every image in your library. Your configured Find panel will look like Figure 10.17.

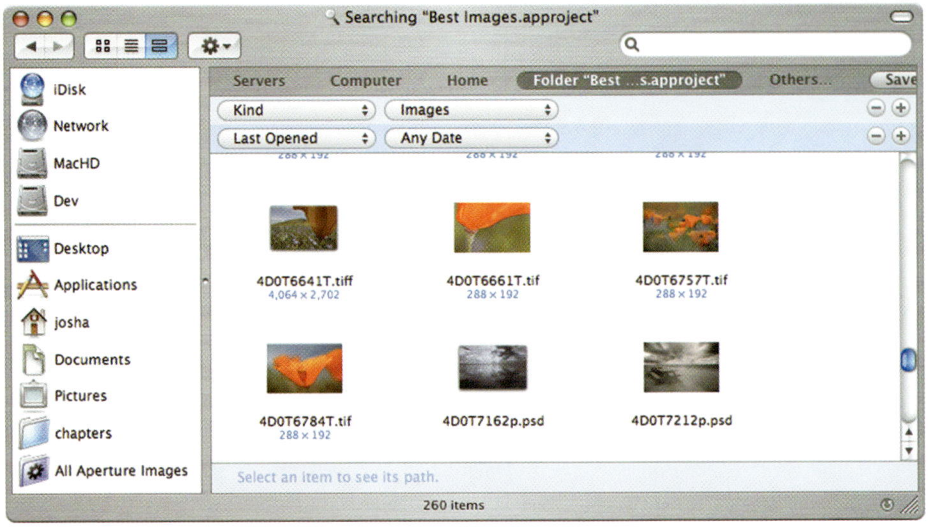

Figure 10.17: The Find panel configured to find all images within a given project

5. Click the Save button at the top right and name your search ***MyProject* Images**, where *MyProject* is your project's name. Check the Add to Sidebar button and click Save.

In addition to being able to quickly get to all of your Aperture images, you will be able to get to the images within one particular project. Plus, the Filter field in the Finder works inside smart folders, allowing you to search for one particular image within either your library or project.

If you accidentally delete the smart folder from the sidebar, you can retrieve it at any time. Your smart folders are saved in Home > Library > Saved Searches. To restore a search to the sidebar, go to that folder and drag the search to the sidebar to restore the smart folder.

RAW Files as Smart Objects

In Photoshop CS2, Adobe introduced a new technology called Smart Objects. Smart Objects let you nondestructively manipulate data because they allow you to access the original content. For instance, if you were to take an image, place it into a Photoshop file, scale it down, and then scale it up to its original size, you typically would expect the scaled-up image to be pixilated. With Smart Objects, Photoshop preserves the original image data and uses it to generate the scaled up image, giving you the original, non-pixilated image.

In this section, we will show you how to place a RAW file as a Smart Object so that you can easily access the RAW data and Adobe's RAW converter for your image.

1. In Aperture, assuming that Photoshop CS2 is set as your external editor, open an image in your external editor by selecting it and choosing Images > Open With External Editor (⌘+Shift+O).

2. Export the image's master from within Aperture (if you set up a smart folder to access your images directly as we described in the previous section, you can skip this step).
3. In Photoshop, select File > Place.
4. Browse and find your RAW file. If you exported the master from within Aperture, the RAW file is wherever you placed that file. If you set up a smart folder, use the smart folder (you'll need to use the OS dialog in Photoshop), as shown in Figure 10.18.

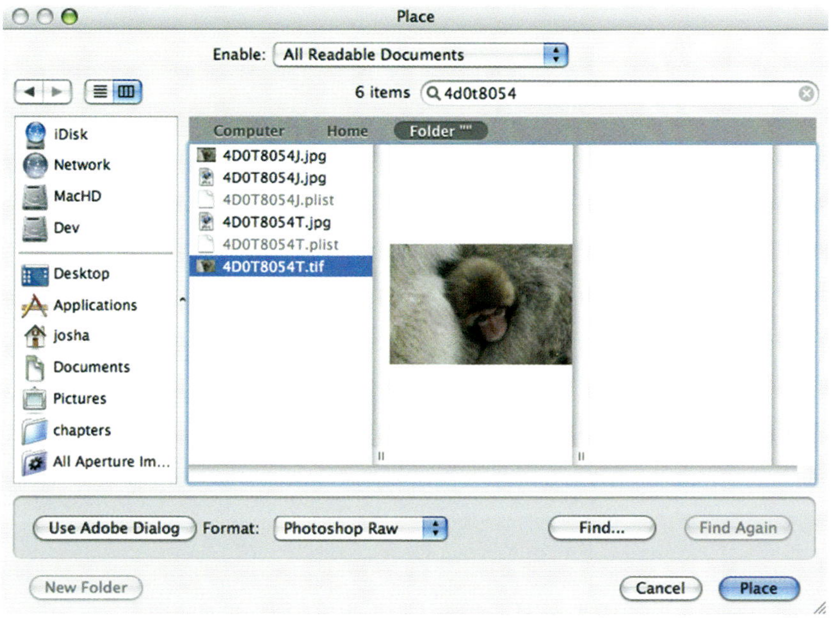

Figure 10.18: Using a smart folder and the filter field to find a RAW file

5. Adobe Camera Raw will appear. For the moment, it won't matter what conversion settings you select; you will be able to modify them later. The resolution setting, however, will matter. By default, Aperture exports its images at 72 dpi. Set Camera Raw to use the same dpi setting that Aperture uses (the default is 72 dpi, but if you changed Aperture's external editor dpi preference, as we discussed in Chapter 6, your setting might be different).
6. Click Open. When the progress bar goes away, you will see your converted image in Photoshop with a large X over it (Figure 10.19). Press Return to confirm the RAW file placement, and the X will go away.

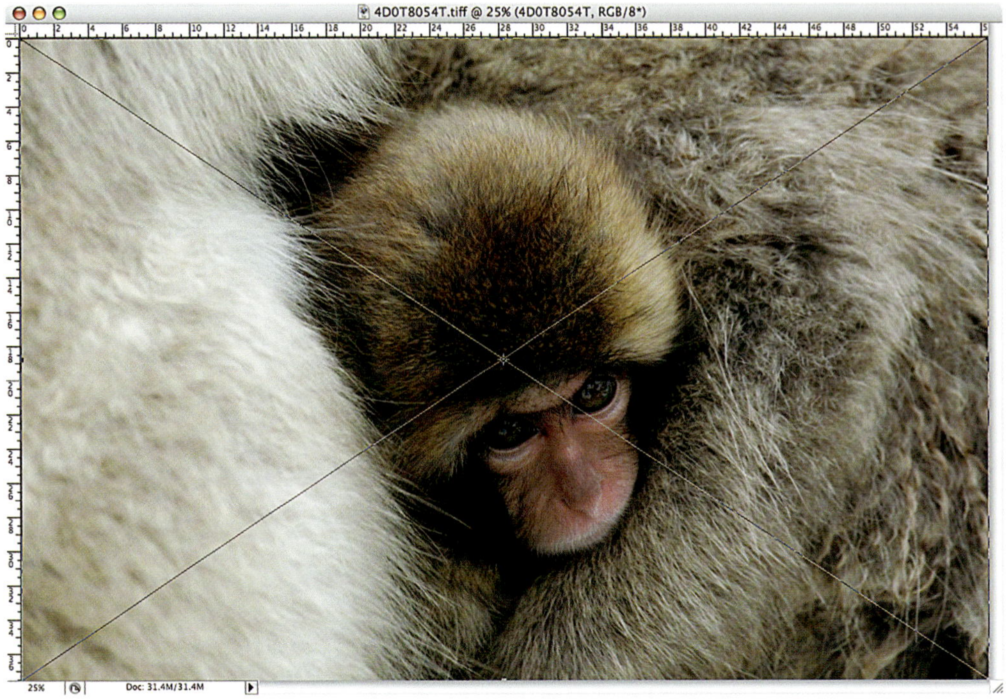

Figure 10.19: Photoshop places a large X over your image until you confirm placing the object. You can move, rotate, and scale the object before confirming.

7. You will have two layers, one labeled Background with the converted image from Aperture and one with the image's name. The layer with the image's name will have a small badge in the Layers palette (Figure 10.20) indicating that it's a smart object. Delete the Background layer, as you no longer need Aperture's conversion.

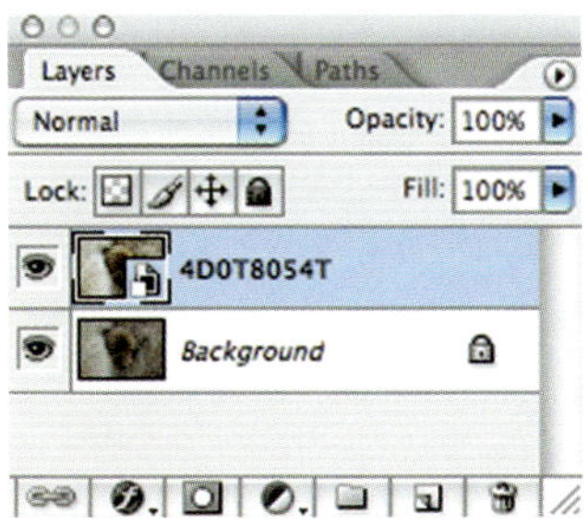

Figure 10.20: The Layers palette with the smart object layer and Background layer

8. Select File > Save. If prompted, it is ***not*** safe to discard your layers. For now, close your image.
9. Back within Aperture, both the file you opened in an external editor and the new version that Aperture made for the external editor will be selected. Click in the empty area of the Browser or on another image to deselect both.
10. Because your RAW file is embedded in your externally editable file, you can delete your original RAW file from within Aperture (it's the version without the Externally Editable badge (⊙). Select it and choose File > Delete Version. Aperture will

ask you if you're sure that you want to delete the version and master file. Click Remove to confirm.

11. Select the version that you can open in an external editor, and open it by choosing Images > Open With External Editor (⌘+Shift+O).
12. In Photoshop, choose Layer > Smart Objects > Edit Contents or double-click this layer's icon in the Layers palette. Photoshop will open Camera Raw, allowing you to adjust your image's conversion settings. When you make your changes, Aperture will automatically update its thumbnail to match your new image settings.

This method is quite handy, as it lets you nondestructively use Adobe Camera Raw. However, it has a downside. You are storing a converted copy of the image as well as the RAW data, and using this technique takes a lot more disk space than using Aperture's RAW converter, which doesn't actually store a converted copy of the image until you absolutely need it (such as for opening in an external editor). Thankfully, for most images, Aperture's RAW converter is perfectly fine, and there is no reason to use this technique to access Adobe Camera Raw. However, for some images, especially ones that Aperture's RAW converter has problems with or for when you want to use the Camera Raw controls instead of Aperture's controls, this technique is quite useful.

Troubleshooting Aperture

Unfortunately, despite the amazing skill of Aperture's developers and Quality Assurance engineers, Aperture can still have problems. The Apple support forums are great sources of information that you can access from http://www.apple.com/support/. However, there are a few steps that you personally can try if you have problems.

The very first thing you should always check is to see if you have enough free disk space. Having fewer than about 200MB free, either on the hard drive you boot from or on the hard drive that contains your Aperture Library, can cause your entire computer to have problems, such as failing to perform various tasks and becoming quite slow. If you do have enough free space, you'll need to dig further.

Image-Specific Problems

When troubleshooting, you should determine if the problem you're having is specific to an image or if it is related to the whole library. For instance, if you're performing a task (such a exporting a group of images), and Aperture repeatedly crashes when it reaches one particular image, chances are that the image is bad. As a first step, turn off any adjustments you made on the image and try again. If Aperture doesn't crash this time, try turning the adjustments on one at a time until you've restored your adjustments and Aperture doesn't crash or until you find the adjustment that causes Aperture to crash. If one particular adjustment always causes Aperture to crash on a given image, use the Aperture > Provide Aperture Feedback menu item (which opens up the web page in Figure 10.21) to tell Apple about the problem. In your bug report, provide clear steps to help them reproduce the problem and also offer to provide the image. If the problem affects more than one image, say so.

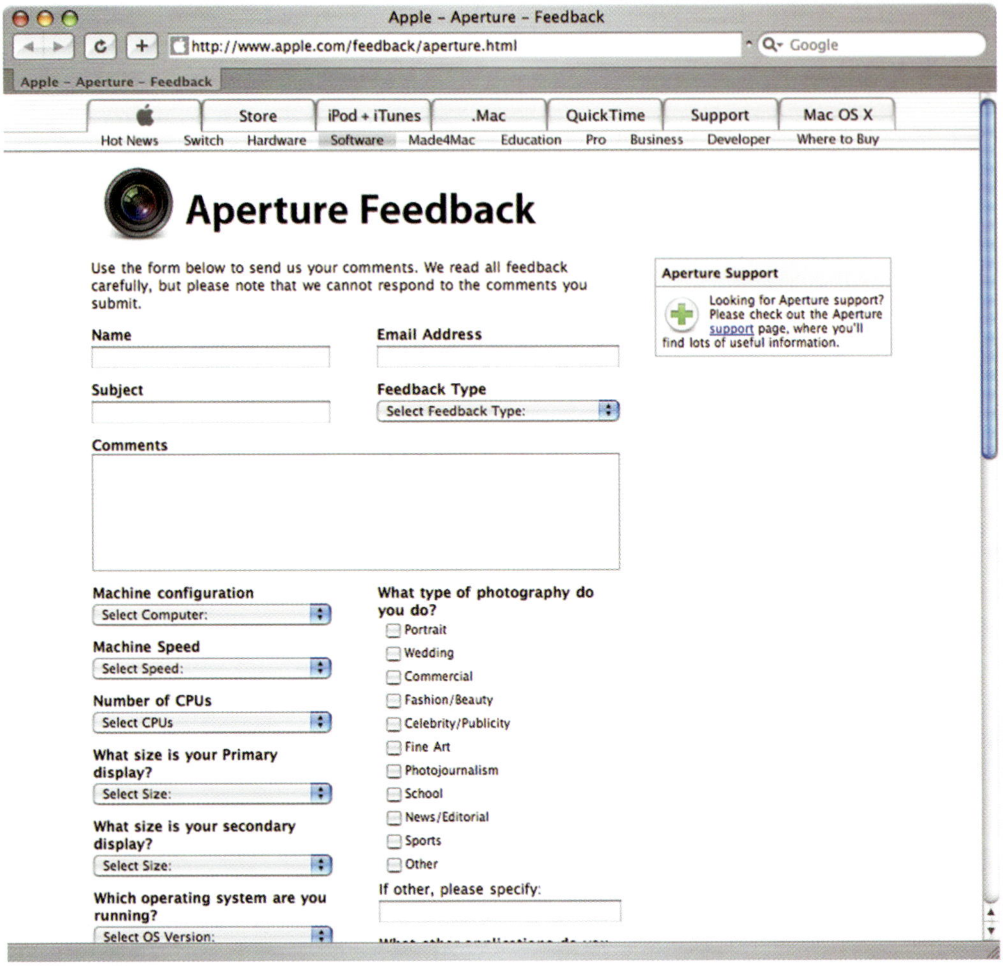

Figure 10.21: The Aperture Feedback page

If turning off the adjustments doesn't solve your problem, verify that the image file itself is okay. To do so, use the techniques from the "Exploring the Photo Library" section (we recommend the smart folder trick) to find your image. Try to open the image directly in another program, such as Preview or Photoshop. If you can't open it, your file is corrupt, and you should restore it from a backup.

However, if you are able to open your file, reimport the file into Aperture. To do so:

1. Copy the image to the Desktop or some other location outside your photo library.
2. In Aperture, select the image and delete it (File > Delete Version).
3. Use the techniques you learned in Chapter 2 and either drag the image from your Desktop onto the project or use the Import panel to reimport it.

If you're still having problems, file a bug report using Aperture > Provide Aperture Feedback or check the Apple support pages. If you want to continue trying to fix the problem, Aperture will sometimes log information to the Console application. You'll find the Console in `/Applications/Utilities`, and it looks like Figure 10.22 when running. The Console can contain a lot of information; make sure to look for lines that contain "Aperture."

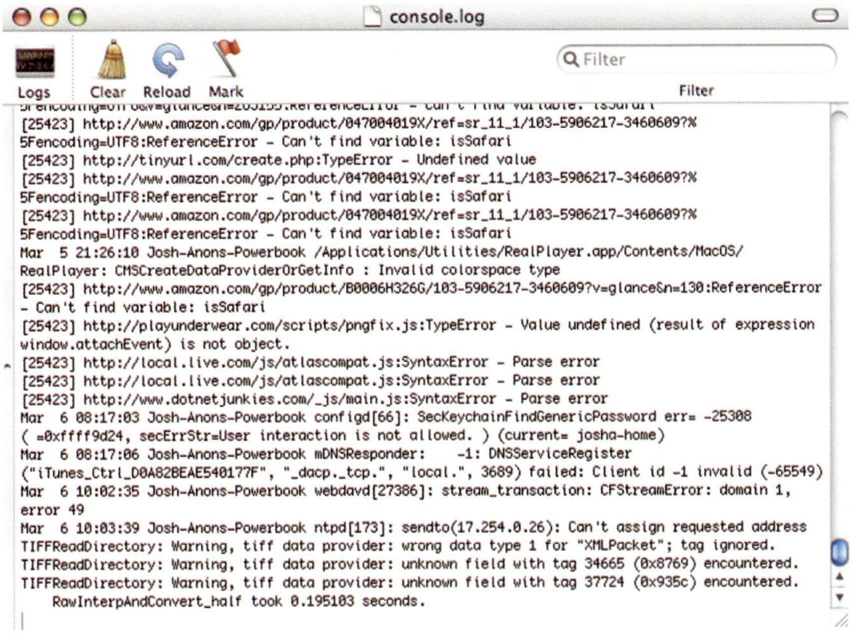

Figure 10.22: Console, showing various errors and warnings from the running applications, including Aperture

Global Problems

The other set of problems are global ones. These types of problems range from not being able to launch Aperture to having problems, such as showing the wrong thumbnails, with a large number of images. If you are having image-related problems and have a recently updated vault or backup of your library, we suggest that you first try restoring your library from your backup. However, if you're still having problems or don't have a backup, there are some troubleshooting steps to try.

The easiest first step is to try removing Aperture's Preferences file; however, this step is more useful when you're having problems with Aperture itself instead of a group of images or thumbnails. You will have to redo any custom configurations you've done, but a corrupt Preferences file is one of the most common problems. To remove Aperture's preferences:

1. Open a new Finder window.
2. Navigate to Home (Go > Home) > Library > Preferences.
3. Find and delete the com.apple.Aperture.plist file.

Relaunch Aperture and see if you still have the problem. If so, or if your problem is related to a group of images, the next step is to try to rebuild your library. Hold down ⌘+Option while launching Aperture and Aperture will automatically rebuild your library (this might take a while if you have a large library).

If you are having a thumbnail problem and rebuilding your library doesn't fix it, you can try forcing Aperture to regenerate your thumbnails. To do so:

1. Close Aperture.
2. Browse to your project using the techniques in the "Exploring the Photo Library" section. (Control-click your Aperture Library.aplib file and select Show Package Contents. Then, browse to your project, Control-click the approject file and select Show Package Contents.)
3. Rename, but do not delete, the AP.Minis, AP.Thumbnails, and AP.Tinies files to old.AP.Minis, old.AP.Thumbnails, and old.AP.Tinies. Rename the files instead of deleting them so that if something else happens, you have a backup.
4. Launch Aperture and switch to the project with the problematic thumbnails. You will see gray placeholder images (Figure 10.23) while Aperture opens each image and regenerates the thumbnails.

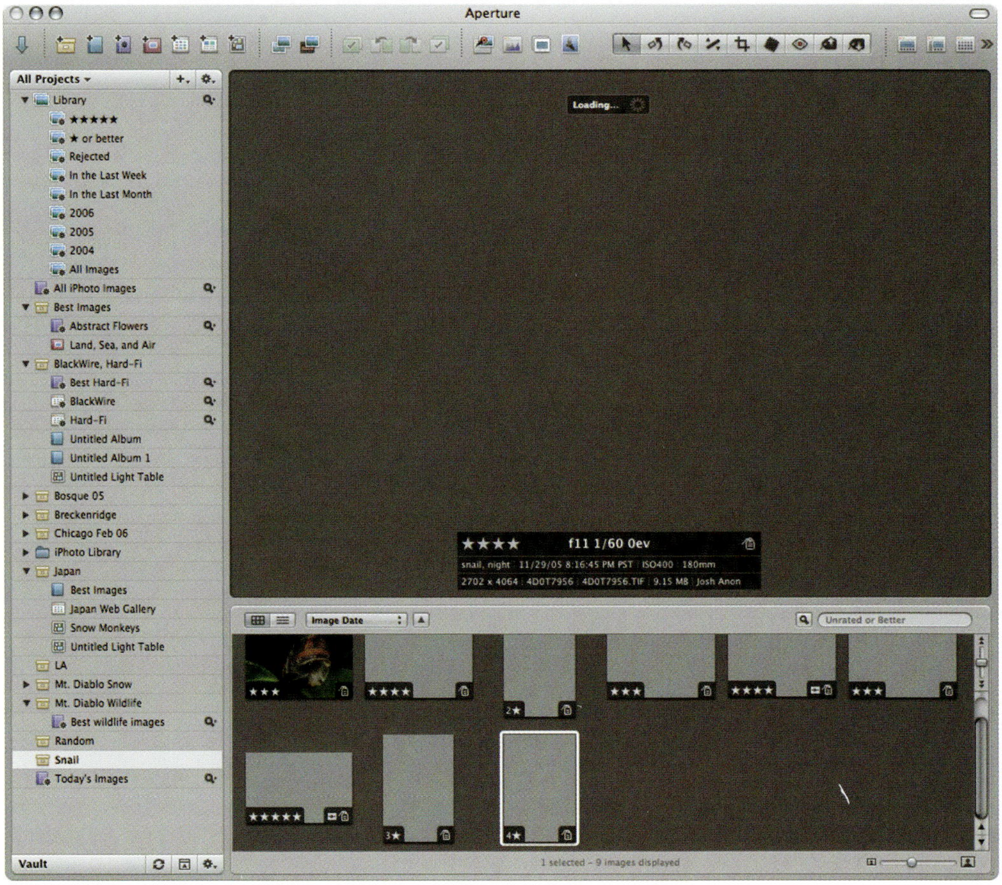

Figure 10.23: Aperture displays gray placeholder images while regenerating thumbnails.

At this point, assuming Aperture was able to regenerate your thumbnails, it's safe to delete the old.AP files from Step 3. If Aperture can't regenerate your thumbnails, your disk might have a problem (try running Disk First Aid from your system CD), you might be low on disk space, or your images might be corrupt.

If all else fails, you can use this last technique to force Aperture to re-create its library database.

1. Close Aperture.
2. Browse into your Aperture Library.aplib file by selecting it in the Finder, Control-clicking, and selecting Show Package Contents.
3. Rename the Aperture.aplib folder to **old.Aperture.aplib**.
4. Launch Aperture, and your Project panel will be empty. Aperture will open a Library Alert window similar to Figure 10.24 and prompt whether you want to recover your files.

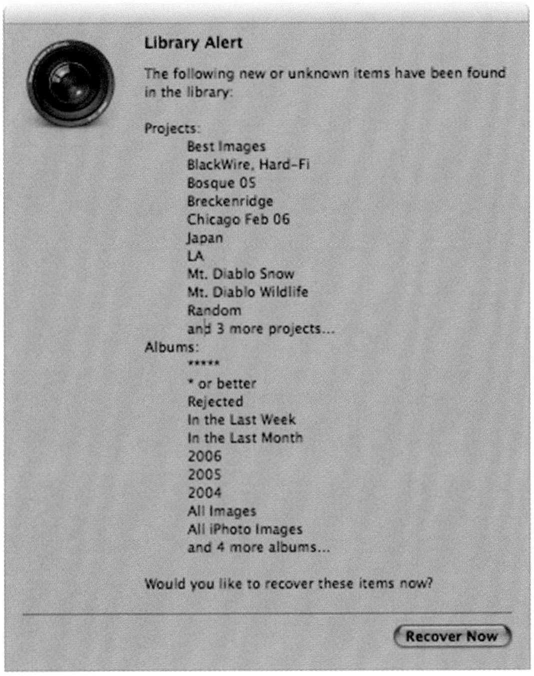

Figure 10.24:
The Library Alert window

5. If you want to completely regenerate your library, click Recover Now. If you changed your mind, force-quit Aperture by Control+Option clicking its Dock icon and selecting Force Quit. Then, within your Aperture Library, delete the temporary Aperture.aplib folder that Aperture created and rename old.Aperture.aplib to Aperture.aplib.
6. If Aperture is not able to recover your images properly, quit Aperture and restore your old library file. To do so, within your Aperture Library, delete the new Aperture.aplib folder that Aperture created and rename old.Aperture.aplib to **Aperture.aplib**.

This recovery process is slow, and we highly recommend that you do not interrupt it.

Index

Note to the Reader: Throughout this index **boldfaced** page numbers indicate primary discussions of a topic. *Italicized* page numbers indicate illustrations.

A

B

C

D

E

F

G

H

I

J

K

L

M

N

O

P

Q

R

S

T

U

V

W

X

Z